Healing Touch

Enhancing Life through Energy Therapy

Edited by:

Diane Wind Wardell, PhD, RN, WHNP-BC, AHN-BC, CHTP/I
Sue Kagel, BSN, RN, HNB-BC, CHTP/I
Lisa Anselme, BLS, RN, HN-BC, CHTP/I

HEALING TOUCH
ENHANCING LIFE THROUGH ENERGY THERAPY

Editors:
Diane Wind Wardell
Sue Kagel
Lisa Anselme

iUniverse books may be ordered through booksellers or by contacting:

iUniverse
1663 Liberty Drive
Bloomington, IN 47403
www.iuniverse.com
1-800-Authors (1-800-288-4677)

Because of the dynamic nature of the Internet, any web addresses or links contained in this book may have changed since publication and may no longer be valid. The views expressed in this work are solely those of the author and do not necessarily reflect the views of the publisher, and the publisher hereby disclaims any responsibility for them.

Any people depicted in stock imagery provided by Thinkstock are models, and such images are being used for illustrative purposes only. Certain stock imagery © Thinkstock.

ISBN: 978-1-4917-3633-3 (sc)
ISBN: 978-1-4917-3634-0 (e)

Library of Congress Control Number: 2014909795

Print information available on the last page.

iUniverse rev. date: 10/11/2018

Dedication

We dedicate this book in memory of Janet Mentgen, BSN, RN, CHTP/I (1938-2005) for her vision, passion, and mission to spread healing light worldwide. We also dedicate this book to all Janet's teachers and Healing Touch instructors in appreciation of their compassionate service. This work lives on through the thousands of practitioners and students who have followed her maxim to "Just do the work!" May this work enhance the lives of all who encounter its healing benefits.

Contents

Contents

Acknowledgements

Writing this book has been a labor of love as our goal of completion in one year morphed over time to a sense of allowing the book to be born when ready. We are so blessed to have the many contributors who were willing to share their expertise. We acknowledge all those who came before, the many researchers, theorists, scientists, and health care professionals who have worked to unfold an energetic and holistic paradigm for healing and wholeness.

We are grateful for our gracious and generous supporter who believes in Healing Touch and provided funding for this book to become a reality. We are also thankful to our editor, Nina Selz, for her time and dedication in reviewing the manuscript. Thank you to the photographer, Gay Wind Campbell, for capturing our vision through her unique cover art. Our publishing team at iUniverse provided invaluable guidance.

Our weekly conference calls began with a meditation, connection and intention for the highest good of all. We appreciate the growth opportunities and support received in the process.

We would especially like to thank our families and friends for their love, support, and patience in this endeavor as we worked to balance family, employment, and self-care with writing. Without their support this journey would not have been possible.

Contributors

As editors we greatly appreciate the contributors' efforts to bring the story of Healing Touch to the world's readers. The book represents a collective and international undertaking. Many of the writers who were chosen to share their expertise and experiences are leaders, instructors and practitioners of Healing Touch International, Inc. (HTI) now known as Healing Beyond Borders: Educating and Certifying the Healing Touch™. (See Key to Abbreviations at end of list).

Joel G. Anderson, PhD, HTI-P, is an Assistant Professor of Nursing at the University of Virginia, the Research Director for HTI, and serves on the Healing Beyond Borders Board of Directors.

Veda Andrus, EdD, MSN, RN, HN-BC, is Vice President of Education and Program Development at The Birch Tree Center for Healthcare Transformation and a Past-President of the American Holistic Nurses Association.

Lisa Anselme, BLS, RN, HN-BC, CHTP/I, is the Executive Director and Nurse Consultant in Integrative Health Care for Healing Beyond Borders. She has a background in biomedical ethics, pediatrics and transplantation. She teaches internationally.

Mary E. Brekke, PhD, RN, AHN-BC, CHTP, is Professor Emeritus, Metropolitan State University at St. Paul and Chair of the American Holistic Nurses Credentialing Corporation.

Anne L. Day, MA, BSN, CMT, HNB-BC, CHTP/I, is Past President of HTI and the Founder of Healing Touch Hawaii. She is the owner of *Healing Journeys*, and teaches internationally.

Suzanne Holck Due RN, CHTP, is the President of Healing Touch Denmark.

Jonathan Ellerby, PhD, is the CEO of Tao Inspired Living, a wellness company and community in the Riviera Maya of Mexico and the author of *Return to the Sacred: 12 paths to spirituality*.

Joan C. Engebretson, DrPH, RN, AHN-BC, is the Judy Fred Professor in Nursing at the University of Texas Health Science Center Houston, School of Nursing and a published researcher.

Valerie S. Eschiti, PhD, RN, AHN-BC, CHTP, CTN-A, is an Associate Professor at the University of Oklahoma Health Science Center, College of Nursing and a Healing Touch practitioner studying the work of the late Martha Rogers.

Mildred (Maggie) I. Freel, MEd, RN, CHTP/I, and *Reiki Master*, is Professor Emeritus, University of Iowa. She was a member of the American Holistic Nurses Association Certification Task Force and a Past Chair of the HTI Certification Board.

Mary Frost, MS, BSN, RN, HNB-BC, CHTP/I, teaches internationally and is a past member of the HTI Board of Directors.

Laura K. Hart, PhD, RN, CHTP/I, and *Reiki Master*, is Professor Emeritus, University of Iowa and the Chair of the Healing Beyond Borders Certification Board. She is a former member of the HTI Board of Directors.

Alexandra Jonsson, BScN, CHTP/I, is the President of Healing Touch Canada, a Past Board member of HTI, and a Past President of the Canadian Healing Touch Foundation.

Bonnie Johnson, RN, MS, AHN-BC, CHTP/I is a practitioner, instructor and Child Development Specialist with a holistic nursing practice.

Sue Kagel, BSN, RN, HNB-BC, CHTP/I, has a Healing Touch practice at Canyon Ranch Health Resort and is on the faculty of the University of Arizona Center for Integrative Medicine and, Tucson, Arizona. She is a Past President of HTI.

Rauni Prittinen King, MIH, BSN, RN, HN-BC, CHTPI, is on the Healing Beyond Borders Board of Directors. Although currently living in the United States, she is originally from Finland.

Savitri Kumaran, RNC, CHTP/I, is a practitioner and instructor practicing in Hawaii. She is a Past President of HTI.

Deborah Larrimore, BSN, RN, LMBT, CHTP/I, teaches internationally. She is a past HTI Board member and the first Director of Healing Touch Education at Wake Forest University Baptist Medical Center in North Carolina.

Der-Fa Lu, PhD, RN, CHTP, HTI Instructor in Training is Assistant Professor at University of Iowa College of Nursing and has co-taught Healing Touch to nurses in various clinical settings in Taiwan.

Angela Mattos, CHTP, is Director of Administration, Healing Touch Canada.

Mary Erickson Megel, PhD, RN, CHTP, is Emeritus Associate Professor at the University of Nebraska Medical Center College of Nursing and served as Research Director for HTI.

Susan Morales-Kosinec, RN, MSN, CHTP/I, is Professor of Nursing at Centennial College in Canada, a founding board member of HTI and the Canadian Healing Touch Foundation, and a past international board member of the American Holistic Nurses Association.

Mary O'Neill RN, CHTP/I, is Immediate Past President of Healing Beyond Borders, maintains a private practice, and is on staff at DePaul Health Center, St. Louis, Missouri, where she offers Healing Touch to palliative care patients.

Christine Page, M.D., is a holistic physician, international presenter, and author of seven books, including *Frontiers of Health* and *The Healing Power of the Sacred Woman*.

Annis Parker, RGON, DipEd, ADN, CHTP/I, is a founding member of Healing Touch New Zealand, and she extends her practice to domestic and wild animals. She is a former international representative to HTI.

Sarah E. Porter, PhD, MS, MPH, RN, CHTP/I, is Associate Professor Emeritus, Oregon Health & Science University School of Nursing. She is an educational advisor and editor.

Marty Rather, CHTP/I, teaches Healing Touch in India and around the globe. She is an author of healing adventure novels.

Carol Reamer, MA, BA, CHTP/I, CEMP/I/S, is an American and religious sister engaged in missionary work in the barrios of Peru.

Gary E. Schwartz, PhD, is a Professor at the University of Arizona, Tucson and the Director of the Laboratory for Advances in Consciousness and Health.

C. Norman Shealy, MD, PhD, is a holistic physician and pioneer in chronic pain management, Past President of Holos University Graduate Seminary, and founder of the American Holistic Medical Association.

Maki Shimamura, BA, CHTP, HTI Instructor in Training is co-founder and operator of Healing Touch Tokyo and a Healing Touch Practitioner in Japan.

John H. Shukwit, MA, LPC, is a therapist at the Canyon Ranch Health Resort in Tucson, Arizona.

Vicki Slater, PhD, RN, AHN-BC, CHTP/I, has published on potential mechanisms of Healing Touch and offers a class on "Physics and Spiritual Healing for Healers."

Terry Sparks, JD, MDiv, CHTP/I, is a Staff Chaplain at the Oklahoma City Veterans Affairs Medical Center. She sees patients as a Chaplain and Healing Touch provider and teaches Healing Touch to Veteran Affairs employees.

Karen Stewart, HTI-PA is a co-owner of Healing Touch Canada. She is a Past President of the Canadian Healing Touch Foundation and co-founder and former Board Member of the Healing Touch Association of Canada.

Mary Szczepanski, MS, BSN, HN-BC, CHPT/I, is a psychiatric nurse, coordinator for the Bartlett Regional Hospital in the Juneau Alaska Healing Touch Program and owner of Healing Touch Alaska. She is a Past Chair of the HTI Certification Board.

Lisa Thompson, RN, CHTP/I, LMT, is a nurse with over three decades of pediatric hospital experience and a Healing Touch practitioner and instructor.

Miki Toda, MRP, MA, CHTP, HTI Instructor in Training is co-founder and operator of Healing Touch Tokyo and coordinates workshops of the HTI Healing Touch Certificate Program in Japan.

Myra Tovey, BS, RN, HN-BC, CHTP/I, is an author and owner of Heart-Centered Living. She was a member of the leadership council of the American Holistic Nurses Association when Healing Touch was developed.

Kathy Turner, RN, NP, CHTP, is a research nurse practitioner in Women's Health at Stanford University Medical Center in California and Past Director of Healing Partners, a Healing Touch community service program.

Rosalie Van Aken, PhD, RN CHTP/I, is an educator at Southern Cross University, Lismore, New South Wales, Australia. She is a past international board member for HTI and a founding member of the Australian Foundation for Healing Touch, Inc.

Wietzke van Oene, CHTP/I, is President of the Dutch Professional Organization of Body Oriented Psychologists. She currently serves as an advisor to Healing Touch Netherlands Board and has served as president and treasurer.

Diane Wind Wardell, PhD, RN, WHNP, AHN-BC, CHTP/I, is a Professor of Nursing at The University of Texas Health Science Center Houston, School of Nursing, and an author. She teaches internationally and is a Past President of HTI.

Nina Weil, CHTP, is a Certified Circle of Life Health and Wellness Coach.

ABBREVIATIONS/CREDENTIALS

ADN	Advanced Diploma of Nursing
AHN-BC	Advanced Holistic Nurse-Board Certified
BLS	Bachelor Liberal Studies
CEMP/I/S	Certified Energy Medicine Practitioner/ Instructor/ Specialist
CHTP	Certified Healing Touch Practitioner
CHTP-I	Certified Healing Touch Practitioner Instructor
CTN-A	Certified Transcultural Nurse-Advanced
DipEd	Diploma of Education
DrPH	Doctor of Public Health
EdD	Doctor of Education
HBB	Healing Beyond Borders
HN-BC	Holistic Nurse-Board Certified
HNB-BC	Holistic Nurse Bachelors-Board Certified
HTI	Healing Touch International, Inc.
HTP	Healing Touch Practitioner
JD	Juris Doctor (lawyer)
LMBT	Licensed Massage and Bodywork Therapist
LMT	Licensed Massage Therapist
MD	Doctor of Medicine (physician)

MDiv Master of Divinity

MEd Master of Education

MIH Master of Integrative Health

MPH Master of Public Health

MRP Master of Regional Planning

MSN Master of Science in Nursing

PhD Doctor of Philosophy

RGON Registered General & Obstetric Nurse

RN Registered Nurse

Name Update

In 2017 Healing Beyond Borders re-visioned the Healing Touch Certificate Program course content which included technique name changes that reflected the original developer's work and, in some cases, resulted in select modifications to the technique (Anderson, Anselme, & Hart 2017). The Healing Touch techniques that directly refer to information in the following chapters are referenced here so that those studying the Healing Touch International, Inc 's curriculum will have a reference point to the prior technique names. In addition, classes have been renamed to provide greater clarity regarding the content of the classes:

Course Titles

Course 1: Foundations of Healing Touch (formerly Level 1)

Course 2: Energetic Patterning and Clinical Applications (formerly Level 2; or 2A)

Course 3: Advanced Healer Preparation (formerly Level 3; or 2B)

Course 4: Case Management and Professional Practice (formerly Level 4; or 3A)

Course 5: Self-Evaluation and Professional Development (formerly Level 5; or 3B)

Original Technique Name	Revised Technique Name
Deep Cleansing Techniques	Deep Auric Repatterning
Double Hands	Hand Cupping with Two Hands
Etheric Fingers	Etheric Hands Scooping
Hands Above and Below	Push Pull with Hands on either side of block
Etheric Template Clearing	Etheric Template Repatterning
Full Body Connection	Chakra Energizing
Laser	Sword Finger(s) Laser
Level 2 Back Technique	Spinal Flush
Lymphatic Drain	Lymphatic Clearing
Magnetic Clearing	Modified Mesmeric Clearing
Magnetic Passes	Field Repatterning
Hands in Motion	Hands Moving
Hands Still	Holding
Mind Clearing	Noel's Mind Clearing
Pain Drain	Siphon
Scudder	Scudder Meridian Clearing
Spinal Cleansing	Spinal Clearing and Energizing
Ultrasound	Beak Finger Laser
6th and 7th Level work	Celestial and Ketheric Template Repatterning

Foreword

BY *GARY E. SCHWARTZ, PhD*
Professor of Psychology, Medicine, Neurology, Psychiatry and Surgery
Director, Laboratory for Advances in Consciousness and Health
The University of Arizona

Every now and again a book is written which defines a field so comprehensively and inspirationally that it becomes a veritable "bible" for the field it represents. *Healing Touch: Enhancing Life Through Energy Therapy* combines extensive knowledge and expertise with deep compassion and vision. The Editors and their collection of contributors have performed a great service in writing this book, not only for Healing Touch per se, but for the health of humanity, nature, and the planet as a whole.

My intent here is not to provide a detailed introduction and overview to this superb volume. Quite the contrary, my purpose is simply to celebrate it, not just from the perspective of a National Institutes of Health (NIH) funded biofield scientist, but as a significant experiencer of Healing Touch as well. You are about to read the most complete, up to date, comprehensive and creative compendium of Healing Touch ever written.

I should confess at the outset that I am "biased" in that I hold a special place in my mind and heart for Healing Touch. The fact is that my introduction to energy therapies in the mid 1990's began with Healing Touch. I completed Level Three A (Level 4) training in Healing Touch as a prerequisite for my being able to conduct sensitive and responsible research on it and other energy therapies.

I subsequently received training in six other energy therapies, and after a decade of basic and applied research, I published a book summarizing our findings titled *The Energy Healing Experiments: How Science Reveals Our Natural Power to Heal*. However, the more I learned about energy therapies, the more I came to understand and appreciate the scope, depth, breath, quality, ethics, and beauty of Healing Touch.

In my role as a professor of Psychology, Medicine, Neurology, Psychiatry, and Surgery at the University of Arizona, and director of the Laboratory for Advances in Consciousness and Health, I had the privilege to come to know and work with many skilled and gifted healers. However, thanks to my role as Corporate Director of Development of Energy Healing at Canyon Ranch, I had the special privilege to come know and work with Sue Kagel.

Sue is a highly admired (and in many of her patient's eyes, revered) senior nurse and Healing Touch practitioner at Canyon Ranch who has played significant leadership roles in Healing Touch International. Thanks to Sue's devotion to Healing Touch and her active involvement in its activities, we were able to conduct a series of pioneering experiments on intention and Healing Touch which are summarized in a chapter in this book.

This book honors the pioneering nurses who initially founded Healing Touch, and it elevates their historical contributions through the continued evolution of Healing Touch as convincingly expressed in this book. Be prepared to be enlightened and inspired. If any book deserves to be subtitled a "life enhancing" book, this is it.

Introduction

This book was created to provide readers with both general and specific information on Healing Touch, a widely used and practiced holistic and energy-based approach to healing. The "work" of Healing Touch crosses all cultures, influences all aspects of self, and assists in creating wholeness for individuals, families, communities, and the world. Contributors to the book were selected for their expertise in Healing Touch and holistic healing. We are deeply grateful for the wisdom, guidance, and passion they have shared. As a result, this book provides a truly collective source of information.

Our intention is that individuals exploring various healing options and those interested in understanding or enhancing their personal healing will use this book as an invaluable resource. Health care professionals seeking energy therapies to enhance their practices and the wellness of their patients will find clinical applications and relevant research. Practitioners of the healing arts interested in a deeper understanding of holistic energy therapy and in gaining additional skills will discover useful and enlightening information. Practitioners and students studying Healing Touch and other energy therapies will find general information to evolve their practices and deepen their work. Specific intervention suggestions for various health issues and general self-care principles are also provided.

The content in the book builds on the curriculum of the Healing Touch International (HTI) Healing Touch Certificate Program presented by Healing Beyond Borders. However, the content is appropriate for all audiences. Those interested in learning Healing Touch as a healing modality are invited to attend Healing Touch classes that are presented worldwide. Completion of all five levels of the coursework can lead to credentialing as a Certified Healing Touch Practitioner (CHTP). Information can be found at www.HealingBeyondBorders.org.

The book's opening chapter contains stories that relate the development of Healing Touch around the world and provide an understanding of the impact that energy healing can have on individuals and communities. The chapters on clinical applications of Healing Touch profile and deepen the work, highlight the research, and promote the integration of energy therapies as adjuncts to standard medical practices. Information on self-care assists in personal wellness, balance and harmony, while evolving the self toward a more compassionate, heart-centered, and aware existence.

Healing Touch uses a holistic approach to physical, mental, emotional, and spiritual aspects of health. Through their personal practices, thousands of Healing Touch practitioners over the past 20 or more years have found that Healing Touch is effective in a wide range of health issues. These observations are now supported by rigorous research as well as demonstrated through client reports of their experiences.

Our hope is that this book will be inspiring and offer insights into Healing Touch as an energy therapy that enhances life from birth to end-of-life. Techniques and tools are presented that can be used to diminish suffering and support optimal wellness. Holistic and energy based therapies, especially Healing Touch, nurture health, wholeness, expanding consciousness, and awareness of our interconnectedness. Through being proactive in our self-care and compassionate in our interactions with all we encounter, we recognize that energetically, the way we choose to be in the world effects the whole.

CHAPTER 1
AN INTERNATIONAL PERSPECTIVE

Healing Touch energy therapy is a universal language of healing that weaves its threads through all cultures and settings. Wherever people are inspired and willing to introduce Healing Touch, and others are open to receive it, the benefits can be endless. General information is provided, leading to an exploration of the richness of the work as Healing Touch practitioners in many countries share their vision, passion, practice and experiences in the spreading of Healing Touch worldwide. The stories are given in their own words and provide insight into how one dedicated and passionate person can make a difference. Objectives of this chapter are as follows:

1. Define Healing Touch.
2. Explore the nature of healing as it applies across cultures.
3. Recognize commonalities among cultures.
4. Understand the global nature of healing through personal stories.
5. Identify models of healing used world-wide.

Healing Touch Definition

Healing Touch is a relaxing, nurturing energy therapy which can effect positive change in people's health and well-being. Using a holistic or "whole person" approach, the practitioner uses gentle touch either on or off the body to assist in restoring harmony and balance in the physical, mental, emotional, and spiritual aspects of the self. Healing

Touch is based on a heart centered, caring relationship between a practitioner and person. People receiving Healing Touch are clothed and are typically reclining, but they may also be seated. Practitioners gently place their hands either directly on the body or work above the body. During the session the person may experience any number of sensations, such as changes in skin temperature, feeling enlivened or calmed and relaxed, becoming more deeply connected to self and others, soothed, peaceful, comforted, and empowered. Sessions may be as short as a few minutes or extend up to an hour.

The mechanism by which Healing Touch works is unknown, but it is thought to interact with the energy field that permeates and surrounds the individual's body. The energy centers located over the joints and major nerve plexuses of the body are called the chakras. The practitioner focuses on clearing the energy field and chakras, bringing about harmony and balance, and generally causing a relaxation effect. This, in turn, supports the body's natural healing ability and self-healing process.

Healing Touch does not require physical manipulation of the body and is safe for all ages. Healing Touch works in harmony with standard medical care as well as with other complementary, holistic and integrative therapies.

Healing Touch offers the benefits of reducing stress and promoting relaxation and calm. It is often used in the surgical setting or with medical procedures and has been shown to enhance recovery, wound healing and decrease pain. It is a beneficial complementary therapy for injuries, eases symptoms from acute and chronic conditions, and creates a sense of well-being. Healing Touch is also used in cancer supportive care, decreasing the side effects of chemotherapy and radiation, easing emotional issues, and supporting quality of life and transitions. Some experience a deepening spiritual connection.

Healing Touch grew out of the holistic nursing practice of Janet Mentgen, RN, in the 1980s, in Denver, CO, United States of America (USA), and contains the work of an array of healers and ancient traditions. Janet and other early instructors then began their life work in spreading Healing Touch around the United States and internationally. In 1996, Janet Mentgen founded Healing Touch International, Inc. (HTI), with

Healing Touch education and credentialing as its mission and with her vision of service in spreading healing light worldwide. The continuing education program was renamed the HTI Healing Touch Certificate Program, and certification credentialing was also transferred to HTI. Janet remained actively involved until her passing in 2005. In 2013, HTI was renamed Healing Beyond Borders: Educating and Certifying the Healing Touch™ (HBB).

The HTI Healing Touch Certificate Program offered by Healing Beyond Borders contains five courses that are taught throughout the world by Certified Healing Touch Instructors, teaching to the same course objectives and content. Completion of the program can then lead to certification as an HTI Certified Healing Touch Practitioner (CHTP). This training usually takes a minimum of two years to complete and includes a one year mentorship program. Further development can lead to Instructor Certification (CHTI).

Introduction to an International Perspective

By Rosalie Van Aken, RN, PhD, CHTP/I

This section explores the nature of healing as it applies across cultures and recognizes the commonalities and global nature of healing through story. Exploration of common denominators, or "golden threads" of healing that unite healers and methods of healing across cultures and times, can be seen under several principles (Carlson & Shields, 1976). The second part of the chapter describes the development of Healing Touch in various lands from different individual perspectives and illustrates the variety of models and ways one can be of service. The narrations reflect individual stories and cultures as the speakers committed to "spread healing light" within their country. For some, it was like a fast growing wildfire fueled by favorable winds, and for others, it was a small and persistent drip that began slowly, yet continues to flow.

Principles from an Historical Perspective

A major principle is the provision of an environment where healing can take place. As stated by Dass (1976), "Just as in a garden, we do not 'grow' flowers; rather we create the conditions in which a flower can grow" (p.171). Healing in many ancient tribal cultures involved rites whose purpose was to make the body an unpleasant place for evil spirits to live, thereby using the body as the environment for healing an ailment (Keegan, 2001). The provision of an environment where healing can take place is evident in Eastern and Indian systems of healing. These systems are based on the concept of balance within the person and between that individual and the universe.

Chinese Traditional Medicine is one of the oldest and most extensive systems of medicine, with a quarter of the worlds' population using it in some way. This system is founded on the belief that everything is based on the balance of Yin and Yang, the two dynamic energies of the universe. In India, Ayurvedic medicine has been practiced for over 5,000 years and is still used extensively today. In this system, practitioners believe that illness is the "result of falling out of balance with nature" (Keegan, 2001, p.6).

Another common principle of healing across cultures might be called a spiritual aspect. Many cultures do not separate spirituality and medicine. For example, Tibetan medicine is based on philosophical beliefs of Buddhism as well as on the emotions, attitudes, lifestyle and spiritual beliefs of the individual. Fontaine (2000) states, "Spiritual diseases are mediated by a qualified teacher who uses meditation and yoga to balance body, mind and spirit" (p. 61). Native American traditional healers also do not separate medicine and spirituality. Many different treatment types derive from using medicine objects that relate to the Great Spirit in a sacred way. Often, a sweat lodge is used to cleanse the body, mind, heart and spirit.

The final common principle of healing, for purposes of this discussion, is the healing relationship. Healers in most traditions are highly trained and respected. In ancient tribal cultures, healers were identified when very young and trained from childhood. Healers prepared themselves in specific ways before providing treatment. For example, Tibetan healers used prayer, and Native American healers fasted and asked for guidance (Fontaine, 2000). The relationship between healer and patient is at the forefront of many healing traditions. Faith and trust appear to be major components in the healing process throughout all cultures (Keegan, 2001). Krippner (1989), observing healers on six continents, found one or more of the following common denominators: certain personal qualities of the practitioner facilitate the client's recovery, positive client expectations assist healing, and a sense of mastery empowers the client.

The richness of Healing Touch is that it lends itself to flowing to and across continents and cultures and maintains its standardization while it melds with the flavor of the area it serves. Healing Touch is one way that connects to various traditions of healing. As its foundation is from ancient sources, Healing Touch provides a renewal of knowledge into the importance of human touch and interaction.

Indigenous People and Healing Touch

I am very fortunate to live in a country where an ancient indigenous culture exists. I acknowledge the traditional owners of the lands within the continent of Australia and the ancestors of those owners. The indigenous peoples of Australia arrived in this land between 40,000 and 60,000 years ago when no other people lived here; therefore, they have been named the traditional owners. It is with deep respect that I share the little I have been told and experienced of the healing traditions of the indigenous peoples of this land. It is this respect that leads me to provide an English explanation for concepts and not use any indigenous words. I thank the indigenous Healers and Elders who have spoken with me and gave me permission to share their concepts.

Early in my experience as a practitioner of Healing Touch, I learned of the similarities between Australian Indigenous Healing and Healing Touch. I was asked to work with an indigenous gentleman with a mental health issue. Ten minutes into the session, he asked me why was I "doing his people's healing work." He explained that the feeling of "things moving through his body" was the same as when he had experienced indigenous healing. He also experienced a "buzzing" in his ears, of which he was initially concerned. He thought it was a hallucination, but then he realized it was something trying to "unscramble his brain." When asked to describe this feeling, he said it was "like a line of light collecting his thoughts and putting them in a straight line." He also stated that one of the main reasons for his "sickness in the head" was not being in his homeland, where the dream lines keep "everything straight."

For the aboriginal people, the earth is the foundation for all spiritual studies, including the dream lines. As stated by an indigenous Healer (who asked to not be identified), "the Earth is a living Spirit, and we communicate with the Spirits of trees, rocks and water" (personal communication, April 10, 2011). A major force in bridging the understanding between indigenous and energy healing, specifically Healing Touch, is the work of Bob Randall, an inspiring Elder and one of the listed traditional owners of Uluru (Ayres Rock). Bob shared information about his people's sacred relationship with the land to me personally, as well as in small groups, conferences and in writing. He talks of the "sacred world of creative energy" and how his people do not separate the material world of objects and creative forces (Randall, 2003, p. 3)

Bob tells of how his people see with their "inner eye", which he says white people call "intuitive awareness". He says this is how his people understand situations, study people, and are able to communicate with their country. The term "country" is used by indigenous people to describe the homeland of their specific group or "mob". Also, Bob describes in his book *Songman* (Randall, 2003) how indigenous people view everything holistically, particularly health and well-being. Therefore, not being connected to one's "country" removes an aspect of well-being, specifically the link with spiritual forces.

Similarities between Indigenous Healing and Healing Touch

During one of her early trips to Australia, Janet Mentgen visited Uluru. She walked around the base and was able to obtain a sense of the land. Janet informed me that she could "almost feel the heartbeats of the land under her feet" (personal communication, October, 1996). White Australians also have a strong connection to this land, although not in the same way as indigenous people. I believe that the "groundedness" of Healing Touch is one of the major reasons it appeals to we white Australians so much. On a personal level, when I center and become grounded in the present moment, I feel the support of the earth in strengthening and focusing my energy.

One indigenous Elder described to me (personal communication, March 5, 2010) an activity of her people's healers and elders that equates in my mind to what we call centering. She describes this as an "inner, deep listening, and quiet still awareness" that brings peace and understanding without a thinking process. This activity is usually carried out in nature while focusing on being in the environment and acknowledging the presence of the sacred. For me, when I center, I begin to receive energetic information from the client's energy field.

How to gain health-related information from the indigenous people of Australia is a vital process and requires considerable understanding and tact. Bob Randall (2003) states that it is important to first ask a person about his "country", as that is his major connection. This is not dissimilar to our Healing Touch intake interview, where we ask about the client's living situation. When working with indigenous people, it is important to take more time asking about "country." Bob advises moving onto gaining information about family as this is the next most important connection, and then casually asking about "what brings you here today" (p. 217). This awareness has led me personally, using deep listening and an open heart, to spend more time asking all clients more about where they feel they "belong" and to who or what they feel connected.

Deep listening is a traditional part of the Australian indigenous culture, with young people being taught through story, song and dance. These stories are told over and over through the seasons, and as years go by, those young people become the story tellers. An indigenous Elder told me (personal communication, March 5, 2010) that her people still gather around the campfire and hear the sacred stories. Listening and watching is the way of learning, not asking questions. In Healing

Touch, deeply listening to the story our clients share, both verbally and energetically, allows us to be of the greatest service.

An aspect I have noticed in learning through watching is that students of Healing Touch often use exactly the same movements as their instructor. One delightful example was when an instructor, who has arthritis in her hands, demonstrated the laser technique. Each and every student slightly curved their fingers when performing the laser technique, although the instructor said the technique was done with a straight finger and showed a diagram to reinforce it.

Waiting is also an aspect of the deep listening concept. The indigenous Elder who shared this concept with me described it as waiting for the right time and doing everything in the right order. She talks of us all waiting together in stillness and deep listening as the healing of traumatized Indigenous Peoples take place. This concept of waiting is also used in Healing Touch, as our clients set the pace for their healing process.

The healing techniques used in Healing Touch may differ slightly from those used by indigenous healers, but the healing process itself can be seen as energetic. Bob Randall tells the story of a female family member who had a severe knee injury. Health professionals wished to perform surgery. An indigenous Healer scanned her body, talking of hot and cold areas, then asked her to turn over. After removing something from her spine, he spat blood onto the ground and quickly covered it. After 15 minutes the Healer told her she would be "alright", which she was. No surgery was required (Randall, 2003).

Bob Randall, in describing some of his experiences travelling with members of the Healing Touch community in the United States and Australia, talks of how he felt an immediate connection to Healing Touch practitioners because the healing work is very like indigenous healing. He states this as follows:

> I personally became involved with this group in a personal way because I could see their natural way of healing is very much like the way our healers scan the body for heat and cold and massage the affected area to relieve symptoms (p. 200).

As you can deduce, there are very many similarities between Australian indigenous people's traditional concepts of healing and those of Healing Touch. However, many indigenous people are disconnected from these concepts, and this is creating much pain and suffering. One of my major hopes is that the Healing Touch community can assist in providing a healing bridge between the Australian indigenous people and their traditional healing practices. Exploring common threads in healing cultures will allow us to keep returning to the fundamental basis of healing and remain in touch with what healing is all about.

Spreading Healing Light Worldwide

By Anne Day, MA, BSN, CMT, HNB-BC, CHTP/I

The following section presents a beautiful tapestry of various stories of how Healing Touch spread globally. The stories are not presented in chronological order but represent the flow of healing work to various countries. The various colors and textures of the tapestry are made up of the variety of facts, perceptions, and stories contributed by those who walked the path of spreading Healing Touch worldwide. Each country is represented by those who were encouraged to share their memories of that special time of "birthing" of this very important healing work and of the evolution that occurred throughout the community of colleagues and supporters. As with all storytellers, the heart-felt sharing of each contributor has its own flavor and view, as each had a slightly different perspective of this time, based on their own perceptions and experiences.

In the early years many traditional health care providers were not open to the idea of holism and were resistant to the new healing practices that were re-emerging at that time. Thus, those who stepped forward as pioneers were tested with many questions and much skepticism. All held a strong sense of "knowing" that these concepts would emerge with acceptance and respect as the new millennium approached. With the rediscovery of holistic health and the importance of including mind and spirit as well as the body, the concept of healing came more clearly into view. Healing included a reconnection with deep peace in one's life and a realization that the mind, the emotions and one's spiritual

9

connection are deeply connected to the total picture of healing. One could be "cured" without being healed (feeling peace with one's life and healing journey), and conversely, one might experience deep healing without a physical "cure". The new awakening into holism brought a surge of desire to redefine roles and to pursue the path of healing. The stories that follow are heart-felt stories of how each person experienced their journey and awakening by bringing Healing Touch forward.

Healing Touch in Australia

BY ROSALIE VAN AKEN, RN, PHD, CHTP/I

The first two Certified Healing Touch Instructors (CHTIs) in Australia were from the United States. Dr. Mary Jo Bulbrook, a visiting Professor at Edith Cowan University in 1991, was accompanied by Donna Duff, RN, and both of them were CHTIs (once AHNA credentialing was developed). The Holistic Nurses Association of Australia (HNAA) was also birthed in 1991. In 1993, Donna offered to return and teach Healing Touch in Victoria and Western Australia. Mary Jo assisted her. Barbara Rogers and I attended her classes.

The word initially spread through HNAA and through the university networks both in Western Australia, Victoria, and New South Wales. As interest grew, Donna and Mary Jo returned to Australia many times to assist in laying the foundations for a strong Healing Touch community. Janet Mentgen initially visited Australia in 1994 to teach the first Level 4 class. She visited again in 1995 to teach the foundational instructor class. It was the support from these wonderful teachers that allowed the community to grow quickly.

A group of women who "took the bull by the horns" and became the leaders in Australia were Hazel Brandreth, Elsie Colgan, Cath Webber Martin, Barbara Rogers, Rosemary Stewart, and myself. By 1996, the idea of having an Australian organization to administer the Healing Touch classes began to emerge. In 1997, the Australian Foundation for Healing Touch (AFHT), a non-profit membership organization with elected officers, was incorporated and registered in Western Australia. In 1998, AFHT became an HTI Affiliate Member of Healing Touch International and has maintained that affiliation through the present time.

I was the first CHTI in the region and teach in both Australia and New Zealand. Other instructors quickly followed and taught classes on both sides of Australia and in New Zealand. Between 1998 and 1999, I visited the United States on many occasions to train with Janet Mentgen for instructing class Levels 3 through 5. Once I met Janet, I was truly inspired to make Healing Touch my life's work. The simplicity and humility of the work was what inspired me—the ordinariness of the work that touched the deepest healing presence within the recipient and the practitioner. One of the major reasons was that I believed mental health nursing had lost the heart of our work with an increasing reliance on medication. Nursing in general needed Healing Touch to balance the reliance on technology.

Janet continued to visit Australia regularly until 2002 to teach instructor classes and advanced workshops. In 2002, Janet told me that it was the right time for me to move into teaching instructor classes. In 2008, I visited the US to attend the pilot instructor training program and taught the first Australia Level 1 instructor class that same year. Currently, four CHTIs work in Australia teaching varying levels of the HTI Healing Touch Certificate Program.

Australia Foundation for Healing Touch's Mission

The mission of AFHT Inc. is to connect communities to energy healing, specifically that of Healing Touch. Acting as a bridge between indigenous people and their own healing traditions is a personal mission. During the 90's, the mining boom in Australia exploded, which brought a lot of money into the country. With the growth of materialism, the connection to the land was increasingly lost. Healing Touch helped to reawaken and reassert the connection to the land through the grounding of oneself as a practitioner and recipient. As self-reliance has always been a big part of the Australian culture, the empowerment aspect of Healing Touch aligned with it. The other major aspect was the Australian culture of "mateship" that was reinforced within the Healing Touch community.

As AFHT Inc. has been endorsed by the Royal College of Nursing

Australia, active strategies are in place to attract nurses to the HTI Healing Touch Certificate Program. The organization is also applying for endorsement from the Australian Traditional Medicine Association (ATMS) and investigating endorsement from the Massage Therapy Association. Several volunteer programs are in place in New South Wales and Western Australia. An additional mission is to expand these programs as practitioners become available. Healing Touch is being used in hospitals, hospices, nursing homes, private practice, and in homes. All in all, the journey of Healing Touch in Australia has been exciting and fulfilling for all involved. There have been no real barriers. It is with gratitude that we acknowledge those who contributed.

Peru, South America

By Carol Reamer, BA, MA, CHTP/I, CEMP/I

Peru, a third-world country in South America, from roughly 1980–2000 was devastated by a civil war. As Vilma, a Peruvian Healing Touch Practitioner (HTI-P) explains:

When Healing Touch arrived in 2000, the Peruvian people were experiencing many fears and anxieties from traumas within their society. Each person began with an itchy knot in his throat and had to learn again to express what had locked up inside because of the terrorism that caused resentments, rage, feelings of vengeance, fear, sadness, and loss. My question was, "Where do we start to rebuild trust, justice, family, homes, and jobs?" It was a massive task. Without knowing what was to come, we were ready to try something new that offered hope.

For 20 years I had been living among these wonderful people. We shared daily life, good times and bad, but I had never gotten used to working with the dying without tools to help. Health care here was almost non-existent for the poor. What was available was too costly or slow in coming. For many, that continues to be true. But at least we now have thousands of Healing Touch students and practitioners from all walks of life working in the community using basic Healing Touch techniques to alleviate pain. Also, many Healing Touch Practitioners give full treatments to patients in their neighborhoods and in other areas. Some groups are working together in centers, some are working in homes, and others continue to go regularly to areas that were affected by an earthquake that hit in southern Peru several years ago.

Beginnings

When Barbara Cavanaugh, RN, Certified Healing Touch Practitioner (CHTP), returned to visit Peru in 1998 after retiring from 31 years of working as a nurse with Peruvians near Lake Titicaca, she heard of a life-long missioner who was suffering from a fall from the second floor of her home. Piedad had undergone back surgery and physical therapy, but months later, she still could not stand without a lot of pain. Barbara offered to help, using something she had just learned in the United States called Healing Touch. After only a few sessions, Piedad was so much better, and one of her companions begged Barbara to bring someone to teach us how to do Healing Touch.

In 2000, Barbara Cavanaugh brought Mary Jo Bulbrook, CHTP/I, to Peru. I was working in the northern Andes at the time and was not able to attend the classes, which were called Manos Sanadoras (Healer Hands) and were held in the coastal capital of Lima. However, during the next several months, I completed Healing Touch Levels 1 and 2 during my home visit in USA. When Barbara and Mary Jo returned to Peru in 2001, I served as a translator for the classes.

Personal Benefits and New Tools

I had never intended to work in the health field. However, when I began to travel in the third-world, living with the poor and listening to their stories and pain, I felt impotent. The people approach their reality in a totally different way than we do in the United States. For lack of money or adequate health care, many just accept the inevitable. They have lived with powerlessness all their lives. They often ask us to come to pray with the sick and/or dying. I had held too many young people in their last moments, helping them to relax and to peacefully go with God. It also meant helping their families to let go and give their loved ones permission to move on. When Healing Touch came to Peru, we finally had something more we could do to help. We could now help the sick to get better, or at least lessen their pain, and teach others to help as well. We also had a new tool to bring inner peace and acceptance to patients and their families.

Anything that empowers people to do for themselves intrigues me. I invited some friends from our neighborhood to take the classes with me. Together we returned to Peru to work together. They are the ones who really convinced me of possibilities that could change life as we knew it. I learned so much from them.

Eileen Kearney, Sue Scharfenberger, and I learned Healing Touch while we were translating simultaneously from spoken English to Spanish and translating books and materials into Spanish. We then began teaching Healing Touch in Spanish. The Peruvians had the great blessing of many other United States instructors coming to Peru in those early years as well as the constant advice, visits, and critiques from Mary Jo to help with the classes. Three of us missioners who were then living in Peru, Eileen, Emiliana González and I, became Certified Healing Touch Practitioners and soon after, Certified Healing Touch Instructors. Janet Mentgen gave us her full support so that we could work through the process as quickly as possible. Her great faith in our ability to be effective practitioners and instructors without having nursing training gave us tremendous confidence and opened the field for thousands of others to follow.

Cultural Acceptance

Historically, Peru is a land whose people have believed in energy and healing. The shamans are very respected as natural healers in all parts of Peru. There are also brujos who practice both positive and negative energy work. Many fear their Evil Eye and the vengeance their enemies pay the brujos to perform.

The main religion today is a mixture of Catholicism/Christianity and belief in the nature Gods of their ancestors. They continue the rituals of honoring the land (Pachamama—Mother Earth), the mountain spirits (Apus), the sun (Inti), and many others. The shamans are a combination of doctor and priest. Peru has 11 official languages, and there are many others as well. Each group has its own belief and practices of using energy and respect for nature. Because the vast majority of people are Christian/Catholic, we speak much more of God in our classes than is usually done in other places.

Healing Touch began in the poor neighborhoods of Peru because the first contacts were with the religious women working in them. Many of these women have extensive networks within their congregations. The Sisters took the Healing Touch classes in droves, and then they took it home and invited the women they worked with in their groups. Healing Touch in Peru has taken hold among the people whose only medical training came from their mothers and their own experience. We had no contacts with medical professionals until relatively recently. It has grown from the bottom up.

Spreading the Work

We took our work to the street. The city halls have many health fairs in tents where people receive short health evaluations and explanations of what kind of doctors they need to see or what kind of self-help they can do. We give continuous 5–10 minute healing treatments in these tents for pain and stress relief. In a single morning, 2 to 25 students/practitioners treat dozens of people who go away feeling better. Our people have been invited to schools, parishes, police stations, universities, businesses, orphanages, and hospitals, to name a few, to continue this work.

In the beginning, the main source of students was within the groups with whom we were working—in parishes, mothers' clubs, youth groups, classes in schools and universities, and neighborhoods. Women were especially drawn to the work as many had never finished high school and felt that they were too old (age 35) to learn anything new. At first, their families didn't take them seriously. But as their family members had aches and pains, they asked for a treatment and became believers—and even students. Classes are often given free or by sliding scale so that they are available to everyone.

One of the biggest benefits was the shift in attitudes of many of the women. They began to believe in themselves and to hold their heads up higher. They had new incentives to begin other works as well. The most difficult challenge was doing the work for Healing Touch Level 5. It seemed insurmountable. Many had never read a book in their life. The idea of reading 15–20 books scared them to death! More than one made the comment that they never knew one could learn from reading books! The pride that flowed from them was palpable. Self-confidence and respect from others changed their perspective of what they were capable of accomplishing. They now are conceiving new ideas for projects and taking their place within the community at large.

Organizing PROSH

In 2002 Mary Jo, in the first Healing Touch Level 4 class in Peru, challenged us to create Healing Touch Peru as a non-profit organization named *Promoviendo Salud Holística* (PROSH) to support us acting as coordinators, leaders, and teachers of Introduction classes and to provide logistics in between her visits to continue classes. This became our Community Service project for Level 5. PROSH is an affiliate member of Healing Touch International.

We soon had invitations through our contacts with groups in other parts of Latin-America to carry Healing Touch to Ecuador, Chile, Bolivia, Argentina and Paraguay as well as to Ireland, Spain, Zimbabwe, and the US-Mexican border. Besides giving classes in these countries, there have been many students who have travelled from near-by countries, such as Colombia, Venezuela, Brazil, and Uruguay, to take advantage of Healing Touch classes.

Today we have three more instructors, including our first Peruvian. With 12 years of experience, we are beginning to have more students from the medical professions. Our results with patients and the Latin American people's innate belief in energy draw others to return to their ancestral richness to heal with their hands. Vilma states it as follows:

Healing Touch is the hope of life, the transformer of life,

this gift of faith in our hands. I believe in this gift. I know that it is good to laugh. When I heal people they always ask 'What did you do to me?' Even a nine year old who falls on the playground asks for Healing Touch. Faith, energy movement, and love go a long way.

Two Personal Stories

Gladys and Paula are two Peruvian Healing Touch practitioners in Lima-Callao, Peru. Their eyes light up as they explain how Healing Touch has changed their lives. The following is from their perspective and in their words:

Gladys: What an incredible way to help others! In 2000, the parish no longer allowed us to work within its structure so I had free time to become involved in something new. The biggest need is how to deal with stress. People need tranquility and help to solve their own problems. One of our biggest challenges is helping people recognize their own needs. Many don't want to pay for the service, saying they don't have the money, but that's not true. It's a matter of learning to prioritize their lives and resources. I have learned to give thanks to God in every minute. That is the key to tranquility and peace. Through Healing Touch, I have a better understanding of nature, the physical body, and how to fit in with life with new understanding and new tools. Everything is in harmony. As practitioners, we have to respect our patients, and give them the freedom to speak or not.

Paula: I came into Healing Touch later, but I fell in love with the idea of energy when I was a child. Energy is life. God puts energy in creation, animals, everything and everyone. Personal wounds are healed within. What does this energy have? One discovers a mutual help, love of God. I have always been fascinated with medicine. I wanted to learn how it works. I have had a curiosity and passion to learn to help others since

I was a child shepherd in the central Peruvian Andes Mountains. Healing Touch has given me the means to treat many people.

Canada

BY ALEXANDRA JONSSON, BScN, CHTP/I; SUSAN MORALES-KOSINEC, RN, MSN, CHTP/I; ANGELA MATTOS, CHTP; AND KAREN STEWART, HTI-PA

Janet Mentgen taught the first Healing Touch class in Canada in September 1990. While Healing Touch began in Canada with the enthusiasm of a few key individuals, it spread across the country as a result of the many volunteer coordinators and students who shared their passion. This is their story.

Susan Morales-Kosinec (Mayer) met Janet through her involvement as an International Director with the American Holistic Nurses Association (AHNA) Board of Directors when Janet was the South West Regional Director in the United States. They became friends as they worked together on the Board and found they had a common interest in Therapeutic Touch (TT). At that time, a curriculum was being developed from the energetic techniques Janet had been teaching at the Red Rocks Community College in Denver, Colorado, United States. It was to be submitted to the AHNA Education Committee and developed for approval as a course of study for their members. At one of the development meetings, there was a discussion about what the course should be called, and Susan coined the phrase "Healing Touch." After AHNA approval, Susan, excited about its promise, wanted to bring it to Canada.

First Class

At an AHNA meeting in February 1990, Susan, in a casual conversation with Alexandra Jonsson (Sandra Johnson), a friend from Canada who also was a TT Practitioner/Instructor, suggested Janet be invited to teach Healing Touch in Toronto, Ontario. Alexandra phoned Janet who immediately accepted, making Canada the first "international" country to which she traveled.

Janet suggested Alexandra find a college to host the course, and Durham College agreed to do so. Prior to the class, the college decided there weren't enough registrations, so they cancelled it. When Alexandra called Janet, her response was "I am coming, even if it's just you and me. I already have my ticket." Alexandra, an excellent networker, immediately hung up and began phoning everyone she knew. At the last minute, she found a space for the 17 students who had registered. Out of that group, 16 went on to Level 2, 15 completed the curriculum, and 3 of them, Alexandra, Marguerite Langley, and Ava Zaritzky, eventually became Instructors.

Without any direction about what would be needed at that first class, when Janet asked on the second day, "Do we have any tables?" Alexandra didn't know what she was talking about. So the students had to work with pillows and blankets on the floor and couches.

As a result of that first class, Janet and Alexandra became great friends and Janet began her long tradition of not only staying with Alexandra in Toronto but also extending her visit after a course just to hang out, eat ice cream, and have some fun. To keep the momentum going after the 1st class, Alexandra began booking a Level 2 and 3 with Janet approximately 6 months apart.

Susan Morales, in the meantime, had moved to Vancouver and in March 1991 was an instructor-in-training in a class in Bellingham, Washington, United States, which Janet and Barb Dahl co-taught. Three others from British Columbia, Rochelle Graham, Karla (Akash) Sonnichsen and Linda Turner, were registered in that class. (Rochelle and Karla went on to become instructors.) Everyone was determined to get there even though Rochelle had to drive through freezing rain the entire way. The weather was so dire that the highway was closed after they left, and cars were driving off the road. Following that initial course in Bellingham, Healing Touch in British Columbia expanded rapidly, thanks to the enthusiasm of many.

Formation of Healing Touch Canada, Inc.

In the spring of 1991, when Janet was teaching a Level 2 Class in Toronto, Susan was inspired to start a business as a more professional way of spreading Healing Touch across Canada. While discussing the idea with Janet, the two of them decided to become partners in the venture. They incorporated Healing Touch Canada, Inc. (HTC) in September of 1993 with Susan as Executive Director.

Healing Touch Canada, Inc. (HTC) became a Certified Canadian Educational Institution devoted to the support of healing through the teaching of energy based techniques. It was founded on the belief that all people have the ability to facilitate healing through compassionate intent and that energy-based healing can be integrated with other forms of health care. HTC is committed to individuals seeking further education and to helping communities with training, promotion and development of energy-based healing.

Initially, all the courses in Canada (except in Newfoundland Labrador) were organized by HTC, and the instructors were contracted to teach for HTC. Based on the model Janet had used in the United States, a core group, comprised of Rochelle Graham, Alexandra Jonsson, and Susan Morales, was formed to guide the company and work with Janet.

Meanwhile, on the east coast, Donna Duff had asked her sister Liz Duff to coordinate classes, and in October 1992, Donna and Mary Jo Bulbrook came from the United States to co-teach Newfoundland's first Healing Touch class. (There were 24 in that class and although Liz recounts that she initially had no idea what Healing Touch was about, she was hooked during the class and went on to become an Instructor.)

In February 1995, Angela Mattos (Markoff), one of the students in the first Canadian Healing Touch course, joined HTC as an Administrative Assistant and has been one of HTC's guiding lights for 18 years. In January 1997, Angela became a member of the HTC Core. Later that year, with HTC on its feet, Janet decided to step back from co-ownership to allow HTC to grow in its own unique way, as other international Healing Touch groups were doing.

At the end of 1999, Susan decided the time had come for her to also step aside. Eventually ownership of HTC was transferred to Alexandra Jonsson and Karen Stewart, who met annually with Janet to discuss the direction of Healing Touch in Canada until 2005. They have continued to work for and promote Janet's vision of Healing Touch being mainstream and in every household. Although much has changed over the years in the way courses are planned and offered, HTC has maintained its focus on providing services to students and Canadian Instructors. Its mission has remained the same: to facilitate and support healing through the education and integration of body, mind and spirit. HTC has offered classes in the provinces of British Columbia, Alberta, Saskatchewan, Manitoba, Ontario, New Brunswick, Nova Scotia, Prince Edward Island, Quebec, and Newfoundland.

Birth of the Canadian Healing Touch Foundation

In April 1995, after a very generous donation of $5,000 to encourage the growth of Healing Touch in Canada, the Canadian Healing Touch Foundation (CHTF), a non-profit charitable organization, was incorporated. The original Board members were Rochelle Graham, Alexandra Jonsson, and Susan Morales. After a group of volunteers painted a 36 foot, 11 circuit labyrinth it became the cornerstone of a December *"Preparing for the Season of Light"* Labyrinth Retreat in Niagara Falls, Ontario and a fundraiser for the Foundation. Since it was a huge success this special retreat continued for a number of years.

Encouraged by the support for the Labyrinth Retreats, in 2001, the Foundation organized the 1st Annual Gathering of the Canadian Healing Touch community in Niagara Falls, Ontario with Janet Mentgen as a keynote speaker. As part of that Gathering, the CHTF Board planned a Silent Auction to raise money for the Foundation. Janet had such a good time during the bidding process; she took the idea back to Healing Touch International, who also incorporated it into their annual conferences.

Creating Healing Touch Association of Canada—Membership

The next piece to fall into place was the formation of a not-for-profit membership organization, the Healing Touch Association of Canada Inc. (HTAC) in October of 2002, and HTAC was recognized as an affiliate of Healing Touch International. The initial Board members were Alexandra Jonsson, Karen Stewart, Lou Ann Thompson, and Catherine

Awai. Janet, who was always supportive of anything Canada wanted to do to *"spread healing light,"* was the first "Angelic" member. HTAC's purpose was to promote Healing Touch across Canada and to provide support to members practicing Healing Touch in Canada, including nurses, other health care professionals and lay persons dedicated to providing heart-centered care. HTAC publishes a Membership Directory, distributes the *"Nexus"* newsletter, and organizes a biennial Canadian conference in various cities across the country.

Canadians have been involved in various aspects of the development of Healing Touch since the early days. The original Healing Touch circle logo was a result of Janet seeing a logo that Ava Zaritzky had on her professional profile book at a Level 5 class in September, 1993. On seeing the words "Healing Touch" in a circle, Janet instantly said "That's it!" Ava had seen this at a class in Australia on something of Hazel Bendith's, and it evolved from there. Ava was also involved with bringing forward the idea of having an annual day to celebrate Healing Touch Internationally, and March 6 was adopted as HTI Day by Healing Touch International on its 10th birthday in 2006.

Healing Touch continues to grow in Canada. Without the enthusiasm and support of all the instructors, coordinators, students, and families, it would not be what it is today! From the initial vision of Susan and Alexandra, to everyone who has been involved, including those who continue to "just do the work," Canada is an important partner of HTI.

New Zealand

By Annis Parker, RGON, DipEd, ADN, CHTP/I

Being geographically close to India, many of the Indian philosophical beliefs had been, were, and are being studied in New Zealand. The Maori culture also has a very balanced, spiritual, and integrated way of viewing the world, a view similar to the beliefs of many indigenous cultures of the world. However this view has been (and still can be) kept separate from the main stream of any work. Many beliefs are common to both the Maori view and Healing Touch, which made Healing Touch easily accepted. There are adaptations, mostly in that we use a very clear language and in how we use pillows. For instance, no pillow that has been under the legs is moved to under the head.

Healing Touch came into New Zealand (NZ) in 1994 through Annie Gibbs and June McCarthy, who had previously attended Levels 1 and 2 in Auckland, Australia. The first class was taught in Hawke's Bay on the North Island of NZ by Mary Jo Bulbrook, who taught level 1 and 2 in the Harding Hall in Hastings. The Healing Touch certificate of attendance was under the American Holistic Nurses Association (AHNA). For me, the classes just "turned up." I guess I was phoned because I was a nurse (and the only nurse in that first workshop).

I was in the very first group of people in the South Island of NZ to attend a Level 1 workshop. None of us had ever heard of Healing Touch before! I was raised with knowledge of auric fields, chakras, clairaudience, telepathy and clairvoyance. I always felt that nursing was incomplete, so that when I was asked if I would like to attend a workshop that grew out of nursing, worked with auric fields and chakras, and had standards of practice, codes of ethics, etc. —my worlds came together! It caused me to embrace Healing Touch with both hands. I understand from others in NZ that they embrace Healing Touch because of the practical, no nonsense way they are taught, and also because they can do it anywhere and at any time. It enhances the health of loved ones and also enhances the provider's work, especially if they are inside the health professions. Healing Touch also benefits their own health and learning by broadening their views of life.

Upper Levels and Carrying the Work Forward

Although a number of the students were not able to attend level 2B classes (level 3 now), we were able to do a level 3A (level 4 now) workshop that was taught by Janet Mentgen in Opotiki, NZ later that year. The class was held on a Marae (a traditional Maori meeting place originally in the open space but is now often a specifically constructed building for tribal meetings). We all slept in the Marae and had "interesting" experiences, including not enough food and no hot shower. We learned later we were supposed to be on another Marae, but due to a sudden death there, plans were changed. The Marae where we were didn't really want us as it was "against their principles." And then, Janet lost her voice in the middle of teaching, so Mary Jo filled in to finish the class, and Donna Duff taught the lower level class.

June McCarthy became a Certified Healing Touch Instructor. The original NZ National co-ordinator was Shiva/Reo Jamieson, followed by Lynn Ward under Mary Jo Bulbrook. Lynn became a regular assistant to the levels that were taught in the North Island of NZ. Healing Touch was also brought to the South Island, and the first class was taught by Rosalie Van Aken from Australia in Christchurch, NZ in 1995. At six monthly intervals, the next two levels followed. By this time I had become the coordinator for the South Island.

I went to the USA to attend Level 4 in 1997, attended a number of other advanced practice courses and intensives, went to the Healing Touch International Conference, and travelled extensively. When I returned to NZ after some months, I commenced a full time practice using Healing Touch with people and animals (domesticated, farm, and zoo animals). This allowed me to meet many members of the health professions and to encourage their interest and participation. All courses were held on the hospital site where I was employed and in 1999, I became a Certified Healing Touch Practitioner. Shortly thereafter, Janet Mentgen invited me to attend the Instructor Training in Hawaii. I became a Certified Instructor and taught my first Level 1 in Christchurch, and over time, became trained to teach through Level 3. I was appointed to the Healing Touch International Board of Directors as the International representative from 2001 to 2007, when representation passed to a Swiss colleague. Levels 4 and 5 are still taught by an overseas instructor or students go to Australia for those levels. Healing Touch courses have now been taught in Southland, Otago, Nelson, and Canterbury in the South Island and Taranaki and Hawkes Bay in the North Island.

It is interesting to me that we have very few Maori folk involved in Healing Touch. It may be that the cost of a workshop is the major factor. However, we now have many more participants in the South Island, and the best promotion is by word of mouth, which in itself demonstrates one's beliefs, and as Janet would say, by "Walking the Talk." It takes time to build the Healing Touch community when there are only a few practitioners or students in an area.

Organizing

In 2001/2002, Healing Touch New Zealand commenced the journey to being independent and autonomous. After a long and somewhat torturous journey, an inaugural Annual General Meeting was held in Christchurch in 2003. The organisation was deliberately set up as a NZ organisation and not as a private business. The Chairperson of Healing Touch New Zealand, Inc. may hold that office for only three years. At the time of writing (2012), we have just appointed our fourth Chairperson, and the organisation is making further plans to support current members, increase membership, maintain contacts through difficult times of natural disaster, and encourage classes throughout the country. Healing Touch New Zealand is an affiliate member of Healing Touch International.

June McCarthy and Kitty Kingsbury, who became instructors, have both retired from that role. This leaves myself and Debbie Carter, both living in Christchurch, the only instructors in the country. Classes are being taught in both the North and the South Islands and are starting to build numbers again. A couple of Certified Healing Touch Practitioners (CHTP's) are being encouraged to train as instructors to ensure succession is in place. New Zealand is working closely with Australia in as many ways as possible, and this includes the training of instructors.

Challenges and Benefits

I am always challenged when there is no one to assist. I find it best to answer questions with honesty. If others are unable to expand their thinking, then walking away and not worrying about their lack of understanding is always good. I ask students and practitioners talking about Healing Touch to stay within THEIR scope of practice and not to venture into the health professions, if that is not their training and experience. Personally, when I speak about the work, I come from the physics and quantum physics side to the anatomical/physiological effects when speaking with more scientifically focused people. This tends to reduce resistance and cause interest. Changing the approach depending on the audience has always worked for me. If they are farmers, I relate to animals or people working with them; if it is a religious group, I take them to more ancient times when things were simpler; and so forth.

Healing Touch has been successful in New Zealand primarily because people became excited not only about the work but also how it could benefit their friends and those around them. The health professionals see the benefit, even though there was some "fight" with the medical model. This is very slowly changing as Healing Touch is now accepted as part of student health at Canterbury University. We keep working to spread Healing Touch into other hospitals and universities when it is feasible to do so.

United States of America

By Diane Wind Wardell, PhD, RN, WHNP-BC, AHN-BC,
CHTP/I, Lisa Anselme, BLS, RN, HN-BC, CHTP/I,
and Sue Kagel, BSN, RN, HNB-BC, CHTP/I

In 1988, Janet Mentgen, RN, BSN was honored as the American Holistic Nurses Association (AHNA) Holistic Nurse of the Year and invited to work with the AHNA Education Committee to create a formal continuing education certificate program. The certificate program, based upon the energy-based techniques Janet taught at the Red Rocks Community College in Denver, Colorado, followed the nursing process and contained a broad group of interventions adapted from a variety of energy healers and healing traditions.

Anne Day related some early recollections of her time with Janet Mentgen prior to the AHNA Healing Touch Certificate Program. Anne offered that her journey began in 1984 when she took her first class in healing. She stated:

> A video was shown of Dolores Kreiger demonstrating Therapeutic Touch, and we were guided in exchanges of sensing the energy and of giving and receiving with

a partner. When I saw the Therapeutic Touch classes offered at the local community college, I was enthusiastic to attend and learn more!

Janet was the teacher for the first class in Therapeutic Touch. I knew that this was opening up a whole new path of learning for me. I continued with Advanced Therapeutic Touch with great enthusiasm! Once you had taken both Basic and Advanced Therapeutic Touch from Janet, if you wanted to go further on this path, you came to her shared office space called "The Health Control Center". There, Janet began to expand her repertoire of classes to include more techniques from Brugh Joy, Barbara Brennen, Alice Bailey and other healers as well as her guidance of her own new techniques. Janet was evolving herself as a healer and was very enthusiastic about teaching others her wisdom and experience. The classes continued to expand, as we all wanted more, and included Back Techniques, Advanced Back Techniques, Therapeutic Touch Practitioner I and II, and Biofeedback, Beginning and Advanced. We all saw Janet as a very gifted, intuitive healer and teacher.

Janet's style from the beginning was to allow students to ask for what they needed and not to give more information than that student was ready to receive. She taught us the value of our own personal development as healers.

A personal story about Janet follows by Judy Turner, who first started studying with Janet in 1986.

As an AHNA Regional Director, Janet decided to have a Regional Conference near Santa Fe, New Mexico. It followed the format she used at Shadowcliff [a retreat center in the Rocky Mountains of Colorado]. We met as a group after dinner on Friday night. She had our group of about 50 or more sit in a circle. We each had to tell why we were Holistic Nurses and what our goals were for this conference. Many of us did not realize we were wounded healers seeking comradeship in our personal healing process. Then one participant from Texas said she had just recently received a diagnosis that she didn't know how to handle or to tell her family. She confessed that she was full of cancer and it was so pervasive there wasn't a treatment regimen. She asked us to help her. Janet didn't get ruffled. She just said, "Mmmm Hmmm." We were all in tears.

The next day we followed the order of workshops that had been set and when finished, Janet said now she would like to do a group healing for our Texas friend. She asked her practicum students to come forward and set the room for a healing. Janet had them place one or two hands on the woman, then had those of us who had had classes with Janet touched the shoulder of one of the practicum students and the rest held space [supported creating the energy for a healing space by becoming centered and peaceful]. Anyone who didn't want to participate could leave, but no one left. Janet stood at the woman's feet and directed the energy. After what seemed like a long time, maybe 10 to 15 minutes, Janet said, "I think that is enough," and we slowly released the energy.

The lady didn't wake up. We waited and waited. Finally, Janet came near her, entering into her energy field and called her name. Janet touched the lady's foot, and she woke up bewildered. Janet made sure she was grounded and then said, "I think there is something that you need to change. Do you know what that is?" The lady said she thought she did. Janet said, "Go and do it then." She then released all of us.

After about a month, I casually asked Janet if she had heard from the lady in Texas. She said, "Now, Judy, you know you are to let go of the outcome." And then a few weeks later, when I stopped in, Janet said, "There is a note for all of us on the bulletin board." The lady in Texas had waited to complete her second check-up and had been cleared of all cancer. She attributed this to Janet and her students!

Healing Touch Certificate Program and Certification

At a committee meeting of the AHNA, Susan Morales-Kosinec (Mayer) from Canada suggested the name "Healing Touch." Healing Touch became a certificate program of AHNA in 1990, spreading throughout North America and then the world. In 1992, AHNA created a credentialing task force, to develop the certification criteria for Holistic Nursing and Healing Touch and create an AHNA Certification Board, which then provided certification for Healing Touch Practitioners (CHTP) and Instructors (CHTI) from 1993–1996.

The Healing Touch Certificate Program grew rapidly and was popular with laypersons as well as nurses, which created a disparity with AHNA's mission, and AHNA released the program in March 1996. Janet Mentgen founded Healing Touch International (HTI) as a non-profit organization to receive the Healing Touch Certificate Program and Healing Touch practitioner and instructor certification as well as provide educational and membership opportunities to the general public.

The first annual HTI conference was in January 1997. During that time, HTI went through an incredible time of definition, growth, identity clarification, and maturation. Clear visioning, deep commitment, and lots of loving service guided this expansion so that HTI could clearly identify a program that could stand on its own, with a body of knowledge and research that validated the practice of Healing Touch. During those years the foundations of the organization were created—the mission statement, goals, code of ethics, standards of practice, scope of practice, and its core values. Each person who committed to "Spreading Healing Light Worldwide" helped to actualize the expansion and respect of this healing work.

AHNA provided endorsement of the HTI Healing Touch Certificate Program through June 2017. Following course revision, the certificate program underwent a continuing education review and subsequent reapplication for endorsement, which was then again awarded in November 2017. In 2013 HTI updated its name and is now doing business as Healing Beyond Borders (HBB). HBB continues to offer the curriculum and certification in the original format, content and process.

There are numerous individuals who helped support and develop Healing Touch in the United States over the last three decades. An attempt to identify all of them and relate their stories is an insurmountable task in a few short pages. We honor all those who have contributed in service to this work as officers of the Board of Directors and Certification Board, committee members; instructors, coordinators of classes, presenters for the work to individuals and groups; supporters, both financial and emotional, and as wisdom holders; and to all who have offered a Healing Touch session to themselves or another.

Europe

Healing Touch in The Netherlands and Denmark

By Wietzke van Oene, CHTP/I and Sue Due, RN, CHTP

The history of healing in Europe goes back to the Middle Ages, a time of mainly sorcerers and medicine women. However, today in the European countries there are no healers left nor any form of natural medicine traditions that contributed to public health in the past. This is because any form of alternative healing was banned, and individual healers were convicted as witches and then either executed in public or burned alive. In the south of Europe, there is a strong religious presence that still today upholds these restrictive beliefs. Another example is found from the region of the Pyrenees, the Cathares, where "free thinkers" were killed in the 12th century by religious groups. The history of banning and killing is carried forward into our energetic European DNA. Only in the Scandinavian countries do we find the Sumos, who were able to safeguard their own healing tradition utilizing Shamans and healing circles. They have been able to survive the many attempts to be banned. What probably contributed to their survival was Mother Nature's protective barrier of freezing cold temperatures and remoteness.

The Beginning in the Netherlands

A first reaction to the word "healing" often creates resistance, without the person consciously knowing why or where this belief comes from. There are moments when each person assesses if it is safe to talk about healing. This could be one of the main reasons why new forms of healing, such as Healing Touch, came from overseas. Diane Schaap, RN, CHTP from the United States, who had studied Healing Touch, moved with her Dutch husband to the Netherlands in 1992. A first Healing Touch workshop was offered in 1994, followed by a Level 2 in 1995.

A workgroup was formed and founded Healing Touch Netherlands (HTN) in 1996. Healing Touch Netherlands is a not-for-profit association and has a board of 3 to 5 people. The development of Healing Touch in the Netherlands has been through ups and downs, with few but very motivated and inspired participants in the first years. Just before the new millennium, the first Level 5 group finished training. The participants in the Netherlands have mainly been therapists and self-employed complementary health care workers. Only a few nurses participated in the early classes or on the Board of HTN.

Healing Touch in Finland, Germany and Sweden

In the same period, Healing Touch workshops were offered in Finland by Rauni King, RN, CHTP/I. Rauni was born and raised in Finland and then immigrated to the USA when she was 19 years old. The same happened in Germany, where Ines Hoster was born and raised, and left the country at 19 years old. Once Rauni and Ines encountered Healing Touch in the United States, they brought this spark back to their homelands. In Sweden and Denmark, Healing Touch was introduced by David Rabinowitsch, RN, CHTP/I from the USA, who continues to have family there. David was instrumental in the creation of Healing Touch Sweden, an affiliate member of Healing Touch International.

Rauni has now taught 23 Healing Touch classes in Finland, about one a year since 1999. Rauni relates that most of her students are nurses with a few doctors and several physical therapists. She says, "It was not until summer 2012 that the first Healing Touch class was in a healthcare setting, a cancer hospital in Helsinki. This course was coordinated by a physician from Finland who completed Level 5 several years ago." Rauni's critique of the health care system in Finland is that it is "very advanced, traditional, and conservative. There are various alternative healers that the average consumer uses frequently. Integrative medicine is a new concept in which both philosophies can work hand in hand. Healing Touch has been slow to be accepted, but more and more nurses and doctors are bringing this work to their patients and friends." In December 2012, a journal called *Kotilaakari*, or *"Home Doctor"*, published an article about Rauni's work in Healing Touch and integrative medicine. Rauni believes, "It will be yet to see how much this work will blossom in the months and years to come."

Return to Holland

In 1999, Wietzke van Oene, Dutch in origin, returned after 10 years from New Zealand to the Netherlands. She had been involved in the creation of Healing Touch in New Zealand on the North Island in the mid-1990s. The spark to get involved in Healing Touch started with her professional search as a body-mind therapist to find out more about the energy field. Healing Touch gave her practice literally "hands and feet," and Healing Touch became her passion and guiding light. The gateway for her to go back to the Netherlands involved sudden and unexpected changes in her personal life. There was nothing left for her in New Zealand, and all moves were leading nowhere. Even her chance for her solo experience as a Level 1 Instructor in Training did not move ahead. The moment she got to the Netherlands, everything started flowing again. She did not know then, that simultaneously, *Healing Touch Netherlands* was going through a crisis. With a second CHTP committed to HTN, the organisation got an additional life spark. In 2001, the HTN Board recommitted to work for the future of HTN; they translated the Healing Touch Level 1 notebook and the Mission and Objectives into the Dutch language.

Dianne Schaap was getting ready to teach as CHTP/I and Wietzke van Oene had only her solo Level 1 to accomplish. Several overseas instructors were invited to teach and to help HTN and the instructors move forward. They believed in us, and that was wonderful. We could experience the international relationship with other countries in many ways. The stories about the Dutch culture would be told overseas, especially the way we answer evaluations after a class; this is very straight forward, with the intention of providing constructive critique. Dutch students like to honestly support an instructor's evolution, and happily write full pages on their evaluations.

Spreading the Work

In 2002, HTN had two HTI Certified Healing Touch Instructors (CHTP/I), and they were the first CHTP/I based in Europe. This provided the gateway for HTN to start growing with tools in our own language and culture. We were able to feel the sense of community and to support and see each other grow. This enriched everyone's lives—instructors, students and our communities at home or at work. To share Healing Touch with others and to see them go home with something that works and is heart-centered, consequently brings out the best in each person.

Denmark

In the same period, David Rabinowitsch offered a first class in Malmø, Sweden in 2002. Suzanne Holck Due, RN, attended the second Healing Touch class. She had been drawn by a small advertisement in the official publication of the Danish Nurses Association, *Sygeplejersken* (*The Nurse*). It mentioned that the American nurse David Rabinowitsch had offered a Healing Touch workshop a few months earlier at the International Council of Nursing in Copenhagen, Denmark. There was now a Healing Touch course planned in Malmø, Sweden. After half an hour in this first Healing Touch class in Malmø, she knew that she HAD to bring it back to Denmark! She completed the program and became an HTI Certified Healing Touch Practitioner in 2011.

Sue remembers the start well: During the first break, she approached David and asked, "Do you think you would ever come to my little town in Fyn, in Denmark?" He enthusiastically smiled and said he would love to come to teach, if she would organize a class. And so the seed was planted. In this very same class was a nurse educator from the north of Denmark, Birgitte Rasmussen, who was one of the founders and current President of the Danish Nurses Association Complementary and Alternative Interest Group (Fagligt selskab for sygeplejersker med interesse for komplementær og alternativ behandling -FSKAB).

In 2004, Sue advertised in *Sygeplejersken* the first Healing Touch Level 1 course, which was to be held in Svendborg, Denmark. What was really exciting was that she got a call from Kirsten Jung from Copenhagen. Kirsten, a massage therapist, read her mother's copy of *Sygeplejersken* and had already followed some courses and completed her study in the Netherlands. In 2006, Kristen was the very first Certified Healing Touch Practitioner in Denmark.

It has been a Due family affair in Denmark, with the support and computer skills of Sue's husband Søren Due, who has been co-coordinator and board member of Healing Touch Denmark from the very start. Sue says: "without him we had no Healing Touch in Denmark. For our small family, as for many others, Healing Touch has been a transforming experience!"

The first Level 1 class was a nice intimate group, including Birgitte Rasmussen's colleague, Hanne Tangaa. In 2005, both Healing Touch Level 1 and Level 2 workshops were given at the local hospital in Svendborg. During the next two years, a network and practice group was established in the local hospital. By 2006, the Healing Touch network developed into Healing Touch Denmark (HTD). The founders were from the original two classes, including Arnbjørg Vest, Dorthe Fischer, Marianne Thomsen, and Søren Due, and all are still active as members of the board or helpers at the Healing Touch classes. Suzanne Due was the first (and current) President, Kirsten Jung was the first Vice President, and later Hanne Tangaa became Vice President. As of 2012, around 85 people have taken Healing Touch Level 1 in Denmark. There has been one Level 3 in Denmark. Students for Levels 4 and 5 went to classes in Sweden and The Netherlands. The goal of Healing Touch Denmark is to bring Healing Touch into the healthcare system and to spread the light all over Denmark, as well as have practice groups in the bigger cities.

Healing Touch Europe Conference

 In 2005, Healing Touch Netherlands organised the first Healing Touch Europe conference, with European and USA speakers and about 100 participants. This was to bring Europe together on common ground and invite others internationally to experience the European hospitality and Healing Touch community. Healing Touch Netherlands had been building their community for well over 10 years by now, and to share our love and enthusiasm with each other was uplifting and inspiring to each and all of us. A point of interest is that all countries within Europe speak different languages, and even within a country as small as The Netherlands, the dialects in the North and South are totally different. We drive 2 hours by car north, west or south, and we have to speak Danish, German, Flemish, Wallonian or French. This is sometimes difficult to understand for the countries where the same language is common for days and days. The 2nd Healing Touch Europe conference was held in 2009 with 75 international participants, and again was a true celebration of the spirit of Healing Touch and made the vision to share light worldwide visible.

The Netherlands

The Healing Touch classes in the Netherlands are mainly followed by independent professional therapists or people who are in interested learning more about healing in general. To draw more nurses into the program, HTN applied in 2007 for Accreditation at our largest Nurses association, V&VN.

It is wonderful that all Healing Touch activities organised by HTN became accredited by the V&V Quality register. A little later, the Level 1 curriculum was included in a Complementary Healthcare basic course by CZ, also being an accredited organisation. The participants of this course are all nurses and professional caregivers interested in holistic care. Many of the students in the first Healing Touch Level 1 class given in 2010 are hoping to finish their Level 5 in 2013.

Spreading the Work

In 2011, Healing Touch was launched into Belgium with a first Level 1 class. Nancy Strybol, RN, CHTP/I who lives in the Netherlands, took Healing Touch to her homeland. There are several projects, some on-going and some by occasion, one being a research project about the effects of Healing Touch for coma patients. A community service project is underway where Healing Touch Practitioners give Healing Touch to the elderly in an elderly care unit. Other projects are irregular but on-going for the Toon Hermans House, where cancer patients and ex-cancer patients gather to network and support each other. Introduction classes have been given at several places, including to students at a School of Nursing. Recently, Healing Touch practitioners are active in clinical lessons on Healing Touch inside and outside the hospital setting. Altogether, we are gaining more confidence as we see positive feedback from every project, and Healing Touch in general is coming more and more into the picture. The philosophy of the board is it is better to go slow and steady than run too fast and lose it along the way.

What HTN hopes to accomplish now is that many care professionals want to be or remember to be healers and follow the HTI Healing Touch Certificate Program; that Healing Touch practitioners will be supported in doing the work with confidence and respect for all that is; and that through us, the Healing Touch work will spread and carry light to where it is needed, close to those who are sick, traumatised, out of balance and those who seek to heal. What we hope to achieve is to be accredited as a mainstream post professional learning program, so that many professionals can integrate Healing Touch work within their practises, and even more people can benefit from it.

The history of HTN and Europe was carried by many people, and today, there is more knowledge, openness, and information available everywhere about complementary health and healing. The current HTN board members are keeping their focus and looking now at expansion. This is possible because students are moving forward with supportive mentors. Now is the right time to ride the wave, trusting that we are on the right wave, and all connected through the ocean, on the right globe.

A dream you dream alone is only a dream. A dream
you dream together is reality. — John Lennon

United Kingdom and Ireland

By LISA ANSELME RN, BLS, HN-BC, CHTP/I

England

Rev. Alison Facey (Ali) began taking Healing Touch classes while living and working in Chile. After returning home to England, in 2011 she contacted Terry Sparks CHTP/I, MDiv, and planned a sabbatical in the United States with the purpose of visiting areas of Healing Touch concentration to gain practical information about how it is being used within health care settings. I met Ali during her travels with Terry, and the three of us envisioned bringing Healing Touch to England. Ali subsequently entered a mentorship relationship with both Terry and myself, and we began to champion her work and vision.

In October 2012 and April 2013, I taught two Healing Touch Level 1s, a Level 2, and a Level 3 outside of London. We held introductory classes for parents and teachers, met with the program director of Cherry Lodge (a charitable organization offering complementary therapies to individuals with cancer), spoke with nurses about complementary therapies and Healing Touch, provided sessions to patients undergoing traditional cancer therapy, and shared skills with pre-school staff caring for special needs children. Joining us in each Healing Touch class was school teacher Mim Hodgson, HTI-PA, who had first studied Healing Touch in Chile, and Maria Ibbotson, CHTP, who had studied Healing Touch in the United States and had recently moved back to England.

Ali recently traveled to the United States to attend her Level 5 course and is now completing her materials for certification. Levels 1 and 2 classes are now scheduled in 2014, and Terry Sparks will be the instructor for these courses.

Ireland

Healing Touch was first brought to Ireland by Sister Eileen Kearney, CHTP/I. Years later, in August 2010, a student and mentee, Felicia McCarthy (Flish), completed her Level 5 in Colorado, United States, returned to her previous home in Galway, Ireland, and became qualified as a Certified Healing Touch Practitioner.

In October 2012, Flish and I held an introductory workshop at the Cottage Pub, visited Cancer West, a facility that offered complementary care to individuals with cancer, and followed with a Level 1 class I taught in an Alexander school. In April 2013, I returned to Ireland and presented an introduction to a Caritas group of women caregivers. Flish presented an introduction within a prison system, and we held a Level 1 and 2 class. Flish entered instructor training in October 2013 and has been pursuing her studies. In September, 2014, I will be returning to Ireland to advance students to Level 3 and will be assisted by Flish in a Level 1 class to further her training.

The classes and people in the UK and Ireland are very precious, and even though we all spoke English, we would often need to translate our colloquialisms to ensure understanding. As usual, however, the energy itself was the teacher, and transcended language. Thanks to the work of Ali and Flish, Healing Touch is growing and expanding in the UK and Ireland.

Taiwan

By Der-Fa Lu PhD, RN, CHTP, HTI Instructor in Training

The seed of Healing Touch in Taiwan was planted in 2001 after I took Healing Touch Level 4 and 5 with Janet Mentgen. Soon afterward, I moved to Taiwan to complete a 2–year commitment to teach nursing at Tzu Chi University in Hualien City, Taiwan. At that time, I shared my interest and knowledge of Healing Touch with my graduate student advisees. Responding to their interest, I began incorporating Healing Touch concepts and techniques into teaching, research, and practice. A presentation was made to a group of clinical nurses at a regional hospital in 2003. After resuming my teaching career in the United States, I kept in touch with my former students in Taiwan. A few of them wanted to receive formal Healing Touch Level 1 training.

After two years of planning, Carol Flack, CHTP/I, and I traveled back to Taiwan in 2009 and conducted several Level 1 workshops in hospitals and nursing schools, where I served as the full time interpreter and class helper. The story of these experiences was published in the Healing Touch International newsletter, *HTI's Perspectives in Healing*.

Planning for this venture started in March 2008. Although Taiwan has a long tradition of energy based medicine, Healing Touch was a new concept in Taiwan. Originally we viewed the trip as a volunteer mission. With some persistence, we were able to obtain funding to cover most of the travel expenses from different organizations, including the Bureau of Health in Taitung County.

The coordinators for these classes were Molly Mow, MSN, RN and Sho-Hua She, MSN, RN, former graduate students at Tzu Chi University. Both Molly and Sho-Hua reviewed the teaching material before the workshops. Molly created a PowerPoint presentation in Chinese for the workshops. They were also classroom helpers and monitored return demonstrations by students. Onsite support for the second and third workshops was provided by directors of nursing departments, whose participation provided important role modeling for others. Some details about the various workshops offered in 2009 included the following: offering of 3 hour introductions to Healing Touch at Taipei Municipal Hospital (8-E General Medicine Unit, Taiwan), to nurses and community adults, and at Yensen Veterans Hospital (Yilan, Taiwan) to 35 nurses; Level 1 training workshops at the Yilan School Nurses Association for 85 students, who received Level 1 certificates with their Chinese names and nursing continuing education credit and was facilitated by Flack, Lu, and Mow; classes taught at the Taitung Veterans Hospital for 55 students, most of whom were staff nurses; and a third class held at Fooyin University (Ta-Liao Hsiang, Kaohsuing Hsien 831). Although 40 nursing faculty and students attended the first day of class, the second day was cancelled due to a typhoon.

Upon returning home, I was certified as a Healing Touch Practitioner (CHTP) through Healing Touch International in April 2010. In July 2011, I was admitted into HTI Instructor Training. The first wave of

Healing Touch workshops in Taiwan was a success, and the beginning of a network was established. A few students from previous workshops have indicated interest in receiving more training. It will be possible to host two levels of training in Taiwan, after Carol becomes qualified as a Healing Touch Level 2 instructor and after I become certified to teach Level 1. Ms. Mow is now working to conduct a pilot study to test the effect of Healing Touch on sleep and pain for older adults in assisted living facilities. There is an increasing interest in Healing Touch in Taiwan. I am working with my former colleagues to investigate the possibility of creating a local chapter and to network with the HTI affiliate organization in New Zealand.

Japan

By MIKI TODA, CHTP, HTI INSTRUCTOR IN TRAINING; MAKI SHIMAMURA, CHTP, HTI INSTRUCTOR IN TRAINING; AND SARAH PORTER RN, PMHNP, PhD, MPH, CHTP/I

Prior to the 19th century, Japan was heavily influenced by Chinese Medicine. Therefore, Japanese people generally understand the concept of energy. However, it is a different story whether they believe it or not. Even though these days various energy therapies are available in Japan, people are poorly informed about the differences among them. Only a narrow range of people use energy therapy. For the general public, much explanation of "energy healing" is required.

The initial gateways for Healing Touch to enter Japan included coincidences and synchronicities, "going with the flow," persistence and following-up on opportunities. In 2003, Sarah Porter, RN, was hired as a visiting professor at a well-known private college of nursing in Tokyo. She intended to have Healing Touch develop in Japan and vowed to share it in any way possible. For Miki Toda and Maki Shimamura, everything started with meeting Sarah. Miki met Sarah at a spiritual workshop and asked her if it was true that energy healings were used in hospitals in the United States of America. Sarah smiled and simply answered "Yes." Sarah mentioned to them that she was learning energy healing and wanted to be an instructor of Healing Touch, then kindly offered to hold a monthly practice group of healing in general. Both Miki and Maki attended Sarah's practice group where she shared her passion of Healing Touch with the attendees, who were mostly Reiki practitioners.

Maki immediately fell in love with Healing Touch. She couldn't wait for Sarah to become a certified instructor, so in 2007 she flew to Maui to take Healing Touch Level 1. She was very impressed to know there were so many varieties of ages, conditions and professions involved. Healing Touch was the most beautiful healing she had ever experienced. At the same time, Miki attended a Healing Touch Level 1 class in Oahu, Hawaii in which Sarah was an assistant instructor. The demonstration of Chakra Spread in the Level 1 class moved her and pushed her forward to action. Upon their return from the classes, Miki and Maki made up their minds to spread Healing Touch in Japan and formed Healing Touch Tokyo to serve that purpose.

After taking Healing Touch Level 1, both Maki and Miki worked together as coordinators. As Healing Touch Tokyo, they invited Sarah, who had become an instructor, to teach a Level 1 class before the end of 2007. The first class was full, and a few were on the waiting list. Since then, Healing Touch Tokyo has been holding HTI workshops in Japan. We are lucky to have HTI certified instructors who support us from their hearts. Registered nurses Lori Protzman, Dr. Sarah E. Porter, Anne Warren, Anne Day, Savitri Kumaran, and Lisa Anselme have come to teach. As of 2012, Dr. Hamada, an integrative physician in Okinawa, has sponsored and coordinated two Level 1 workshops in Okinawa.

In 2011, Healing Touch Tokyo, with the support of Sarah, Zita Wenzel, PhD (Level 4 student living in Tokyo), and other instructors, created a standardized content for the Healing Touch Introductory workshop and workshop guidelines. Currently, 15 Healing Touch Level 3 students have learned the contents and guidelines and are qualified to hold the introductory seminar. Their mission then, as it is now, is to facilitate the spread of Healing Touch in Japan.

In June 2012, having coordinated the workshops since 2007, Healing Touch Tokyo held the first Healing Touch Level 4 class in Japan, the first Level 5 in 2013, and continues with developing HTI Healing Touch certified practitioners. Healing Touch Tokyo hopes that energy healing is understood and accepted within conventional medicine in Japan and sees that it is time to incorporate Healing Touch into the medical settings. Currently, two students have become Certified Healing Touch Practitioners, Miki and Maki, and both received their pins during the Certification Ceremony at the 16th Annual Healing Touch International Conference in Colorado. By the time more students become certified practitioners, a formal non-profit organization might be established to support their activities and to spread Healing Touch into the clinical settings. Healing Touch Tokyo currently prepares to have more coordinators of workshops.

Maki would like also to have more independent coordinators all over Japan as she would like to share her experience as a workshop host with others and develop more coordinators. She has a dream that at least one hospital will provide Healing Touch in the Tokyo area in the near future. She also has a vision to have a Healing Touch conference in the Tokyo area! She wants Healing Touch to have a large presence in Japan.

One of Miki's personal missions is to keep spreading in Japan not only Healing Touch but also the importance of compassion, love and self-growth for healing. Through spreading Healing Touch, she would also like to spread the notion that caring for oneself and others is not difficult and is easily done just by hands and with heart. In general, energy therapy is not easily accepted. Miki feels the need to cultivate places to offer Healing Touch in Japan, not only in hospitals, but also in facilities for elder care and disabled persons. Many Healing Touch students seem to like having Healing Touch volunteer opportunities in those facilities.

The plans to continue the expansion of Healing Touch in Japan are multi-faceted. Sarah began teaching Introductions to Healing Touch at The College Women's Association of Japan; Foreign Nurses Association of Japan; and at St. Luke's College of Nursing. Of most importance is to continue the monthly practice group organized by Miki, Maki and several other Japanese energy healers.

Healing Touch students are so passionate about Healing Touch that their enthusiasm has assisted Healing Touch Tokyo to continue to expand. Some of the students are nurses who had been waiting so long for an energy therapy based on the nursing process. They gave us encouragement and advice to continue this work. Obviously the passion of instructors is invaluable, for which Healing Touch Tokyo is highly appreciative.

Our work is supported by the Divine Flow which appears as the incredible commitment of people in Japan who love Healing Touch and who work very hard to create workshops and practice groups. The philosophy and teachings of Healing Touch is Miki's motivation and passion. After having completed the HTI Healing Touch Certificate Program, she discovered that she also loves "the educational program" itself and would like to spread it. Maki recognizes the need for a certification process adaptation that addresses languages other than English (which is part of the strategic planning for Healing Beyond Borders) to assist in removing any bottlenecks to students progressing in their training until a critical mass is formed and more certified Japanese practitioners can assist in the mentoring and certification process in their native language.

Thailand

BY SAVITRI KUMARAN, RNC, CHTP/I

Dr. Ladawal Ounprasertpong, who is in the Department of Nursing, Faculty of Medicine Ramathibodi Hospital, Mahidol University, Bangkok, Thailand, attended a Level 1 Healing Touch class in Honolulu, Hawaii in the early 2000's while studying one summer at the East/West Center at University of Hawaii. Hawaii is a natural vacation destination and provides intellectual experiences for those on the Pacific waters, including Japan, Taiwan, Thailand, and Cambodia. Dr. Ladawal extended an invitation to me to be a speaker at the *First International Conference on Prevention and Management of Chronic Conditions* in Bangkok, Thailand in January 2006. An introduction to Healing Touch was held with the help of Annis Parker, RN, ADN, DipEd, CHTP/I, a Healing Touch Instructor from New Zealand. I presented a keynote talk on Healing Touch while Annis demonstrated some techniques during the presentation. A 3 hour break-out session was also conducted, which was well attended by participants from many different (up to 17!) countries. Although the health care practitioners from this region often have a more holistic view than many in western countries, this was their first exposure to Healing Touch.

Dr. Ladawal also organized a Level 1 Healing Touch class for members of their holistic nurses' association that was attended by 100 members. The class was held in the banquet room of a hotel. The students were very attentive and were able to understand the concepts and techniques with ease. Dr. Ladawal told me later that many of the nurses were using Healing Touch with their patients.

In 2007, I returned to Thailand at Dr. Ladawal's invitation. Another Healing Touch Level 1 class was organized, this time at one of the larger nursing schools. It was attended by over 100 students. I also spoke at a large hospital in Bangkok.

Dr. Ladawal would love to have additional instructors come to teach Healing Touch. The nurses have been very receptive to Healing Touch, find it culturally and ethnically acceptable, and are utilizing it with patients. While there is interest in continuing Healing Touch classes, and it is welcomed by Dr. Ladawal and her colleagues, there is currently no funding to support its further development. I would love to go back someday.

India
BY MARTHA RATHER, CHTP/I

A Story of Teaching in India

In 2004, we initiated a class series taught at Martuvam Healing Forest in Auroville, Tamil Nadu, India, at the request of a young man, Sivaraj and his wife Malar, who were just beginning to build their healing center. I took a small group of Healing Touch teachers and students to teach Healing Touch classes, which was followed by a tour of the ancient temples of Southern India. This on-going series of Healing Touch classes has continued every other year since then.

Healing Touch India originally began in 1999 when Kathleen Rosemary, CHTP/I attended a conference on intentional communities held in Auroville. Kathleen is one of the original members of "The Farm" intentional community in Tennessee. This international conference was organized by an American woman, named Bhavana, who had lived in India for over 20 years at that time. She was active in organizing the native women to receive better jobs and better health care. Her "adopted" son, Sivaraj, met Kathleen and had a private introductory class. In his interview, he tells about how he recognized that this was what he had been searching for to complete his alternative health center.

Although Kathleen received a small grant from Healing Touch International Foundation to continue her work, she was not able to return. Savitri Kumaren offered to help and held an Introduction to Healing Touch class in Auroville in 2000 for anyone who wanted to come.

The year 2001 brought terrorist problems around the world. Normal flights to India were cancelled. We all stayed home.

In 2003, I won a scholarship to attend a week long seminar in Northern India. When I returned to the United States, I attended a Healing Touch leadership meeting in Nashville and told everyone how much I loved India. Kathleen was there and immediately offered me an opportunity to teach in Auroville. She said that Sivaraj wrote to her twice a year asking for more teachers. Since I was now acquainted with this tour company, I had a unique opportunity to offer a teaching experience in India to anyone who wanted to join in. My personal goal was to bring at least 6 people with me each time so that my trip would be a gift from the tour company. The long term goal was to find other people who wanted to continue with this community. How many times would I be able to go to India? How many years would it take to find the right person who would become the local teacher? How many years would it take to truly make a difference in this native culture? Bhavana had worked tirelessly for 20 years, and the problems there were still extensive. Nevertheless, we offered a program and through the years, many Certified Healing Touch instructors have generously participated. In 2004, Sivaraj, Malar and three small children were still living in a grass hut, but the concrete building that would become their home was half built. Ruth Muhr and Dan Snyder held a class for the Europeans in the nearby yoga hall. There were 16 students in this class from 8 different countries.

The native class was co-taught by Martha Rather and Margaret Leslie. Fifteen students attended, including Sivaraj, a passionately interested lady from Sri Lanka, our translator, and several young men from the village. During 2005, Kathleen Rosemary and I raised money for the next class series in India. We collected Healing Touch notebooks for Levels 1 and 2 that several of us planned to carry in our luggage. We also collected cash donations and sales from used books so that we could donate $750 to build a free-standing classroom next to the Sivaraj home. When we arrived, the classroom with a concrete slab floor and thatched keet roofed with open sides for natural air-conditioning was complete for us to use. We also were able to provide scholarships for two women from Sri Lanka. In Feb. 2006, we returned for a more comprehensively planned class series. The HTI certified teachers attending were Deborah Larrimore, Janna Moll, Judy Meno, Margaret Leslie, Geraldine Hartmayer, and Martha Rather. The first weekend we split into 3 locations, teaching Level 1 to a total of 85 students. We spent the week being tourists and shopping. Then the second weekend we taught Level 2 in 3 locations to a total of 65 students. Three locations were needed because Indian men and women use separate classrooms.

In Feb. 2008, through the help of Kathleen and Healing Touch International Foundation, we received a grant to help with another class series. Once again the lady from Sri Lanka came to study Level 3 and brought her friend. She was already teaching introductory classes and practice sessions in the mountain region of Sri Lanka where she lived.

The instructors attending in 2008 were Vicki Slater, Mary Frost, Geraldine Hartmayer, Margaret Leslie, and Martha Rather. During those two weekends, seven classes were taught at different locations. This was an attempt to follow social protocol and teach the native men separately from the women and to teach the English speaking people separately. A total of 82 local and international students from 8 countries attended these classes. Mary Frost taught the first Level 3 class here. In Feb. 2010, a smaller group went to Auroville. The instructors were Mary Frost, MaryAnn Carlson, and Martha Rather. The classes taught included Introduction to Healing Touch to a group of 20 nursing students, Level 1 to the English speakers, and Level 3 to the Tamil women. It was truly amazing to see the personal growth in these Tamil women. Their poise increased and they radiated a new level of self-esteem. Their lives and the lives of their children had been changed forever. In 2012, Mary Frost took 3 friends with her to India. They were hosted in Auroville by Sivaraj and Malar as well as Debi Hood from Nashville, who was already visiting there. Mary taught 3 Level 1 classes.

To make classes accessible to all with an interest and to be of service, the classes taught to the native Tamils were free of charge and included lunch both days for all teachers and students. Lunch was paid for by donations raised by Marty Rather during the year. The classes taught at Verite Hall for the Europeans had a small charge that the Verite people collected for hall rent.

Auroville Students

We found two distinct types of students. The first type was the European visitors who had come for the winter to vacation and take classes in various yoga and healing arts. The classes for these students were conducted in English in an architecturally beautiful classroom. These classes were very similar to any Healing Touch class conducted in the United States.

The second group of students was the natives from the local villages, the Tamil-speaking people whom Sivaraj and Malar represented. We were told later how revolutionary our thinking was. No one had ever agreed to teach the local natives before. Earlier teachers (of all sorts of subjects) had been interested in teaching only the European students. We wanted to dig into the "grass roots." We also, quite innocently, showed up for the first class in native Indian dress, mainly because it is beautiful and functionally cooler. It touched the hearts of our sponsors and translators so deeply, as they perceived this showed respect for their culture, that one could see their eyes misting. We did not realize the enormity of this moment until it was explained later. The class began with our translator, who was a local schoolteacher and priest, leading us in a special blessing for success.

The first class was held on the roof of a building known locally as "the arts and crafts building." A keet roof of local tree fronds had been erected overhead to provide shade. The sides were left open to allow a breeze as the only air-conditioning. There were grass mats laid on the floor on which students could lie to receive their healings, with the healer also on the floor sitting next to them. We gratefully had chairs in which to sit for the beginning techniques.

Teaching in another language, such as Tamil, required mental gymnastics because it contains sounds not present in English. However, it did not take long to observe and feel how the language of the heart and the communication between the eyes was convincingly accurate. Soon the translator was needed primarily for the transmission of facts, but the demonstration of techniques seemed to be understood without translation and found eager students willing to get their energetic hands on each other.

The basic theory of chakras was not met with any skepticism at all, as we sometimes find in the United States. Chakras are mentioned as part of their cultural life. However, the idea of using a person's energy to relieve pain or improve his or her life in some way was a foreign idea. They eagerly wanted as much knowledge as they could get.

We found the students to be very intelligent. Their questions showed careful discrimination, and they seemed to remember everything. Repetition was rarely necessary. Many of them spoke some English, some more than others. On subsequent trips, we found that they had practiced and were speaking the language of energy, and they were always wanting more information and more personal healings.

I was especially astounded when I taught the first Level 2 class there. I had been hesitant to teach diagramming the energy field. Would they really understand what I was trying to communicate? However, the drawings of their first assessments surpassed my wildest expectations: they provided more detail than any beginning students in my previous experience.

We were surprised to discover that most of these Tamil people carried their aches and pains in the same spots that we Americans do, including headaches (even migraines) and neck, shoulder, and lower back pain. One year, the women showed so much joy as they found their pain dissolving that during lunch, they began to sing and dance, inviting us to join.

As this class series continued and several of the women completed Level 3, we noticed how their personal lives have been affected. Employment and earning a living is a foundational problem in every country. Our Level 3 graduates seem to hold themselves with better self-respect and stability within their families and jobs.

We have continued to teach European students in Auroville as well, although there is a different group every time. These students go back to their home countries and could possibly connect with Healing Touch in that area. We have had no follow-up connection with them.

Interview with Sivaraj and Malar

The following is a recorded interview.

Interviewer: What was the gateway that allowed Healing Touch into your community?

Sivaraj: I was a student of Siddha medicine (South India's version of Ayurveda) using healing herbs. The section of Auroville land entrusted to me and my family was devoted to growing herbs. Then in 1999, I met Kathleen who was attending an Intentional Community conference here. She told me about how to heal with the loving intention of the heart. It was all about love! I was very much interested in building this healing community. That's why I'm interested in bringing you people here and so we can learn together. The energy work helps us ground and feel support as a community.

Interviewer: Please describe your healing center community.

Sivaraj: At Martuvam Healing Forest, we teach people about how to recognize, grow, and use healing herbs and spices. Now we also have a classroom that can be used to teach classes on various subjects, especially Healing Touch. We used to have a dream of having a clinic where we could give healings and spa treatment to visiting tourists. But that involves having another building and licenses that we don't have. It is part of the dream still. We will see what the future brings.

Interviewer: So do you have a timetable to make this happen?

Sivarji: Plans cannot be that definite here. We did not

plan for the cyclone that hit us. (Dec. 30, 2011). It took 50% of the trees and plants out of the whole area. It will be a huge cost to rebuild, but that is what will happen. We can do it. We are focusing on our "MalarIndia" business (local women sewing quilts and making jewelry) to bring in money for food for our children as well as new plants. It is that basic here right now (March 2012). But we are building up again. We know we need only love.

Interviewer: What about those women who were our Level 3 students?

Malar: Yes, we see them all the time. Right now there are some jobs in Pondicherry—work on fixing some roads. They work there and then stop by on the way home, begging me for a healing for their aching bodies. I give healings whenever they come. I am happy to share the love.

Sivaraj: I see changes in my wife. She is really grounded now and has more inner strength. We want you and all the Healing Touch people to keep coming here and teaching us more. I really need this support from your group. We would like people to come regularly. Anyone who wants to "give" of their work can come. We have places for you to stay and work with us. I'm very happy to keep the love going! People can contact us at sivarajmalar@yahoo.com and www.martuvam.org and on Facebook as "Sivaraj Malar".

Southern India

BY RAUNI PRITTINEN KING, RN, MIH, HNB-BC, CHTPI

I have been traveling to Southern India for the past 10 years with the development of the Sri Narayani Hospital and Research Centre. Sri Narayani College of Nursing started with nine students in 2006 and has now about 350 students. The college of nursing offers a mid-wifery degree and two nursing education certifications, including a Bachelors of Science in Nursing degree. I have provided Healing Touch workshops for the nursing students and their instructors on two different occasions. Level 1 within the last two years had about 60 students in each class. In February 2012, students were able to enhance their skills by providing Healing Touch for patients in the Sri Narayani Hospital. My plan is to continue teaching Level 1 to the new nursing students and their instructors and offer a Level 2 class in the future.

Dharmasala, India

By Mary Frost, RN, MS, HN-BC, CHTP/I

Since 2005, classes have been held in Dharmasala, India. The classes were initiated by Tekla from Vancouver, Canada. She invited me to teach and I traveled there several times, one very exciting venture! The classroom which we used was sun-filled with many windows, and occasionally a monkey would swing by on the stairwells and electrical lines outside.

The students were very well aware of the concept of "energy", and their word is "Lung" for the movement of life force throughout the physical body. They found Healing Touch to be relaxing, restoring and uplifting. It was a great pleasure to be with them. Many of them were either first or second generation refugees from their home country of Tibet, from which they escaped from the Chinese rule over the high mountain passes into Nepal and then to their new home in India. Tekla had lined up translators for the classes, who were themselves very interested in healing and excited to be participating.

During Level 3 class, when I began the discussion of "angels and Spirit helpers," I asked the students if they were aware or understood the concept, and they all knowingly nodded their heads. The spokesperson for the group explained that their understanding is of the *Khondomas*, who are like the winged ones who travel in groups of five and are blue. That was an especially potent sharing as it showed the universality of the concept. We were invited to return next year to teach and also to present to a Buddhist nuns leadership conference.

Meeting His Holiness, the Dalai Lama

Through Tenzin, Mingma, and two Tibetan monks, now our friends, we were able to get a miracle audience with His Holiness the Fourteenth Dalai Lama! I told His Holiness that I came representing Healing Touch International and that we had been offering Healing Touch teaching at Men Tsee Khang Tibetan Medical College (and that two of us have taught there in the past), the Tibetan Women's Association, and to others in the community. He said with great emphasis, "Very Good". He took both Claire Barry's, my Healing Touch friend from South Africa, and my hands and had his photographer take our photo with him. I have the photo and still cannot believe that this happened! This opportunity was less than 24 hours in the arranging, and we learned that most people apply for this honor years in advance, and many are turned down. So—I am taking this as an honor for HTI and all of us and our work!

Mary Frost, Dalai Lama, Claire Barry

Ecuador

BY SUE KAGEL, RN, BSN, HN-BC, CHTP/I

Karin Delgadillo held a dream for over 5 years to bring Healing Touch to Ecuador. The dream began when she experienced a Healing Touch session at Canyon Ranch Health Resort while participating in a private retreat to bring healing to Global Women's Rights Activists. Inspired by the experience she received during her session, she felt it would be of great benefit to the communities of marginalized people she served through the Fundacion Chasquinet, a non-profit organization bringing programming for personal transformation and empowerment as well as placing Wi-Fi internet connection in rural and poor communities in Ecuador. The spark and passion motivating her was to make a difference in the lives of women, children, orphans, and "children in and of the streets," many of whom had been abused. She also wanted to assist the men in the communities.

Chasquinet (the Chasquis were the strong Mayan messenger runners) is part of Somos Telecentros, a group linking South America and the Caribbean through computer networking. This group is also part of an umbrella worldwide organization. Karin's role at the time as Executive Director and as group facilitator of Chasquinet placed her in a position of influence. Through the tele-centers in the communities, Chasquinet staff members created flyers and sent announcements regarding classes to spread the word of the upcoming classes.

I was invited to teach Healing Touch in several of the communities that Chasquinet served in Ecuador. Funds for classes were raised by students in the United States through creating and selling pendulums. Personal funds were used for airfare, travel and lodging. In June, 2004, (winter in Ecuador), I taught 5 classes over a 2 week period in various locations around the country assisted by my daughter Stephanie Pagac, a Level 3 student. Four classes were introductory, and one was a full Level 1 class for the Chasquinet staff. Karin, and Marcelo Galarza, a staff member who worked closely with the communities, served as our guides, translators, and photographers. Marcelo had no idea what he was in for, knew nothing about Healing Touch, and had only a working knowledge of English. However, as we traveled for hours between locations, we had the opportunity to talk about Healing Touch. Two weeks later, he could almost teach classes himself from translating so often, and he had a deep appreciation for Healing Touch work. Because language was a barrier, as some students spoke Spanish, some Quichua (a local dialect), and many did not read, Marcello created pictorial references that could be sent by internet and printed out to support practice groups.

Teaching in Ecuador was a very different experience than teaching in a classroom in the United States. Because scheduling classes in Ecuador was controlled by community leaders, we were required to meet with these government officials prior to teaching. After interviews, explanations of the work, and relating our intention of benefits to their communities, the officials gave permission to hold classes. The officials set the days and times; class started after work (3pm) and were finished before dark so that the women wouldn't "disappear" walking home. Women were given a day off during the weekend to cook, wash clothes in the open air laundry tubs, care for their families, and be ready for the new work week.

In each area, our teaching shifted to an introductory format that was based on the hours and content for meeting the needs of each community. In Toctiuco, a poor barrio on the slopes of Quito, the class was comprised of community leaders, a young man who wanted to help the high-risk teenage boys with whom he worked, and a group of child care workers. We evaluated the needs of the group, and identified a need for pain relief for legs and shoulders as people carried huge loads on their backs up and down the steep slopes. Class was short, focused and exciting. Although I had hoped to continue teaching a few more techniques to the same group the next day, class size doubled with our students bringing in family members, babies, grandmothers, husbands, and friends. We went with the flow.

This pattern repeated in each new community. Each community session focused on the needs of the specific community gained from questioning and dialogue with the government and community leaders as well as the students at the start of class. For example, women and children had issues of domestic violence. One of the women commented on the second day of class that she had offered Healing Touch to her husband on his return from work, drunk as usual. She related, "His back pain disappeared," and she added with a laugh, "He fell asleep and didn't beat me!"

In Colinas de Norte, a barrio on a mountain slope near Quito, class was directed toward child care workers, women elders, and indigenous women who spoke a different dialect. The class focus was on children, heart-centered presence, Chakra Connection, and Pain Management Techniques. We worked on large gym mats on the community building floor. Although it was winter, we had no heat or blankets. We found that Healing Touch was communicated through the energy of the class and demonstration of the techniques.

At Guacaracha, near Esmeraldas on the coast, the weather changed dramatically. We focused both on family issues and on headaches from heat and dehydration. Over the continental divide, we taught in Chaco, a rural town with a little four bed hospital. The medical workers were invited, and we taught to a physician, nurse, paramedics, a veterinarian, and a Peace Corps worker as well as members of the community. People in this area were totally comfortable with energy work, relating it to the work of the shaman using a guinea pig or an egg to pass over a patient to clear his or her energy. Our veterinarian loved to sense the energy of his various partners and claim with great humor that they "Felt like a chicken, or a monkey, or a burro!"

Carrying it Forward

After Karin invited me to teach, she enlisted the support of other staff members, Lilyn and Luly, as well as Marcello, to give Healing Touch introductions to over two thousand people. Many of the communities and people with whom they work have little to no medical care. People's stress levels are incredibly high, and they are often in survival mode. We heard comments, such as "Healing Touch is the only time I receive a loving touch" and "My husband used to beat me, now he asks for Healing Touch." Many who didn't believe Healing Touch would work for pain, headaches, and anxiety have been amazed and surprised at the benefits. Family members are learning Healing Touch to help elderly parents, and many younger men participate to help brings tools of relief to their wives and children. It is surprising the number of males in the classes, as compared to classes in other countries.

Changes noticed by the community members and the Chasquinet staff include a decrease in aggressive, violent behavior in the families who have learned Healing Touch, as well as stress relief and physical symptom relief. The Chasquinet staff's dedication and efforts continue to spread healing light through Ecuador, and they continue to introduce the concept of Healing Touch via telecommunication links to Central and South American and the Caribbean.

Presently, Healing Touch principles are integrated into Chasquinet workshops on personal and community transformation and are taught to be integrated into speech and actions. Each workshop begins with a grounding, breathing and body awareness/connection exercises. This begins the workshop journey with relaxation and enthusiasm. When used with anger management, Marcello reports, "before exploding, feel the feet and body, breathe and relax to act more intelligently and less aggressively." This has been very helpful in reducing domestic violence. Breathing is also encouraged to reduce fatigue.

The population is transient in the communities where Healing Touch was introduced. Some of the Telecenters closed, other leaders have moved, and it is difficult to maintain relationship with those who have been instructed. Yet, people are carrying the Healing Touch tools and memories with them.

South Africa

By Mary Frost, RN, MS, HN-BC CHTP/I

The Beginning (Spark)

I had the great blessing of being born of parents who had knowledge of war, peace, healing, and international relationships. My family was dedicated to international aid and relations and through this experience, I was exposed to people and cultures worldwide. That, coupled with extensive traveling and backpacking worldwide in my youth, prepped and schooled me in what has become a deep passion for world travel and exploration.

In 1990, I met Janet Mentgen at the American Holistic Nurses Association conference. This meeting and Healing Touch introductory class was a life changing experience. My soul "signed me up" for anything else that was to follow. It is the international work that has stretched and challenged me most and offered the sweetest and most precious of gifts. Whether traveling and teaching in Eastern Europe and Romania not long after the fall of the communist regime, on the island country of Bermuda constantly under the threat of tropical storms, in the multicultural Republic of South Africa with such desperate need, or in the various tropical and mountain regions of India, I have been called upon to "be in the moment" and adapt to any unexpected situation. This means being able to create what is necessary to teach in any environment and find the consistency in the basics of the work to connect heart to heart with anyone and into the universal understanding that we all contain within our human Spirit.

South African Experience

Healing Touch came into South Africa through Mary Jo Bulbrook in the 1990's. In 2004 the work was continued by Robin Goff RN CHTP/I and I. Classes were held across the region in Cape Town, Soweto, Johannesburg, Mowbray, Bonnytown, Riversonderend, and the Kalahari.

From that initial trip in 2004, a project was born, *Yebo Gogo*, which in Zulu means "Yes, Grandmother," in honor of the huge number of women caring for their grandchildren whose parents have died of AIDS. Now GOGO is an acronym for "Grandmothers United in Global Oneness". In February 2005, Robin, Linda Elaine Smith and I returned for a second time to bring hope and Healing Touch to South Africa. The focus was to teach Healing Touch techniques to caregivers of persons suffering from and dying of AIDS as well as to those who care for some of the millions of orphaned children in Africa. We traveled to Johannesburg, Soweto, and Cape Town to teach and distribute donated medical supplies and gifts made by American school children. We continue to return to teach Healing Touch and support this organization.

Cape Town's Growth

Jessica Abramson, RN, CHTP, was one of the students in the 2005 class who describes the culture of Cape Town as a multicultural city that includes Africans (indigenous and those from many other African countries who have migrated here and speak many different languages), English, Afrikaans, Muslims, Jews, Indians, and other subgroups. Each cultural sub group has its own healing traditions and healers along with various herbalists, naturopaths, massage therapists, etc. And, of course, for those who can afford it, there are the large western medicine hospitals. It was when her own son was gravely ill that Jessica sought out across cultural lines, received healing for him, and opened her views to other approaches. Jessica shares her spark and journey:

> I came back to the Healing Touch courses as they were offered in Cape Town. It was at Level 3 that I "got it" and felt I could do this and offer it to patients and others on a regular basis—and put it into my practice. I have also accompanied Mary Frost to offer Healing Touch in the poor townships of Cape Town for elders and women who care for orphaned children. I take every opportunity to bring Healing Touch to other South African cities and provinces. Our hope is to have our own instructor one day. Healing Touch has been one of the greatest gifts of my life.

Claire Barry, Healing Touch Practitioner Apprentice (HTI-PA) in Cape Town, has worked regularly on a voluntary basis with many community organizations. Predominantly the organizations are orphanages or care centers for children infected or affected by HIV/AIDS. Children whose parents have died of AIDS are most often looked after by their grandparents, in particular their grandmothers. These grandmothers and caregivers suffer immensely from stress and stress related diseases from looking after children in desperately inadequate conditions. It is with these grandmothers as well as the children's caregivers that Claire has offered and taught Healing Touch introductory classes. Her goal is to become a Certified Healing Touch Instructor and to perpetuate the work of Healing Touch International on the mother continent.

Soweto

On one trip to South Africa, I taught an eight-hour basic Healing Touch class for caregivers in Soweto, a township formed during the segregating time of Apartheid in the outskirts of Johannesburg for the relocation of dark-skinned Africans. The job of these strong and compassionate caregivers is to walk out into nearby informal settlement camps in mostly ill-fitting shoes with heavy backpacks of supplies and to care for homebound ill and dying persons. For the next couple of days after the class, I accompanied two of the caregivers on their patient rounds to observe, learn their work, offer them suggestions for comfort care, and to encourage them in using Healing Touch to treat pain, restlessness, insomnia, and other conditions. I was most humbled when we walked through rows of shack homes on wash water muddied paths to find our designated care recipients. The caregivers were most appreciative to know the basic Healing Touch treatments to use as a part of their care. Every morning before they leave their office on their rounds, they all gather to sing and pray and connect with a fortifying source of Spirit to sustain them for the day ahead.

The Kalahari Experience (Gateway)

On a subsequent trip to South Africa in 2010, I had another incredible opportunity to teach and share Healing Touch in the Northern Cape Province with my dear friend, Claire Barry, who had told me many times about her experiences with the Khomani San, "first" peoples of the Kalahari Desert region. She not only served the people of the community through a job with United Nations Educational, Scientific and Cultural Organization (UNESCO) for three years, she also connected and studied with the healers and elders of the community on many subsequent stays and sought out grant funds to support projects of all kinds. She made preparations for me to come and offer a Level 1 Healing Touch in the small town of Andriesvale.

The San, gatherer-hunters for untold thousands upon thousands of years, have been robbed of their heritage by fences, European colonialists, slavery, roads and their foreign crews who carried alcohol, nutrition deprived "western" foods, and HIV/AIDS. The San still gather desert foods, such as tiny watermelons and larvae in cocoons to roast over the fire.

My first experience was to help organize a Healing Touch clinic for women and children on the grounds of "the office", a small one room building that holds two computers and two women staff, all continuing from the UNESCO project. The clinic space is a large tree with spreading shade limbs and a handful of mismatched chairs. We arrived, and the recipients of the Healing Touch treatments trickled down the dusty road with hats or colorful scarves on their heads while carrying swaddled babies. There were four of us doing the treatments as I had brought two other students of Healing Touch along for part of the trip. Many of the women recipients reported to Claire of headaches or body pains subsiding and getting sleepy and relaxed, or feeling good.

A few of the women who availed themselves of the open air clinic hours and two men also attended the Level 1 class the next weekend. We finished day two without the men and added an elder granny, Oma Nas. She was asked to speak about her knowledge of San healing traditions for our benefit and the younger women present. She described in her native language, at times sliding into a nearly extinct language of many clicks and other sounds, the traditional Trance Dance (still practiced by some San groups) and how a medicine man would suck out the "disease" from a person lying in the middle of the dance circle and then run quickly out of the circle to expel it from his nose and mouth by coughing. She also spoke of the gathered herbs used in various ways and of those who had the gift "to see" and use their hands on the bodies of others to coax a healing or cure. Claire shared her experience as follows:

> At present in this community there are three healers—two women and one man who is also a herbalist—who practice healing as their livelihoods. Many other people treat family and friends on an unofficial basis. Their method of energy healing is called *Smeer*, an Afrikaans word which means to rub with a substance. Smeer is a combination of energy

healing, massage and manipulation. One of the aspects of my personal work in this community is to encourage the recognition and continued use of Traditional Healing methods. Intros and the Level 1 class were attended by mostly young women. My hope is that these young women will take on the roles of community Healers as they mature. The older woman who attended the classes also practice smeer. I've used Healing Touch extensively within this community, which I see has had an impact on the continued use of energy healing here.

Chapter Summary

Healing Touch work continues to ripple and flow, bringing new opportunities in healing through the passion of the students, practitioners, and instructors as they move around in the world or feel drawn to introduce Healing Touch through their families, friends or professional connections. It is the spark of the individuals and their motivation that continues to *spread Healing Touch worldwide.* Those who carry Healing Touch forward frequently mention that they feel called to follow a dream or have a vision of sharing the work with a particular population. Some start as service projects, while others bring together friends or colleagues which evolves into formal class training. Some other avenues to spread the work have been through the Peace Corps, universities, medical centers, and service projects.

Classes have also been taught in Trinidad/Tobaggo, Tibet, Nepal, Romania, Sri Lanka, Uganda, and Cambodia, where small groups continue the work informally or communities are beginning to grow. The sparks will continue to ignite the flow of the Healing Touch work through the passions and calling of individuals and their dedication to providing health and healing across communities, cultures, and continents for the highest good of all.

Healing Touch has spread worldwide by the efforts of individuals just like you. Some have had visions of travel to distant lands where this work could be of benefit, and some just went where they were asked to go. The only requirements for working internationally are a desire and passion to spread healing light, keeping in mind the needs of those being taught and served and with respect for their cultures and location. Each individual has a unique gift to offer. The best place to start is in the home, wherever you may be.

CHAPTER 2
HISTORY OF HEALING TOUCH EDUCATION AND CERTIFICATION

Healing Touch evolved from long lines of traditions and cultures, and many different bodies of energy work. Energy therapies have been present around the world, both formally and informally, for thousands of years. Several of these were discussed in Chapter 1. The history of how these concepts were brought together into a standardized Healing Touch course of study and certification are explored in this chapter. Healing Touch Practitioner and Instructor Certification was originally offered through the American Holistic Nurses Association (AHNA) from 1993 to 1996, at which time it was transferred intact to the newly created Healing Touch International, Inc. (HTI). In 2013 Healing Touch International changed its name to Healing Beyond Borders to better represent its mission and vision, with all other aspects remaining the same. The course work remains as the *HTI Healing Touch Certificate Program*. The objectives of this chapter are as follows:

1. Describe the mission of Healing Touch International, Inc./ Healing Beyond Borders.
2. Outline the development and importance of Healing Touch Practitioner and Instructor certification and credentialing.
3. Discuss the significance of the timeline development of Healing Touch International, Inc.

Art and Practice of Healing Touch

Healing Touch focuses on healing, rather than on providing a cure. A cure assumes that a certain practice, for example a medication or surgery, can eradicate the disease or illness. Healing, however, unfolds through a person's innate ability to discover the self and return to harmony and balance (Dossey, 1993). Healing is about becoming whole throughout all aspects of self. When healing occurs, it may be on multiple levels. The person may be freed of symptoms but this may not be the ultimate goal. The practitioner intends the highest good for a client, not just symptom relief. An example of healing versus curing is seen in the following story:

> A busy physician had suffered a recent fracture in her hand and was in a great deal of pain. A practitioner offered her a brief Healing Touch session. Rather than experiencing pain relief, the physician received insight into what was needed for her healing. The physician realized she needed to go home to rest and care for herself and allow herself to heal, rather than pushing herself to continue working.

All healing is self-healing, whereas curing the symptom could include taking medication to remove the pain and, thereby, allowing her to work. However, her underlying problem would remain. Instead, by engaging the healing process, there was now an awareness of the individual's need to do his/her part.

Healing Touch can be used in a variety of situations as it is a non-invasive intervention and does not require manipulation of the physical body. It can safely be used with individuals of all ages, from the smallest newborn (Hanley, 2008; McDonough-Means, Aicken, & Bell, 2006) to the frail elderly (Wardell, Decker, & Engebretson, 2012).

Becoming a Practitioner

The HTI Healing Touch Certificate Program offered by Healing Beyond Borders has a standardized curriculum so that classes, taken anywhere in the world, are consistent. The training program has 5 levels, including a one-year mentorship program. Level 1 focuses on recognizing energy concepts, the Healing Touch process, and developing skills in performing basic Healing Touch techniques. Level 2 increases the breadth and depth of study and focuses on the interview, back techniques, and performing a healing sequence. Level 3 focuses on cultivating and clarifying the energy of the practitioner, development of higher sense perception, sequencing, and additional techniques for clearing the field. Level 4 is designed to prepare the student to become a practitioner and establish a practice setting. Additional Healing Touch techniques are also learned at this level for preparation and healing work. Level 5 focuses on completion of the projects in Level 4 with a more in-depth understanding of principles and practice components of Healing Touch.

The training process usually takes a minimum of two years to complete, although the pace for completing training is flexible. Completion of the 5 levels of the program confers the title of Healing Touch Practitioner (HTI-P). An HTI-P has the necessary prerequisites to apply for certification as an HTI Certified Healing Touch Practitioner (CHTP). Upon meeting necessary criteria and demonstrating competency in the principles and practice of Healing Touch, the HTI-P applicant is awarded the credential of CHTP, which is to be renewed every 5 years through continuing education and peer review. For those desiring to become a Certified Healing Touch Instructor (CHTI), additional instructional process and certification are required.

Overview of Healing Beyond Borders

As a non-profit service organization for Healing Touch members and students, Healing Beyond Border's mission is to spread healing and light worldwide through the heart-centered practice and teaching of Healing Touch. The purpose of Healing Beyond Borders includes, but is not limited to, the following mission:

- Provide continuing education for nurses, health care professionals and others.
- Promote and provide resources in research in Healing Touch and health care integration.
- Provide certification of Practitioners and Instructors in Healing Touch.
- Provide community education of energy based therapies.

Healing Beyond Borders utilizes a Code of Ethics/Standards of Practice, Scope of Practice and Instructor Guidelines to guide the ethical application of Healing Touch. The standards are set in place in order to insure safe and ethical practice. There are 12 standards/codes that include the following: how practitioners integrate and practice Healing Touch within their professional practice; the collaborative nature of Healing Touch within conventional care; the importance of self-care; the equality and acceptance of the client as an equal partner in the process of healing; how information is provided to clients; the process of a Healing Touch session; setting intention for the highest good of the client; creating a healing environment; the principle of healing as a unique self-healing process; maintenance of confidentiality; providing quality care; and focus on one's professional responsibility in representing Healing Touch to the public (www.healingbeyondborders.org).

The Scope of Practice statement defines the levels of Healing Touch practice that include the student, apprentice, practitioner, and certified practitioner. The statement also includes instructors and instructors in training. The Instructor Guidelines identify principles of conduct for instructors that include expected professional behavior within the classroom. The Core Values of Healing Beyond Borders are integrity, heart-centeredness, respect of self and others, service, community, and unconditional love.

Recognizing the importance of evidence-based practice, Healing Beyond Borders champions the study and research of Healing Touch. In 1997 a Research Director position was created to support and promote research in Healing Touch. In 2010 this evolved to the organization's Research Committee, which continues to assist and promote research in Healing Touch. Healing Touch studies are reviewed in Chapter 9.

The organization also encourages integration of Healing Touch as a complementary therapy to standard medical care and since 1998, has provided consultation services to individuals and health care facilities. In addition to the standard HTI Healing Touch Certificate Program, Healing Beyond Borders offers additional continuing education opportunities through the Annual International Energy Healing Conference and the Professional Development Series.

The Healing Beyond Borders website provides access to a database of classes, practitioners, clinics, and support groups worldwide and links with affiliate countries offering Healing Touch. Through collaboration with like-minded individuals, Healing Beyond Borders members hold true to the organization's vision to *Spread Healing, Light, and Love, Creating Wholeness on Earth.*

Credentialing: The Valuing and Credibility of Our Work

By Mildred I. Freel, MEd, RN, CHTP/I, RM

Credentialing enables HTI (now Healing Beyond Borders) to be accountable to the public for the safety and competence of HTI practitioners and instructors. This process has been in place for over two decades. In 1992 AHNA appointed a credentialing task force to develop a process by which the graduates of the Holistic Nursing Program and Healing Touch Certificate Program could become certified. The credentialing task force's activities in the early 1990s included developing, designing, implementing and measuring the five levels of the Healing Touch course curriculum. These two groups agreed that a credentialing program needed to be in place and operative for these two educational programs within the near future.

Changes in Health Care and Need for Credentialing

The AHNA leadership could see that alternative and complementary health care modalities were gaining in recognition and their use was becoming consumer driven. Credentialing would be essential for the services of these holistic nurses and Healing Touch practitioners to be accepted into mainstream health care.

Credentialing Definition and Quality Maintenance

Credentialing is a process such as licensure, accreditation and certification. It may be a government based legal requirement for a person, program, or agency to engage in a service offer to the public, or may be optional or voluntary, where the individual seeks the designation for the benefit it bestows (Styles, 1986). A major goal of credentialing is to protect society from sub-standard service and fraud (Brown, 1975). Credentialing confers recognition of a practitioner's knowledge, skill, and competence in a special area (Nemeth, 2012). The credibility of the credentialing process resides in the following:

1. The credentialing agent's (i.e. Certification Board members) activities are free of conflict of interest.
2. The credentialing criteria and standards have been designated by experts in the field.
3. The decision to offer credentials is based on a valid measurement of the criteria.

Credentialing agents designate whether a person, program of study, or service has met predetermined specific standards or criteria, as identified by experts in the field (ANA, 1979). The agents are expected to provide selfless service, maintain low visibility, and ensure confidentiality of information acquired during the credentialing activity. In regard to those credentialed, quality of service is maintained by the credentialing agency setting standards and periodically monitoring activities of those persons or programs of study. If the public is to be well served, the credential of the practitioner and program accreditation must remain current.

AHNA Credentialing Board Process

Early in the decision making process, AHNA's credentialing task force (composed of instructors from each of the two educational programs), recommended that an autonomous certification board be established for each of AHNA's educational programs and the credentialing process be guided by criteria and standards. The certification boards, composed of AHNA members who were graduates of and credentialed in the AHNA educational program for which they would be conferring certification, were to have complete autonomy over decisions regarding certification of applicants, who were graduates of the respective educational programs. To verify that those certified maintained their competency, a renewal process was developed and required for the continued use of the certification designation.

The Healing Touch Certificate Program was unique in that it accepted as students not only nurses but also other health care providers and persons interested in healing. Persons who were not nurses were required to present evidence that they had been mentored by a nurse for a year. Therefore, the certification option was not limited to nurses.

Certifying Instructors

In the early 1990's, a formal structure of instructor apprenticeship training was established to prepare instructors for the Healing Touch Certificate Program. The purview of the certification board was expanded to include the certification of instructors. Henceforth, instructors were required to be Certified Healing Touch Instructors (CHTI), to renew their Instructor Certification every five years, and to maintain themselves as Certified Healing Touch Practitioners (CHTP) with ongoing practices.

Portfolio Process

Believing that the ability to utilize the healing process is the essential element which determines the competence of a practitioner, the credentialing task force chose a portfolio approach as the measurement instrument for review of applicants for certification. A portfolio is an organized, purposeful, collection of entries that permits open-ended, rather than single answer testing, and allows for individualized, reflective presentations. Reflection is a significant part of the portfolio process as it identifies the rationale for entries, growth, and achievement and illuminates creative thinking. The applicant's entries, documents, displays and examples of work tell the story of change, growth, and acquisition of skill competence as well as the ability to use energy in a therapeutic manner (Bryne et al., 2007). In October 1993, the AHNA Certification Board, using the portfolio approach to validate ability, conferred the first certification of a Healing Touch Practitioner. AHNA continued issuing certifications through April 1996.

AHNA Healing Touch Certification Moves to HTI

In 1996, AHNA determined that the credentialing of practitioners and instructors of the Healing Touch Certificate Program, that included both allied health professionals as well as laypersons, was not within the mission of the AHNA. The AHNA transferred all credentialing activities to the newly founded, non-profit organization Healing Touch International, Inc. All certification procedures, governing policies, and Certification Board members remained in place. The difference was that certification was now offered through HTI rather than AHNA.

Trends in Health Care

In today's healthcare settings, community integrative care centers are emerging, and conventional treatment centers are adopting integrative care departments and programs. The use of complementary and integrative modalities helps nursing and other health care providers to mature in their practice mission and expand their scope of practice, all of which enhances, rather than conflicts with, professional practice. Integration of complementary care modalities impacts conventional care, as Nightingale, the founder of nursing, advised, "to put the patient in the best condition for nature to act upon him" (Nightingale, 1969, p. 133). However, credentialing of complementary and integrative therapists and practitioners as well as complementary care programs is imperative for acceptance.

Credentialing provides a stamp of approval, indicating to the public, other health care providers and health care agencies that the providers of such modalities are safe and competent (Styles, 1986). In addition, research is validating that the work of the Healing Touch Practitioner is not only safe, but it is also efficacious.

In the early 1980s, AHNA leadership foresaw the changes that would impact the interface of Western health delivery systems and complementary and alternative medicine (CAM) therapies and validate the need for credentialing. Some changes that have occurred are as follows:

- In 1984, the North America Nursing Diagnosis Association (NANDA) added the Nursing Diagnosis of "Energy Field Disturbance" to its list of Nursing Diagnoses (Carpenito, 1984). The intervention represents a specific nursing theory—the human energy field theory—and requires specialized instruction and supervised practice. The diagnosis of Energy Field Disturbance is a state in which a disruption of the flow of energy surrounding a person's being results in a disharmony of the body, mind, and/or spirit.
- In 1992, the National Institute for Health (NIH) created an Office of Alternative Medicine and designated federal funding of alternative and complementary health care modalities (National Institute for Health [NIH], 1994).
- In 1994, the NIH published a report classifying alternative and complementary modalities and systems, further recognizing and legitimizing their place in the health care arena (NIH, 1994).
- In the 1990's, theory-based, conceptual systems became part of nursing culture. This paved the way for acceptance of Martha Roger's theory (The Unitary Human Being), which describes the human as an energy field, as applicable to nursing practice (Barrett, 1990).
- In 1996, HTI developed and published a statement of Standards of Care, which included a definition of Scope of Practice and Code of Ethics/Standards of Practice. This provided a professional attribute recognized by mainstream health care.
- In the late 1990s, HTI supported research through establishing a Director of Research and the Healing Touch International Foundation, which distributed funds to support research

projects regarding Healing Touch. It also provided a consultant for Integrative Health Care.

- Also in the late 1990's, State Boards of Nursing included biofield therapies, such as Healing Touch, within the scope of practice for the registered nurse. For example, in 1998, the Iowa Board of Nursing voted to affirm that:

> Therapeutic Touch and Healing Touch were within the scope of practice of the registered nurse when the nurse has the appropriate education and skill to perform the function. As with any nursing activity that requires specialized nursing knowledge and skill, the Board holds the individual nurse accountable and expects the nurse to personally possess current clinical competence to perform the act safely.

- Because the Healing Touch Certificate Program was developed following the continuing education model, State Boards of Nursing allowed Healing Touch classes to be used to meet licensure requirements. The Specialty of Holistic Nursing was added in 2010.
- During the decade of 2000, regulatory boards focused on evidence and competency-based nursing practice. This created the basis for the incorporation, credibility, and use of research findings regarding Healing Touch in health care settings. After 2000, the American Nurses Association (ANA) rapidly expanded its Certification of Specialties, using the portfolio approach (Bryne, 2007).

Current Credentialing Trends

Currently, a number of subspecialties are moving from the test format to the portfolio approach, such as Credentialing for Genetics Nursing (Monsen, 2005). Additionally, new ones are being added, such as the announcement in 2012 by the American Nurses Credentialing Center (ANCC) of portfolio certification for Advanced Forensic Nursing and the

Emergency Nurses Association's New Portfolio Credential for Emergency Nurse Practitioners (ANCC Report, 2013).

Chapter Summary

Many individuals have contributed to furthering the work of Healing Touch through self-less service. This includes not only the directors of Healing Beyond Borders but the many additional volunteers who serve on the credentialing board, committees and work within their communities and also the thousands of students who carry the work forward. It maintains a high level of integrity and acceptance in the health care community and beyond because of its standard curriculum and nursing process format.

CHAPTER 3

FOUNDATIONAL ASPECTS
OF HEALING WORK

This chapter introduces you to various professionals' conceptualization of energy healing. The chapter begins with a focus on nursing, as Healing Touch is originally a nursing intervention. Other sciences, including medicine, biology, physics, and math that explore the nature of healing are included. The perspectives provided are not meant to be all inclusive. For example, a medical intuitive physician's view is not the view of traditional western belief systems. The objectives of the chapter are as follows:

1. Explore nursing theorists' concepts related to Healing Touch as a nursing intervention.
2. Recognize the influence of intention on the formation of thought.
3. Summarize various theories that contribute to an understanding of energy therapies.
4. Identify various theories and approaches that contribute to a holistic approach to health and healing.

Also included in this chapter are the science of intentionality and the physics of healing from an electromagnetic induction perspective. Complexity science, in which change is looked at as a result of a series of interactive events, provides for future explorations and challenges to the traditional way of looking at cause and effect. The view changes from a linear concept (do this then that occurs) to a view of individualized complex adaptive systems (do this and that will affect this, which will affect that, etc.).

Nursing: The Approach and Theorists

Nursing provides one way to explore various aspects of healing as nursing involves the person, his or her environment, and the provider. Nursing incorporates a holistic view that includes personal attributes of the physical (body), emotional (relationships), mental (thoughts), and spiritual (connection to something beyond the self). Nursing is a perfect discipline for housing Healing Touch because of its broad view and role in assisting others in their healing journey. The nursing process is evident throughout the Healing Touch curriculum and includes gathering subjective (interview) and objective (assessment of the field and chakras) information, developing a plan, and providing an action or intervention that uses Healing Touch techniques. Evaluation, both of and from the person, follows the intervention, and the process concludes with teaching and referral. The North American Nursing Diagnosis Association provides the following diagnosis for working with the body's energy system: "Disturbed Energy Field: a disruption of the flow of energy surrounding a person's being results in disharmony of the body, mind, and/or spirit" (Gadwig & Wardell, 2011, p 345).

Martha Rogers: The Science of Unitary Human Beings

By Valerie S. Eschiti, PhD, RN, AHN-BC, CHTP, CTN-A

Of all nursing theories, Martha Rogers' conceptual system, the Science of Unitary Human Beings (SUHB), most closely resonates with the energetic basis of Healing Touch. According to the Society of Rogerian Scholars (2008), Dr. Rogers began nursing school in 1933 and obtained a doctoral degree in 1954. She was a futurist, a nurse ahead of her time. Her hunger for knowledge and understanding led her to study the sciences, math, and physics. She synthesized her learning and experiences to develop a conceptual model or system, describing SUHB as an abstraction of reality rather than a theory. The four major concepts of SUHB as outlined by Rogers (1986) are defined in Table 1.

Table 1. Major Concepts of the Science of Unity Human Beings

Energy Fields	Fundamental units of living and nonliving beings; cannot be reduced to the sum of their parts (e.g. biological, social, physical, and psychological fields).
Openness	Energy fields are not closed, but are open to influence from other energy fields.
Pattern	A characteristic of an energy field that is perceived as a wave.
Four-dimensionality	A nonlinear domain without attributes of space or time; it characterizes human and environmental energy fields.

An important conceptual link between Rogers' SUHB and Healing Touch is the notion of the existence of energy fields. As Rogers (1986) explained, "Energy fields are postulated to constitute the fundamental unit of both the living and the non-living. *Field* is a unifying concept. *Energy* signifies the dynamic nature of the field. *Energy fields* are infinite" (p 4). Rogers classified two types of energy fields: human and environmental. She specified that humans and environments do not *have* energy fields, but rather, they *are* energy fields. Thus, the interaction between human and environmental fields affects the health of human beings.

According to the conceptual underpinnings of SUHB, the energy fields of a client and Healing Touch practitioner interact. For example, suppose a client comes to her appointment from a situation in which she has just been fired from her high-level managerial position in a hectic office. The client wishes to reduce anxiety and gain a sense of balance and equilibrium. As the Healing Touch practitioner assesses the client's energy field, she feels jagged spikes of fast-moving energy emerging from the client's chest and abdominal areas, at the 3rd and 4th chakras. These jagged spikes are in stark contrast to the smooth, curved, and slow-moving energy the practitioner feels in a client who is calm. The practitioner uses the Hands-in-Motion technique, moving her hands slowly and gently above the client's body, to assist the client to re-pattern her energy field to a balanced state. The room is a comfortable temperature, with soothing music playing in the background. By the end of the session, the practitioner notes the person's breathing rate has slowed and deepened, and the spikes of energy have softened into undulating, wave-like curves. The client reports her heart no longer feels like it is "racing", and she has a sense of well-being and peace.

In this scenario, the energy field work of the practitioner and the peaceful environment interacted to re-pattern the client's field in a healthful manner and led to the outcome of a calm demeanor. Through this example, one can understand how Roger's conceptual model can be used to explain interactions and be incorporated into a healing practice.

Additional Reflections on Martha E. Rogers

BY LISA ANSELME RN, BLS, HN-BC, CHTP/I

From the first time I was exposed to her ideas as a nursing student, I was intrigued by Martha Rogers. She was so evidently ahead of her time. She was a truly brilliant nurse theorist and educator. Born in 1914, and sharing a birthday with Florence Nightingale, Martha Rogers also was a visionary and leader in the field of nursing and transformative healthcare. Martha had what could be described as a renaissance education, in that she studied not only the biological sciences, but also liberal arts, art, languages, and psychology while maintaining a very keen interest in space.

As previously described by Dr. V. Escheti, Dr. Rogers' theory is foundational and highly applicable to the nursing profession, our work in Healing Touch, and essentially, all biofield therapies. Within this SUHB framework (Rogers, 1986), human beings are irreducible wholes—contrary to our recent medical model of sub-specialization and inquiry that includes an ever increasing dissection of care of the human body into specialty areas, there is recognition within Roger's framework of an all-inclusive and complete human being that interrelates and is inseparable from the universe and in which the whole is much greater than the sum of its individual parts.

Further exploration of the four components of the SUHB includes the following.

1. An **energy field** is the basic unit of both the living and the nonliving, is both the human and environmental and is ever changing, continuous, open, increasingly diverse and infinite. An underlying principle is that human beings *are* energy fields, rather than have energy fields. This premise is foundational to our work Healing Touch, and it helps to explain how our work within the accessed energy field can create change and healing in any or all areas of the human being: body, mind, emotion, spirit, and transpersonal.

2. **Openness.** Of note is that Rogers describes the energy fields as consistently open, infinite and integral with each other. In our assessment of the client, we may describe an aspect of the field as "closed" or "compromised", but in actuality, this is simply a reference type of description. It is this writer's perspective that there is consistently true openness in the energy centers and other aspects of the field that continues to exist throughout the lifespan, and even for hours following death. The concept of openness is what allows for the opportunity of learning, expansion, and growth.

3. **Pattern** is an abstract, identifying characteristic of the energy field and is perceived as single waves. In Dr. Cowling's 2008 keynote address at the 12th Annual Healing Touch International Conference, he noted that our "appreciation of the ever expanding wholeness in the person, to participate knowingly with conscious awareness of their wholeness, and honoring and respecting the information that they know and hold about themselves, leads to transformation and change that truly frees people." This is the basis for our practice. It is demonstrated as we simultaneously assess the individual and maintain awareness of areas of constriction along the health continuum, while looking beyond to the perfection and whole person, recognizing their true nature, and releasing the vision of the constriction or dis-ease.

Feelings, attitudes, and emotions are not isolated events but are translated into bodily changes that simultaneously affect all parts of the body. Pain and illness are recognized as a natural part of life and are valuable signals of areas of constriction of flow. Modalities based on Rogers' SUHB model include patient participation in pattern appraisal related to the health events and deliberate mutual health patterning to promote harmony, healing, and comfort. In our Healing Touch work, we observe with all of our 5 senses—along with High Sense Perception— and seek, discover, and reveal the unique patterning that exists within each person, while recognizing the similarities between persons and the relationships between persons and their environment. It is the signature of the person that identifies him or her, while still acknowledging the interrelationships and non-separateness from the whole.

4. **Pandimensional.** "Human field image" offers a pandimensional (formerly four dimensional) view of unitary human beings and their non-physical components. The model portrays reality as being pandimensional, nonlinear, and infinite. Dr. Rogers did not believe that we move or evolve into pandimensionality, but rather this is a way of perceiving a reality without limit. She noted how gifted and "hyperactive" children shared common behaviors that were more in line with an accelerating evolution (nonlinear and infinite) rather than something outside of an outdated "norm". This appeared indicative of the increasing speed and frequency of human energy field rhythms that matched higher frequency environmental field patterns. Human and environments are simultaneously and cohesively evolving. She felt that this described the common, changed patterns associated with aging, such as increasing variability of sleep-wake cycles and the perception of an ever increasing racing of time. She also believed that this helped explain precognition, clairvoyance, and (this author would include) clairaudience and clairsentience as being rational and logical in a pandimensional field experience. In our work in Healing Touch, these skills and appreciations are frequently enhanced in the maturing

practitioner, and in the SUHB model, these experiences would be considered within the norm rather than as outliers.

In addition to the above four components, Dr. Rogers (1986) described three principles of homeodynamics, a distinction from homeostasis. With the SUHB, humans are not seeking stasis or fixed movement and stability, rather we humans are seeking an ever expanding frequency and pattern. These three principles are as follows:

1. **Resonancy** involves the ever-continuing change from lower to higher vibratory frequency and wave patterns in both human and environmental fields.
2. **Helicy** is a continuous, changing, innovative, and increasingly diversifying human and environmental field patterning containing non-repeating rhythms.
3. **Integrality** describes a continuous, interactive, and interrelated human and environmental field process.

Within our clinical practice of Healing Touch, this translates into our findings of ever expanding vibratory fields that are unique and diverse—as we practice self-care and in the fields of others with whom we work—and helps to explain the dynamic energetic interrelationship that we find between the individual and his or her environment. Through this work, there is a recognition that change is always in the direction of increasing diversity and complexity of pattern in ever expanding wholeness and infinite potential.

Margaret Newman: Health as Expanding Consciousness

By Mary E. Brekke, RN, PhD, CHTP, AHN-BC

Margaret Newman (1990, 1994, 2008) built on the theory of Martha Rogers. Newman incorporated the concepts of the unity of the whole, unidirectionality, pattern, and mutual process in the client-nurse relationship. Newman emphasized that whereas medicine focuses on diseases and their symptoms, nursing focuses on health. She described her theory of Health as Expanding Consciousness and postulated the following five assumptions (Newman, 2008, p. 3–5):

1. Health encompasses conditions heretofore described as illness, or in medical terms, pathology.
2. These pathological conditions can be considered a manifestation of the total pattern of the individual.
3. The pattern of the individual that eventually manifests itself as pathology is primary and exists prior to structural or functional changes. The pattern identifies the human-environmental process and is characterized by meaning.
4. Removal of the pathology in itself will not change the pattern of the individual.
5. If becoming "ill" is the only way an individual's pattern can manifest itself, then that is health for that person.

According to Newman (2008), health includes disease and illness, and diseases or disruptions are part of the self-organizing process of expanding consciousness. Expanding consciousness gives one a sense of growing in meaning and understanding. Further, it is "*following a path to one's center*" (p 37).

Newman (1990) stated that change occurs "when the old rules don't work anymore, a time when one must make a choice. The task is to learn how things work, to discover the new rules, and to move into a new level of being, understanding" (p.39). Therefore, the person's task, when placed in a chaotic situation, is to come to a new higher order. Whatever manifests itself in a person's life is a reflection of the underlying pattern. Even disease is a reflection of a person's pattern of consciousness.

The role of the nurse is to assist clients to become aware of their individual patterns that (by definition) include the current illness or disruption. Recognition of the presence of and unconditional acceptance of the pattern are at the center of the interaction. This recognition and acceptance result in expanding consciousness, or an "ah-ha" moment, for the client.

According to Newman (2008), one's pattern is held in an informational field and is non-energetic, non-local, and present everywhere. An assumption of health as expanding consciousness is that there is an inter-penetration between the fields of the nurse and the patient when the nurse is fully present to the patient. Newman sometimes refers to presence as resonance, or a vibrational frequency.

Application

Healing Touch can be used to assist a client to achieve a new level of understanding, or *to expand one's consciousness* in regard to an aspect of life that relates to health. As the practitioner becomes centered, grounded and fully present to the client through interpenetrating fields, the practitioner provides the opportunity for the client to enter this center. The client becomes fully present to the moment, to her/himself, and to the greater knowledge and wisdom that is available.

The more practitioners can work from an open flowing system of ever expanding consciousness through their own chakras (by engaging in self-care practices and personal development), the more they can provide clients opportunities to do the same. The practitioner sets the intention for the client's highest good and infinite potential/expansion. The client sets the intention by being open to this expanding consciousness. The practitioner can also use intention to assist clients in their experience of expanding consciousness. For example by offering, "I intend to facilitate the client's opportunity for learning what is useful at this time."

Some questions for a client to explore at the beginning of the session from Newman's perspective might be:

1. What can I learn from this illness/problem/situation?
2. What can I do that is helpful to me?
3. Might this illness/problem/situation be related to_____? (fill in personal situation, such as a stressful job)

These questions could be phrased as positive statements that emphasize one's openness to receive information. For example, a positive statement for the first question could be: "I am open to learning what I need to learn from this illness/problem/situation."

Newman's theory can be incorporated into one's self-care practice.

If a client is dealing with an illness, consider beginning the day with a statement such as, "Today I intend to receive information about causes of this illness (name the illness)." Or, "I am perplexed as to why this infection has returned. I trust that I will receive helpful information when it is most useful to me." Newman's theory of Health as Expanding Consciousness can be useful to gain insights into illness, thereby enhancing one's personal growth. This theory and process can also augment Healing Touch sessions, assisting both clients and practitioners to move to a greater understanding and awareness in their health journeys.

As the client moves to a new order of understanding, the practitioner can be supportive by assisting the energy field to shift to a place of balance. The practitioner can include self-care teaching and applicable homework to assist in the re-patterning of the energy field as well as the lived experience.

Jean Watson: Theory of Human Caring

By Diane Wind Wardell, PhD, RN, WHNP-BC, AHN-BC, CHPT/I and Sue Kagel, RN, BSN, HNB-BC, CHTP/I

In her early work on the Theory of Human Caring, Watson (1985, 1988, 1989) recognized the importance of interaction to restore a person's inner harmony, no matter the circumstances. This restoration is facilitated by helping clients to find meaning in their condition and to gain insight to aid self-healing. Healing Touch philosophy resonates with the premise that all healing is self-healing.

Watson's theory incorporates the soul in the examination of the wholeness of a person. She speaks to the need for balance in body/mind/soul. The nurse's function is that of facilitator and co-creator, rather than that of director. The nurse helps a person to find a way through chaos or illness through assisting him or her in self-care, choices, self-exploration, creative problem solving, and self-responsibility. In Healing Touch, the practitioner focuses on wholeness and works with the client to set mutual goals, including those for the body, mind, spirit, and emotions. Self-exploration and self-care teaching are encouraged to forward mutual goals. Further, the spiritual or soul aspect is included in Healing Touch. The concept of soul is reflected in the practitioner's acceptance of the client's interpretation of religious, metaphysical, or other paths.

For Watson, the provider's caring attributes are shown by actions, attitudes and deeds. It is important for the provider to be accepting and non-judging. Trust can be established by eye contact, gentle touch, genuine dialogue, silence in listening, and energy exchange. Self-exploration and self-care for the nurse/healer is stressed in order for her or him to be fully present when assisting others. In Healing Touch, the focus is on the development and evolution of the healer through learning to focus on self-care as a way of life, introspection, meditation, and journaling for insight.

Watson (1999) described an Era III/Paradigm Caring framework as the Transpersonal Caring-Healing (T-C-H) Model. She later expanded this concept to *caring science as a sacred science* (Watson, 2005). In her theory, Watson (1999) proposes that modalities involving human touch flow from a spiritual path of human development and form "the foundation for transpersonal practice" (p 230). Basic premises of the T-C-H Model as caring include grounding, centering, respect, personal development, and trust. These elements are also reflected in the ethical standards and practice of Healing Touch.

In reference to the basis for caring practice, Watson (1999) states "care and love are the most universal, the most tremendous, and the most mysterious of cosmic forces: they comprise the primal and universal psychic energy" (p 32). Healing Touch is a heart-centered practice that encompasses the attributes of compassion, innate harmony, healing presence and unconditional love (Joy, 1979).

The essential characteristics of the T-C-H model are illustrated in both self-care and in performing Healing Touch with others (Wardell, 2001, Watson, 1999). In personal practice, one might use a Healing Touch technique, such as the *Self-Chakra Connection*, as a morning exercise. When vulnerable, one steps out of the ordinary or customary world by recognizing the importance of energy therapies in healing or by using non-ordinary means for assessment, such as intuition, guidance and pendulums. The ability to cultivate one's ability to ground, energize and center the self and others is an essential practice in Healing Touch. This is taught as part of the *Basic Healing Touch Sequence* and reinforced within each level of the curriculum. The practitioner uses focused intentionality to potentiate wholeness, harmony, and healing in any Healing Touch session. And in performing Healing Touch, the provider is to be mindfully present. That is, practitioners use their observation skills and heart-centered awareness to engage at a deep level that, in turn, cultivates the ability to be authentically present. This involves being non-judgmental, a state that provides the practitioner an opportunity to see things in a new way.

When one connects with the deeper self, working with others is also self-healing. Being connected with the deeper self helps one to move through life's challenges and to recognize personal avenues for self-growth. Healing Touch cultivates an awe of the unknown through assisting others in their own self-healing. Healing moves from one of self-direction and control to a less known understanding of the body response to distress and the ability to heal. Always, when one is heart centered, a caring and acceptance of others is conveyed. In Healing Touch, the practitioner, heart-centered and grounded in whatever physical surrounding, is the healing environment. To begin creating connection and trust, caring may be exemplified through gestures such as a warm smile, eye contact as appropriate, and extending a hand in greeting.

A last premise of the T-C-H model is hearing and honoring your client's personal story. Honoring another's story honors the person as it recognizes the importance of the sharing that changes both the giver and the receiver. Each word has the potential to change another person when it is captured within and expressed from the heart.

Healing Touch practice also provides the opportunity to change both the participant and the provider in ways that foster the development of deeper personal commitment and social awareness. Healing Touch demonstrates the goal Watson proposed for nursing, that of promoting self-control, choice, and self-determination. When individuals are part of a community, they have an awareness of being engaged in a larger, deeper, higher, complex pattern of life.

Watson (1999) identifies six aspects of the caring moment. The first aspect is "the whole caring-healing consciousness is contained within a single caring moment" (p 111). This moment is shared by a story or simply with a gaze that is demonstrated in the *Heart to Heart Meditation* (Joy, 1979). The second aspect of the caring moment is "the one-caring and the one-being-cared-for are interconnected" (Watson, 1999, p 111). The human energy fields of both recipient and provider interact so that healing is by and for each other. The third is "human caring-healing processes are communicated to the one being cared for" (p. 23).

The fourth and fifth statements have to do with a shift in consciousness to a place beyond time and space that results in transcendence. These experiences are often encountered in a healing moment and can be manifested in a variety of ways, including altered perceptions, out of body experiences, and communing with the deceased (Engebretson & Wardell, 2012). Through a sense of "awakenness", it is possible to allow for a spiritual wakening and harmony of mind/body/soul. Time spent in nature, art and creativity becomes valuable in accessing and feeding the mind/body/soul. New levels of consciousness can be reached by those in a caring interaction. An awareness of the soul opens new possibilities for growth. Access of inner knowledge and intuition can bring us to a new place of connection with others, nature, and the universe. Human beings know deep within that the healing of their illness is about getting back to their true self to meet their true purpose and find meaning in life. A goal is to help others to find their pathway, voice, and meaning in life.

The prospect that "caring-healing consciousness is dominant over physical illness" is the sixth aspect and speaks to the miracle of healing which can be on a physical, emotional, or spiritual level (Watson, 1999). It is not about cure; it is about the ability to heal the human spirit.

In summary, Watson sees a person as a unique being to be cherished and respected, and whose dignity needs to be protected. We all need love and caring from ourselves and others. It is necessary to nourish humanity in order to have a responsible and evolving society through caring relationships. This view creates empowerment, trust, support, and protection of human dignity, as value is placed on the caring relationship seen in Healing Touch practice. The relationship is an exchange: human beings can only care for and heal others to the extent that they have cared for and healed themselves. Emphasis is on self-help, self-control, self-knowledge and responsibility. Self-exploration, creative problem-solving, choice and freedom are also encouraged. The process of self-discovery is one of growth and change.

The Scientific Art of Holistic Practice

By Veda Andrus, EdD, MSN, RN, HN-BC

Holistic health and healing have emerged in professional healthcare practices in the United States over the past 30 years (American Holistic Nurses Association, n.d.; Holistic Medicine, n.d.). The word holism, derived from the Greek-Indo-European root *holos* or *hale,* meaning "whole, healthful, healing, or holy", implies a sacred relationship based upon attending to and caring for the whole person, that of the body-mind-emotions-spirit. Health and illness are seen as a continuum, ever changing and evolving, where health is not viewed at one polarity and illness at the other. Instead, health and illness interweave, and a person is not categorized as being *either* healthy *or* ill. The continuum is likened to a dance where, for example, one's emotional or mental state influences the physical body, and a spiritual longing affects one's entire state-of-being. No separations are made among body-mind-emotions-spirit.

Integral within a holistic health model is the consideration of how people's environment (home, work, community, and world) and relationship with themselves influence their health and well-being. Intentionally incorporating an avenue for clients to share their story or their life experience will assist practitioners to form a plan of care. The practitioner—practicing the art of full presence, deep listening, and non-judgmental compassionate care—will hear through story, information and experience that will serve as an energetic guide for the professional relationship.

Health care professionals have defined holistic healing within their practice as an integration of various modalities. Although these modalities provide valuable healing connections, they do not define the essence of a holistic practice. Holistic healing is a scientific art with a body of knowledge grounded in a philosophical and theoretical framework. This framework provides practitioners with a foundation and springboard for relationship-centered therapeutic partnerships with their clients. The art of practicing holistic healing requires consciously and creatively pursuing professional caring relationships within this theoretical foundation. The core of holistic healing is about the quality of the relationship between the practitioner and the person. It is about the practitioner's *way of being*—his or her intention, therapeutic presence, and heartful caring.

Paradigmatic Shifts: Mechanistic to Holistic

Although the word "paradigm" has become common vernacular, recognizing its clinical application is critical. A paradigm is a model, pattern, framework, pair of lenses, or set of ideas that describes some aspect of our world. People have their own paradigm based upon what they have learned and experienced. The predominant paradigmatic worldview is a mechanistic paradigm that has its roots in the 17th century. Isaac Newton (physicist) and Rene Descartes (mathematician) were two forerunners of mechanistic thinking. This way of thinking concretely reduces everything into parts which can be measured. To quote Descartes, "All science is certain, evident knowledge. We reject all knowledge which is merely probable and judge that only those things should be believed which are perfectly known and about which there can be no doubts" (Garber, 1978). Newton provided a consistent mathematical formulation (differential calculus) based upon the Cartesian conceptual framework, and this framework remained the foundation for scientific thought well into the 20th century. Paradigmatic thinking is the foundation of the conventional western medical system.

The early 20th century, heralded by the extraordinary intelligence of Albert Einstein, ushered in new thinking. Einstein's theory of relativity provided a unified foundation of physics, influencing an evolving worldview that is holistic and interrelated (Einstein, 2010). This worldview recognized that paradoxes are an essential element of quantum physics, and the concept of *relationship* became the key to understanding space and time, as well as cause and effect.

Other modern physicists, including Heisenberg, Uncertainty Principle (Lindley, 2008); Bohr, Complementarity; Planck, Theory of Quantum Mechanics (van der Waerden, 1967); Bohm (1983), Implicate Order of Nature; and Pert (1999), Psychoneuroimmunology, have been influential in promoting the view of the universe as an interconnected web of wholeness. This paradigmatic thinking is the foundation of holistic health and healing.

Ontological Holism

The word ontology refers to "the study of the nature of being" (www.dictionary.com). An ontological shift occurs when the true essence of holistic work is recognized as having its roots in the understanding that who we are, our way of being, and the quality of the relationships we develop with ourselves and with our clients, deeply influence the potentiality for healing, both for our clients and for ourselves. This is a basic change of consciousness about what it means to be human. That is, a change occurs when we reconsider "being human" from that of *separation* to "being human" in relationship with all else in the Universe.

There is no separation between our way of being and how this contributes to the relationship we have with our clients. Hence, personal preparations for engagement (intentionality, grounding, centering, and self-care) are critical in creating a healing environment. Quinn articulates this as "the [practitioner] *as* a healing environment" (Quinn, 1992, p. 9). Recognizing the physical environment does not always provide a healing space; therefore, the practitioner, through intentional preparation, *becomes* a healing environment for the relationship. This does not deny the importance of the physical environment, rather from an ontological holistic perspective, it assists practitioners in understanding their unique contributions to the relationship.

Therapeutic Presence

Erie Chapman (2004) writes: "Loving care does not require twice the time, but it does require more than twice the presence" (p. 78).

Clients come looking for both expert technical care *and* to be attentively listened to and touched in some capacity. When the practitioner is not fully present, the client will experience a lack of engagement, which may influence building a trusting relationship and influence the process and outcome of a healing session.

Presence, defined as being in close proximity (including physical touch), triggers a release of brain endorphins (Selhub, 2009). Endorphins, often related to a "runner's high", occur in the brain and resemble opiates that work as natural pain and stress relievers. With high endorphin levels, people feel less pain and fewer of the negative effects of stress. According to Selhub, oxytocin, a hormone that is often associated with childbirth, triggers a series of biochemical reactions that tend to lower blood pressure and enhance relaxation responses. The release of oxytocin can be stimulated by eye contact, direct conversation, massage, and physical touch.

When there is full presence on the part of the practitioner, *both* the client *and* the practitioner experience the release of endorphins and oxytocin, and this supports the holistic paradigm of integrality and interconnection. If a practitioner is not fully present and does not engage in eye contact and physical touch, the therapeutic nature of the relationship for both partners is influenced. The relationship-centered care model is a reminder that it is the quality of the relationship we have with ourselves and our clients that influences and shapes outcomes. Creating a caring-healing environment holds promise of advancing care to a new level and of enhancing both client and practitioner satisfaction.

Caring for Ourselves

Becoming a healing presence takes practice. It starts with caring well for ourselves so that we bring our best to all relationships. If our own vessel is empty, and we are exhausted and overextended, we cannot provide good quality of care for our clients. While a stressful lifestyle is a big contributor to burnout, we must recognize and take responsibility for our own needs. How can we be credible role models for our clients if we are not practicing healthy lifestyle behaviors ourselves?

The mechanistic worldview indicates that who we are, how we care for ourselves, and how we present ourselves is *separate* from how we come into relationship with others. In a holistic paradigm, where the world is experienced as one interconnected and integral whole, the ways in which we care for ourselves will become the core essence that ripples into how we become a healing presence for others. Parker Palmer (2000), author of *Let Your Life Speak: Listening for the Voice of Vocation,* writes "Self-care is never a selfish act—it is simply good stewardship of the only gift I have, the gift I was put on earth to offer others" (p. 30).

Larry Dossey (1982) developed a *Spacetime Model of Birth, Life, Health, and Death.* He notes that "health extends to all other bodies since all bodies are in a dynamical relationship. Individual health is an illusion" (p.148). He elaborates by saying "illness is a collective event, since all bodies are related. Individual illness is an illusion." And finally, "neglect of health negatively affects all persons and is a collective affair" (p.148). This set of insights guides practitioners in the recognition that, from a holistic paradigmatic perspective, the manner in which they care for themselves directly influences the quality of personal-professional relationships.

The Thread that Ties

The paradigm of holistic health and healing guides practitioners to view person-client relationships in their wholeness, which includes understanding and honoring the vital nature of their life story, the environment in which they live and work, and the integrality of their body-mind-emotions-spirit. Treatment of one dimension of being impacts all other dimensions. Two people presenting with the same symptomatology might be treated very differently, based upon their story, beliefs, environment, and sense of self. The whole person is treated, not simply the symptoms or the presenting disease, a state with multiple contributing factors that makes it larger than a single cause. The relationship co-created between the practitioner and the client is a partnership, one where both are influenced by the other and the potential for healing evolves within a mutual process.

Energy Medicine Coming of Age

BY C. NORMAN SHEALY, MD, PHD

For the past 100 years conventional western medicine has concentrated almost exclusively on drugs and surgery as the major therapeutic tools. Although conventional, allopathic medicine has developed a remarkable array of technologically superior diagnostic tools, it has ignored virtually everything that is included in holistic, alternative, and complementary medicine, especially as it relates to the remarkable advances in Energy Medicine. Both diagnostically and therapeutically, the field of Energy Medicine has blossomed into a broad array of procedures and approaches that are increasingly being proven to be significant, including: Spiritual Healing, Therapeutic Touch, Healing Touch, Reiki, Qi Gong, Acupuncture, Ayurvedic Medicine, Body Therapies from massage to manipulation, Herbal Medicine, Color Therapy, Music and Sound Therapy, Homeopathy, Radionics, Crystal Therapy, Aroma Therapy, Energy Psychology, Electrotherapy, and Biofeedback Training.

I sense that the wide interest and use of these alternatives to drugs and surgery are primarily due to a growing distrust, at all levels of society, in the pharmaceutical excesses and an intuitive sense that the "side effects", including a minimum of 106,000 prescription drug deaths each year (Stanfield, 2000) are really unacceptable. Over 40 years ago, Dr. John Knowles (1977), a Harvard-trained internist and cardiologist, wrote that "99% of people are born healthy and become unhealthy because of human misbehavior" (p. 57). And Americans are less healthy today than they were 40 years ago.

At the beginning of the last century, Sir William Osler, known as the father of American Medicine, emphasized that stress is a major cause of disease. In *Aequinamitas,* Osler (1932) considered "Imperturbability" in physicians to be a divine gift. And we now know because of a phenomenal variety of research that lack of AEQUANIMITAS is the major stress reaction in most humans.

As early as 1929, Edmund Jacobson proved that his simple approach, *Progressive Relaxation,* could successfully treat 80% of stress diseases.

Between 1912 and 1969, Dr. Johann H. Schultz collected and proved 2600 scientific references showing that Autogenic Training accomplished the same goal. Despite this and the confirmatory evidence of biofeedback training by Dr. Elmer Green and *The Relaxation Response* by Dr. Herb Benson, American medicine has virtually ignored these safe alternatives (Benson & Klipper, 2000).

My own experience, dealing with over 40,000 patients, shows me that the vast majority of people do not have the motivation or will power to take advantage of these superior techniques. Most people want someone else to do it for them! As Edgar Cayce said, "If you have a surgical personality, have surgery." The evidence for effectiveness of placebos strongly reinforces the idea that patients' belief and faith are far more important than anything. Average placebo is 35% effectiveness, and there are a number of studies with even higher success rates. Actually there are a few drug studies with the placebo having a 70% success rate!

It is important to emphasize the critical necessity for drugs and surgery in some acute and traumatic disorders. In general, conventional medicine shines in dealing with acute illness, about 15% of the whole. Energy Medicine shines in chronic disorders, which represent 85% of problems!

In my opinion, the scientific proof of many of the Energy Medicine approaches is at least as good as that for most conventional medicine. Therapeutic Touch is one of the most accepted Energy tools in hospitals. The early successful blood studies of Dolores Krieger helped establish it as a favorite for many nurses. This is the foundation for Healing Touch practice as well. Of course, it would be particularly fascinating to see whether Qi Gong or Reiki have similar results. Interestingly, I have demonstrated in 116 patients that a total of 5 healers can strikingly affect, from a distance, the computerized EEG brain map, with one healer accomplishing this from a distance of 1000 miles.

Music therapy and Past Life Therapy have significant positive clinical results, as do biofeedback, Emotional Freedom Technique, Cranial Electrical Stimulation, and acupuncture. My own work has largely focused for over 40 years on electrotherapy, specifically with Transcutaneous Electrical Nerve Stimulation (TENS). More recently I've worked with the use of human DNA frequency (54 to 78 GHz) applied to specific acupuncture circuits. I have demonstrated that such specific circuits can raise DHEA and markedly improve 70% of patients with rheumatoid arthritis, 75% of patients with migraine, and 80% of patients with diabetic neuropathy.

Photostimulation (use of light waves) not only raises beta endorphins; it alone can help 56% of patients with depression. Cranial Electrical Stimulation (CES) not only normalizes serotonin; it brings 50% of depressed patients out of depression safely within two weeks, while antidepressants at best help 42% of depressed patients and have a 25% complication rate. CES plus photostimulation brings 84% of depressed patients out of depression! Other GHz results on specific circuits have normalized aldosterone, raised calcitonin, raised oxytocin and lowered free radical production significantly.

It has recently become obvious to me that there is a striking reason why most people need help and are simply not capable of doing the treatments themselves. Oxytocin deficiency has now been identified in every known psychological/emotional disorder! Autism, ADHD, depression, anxiety, addiction, borderline personality, obsessive compulsive disorder, and schizophrenia have all been associated with deficient oxytocin.

I believe that the foundation for oxytocin deficiency is set most often during pregnancy or at delivery. If the mother has a significantly traumatic pregnancy, is anesthetized for delivery or has labor artificially induced, she does not produce a surge of oxytocin to "stimulate" the child's innate oxytocin mechanism. Even if the child is stimulated adequately at birth, major trauma during the first seven years of life can shut down the oxytocin system. Divorce of the parents, currently occurring in 50% of marriages, is the most common major trauma of childhood.

Even in oxytocin deprived individuals, a truly nurturing individual can often coax a deprived individual into feeling nurtured. Therein may lay the most significant contribution of Healing Touch, and many of the other Energy Medicine approaches may contribute similar feelings of being nurtured. Healing Touch practitioners not only send energy to the patient; they send an inherent nurturing, caring feeling!

Meanwhile, I have now demonstrated that the acupuncture

circuits which can raise DHEA, calcitonin, aldosterone, neurotensin or oxytocin, or lower free radicals, can be activated by application of specific blends of aroma oils. The most significant finding is that a blend called Air BLISS, applied to the Ring of Air, not only raises oxytocin; it makes most individuals feel relaxed, calm and at peace. Several massage therapists have reported significant benefits when they massage these acupuncture circuits or use the aroma oils. These, and many other reports convincingly supporting the value of Energy Medicine, have assisted the modern coming of age of safe alternatives to drug and surgery (Shealy, 2011).

Consciousness, the Field, and Intention
BY LISA ANSELME, BLS, RN, HN-BC, CHTP/I

Lynn McTaggart (2001, 2008), author of *The Field: The Quest for the Secret Force of the Universe* as well as an investigative journalist and international spokesperson for complementary therapies, presented a keynote speech at the 2007 Annual Healing Touch International Conference that focused on intentionality in its application to Healing Touch. She also led attendees in a live "Intention Experiment". During this talk, McTaggart explained that she began studying intention when she became curious about the relationship between thoughts, energy, and matter. Stating that she was very traditional and grounded in science, she interviewed scientists, thinking this would be a quick study that would let her easily dispense with refuting any relationship.

But what she discovered astonished her: "If somebody can send a thought to someone and that person gets better, just from that thought, then that completely upends all of our understanding of how the world works." As she investigated the relationship between intention, energy and matter, she learned that science was inadvertently providing support for the legitimacy of intention and consciousness upon matter. Science was suggesting that consciousness is an actual physical energy that changes matter. Consciousness, a thought, is an actual thing. McTaggart stated that consciousness determines how we see the world. "This was new science in the making, and the old science was crumbling before my very eyes."

McTaggart said Charles Darwin created the paradigm of the survival of the fittest, which is "Eat or be eaten. Only the best survive." And further, Isaac Newton taught us that "we live in a very well behaved universe of separate objects that operate by set laws in time and space." McTaggart noted the following:

> This scientific vision is very bleak. It describes us as completely separate, discrete, individual, and alone. Lonely little people in a lonely little universe, this isolating paradigm affects everything. Don't we always applaud the individual, applaud competition, and applaud "be the best or don't survive"? We create our work, countries, societies, and planet based upon the idea of competition and separation. But maybe this is not the final truth.

McTaggart further talked about a new scientific story coming from many prestigious corners of the globe that describes a very different paradigm. At its essence, the new story describes us as pure energy, not something separate but part of the whole, part of a vast energetic field. Everything is connected and effecting everything else at every moment. Time and space are only human constructs and not the real truth. McTaggart illustrated this with a study of monks who sat naked in the snow, wrapped in wet sheets and steamed them dry via raising their body temperature through Tsumo meditation.

In 2007, McTaggart began conducting her own experiments, and has worked with Dr. Gary Schwartz at the University of Arizona Laboratory for Advancements in Consciousness and Health (LACH). She experimented with groups sending intention to a leaf or seedling. Calling them "Intention Experiments", she started with a leaf that had 16 holes poked in it, and asked a large audience to "make the leaf glow." The next week, Dr. Schwartz reported that the leaf "was glowing so much that it seemed to have an effect on the control leaf that actually made it look darker."

McTaggart has repeated this experiment a number of times. She has also used the internet to conduct *Intention Experiments* with thousands of people from countries around the world. The outcomes suggest that distance from the seeds or from the recipients does not seem to matter, and both small and large groups have an effect. In her words, McTaggart tells us:

> Our human potential is just a glimmer of what it could be. We have many more possibilities than science has told us. And our task is to learn how to receive this information again. If we are not separate, think about it, we never win or lose. We don't and shouldn't compete. We have to think about something more than the time and space paradigm we now have. We need another way to be. We have to change the way that we think of me and not me. We have to change the way we interact with others. We've got to change the way we carry out our work, bring up our children, and approach our own death. Basically, folks, we have to change the whole shooting match. We have to change everything.

Healing Touch International's Intention Experiments

By Gary E. Schwartz, PhD and Sue Kagel, RN, BSN, HNB-BC, CHTP/I

Setting one's intention for the client's "highest good" is one of the basic components in Healing Touch and is found in the *Basic Healing Touch Sequence* that provides the foundation for all interactions between the client and practitioner. This concept is taught in the beginning of the first Healing Touch class and carried throughout the curriculum. Utilizing this framework, one can shift from the concept of curing to the concept of healing, in which the realms of possibilities are endless. The focus shifts to facilitating and supporting the person's own healing process rather than "fixing" or "doing to" them.

Intention experiments have been conducted during Healing Touch International, Inc. (HTI) Annual Conferences for a number of years in an attempt to explore and garner a greater understanding of the power of thought and intention. Exactly the same protocols were used in all experiments to prepare for the experiment and during the intention aspect. The intentions, measuring devises and locations of the intending participants have varied.

Seeds

The first experiment was conducted at the HTI Annual Conference in Hilton Head, North Carolina, 2007. Lynne McTaggart conducted the experiment in collaboration with Gary E. Schwartz, PhD at the Laboratory for Advances in Consciousness and Health (LACH) University of Arizona. The general conference attendees focused on a photo of a randomly selected packet of seeds. The intention was set for the seeds to grow faster, stronger and taller than a control group of seeds. The seeds, which were in the lab in Arizona, were then planted.

The results indicated that the Healing Touch conference attendees' concentrated attention on this packet of seeds at the LACH lab in Tucson, Arizona resulted in significant growth compared to the control group (Schwartz, 2007). The Healing Touch experiment resulted in much more directed effect and significantly less "scatter" effect than other similar trials. McTaggert commented:

> I was particularly interested in the effect of the experienced intenders (like healers) and whether they'd make our seeds grow even faster than the "ordinary" rest of us. …In fact, the seeds sent intention grew nearly twice as fast as the control seeds. This extraordinary result not only demonstrates the power of intention, but also suggests that experience counts: certain conditions and training make one a more effective intender (p.10).

Light Box

The additional experiments were orchestrated under the direction of Gary E. Schwartz, PhD and Sue Kagel, RN, BSN, a Certified Healing Touch Instructor, for consistency. The second experiment was conducted at the HTI Conference in Tucson, AZ in 2009 in conjunction with LACH (Schwartz, 2009). The laboratory held a tightly sealed light chamber capable of measuring photons in the visible spectrum as well as gamma/cosmic rays or more simply stated, light. This complex experiment was set up to provide a well-controlled environment with many data points to help insure objectivity and scientific merit and was designed to detect a possible increase in the organization of light, plus gamma/cosmic rays as a function of healing energy.

The conference attendees' intention was to send loving, healing energy along with prayer or divine guidance to an image of the light chamber, which was visually projected on a screen. The actual chamber was located 23 miles away at the University of Arizona LACH laboratory. The experiment successfully revealed a relative increase in the overall brightness of the Fast Fourier Transform (FFT) image compared to pre and post no-intention control recording periods. (See Figure 1 top row). Measurement of the organization of the photons was conducted via 2 dimensional FFT analyses using ImageJ software provided by the National Institutes of Health (NIH).

Random Event Generator

Simultaneously, a random event generator (REG) was used in the conference ballroom by Dr. Schwartz during the energy setting aspect of the protocol. Each time the attendees raised their energy levels to send the intention, the REG registered a sustained change and then returned to baseline when the experiment was completed.

Light Box with a Twist

The experiment was replicated at the 2010 HTI Conference in St. Louis, Missouri, now from a distance of 2000 miles from LACH (Schwartz & Kagel, 2011a). Sue Kagel directed the participants as in prior experiments to raise their energy and intention except that this time, the use of prayer and guidance was not used. Practitioners were to use only loving, heart-centered energy.

The results show that the cosmic/gamma rays again were more organized in structure and brighter, but were not as bright as in 2009. (See Figure 1 second row.) Figure 2 shows the Plot Profiles of the FFT's. For each slide, a common scale was used across the six images. In other words, the obvious visual differences comparing the Active Intention Periods with Pre and Post Control Periods are real (and dramatic)! There is also more complexity in the 2009 Active Period when participants called for divine assistance, and post controls in both groups show more structure, which might suggest a lasting effect of the healing intention.

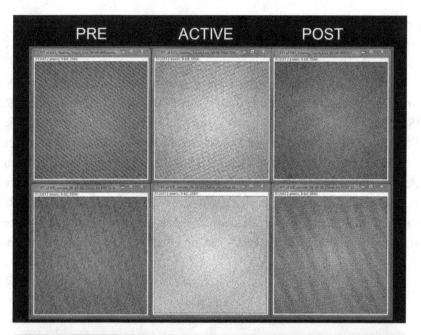

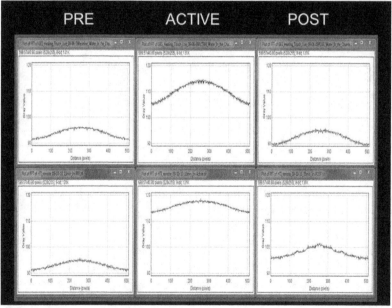

Figure 1

Top Row: 2009 HTI Intention Experiment with Guidance
Bottom Row: 2010 HTI Intention Experiment without Guidance

Measuring with a New Device

In 2011, at the HTI Healing Touch Conference on the Big Island in Hawaii, the Experiment was repeated with different measuring devices and with two consecutive sets of intention (Schwartz & Kagel, 2011b). The intention and protocol were the same, except for a difference in evoking the energy before and during the intention. One set was conducted using loving, heart-centered energy only, and the other set was performed using loving energy with the addition of calling on divine assistance. Participants were shown a slide of the measuring device and were instructed to imagine and intend that they were sending the energy to a client (the machine) or that the client was in front of the machine, but that the energy would go to the machine as well to register the effect. Changes in radiation and magnetic fields were measured on a second by second basis for nine hours on the day of and after the experiment.

The results indicated a somewhat greater increased organization of cosmic activity and increased magnetic field activity during the intention setting by the practitioners and basically replicated the findings of 2009 and 2010, this time using moment to moment recordings of radiation. The observations did not make it possible to compare the two kinds of intention (with and without divine assistance).

Machines to Biology

The 2012 experiment took place at the HTI Annual Conference in Bloomfield, Colorado. The practitioners had expressed a challenge in connecting lovingly with a machine, so a new experiment and measuring tool was developed to be inserted into the existing protocol and intentions used during the previous years. This time a picture slide of Dr. Schwartz sitting in a chair was shown by a slide for the focal point. Simultaneously, Dr. Schwartz was sitting in a chair in his lab approximately 500 miles away. No information was given on his current state of health; however he did look somewhat "frail" in the photograph. The same basic protocol was used. The participants were again directed to use loving energy and divine assistance and were directed to set the intention for his highest good, healthy vitality, and healthy blood.

Finger sticks were used to collect small blood samples from Dr. Schwartz prior, during, and after the intention time. The research focused on changes in the Zeta potential of the blood samples as the measurement tool. Dr. Schwartz was also asked to journal his experience as he received the energy intentions as part of a "distance healing". The sensations he experienced parallel those described during actual sessions: moving through a sense of calming and peacefulness, quieting of the mind, almost sleepy and then becoming more awake and alert and feeling energized while in a very calm state.

There was a change in the Zeta potential of the blood cells, however, the directionality was not that which was expected. Further control trials are needed to further elucidate these results.

Conclusion

The Healing Touch practitioners attending conferences, many with 20 or more years of experience working with intention and energy, have consistently shown that sending loving intention for the highest good results in a significant change regardless of the distance or tools used. Healers regularly utilize this type of format in performing distance healing, always for the highest good of all. Distance healing, done with loving intention, can be focused specifically to individuals, family members supporting an individual, communities with disasters, the weather, and in daily well-wishing for the planet and all its inhabitants. This may be done very generally or specifically, with the focus on healing rather than cure. The HTI Intention experiments continue with creative variations within the consistent protocol as an attempt to provide scientific evidence for the concept of intention and distance healing.

The Physics of Healing Touch

By Vicki Slater, PhD, RN, AHN-BC, CHTP/I

This section will explore the possible physics that underpins Healing Touch. While the idea that Healing Touch as an electromagnetic occurrence will likely fit the experiences of even the beginning student, electromagnetism is a theory. Physicists will not claim that something *is* until it has mathematical support and experimental proof. However, to support the idea that Healing Touch *is*, from a physics perspective, may be fairly simple.

The discussion begins with how the human being acts like an electromagnet. Then we will look at electromagnetic induction and how it may apply to Healing Touch as well as to every interaction in life. Meridians may play a role in the electromagnetic human, including possibly distorting the shape of the aura. We will also talk about how the practitioner influences the Healing Touch treatment. Hopefully the discussion will help explain why "getting on the table" to be a recipient of Healing Touch is important for the practitioner.

Electromagnetics and the Electromagnetic Human: Power and Protection?

Electricity and magnetism were originally thought to be separate phenomena until they were discovered to be two parts of one phenomenon, much as a coin has two sides. Engineers use the electro/magnetic phenomenon to make electromagnets. Electromagnetism is part of what physicists call "classical physics," rather than quantum physics, and is responsible for powering a lot of the gadgets in our life. It is everywhere and may be more universal than we realize.

Most electromagnets have iron at the center of a coil that makes it capable of carrying an electric current. When electricity is flowing, a magnetic field develops around the coil, which magnetizes the iron core and strengthens the magnetic field even more. If you keep adding coils, you can increase the power of the magnetic field many times, giving you much more power than could be expected from just a collection of iron and an electric current.

Humans and animals exhibit electromagnetic properties. We have iron cores of hemoglobin in our red blood cells that are surrounded by the electrical fields of neurons and meridians. People who see energy often report that the electrical field appears blue and the magnetic field seems yellow. For example, look at the blue hue that hugs the bodies and the yellow auras in Barbara Brennan's color plates in *Hands of Light: A Guide to Healing through the Human Energy Field* (Brennan, 1988).

Because our iron core flows throughout our entire body, we have a magnetic field that surrounds us. It may be our aura or part of our aura. Like a magnetic field, our aura is denser closer to the core and drops off in a stair-step fashion rather than gradually. It disappears when we die and our electrical flow stops, and it is diminished when we are ill or when we have low hemoglobin (anemia). It may be part of our defensive system, because our magnetic field might provide a barrier protecting our internal electrical workings, such as the stimulus that causes the heart to beat. (Our aura may be similar to a *Faraday cage*, which is a barrier that protects delicate electrical equipment.)

Electromagnetic Induction

Engineers put the relationship of electricity and magnetism to work through *electromagnetic induction*. This process makes powerful generators provide power to your city and tiny ones power your cell phone. When you put two electric currents near each other, their magnetic fields interact, or interfere with each other. A sudden change in one of the electric currents causes its magnetic field to change, and this change *induces* a current in a nearby circuit. This *induced current* results in a surge in electric currents, or a *voltage surge*. The magnitude of the induced current is determined by many factors, such as how quickly the current in the first circuit changes, how close the two circuits are to each other, and even the amount of air between them. Under the right circumstances, electrons can leap across a gap and reestablish a current.

Electromagnetic induction is used widely. It is used in electric motors, electric engines, cell phones, radios, TVs and many other electric devices. One way that engineers and physicists create electromagnetic induction is to take a long wire and wind it around a core, which is often made of iron. It will help to see this if you take a string and wind it around a pencil. Notice that the effect of winding the string (electric wire) is to have as many electromagnetic fields next to each other as you have windings. The increased number of windings close to each other strengthens the electromagnetic field. You've heard of generators having millions of coils? The engineers coil the electric wire around a core many, many times to generate the amount of power they need. Each electric/magnetic coil can induce a current, voltage, and magnetic surge in the adjacent ones (i.e., power). To maintain the surge, the electric current must be changing, which is one reason we have alternating current. Once the electric current stops changing, the surge disappears. Now, hold the thought of electromagnetic induction while we talk about meridians.

Meridians and the Aura—Power, Protection, and Redundancy

The first time a practitioner senses a distortion in a person's energy field, they have encountered a problem with the idea that the human electromagnet/hemoglobin arrangement can be the entire cause of the aura. How is a distortion created in a field in which moving iron within a neuron/meridian mesh fills the body? The magnetic field produced by this arrangement should be smooth and intact.

The meridians are a series of tiny electric currents. Becker and Selden (1985) measured them at less than 1 billionth of an ampere, or between a nanoampere and picoampere. (For those of us who are not physicists, that is almost an imaginary amount of current.) Meridians are smaller than a hair, so imagine how tiny the current would be that could flow through one of your hairs. Many people have heard that there are 12 pairs of meridians, 12 on each side of the body. If you read acupuncture and Traditional Chinese Medicine literature deeply, you learn that the meridian system is like a mesh. It fills the entire body from the deepest level to the surface of the skin. The 12 outermost and most accessible pairs, called "Jing," are not the only meridians. The smaller ones, called "Lou," are internal and pervasive.

Remember how engineers create an electromagnet? They place multiple electrical currents next to each other. That is how meridians are arranged. Think about the roadways of a city. You have the highways, the feeder roads, the side roads, the road leading into your development, and your driveway. In a similar manner, you have the biggest meridians, which divide into smaller ones, and still smaller ones. What you have are many meridians spread throughout the body, creating a system of electric currents and their magnetic fields. This is the arrangement needed for electromagnetic induction. Like any electromagnet, you have access to more power than would be possible with the relatively tiny initial electric input available in the meridians. In addition to being efficient, the arrangement creates redundancy so that if there is a problem with one meridian, the other magnetic fields are still there and creating a relatively stable electromagnetic field.

Some people who see energy fields report a series of lines in the aura running from above the head to below the feet. They are often perceived as blue threads. This external mesh seems to fill the space from close to the body to the edge of the aura. It is as if we are encased in a series of electrical currents that also help to produce a stable magnetic field.

Some practitioners might sense these energy lines even if they don't see energy. If attention is paid while doing *Magnetic Passes* these tiny fibrils may be noted. Most of these fibrils may feel linear, but there also maybe a sense of knots and holes. A hand scan of the field above the knot or hole may reveal that the field is distorted. Paying attention to an area where the aura is distorted may assist in locating knots and/or holes. To heighten your ability to discover the sensation of the meridian mesh use your hands to explore the space around you. Move slowly and invite your hands to teach you.

If there are "invisible" external meridians, some of the odd things you might have discovered in auras make sense. Remember that there are layers in the aura and that each layer "feels" different from the others. Perhaps the structure and the jobs of the external meridians change at different distances from the body. Damage to the external meridians may cause energy leaks, dips, bulges, twists, holes, or an auric level that has a hole in it where the surrounding ones do not.

So now we have two possible sources of our aura: the hemoglobin and neuron/meridian system and the internal and external meridian mesh. Both produce magnetic fields, but differently, and together they may be providing us with a stable electromagnetic field that both protects us and provides energy.

The Role of Chakras: Alternating Current

Chakras (energy centers of the body) are a third piece of the puzzle of the physics of the human body. Remember that voltage surges require that the electric current keeps changing and that an alternating current provides the needed change. When using a pendulum, ask to be shown how the energy is actually flowing. It is likely to show that at each chakra, the pendulum spins in the opposite direction of the one preceding and following it. This is how an alternating current would work. This alternating swing occurs at the chakras in the joints of the toes, fingers, arms, legs, spine, and in the torso, and this swing occurrence suggests that at least one of the electric flows in the body is an alternating current.

Two Human Electromagnets Next to Each Other—Mutual Electromagnetic Induction

The key to the voltage surge in electromagnets is the changing electric current. If the hemoglobin/electrical structure and meridian systems are valid, what could create the changes other than the possible alternating current of the chakras? Behaviors such as movement, digestion, respiration, elimination, and sex could produce changes in our electrical current, but the changes might be relatively small if the behaviors are routine. Even our thoughts change, which also may provide voltage surges. Another possible source of change is being next to another living electromagnet.

If we are electromagnetic structures, then when two people are near each other, they must interfere electromagnetically with each other. Each could be expected to cause a voltage surge in the other person just by being next to them. If three, four, or many people get together, then, like an electromagnet, you may have multiple sources of electric current with their magnetic fields interfering with each other. Perhaps this is part of the power of a community or of a mob.

How Healing Touch May Employ Electromagnetic Induction

Zimmerman (2000) found that practitioners of Therapeutic Touch, an energy modality similar to Healing Touch, emitted a pulsing frequency from their hands *when they were in a centered state.* This frequency ranged from 0.3 Hz (Hertz) to 30 Hz (the upper range that his equipment could measure), but focused in the 7–8 Hz range (and was not present when practitioners were not in a centered state). Waechter and Sergio (2002) found the same results working with people who have mastered qi (chi).

Sisken and Walker (1995) tested pulsed electromagnetic fields (PEMF) on various soft body tissues and found that they respond to specific Hz, but not to others. Cells shown to heal more rapidly at specific Hz were as follows: bone growth, 7 Hz; ligaments, 10 Hz; and endothelial cells and small capillaries, 15 Hz. Nerve regeneration occurred at .05–2 Hz. In rats, crushed nerves regenerated faster than normal at 2 Hz, but a severed nerve needed 15 Hz. These frequencies are within the ranges Zimmerman found emitting from centered Therapeutic Touch practitioners.

While in a centered state, you may produce an electromagnetic pulse that could create voltage surges in the person next to you. And that surge might be just the right size to speed up healing. When you move your hands, you may be producing even greater voltage surges because you are inducing greater change. You might even produce healing voltage surges in yourself, which may explain why Healing Touch practitioners often appear to be younger than they are.

Voltage surges may even cause spontaneous repair of broken meridians. If a sudden change in the meridian flow creates a voltage surge just the right size to cause electrons to leap the gap between the two ends of a broken meridian, a spontaneous repair of the current flow might occur, allowing the reestablishment of an electrical current. One common Healing Touch experience as a result in the repair of broken electric flow is Wound Sealing. Imagine a wound in a client's field, and how it may feel like a hole. As you move your hands around the auric hole to fill it in, you induce voltage surges at the edges of the wound. The right sized voltage surge may enable electrons to leap the gap between the ends of broken meridians and reestablish the current's flow. This process may be involved in the rapid healing of surgical and other wounds treated with Healing Touch. It also may contribute to the unexplained, gentle, life changing healing we see in people who receive frequent Healing Touch treatments.

The Role of Electromagnetic Induction in Every Encounter: The Role of Your Presence

If electromagnetic induction is a factor in Healing Touch, then it is likely to be a factor in any and every human interaction—or human-animal, human-tree, human-any living thing interaction. This suggests that the nature of your presence may be just as important as what you do. When two beings are next to each other, they may cause voltage surges in the other. Kissing a "boo-boo" may create a voltage surge that speeds up healing. Holding a child in your lap may offer you the opportunity to send loving voltage surges that contribute to healing and well-being. However, remember that it is only the right strength of the voltage surge that causes spontaneous repair. If the strength is too high, damage could occur. This may be why anger and hate can make you feel as if you have had holes punched in you. Perhaps you have. The loving or centered state, as well as the practitioner's actions, may be what make Healing Touch healing.

How to Make Yourself a More Powerful Healer: Increasing Your Electromagnetic Field

Janet Mentgen replied, "Get on the table" when someone asked her how to become a better healer. Compare the difference in the power you sense from the skilled Healing Touch practitioner versus the novice. Both are making the same movements, both are centered, but there is a difference. The skilled Healing Touch practitioner seems to have more power as well as gentler power. Those who are able to perceive electromagnetic fields report that experts have more external meridians than do novices. Perhaps getting on the table and allowing another to create voltage surges in your meridians better prepares you to handle the energy involved in Healing Touch.

Another way to assist you to increase your electromagnetic field is to practice movements performed in Tai Chi, Tai Chi Chih, or Qigong. In these practices, you move your hands through your own field. As such, you may be creating your own voltage surges, inducing healing as you exercise.

Our Even More Complex Structure: The Connective Tissue

Oschman (2000) does an excellent job of portraying the complexity of the human body in *Energy Medicine: The Scientific Basis*. His third chapter is devoted to the electrical role of connective tissue, or "living matrix," which he describes as "a semiconducting communication network that can carry the bioelectronics signals . . ." throughout the body (p. 55). The electrical nature of connective tissue may well be involved in the nature of the aura and the effects of Healing Touch. Perhaps the electromagnetic interference of a practitioner involves not only meridians but connective tissue as well. Obviously we have much to learn about the physics of Healing Touch and of the Healing Touch practitioner.

Classical Physics and Quantum Physics

Electromagnetic induction is a part of classical physics—the atom, molecule, electricity, magnetism and every day phenomena that make our lives so easy and takes astronauts to the moon. Electromagnetic induction may be a valid explanation for much of the healing seen with Healing Touch, but it is likely not the complete explanation. Electromagnetic induction may assist a broken field to repair, but it does not explain how Healing Touch helps a person to heal long standing emotional and spiritual wounds, ones we see healed in people who receive regular treatments. Perhaps the answer will be found in the subatomic world (smaller than the atom) studied by quantum physicists. Many aspects of quantum theories, such as Consciousness-Created Reality and String theory, may apply to Healing Touch. But how quantum theories impact our work may be even more difficult to understand than are the effects of electromagnetic induction. Or it may be that the puzzle of Healing Touch will be found in other classical physics theories unexplored here.

Conclusion

A complete understanding of the science underpinning Healing Touch lies in the future, but electromagnetic induction offers us a place to begin. Healing Touch appears to be a physics event; it cannot be explained with biological, chemical, or physiological sciences. A theory that electromagnetic induction might be a factor in Healing Touch and in all human interactions fits the experiences of practitioners. Hopefully someone will have the interest, laboratory, tools and skills to be able to test whether we influence each other electromagnetically. Is our presence an electromagnetic event? If so, then what effect does Healing Touch add to this natural human state?

Complexity Science in Healing Systems

By Joan C. Engebretson, DrPH, RN, HN-BC

Complexity Science has its origins in modern physics, chaos theory, quantum mechanics, and nonlinear mathematics and has advanced in application with the advent of computer programs that can manage large amounts of data. Data management has allowed pattern identification and computer modeling, which is being used in some areas of economics and weather forecasting as well as in medicine to better understand the complex processes of physiology. The principles, however, have been applied to biologic and social systems, which are better understood as complex adaptive systems (CAS). This is an important perspective that moves from a more linear mechanical perspective to an adaptive living system. This approach has the potential to transform our understanding of health and illness in complex living systems. Many of the conceptual aspects of complexity and CAS are similar to Systems Theory, a concept familiar to nurses. The following are concepts from non-linear dynamics (Engebretson & Hickey, 2011; Lindberg, Nash, & Lindberg, 2008).

- Non-linear dynamics focus on *simple rules*. For example, linear math focuses on 1+1 = 2. Complexity would focus on the simple rule of + or the relationship between the variables.
- Non-linear patterns are *sensitive to initial conditions*. A small difference in starting points can result in significant different trajectories.
- Non-linear dynamics manifest *fractal patterns*. These are repeated patterns at different levels of scale. An example is looking at patterns in a coastline, which has similar patterns at different levels of resolution (sometimes called *scaling*). An example from biology is fractals scaling in branches of blood vessels. These patterns may be mathematical and plotted or modeled on computers.

Complex adaptive systems can refer to individual living organisms or groups of organisms with specific components and characteristics (Zimmerman, Linidberg, & Pisek, 1998). This is similar to Systems Theory and the concept of nested systems. Hence, in a flock of birds, each bird is a CAS and the flock also functions as a CAS. The components and characteristics of CAS include the following:

- Agents: These are the individual units of components of a system. Again the patterns of interaction, rather than the individual components, are the focus. For example, one cannot understand how a flock of birds navigate their flight by examining only one bird.
- Patterns: Patterns and behaviors of the agents are the focus.
- CAS are dynamic and adaptive: CAS can change in response to both internal and external environments. For example, a human in total homeostasis is unable to adapt; however, a human needs to keep the system close to equilibrium—a balance between stability and change.
- CAS are supported by simple rules: These allow a CAS to act as a system. These have been applied to understand how a swarm

of bees behaves, and work is underway to better understand human organism behavior as a system with multiple agents.

- Emergence: This is a property that allows new and novel patterns, properties or processes to emerge in a process of self-organization. These come from the system and are not externally derived.

- Self-organization: This allows CAS to move into new creative patterns, thereby changing the dynamics of the system. These may emerge without central or external control.

- Control is distributed rather than centralized: Agents or components do not act through a central agency within or outside of the system. This decentralized control serves an adaptive function.

- CAS have diversity: This allows for multiple resources to respond to external stimuli and internal adaptations. The greater the diversity, the more robust the system.

- CAS are deterministic: Patterns follow or are determined by previous ones. These follow simple rules and may be predictable on the short run. These allow for modeling.

- CAS are exemplified by embeddedness: This is similar to the hierarchy of systems in Systems Theory that systems are embedded in larger systems in which all levels influence and are influenced by each other.

- Coordination dynamics occur within CAS: These coordinating elements interact at different levels and areas of the system and surroundings. These dynamics allow for a system to adapt to change while maintaining some stability.

- CAS are sensitive to initial conditions: Even a small perturbation in the system has capacity to alter the entire system by triggering changes in patterns, structures and processes. Conversely, large input may have little effect on the system. This is commonly referred to as the butterfly effect.

- Co-evolution occurs in CAS: A process of reciprocal adaptive dynamics often occurs, in which two systems are simultaneously changing and self-organizing. An example is a parasite and the host co-evolve to form a single system.

Application to Organizations

These principles have also been applied to human organizations, and Stacey (2001) has made a distinction by labeling the dynamics in organizations as complex responsive processes. Many of the principles apply. One of the applications focuses on the idea of a strict hierarchal system attempting to function in a mechanical top down control as being poorly adaptive. Recommended is the idea of distributed control, which allows for emergent, innovative creative processes that are more adaptive and make for a more responsive system. However, this does not mean there is no central control, which could devolve into random chaos. Complexity is best served by operating within a zone between random chaos and tight mechanistic control.

Application to Complementary Modalities

Often complementary modalities are based in a holistic approach to health, as opposed to many biomedical treatments and research that are based on a reductive mechanistic approach. Biomedical research is anchored in a specific science perspective using experimental designs in which specific outcomes are hypothesized for an intervention with a very specific mechanism. The human organism is a CAS and therefore has multiple pathways, feedback loops, and dynamics in its actions to maintain adaptive functioning in changing environments.

Energy healing may be better understood through the lens of complexity, as it is predicated on a more holistic perspective in which the energetic intervention can work on the whole person. Hence, energetic healing may improve sleep in one person or on one occasion and improve appetite on another occasion. This fits a complex model in that energy therapies are understood to stimulate the CAS's recuperative powers and are designed to respond to the particular individual need at that time. Energy therapies are able to individualize their intervention as well in response to the recipient's needs. Healing experiences have been investigated and found that they are individualized processes that do not follow a uniform pattern (Verhoef & Mulkins, 2012). This may explain why standardized clinical trials on energetic therapies often yield equivocal results. Complexity science may provide an advantage in future investigations of healing and are being explored by scientists involved with Complementary and Alternative Medicine (CAM) research (Ahn et al., 2010).

Implications for Clinical Practice

Complexity science introduces a new way of thinking about the body and the organization of health care and can be seen as cultural models or mental models that shape the way we think and act. An older dominant model can be related to the Industrial Age; with the metaphor of the machine. A popular notion of physiology once referred to the body as the magnificent machine. This led to a focus on mechanism of action, with the repair or replacement of broken parts. Translated into the delivery of health care, this fostered a focus on standardization, efficiency, and linear approaches to research. As we move into the Information Age, the focus shifts to complexity, and an understanding of the living organism as a complex of internally distributed communication and adaptive patterns. The application to organizations is based on a more complex understanding and may lead to more distributive controlled, creative, and adaptive organizations that focus on innovative adaptive responses and individualized interventions. Engaging in conversations among providers and between providers and patients also reflects a more complex perspective and illustrates the importance of sharing information and forming new innovative, creative and adaptive patterns. The following examples illustrate some of these concepts:

- **Relationship-Centered Care:** The notion of complex responsive process has been applied to relationship-centered care in the clinical setting (Suchman, 2006). This incorporates the notion of self-organization in the social process of the clinician-patient relationship.
- **New Models of Leadership:** An emergent model of leadership in which leaders are open, responsive catalysts and collaborative co-participants and collegial partners, leveling the hierarchy.
- **New Models for Research:** The development of other research designs in addition to the randomized controlled trial, include mixed methods, action research, positive deviance, and appreciative inquiry.

- **New Models for Understanding Physiology, Disease and Healing:** While the application of complexity to physiology is challenging, new models are steadily coming into medical literature. This has great relevance to nursing and to understanding complementary therapies such as Healing Touch.
- **New Models of the Human Organism:** New models of life support, understanding sepsis, and other health issues as well as monitoring systems are emerging from the application of complexity perspectives.

Complexity science is continuing to develop theoretically, and methods of evaluation continue to unfold. Its practical application to energy therapies allows for understanding the varied responses of both healer and client. Unlike other measurements and explanations of scientific principles, complexity science seems to allow for expansion rather than restriction of thought and response. The Healing Touch International's Code of Ethics/Standards of Practice statement that reflects this thinking is "the individual is acknowledged as a complex being, who is part of a social system and is interactive with and is acted upon by internal and external environments" (www. HealingBeyondBorders.org). Healing Touch also focuses on observation of patterns in the individual's life and energy system.

Chapter Summary

A variety of theoretical approaches have been presented to provide for a greater understanding of how the mind-body-environment shapes our experience. Specifically, this chapter has explored how energy therapies, such as Healing Touch, have a basis in select nursing theories, holism, cultural interpretations, distant healing, electromagnetic theory, and complex adaptive systems. Even though significant advances have been made over the last few decades, our understanding of the mechanism of action for how energy work brings about change and/or healing remains limited. An element of trust is still required, and one's personal experience is mediated by a variety of factors.

CHAPTER 4

LIVING IN HARMONY: CARING FOR SELF AND OTHER LIVING SYSTEMS

This chapter identifies the foundational work of Healing Touch as it manifests through the heart. Inherent in the healer's work is the importance of developing and maintaining the self as the instrument of healing. Part of the complex interaction of the human being as a participant in the healing journey is between the self and other humans, animal and plant kingdoms, and the earth itself. Therefore, these elements will be explored in relation to the following objectives:

1. Incorporate an understanding of the importance of conducting oneself in a heart-centered manner.
2. Recognize the foundation of self-healing and incorporate healing into everyday life.
3. Develop self-care practices designed to increase your internal vibration for healing self and others.
4. Honor the roles that animals and other living systems have in maintaining health, assisting in healing, and supporting the environment.
5. Identify the earth as healer and healee.

Heart-Centeredness: Living from the Heart

By: Myra Tovey, BSN, RN, HN-BC, CHTP/I

Janet Mentgen, the founder of Healing Touch International, often said in her teaching and healing practice that the heart chakra, or heart center, was the foundation of her Healing Touch work. In this section, we will explore what the heart center is, how to access the heart center, and how to live a heart-centered life.

What is the Heart Center?

The heart chakra, or heart center, is at the center of the chest. Below the heart center lie the root, sacral and solar plexus chakras (lower chakras), and above it are the throat, third eye or brow and crown chakras (upper chakras). The heart center allows the individual to be a balanced, detached observer of his/her beingness, while denying none of it. This balance is not just emotional or mental; it is also physical and energetic.

First, regarding emotional balance, heart-centered people experience fear, anger, jealousy, and other emotions like everyone else. However, heart-centered people are aware when they experience those emotions, and they have learned to shift back to the heart. They don't judge themselves when they experience "negative" emotions; they don't say "Oh no, I just felt anger!" Instead they experience the feeling, then allow it to shift to the place of emotional balance, the heart.

The balanced mind doesn't race about or have a lot of chatter. If a solution to a problem isn't immediately apparent, heart-centered people "table" the problem until they are in a calmer state. Once in a calmer, more balanced state, they are able to see the solution to a problem more clearly.

Energetic balance means the chakras are all open. If a person is emotionally distraught, angry, or upset, it's likely that his or her second chakra will be "compromised" or closed. If a person has a mind that is racing, it's likely that the sixth chakra is compromised or closed. If all of the chakras are open, the body is in physical balance. This balance often allows the body to heal itself.

According to Joy (1970), the heart center has four attributes. They are as follows:

1. Compassion—the feeling of gratitude for self and others.
2. Innate Harmony—being calm in the midst of chaos.
3. Healing Presence—the feeling of love, gratitude, and appreciation that creates the condition for healing.
4. Unconditional Love—the mystery that unites all things.

The fundamental aspect of the heart center is that the heart unites all things. Most people, when given a choice, prefer a quieter mental state associated with heart-centeredness to that of mental confusion or emotional chaos. Although it is hard to quiet one's mind in today's busy world, accessing the heart center is an effective tool for personal development.

How to Access the Heart Center

Here are two exercises for accessing the heart center. The first is a process called "Centering". Begin by being in a quiet, safe environment (music optional). Close your eyes and with a positive, loving feeling, take 5 even, relaxed, deep breaths (Institute of HeartMath, n.d.). As you exhale, imagine a circle opening at the center of your chest and release any of the worries or stress in your life at this time. Tell yourself there is nothing you have to do at this time—that this is your time to just BE, and relax. Feel the energy of the heart center; one of compassion, innate harmony, healing presence, and unconditional love. Notice what your heart energy feels like. With your focus at the heart center, your mind becomes quiet. As your mind becomes quiet, your body relaxes. If your mind should become distracted, refocus at the heart center. Continue to focus at the heart center for 5–10 minutes. When you are ready, slowly open your eyes and let your awareness come back into the room.

The second exercise is the *"Heart to Heart" Meditation* described in *Joy's Way* (1970). In this exercise, you work with a partner. Sit comfortably, facing each other, and connect hands, palm to palm. Close your eyes, and center your attention on your own heart center. Now imagine the heart energy moving up to your throat, dividing at your throat, and flowing down your arms and into the palms of your hands. Image there is unconditional love flowing from your heart center to the heart center of your partner. The emphasis is on giving and receiving the heart energy, allowing it to flow. Then draw the energy back to your own heart chakra. This exercise takes approximately 10 minutes. Take 5–10 minutes after the exercise to share the experience with your partner.

What it Means to Live from the Heart

When life presents difficulties, the heart can allow an individual to perceive things differently. Instead of reacting to a problem, the person can observe the problem and be pro-active. Solutions are more apparent and clear when one lives through the heart center. As an example, when a problem occurs, the person's third and sixth chakras (solar plexus and 3rd eye) can become compromised. Is this person overly concerned about power or control? Is he or she emotionally fragile? If so, then it's likely that the solar plexus is compromised. If the person is frantically trying to fix a problem, but can't decide what to do, then it's possible that the third eye, the area of clarity and insight, is compromised. Focusing at the heart, while not denying the energy or importance of other energy centers, brings the chakras into a balance. This happens when a person observes the situation in a somewhat detached state. It is in the observer state that a person may arrive at new answers.

Living from the heart center allows individuals to live life in the present time, rather than in the future or past. When focused at the heart center, one does not judge or compare. Judgments are our reactions to good or bad, beautiful or ugly, etc. These reactions come as messages from our family, culture, and society, and often create a separation from others. Judgments such as good/bad, beautiful/ugly, smart/dumb, etc. are dualistic evaluations of self and others. This type of judgment lowers our vibration, and usually comes from the solar plexus. When we compare ourselves to others, we either find ourselves or others lacking. Our family, culture, and society condition us to make comparisons.

Comparison is, once again, a lower vibration that usually comes from the solar plexus.

The two previous concepts (making no judgments or comparisons) must be applied to others as well as to self. When they are put into practice, relationships are brought into balance.

Steps to Living a Heart-Centered Life

There are multiple steps to living from the Heart. The first is an awareness that you need to make a change. If you are living a very stressful life, but have no awareness that change is needed, then there is no life adjustment. Often there will be a physical or emotional crisis in life to make you aware that change is needed.

In the second step, there must be a belief that one can change. Often, people who are in high stress situations do not believe that their lives can be different. Although they may see a need for change, they may feel that they must forever live with the difficulties that life has presented to them. When one believes that change is possible in life, action can be taken.

Along with the belief that one can change is a desire to change (third step). Once an individual feels that his or her crisis situation can be changed, the next step is to want the change.

The fourth step is choice. After the above steps to heart centeredness have been experienced, choices must be made on a daily basis that will reinforce change. This is the step that requires action. Do your choices give you energy or take energy away?

The final step is to engage in daily (or more often) centering. This might be the most important step in living from the heart. No matter where you are in the process of life, heart centering is a daily discipline that must be done to accomplish meaningful change (Tovey, 2007).

Heart-Centeredness: Challenges in Life

When we have a crisis or challenge in life, most of us tend to go into reactive, or fix it mode. While it is important to cope with an immediate crisis, the steps to living from the heart center can be crucial, not only for the immediate problem, but also for a longer term opportunity for growth. Using the five steps as a foundation, we can apply them to most of life's challenges.

Let's take the example of a physical crisis. A physical crisis is often a wake-up call for change. The crisis itself brings awareness about needing to change (step 1). In examining the belief that we can change, do we believe that we can make the necessary changes to prevent future crises, and to heal? (step 2). In regard to the desire to change, often a physical crisis will instill in us the desire to change (step 3). In regard to making a choice, the choice that we make often requires a lifestyle change (step 4). Using daily centering and quieting the mind will allow the body to relax and help us to continue to make the best decision for needed changes (step 5).

Use of Dreams in the Heart-Centered Life

If you want to live a heart-centered life, it may be useful to pay close attention to your dreams, as they often contain important clues to our inner balance and wisdom. As stated in the *Talmud* of Judaism, a dream not understood is like a letter unopened. Here are some key points to remember about dreams and dream work:

1. Everyone dreams, even though you may not remember them.
2. If you are a person who doesn't remember your dreams, ask for a dream before retiring for the night.
3. Begin a dream journal. Keep the journal by your bed, or in a nearby area where you can write down your dream upon waking.
4. Share dreams with a friend or become part of a dream group as this can be valuable for self-growth.
5. Dreams can be categorized in a number of ways—for healing, for revealing your true emotional state, as compensation for your outer life, for telling you to make outer life changes, or as prophetic.
6. Often the shortest dreams are the most instructional.
7. Even if you can't remember a lot of detail in a dream, remembering the feeling that you had when you awoke can help you access the spirit of the dream.

8. When interpreting your dreams, it is helpful to look at each character in a dream as aspects of yourself.

9. Think of dreams as instructions from your own inner teacher.

10. It takes billions of cells to create a dream image. If your mind produces that much energy to create those images, they must be important!

Conclusion

The best way to strengthen a connection with your heart center is to do one of the centering exercises mentioned above on a daily basis. Allow yourself the time to BE and relax, feeling your heart's attributes of Compassion, Innate Harmony, Healing Presence and Unconditional Love.

Remember, working from the heart is an experience, not a thought. In the words of Dr. Brugh Joy (2007): "One cannot think about what it would be like to be totally focused in the heart chakra area, one must feel and be the heart chakra" (p.228).

Janet on Self Care

BY DIANE WIND WARDELL, PHD, RN, AHN-BC, CHTP/I

Janet Mentgen was an expert in self-care management. For over 20 years she journaled almost daily and recorded not only her reflections on how to live but also the wisdom and guidance she received while journaling. This process began in the early 1980's, when Janet was having work-related challenges and relationship difficulties in her marriage. It also paralleled her development as a healer, as this is when she was first "re-introduced" to energy work. According to Janet, she had been a particularly difficult child and was often sent to her room as punishment. It was here she learned to "hover" physically above her bed!

In this section, various aspects of Janet's received wisdom are covered as described in Janet's personal journals. However, this narrative is not meant to be all inclusive of her teachings. Janet's interest was in teaching us how to be "lightworkers" for the planet so that we can help heal the earth. This was to be done by healing the self in order to become a bearer of light. Janet believed that it was the little things that change the earth, and she stressed simplicity in life practices.

Heart Meditation

The following is a meditation that Janet used specifically to help her write. However, it can be applied to any spiritual process.

> First, prepare yourself for meditation by sitting in a quiet space. Then become aware of your breath. Go deeper now into your heart center on your inward journey and feel the presence of those who are there to assist you as your teachers and guides for the highest good. Let them blend into one as you continue to feel connected. Let the blending occur and watch a glowing light made up of their forms as you image them. Let this light continue to brighten as all shapes blend into light. Now let this light intensify in your body, the blending of all presences known to you. Let the light infiltrate all your cells, becoming brighter as it blends with your cells and grows in intensity until all becomes one. Feel the vibration of this light as it continues to become brighter. Now you are also aware of a vibrational quiver in your heart. It is energetic in nature and you can feel the warmth also directly within the heart center. Continue to let this expand and brighten. Now sit quietly in this light and vibration until you feel it is time to stop. You are magnetically held in this light. . . listen and observe only . . . the light has extended all around you now and is present in the inside and the outside of your body . . . you are hearing your inner voice clearly with the heart center . . . the mind is still.

Making Decisions

Janet would often teach about the differences in making a decision from the heart or from other centers. For example, when in your emotional center, you will feel your emotions dominate. In the mental center, your thinking will dominate, and when in the heart, peace will dominate. Janet's journal writings are as follows:

> You need to be in the emotional center to heal your emotions, in the mind to correct your thinking, and in your heart to feel and live within the peace. Therefore, you could describe periods of your life as predominately physical, emotional, mental or peaceful. Which of these best describes you?
>
> Make an effort to move into the heart, the place of peace. The heart is responsible for the transformational process. When this happens, the heart dominates and blends with the physical, emotional, and mental aspects, and the soul becomes the overseer. Then life is lived through the grace of peace rather than the chaos of ego. Learn to ask for help from outside of the ego-self, and go to a source of greater wisdom.
>
> For most of us, we work from the solar plexus or will center. Feel the shift from solar plexus to heart just by seeking the intention to move into your heart center as you do before each healing session. When you are not feeling peace, balance and harmony, it is a clue that another choice needs to be made.
>
> For example, you can use the following process when you are confronted by others. First, pull into your heart center for any response you need to make. Learn to listen with your heart. Not everyone is going to like or agree with the decision(s) you make. If you are in your heart center and have made the decision from that center, you will be fine. It is all right for others to be angry and to express that anger even if you become the target for that anger. Do not become angry also and

respond with anger, but go into the heart center and again listen to your inner voice and respond from your centered state. You do not become angry also, as this would fuel the anger and not accomplish the task at hand. Do not fear another's anger.

Be Kind to Yourself

As Janet evolved in her heart-centered practice, she became aware that it felt like being a beginner again. It is like the first day in school of a new grade, and there is much to learn. The lessons get much harder and the work more intense as you progress. Sometimes the more intense the lesson, the more time it takes to incorporate, which will create a feeling of space or "time off" on the journey.

Janet shared that sometimes it is difficult to understand where you are in your development:

> The difficulty may come in only being able to witness moments and not seeing the overall picture from a distance. What seems insurmountable in the moment is only a minor obstacle overall in our perceptions, so it is important to move forward daily, day-by-day with choices and decisions. Do not try to hurry through as it is a learned way of life and engages patience. Each lesson only creates more lessons, and this continues on. It is not like an instant cure for a problem, but it is a much slower and much deeper resolve. Let go of a specific time frame and allow it all to evolve.

Chakra Healing

A visit to the hot springs (one of Janet's favorite places) provided the backdrop for working with the energy field, including the chakras. The directives she learned for each of the chakras can help provide a framework for self-healing:

Physical: The stronger the body, the better the support and frame for carrying the workload.

Emotional: It is important to learn to feel emotions before their release; otherwise bypassing emotional development leaves a vacancy in integration. Emotions are necessary for full balance and living. Releasing old emotional patterns frees you for being present emotionally. Continue to learn to feel more, do not be afraid to feel.

Mental: The mental layer process is to clear old thought patterns and beliefs that are not true. Remember that you are a servant to others. Stay within that attitude and you will not develop a superior attitude toward others. There are two elements to this practice. You cannot be competitive nor can you expect others to serve you.

Heart: On the heart level, move directly into heart energy and let it radiate from your center. See the light and watch the light as it comes from you. When this light emanates from you, it becomes a magnet that attracts others to the light and can be shared.

Throat: In the throat is the communication center. Feel the art of expression coming to you.

Head: In the head center, acknowledge all the wisdom that comes to you through your teachers and others who bring you messages of good will and thanks. Learn to hear these messages from your brow center and heart, and not from your ego. This will help you to appreciate without feeling superior and prevent pride and reputation from becoming your guide. As you function from the heart center under the guidance of the brow center, you can walk a more loving path.

Providing Service

Janet gave additional information about how to be in service. This is an important component of healing work. Janet wrote her guidance as follows:

> At times we may feel like we are all alone, but we are not expected to have to do this work alone, even though it may feel that way in the moment. There are many available to help you, including the "messengers" that are sent to you at specific times. Look at everyone you encounter as teaching you part of living. Every incident, every little encounter, every sacrifice, and every gesture of service contributes to the whole. When you serve one, you have served many. Do not hold back on your service to others. Work right through the pain into a caring way, thus coming from your heart, your open heart. Let all your work be heart-centered. If it is not, and you are aware of that, stop, become centered in the heart, and then proceed. Heart-centered work is more profound than ordinary work that is driven from the ego although both are beneficial.

Rest

Rest and reflection need to be part of self-care. Janet offered many different directives from her reflections, including taking time out every hour if possible, then, for an extended hour during the day. During these breaks, Janet's writings reflect the goal is as follows:

> *No decisions are to be made at this time, only exploration of ideas.* Without adequate rest, the light of the body begins to dim, and eventually becomes stressed and in trouble. It is also important to have focus, which can appear as "contraction" (or the pulling away from that which attracts) and is a way to adjust the ego and to stay focused on the work. Reflection stops the scattered feeling and brings one into focus. If one is attracted to all the

dazzling lights out there, it is easy to lose focus on the one light, the light that guides us in this mission.

For calmness Janet offers another technique. Image yourself by constructing yourself (hair, mouth, eyes, nose, etc.) in your mind, then look into your eyes in the image (self looking into self) and find your own center.

One interesting aspect of rest is to clean! Janet often reminded others to organize their personal space. For her, it was clearing her desk and organizing her projects so that she was able to *"Plan your future, live your present, release your past."*

Group Vibration

Vibration is an important component in energy healing. Janet was a musician (violin) and seemed to understand the multifaceted aspects of this principle. She journaled the following wisdom:

> Wherever a different group is formed, the harmonic note vibrationally will be different. It is for you to listen and learn to distinguish the sound as well as being aware of vibrational changes. These are mostly unnoticed by most people. Through learning to read and understand the note and vibration, you will increase your sensitivity.
>
> When connecting with individuals, let your vibrational rate come into a higher level. First however, you must match the rate of the other individual, for you can only progress as you blend. The note can be different but the rate must match. Time together helps this to happen. Also, walking together will be helpful in bringing vibrations to a higher level.

Ask

Janet reminds us that we have support that is available to us. One aspect of this support system from the realms of the spirit world (i.e. angels, totems, guides) simply waits quietly to be acknowledged. In reality, you never have to be alone, but it can be a choice you make. Simply remember that there is a support system available to you and ask for help, not only when there is stress or problem, but other times as well. She reminds us that with relief of life problems and stresses, you are then free and ready to move into the joyfulness of life. In addition, she tells us:

> By learning the discipline of self-care, eventually you will be able to practice self-care under any circumstance so that hard times can become a way of finding peace and happiness. Life is never meant to be lived in isolated ways with specific feelings, but with many feelings present. Tears of laughter would be a way of saying this.

Presence and Transformation

On a day early in January, 1992 Janet was directed to spend a day in silence, which became part of her spiritual practice when returning from traveling and teaching. Janet used these days of silence so that she would be mindful of her words and activities. Specifically, she would speak only directly and what were necessary words for the work at hand, otherwise she practiced silence so as not to be distracted by outside influences and to be able to come to a place of internal silence without effort. She was given:

> It is difficult to focus when you are busy in your daily activities. You must be able to discern the difference between chatter and your internal wisdom from your "quiet council", where the heart is connected. In your focused attention to the issue at hand, within the quiet circle, you will access the inner wisdom necessary and worthy of this work.
>
> Move to an even deeper level when you are aware of your inner silence, increasing your ability to know your harmonic sounds so that you can blend to the perfect sound, which is the Logos, a level of attainment beyond most human understanding. You will know the sound when you hear it, until then it is only a knowing that it

exists beyond your consciousness. You must also hear the sound *without* losing the earth connection. This is the passage through the portal and could be likened to the "no sound" effect. You do not know when the opportunity will come, and it is a time of preparation and waiting for the event to occur. Always be prepared and continue to practice this state of silence within the context of everyday life, for you must continue with your earthly assignment as well.

Self-Care to Increase Your Vibration as a Healer

ANNE L. DAY, MA, BSN, CMT, HNB-BC, CHTP/I

An important theme that runs through each of the Healing Touch classes is self-care and the development of the healer. At each level of Healing Touch classes, we talk about this important subject, as it is the foundational piece for doing any healing work. Janet Mentgen always said that we must do this work from the place of the heart. As we became more experienced healers, she said our vibration would be consistently at a higher level and our work would flow more effortlessly and more effectively.

On-going personal growth and development of the healer is a prerequisite to one's maturation in working with energy. One's ability to do this work is directly related to one's own personal development on all levels: physical, emotional, mental and spiritual. Our goal is to help those who have chosen the path of healing to raise their own energy vibrations to higher and more refined levels of energy. As we radiate loving energy, less needs to be "done", as the radiance of our "being" will influence the energy field through our intention for the highest and best for the person. As practitioners become clearer energetically, and are in a vibration of peace and unconditional love in their lives, they will need less and less "techniques" to do the work. Thus, one can accomplish great healing with simple touch, clear intention, and unconditional loving vibration, as the Spiritual Masters (e.g. Jesus, Buddha, Krishna,) have done.

High Level Wellness

A foundational goal is to practice *High Level Wellness*, which is more vibrantly alive than just being "well". High Level Wellness is to dance with life having all the energy one needs for whatever one chooses to participate in. Life is energy; we are energy. When we learn to see life through the eyes of energy sensitivity, we become aware of what fills us and what depletes us. The secret lies in keeping our energy "cup" overflowing, or to keep our "energy valve" open. How then do we learn to live at these higher vibrational levels on a day-to-day basis? It is the commitment to the path of healing, and living holistically and from the heart that will take us gradually to these higher levels.

Self-Assessment

We all have daily challenges to stay in balance with the four areas of our lives: physical (P), emotional (E), mental (M) and spiritual (S). Life is a constant change and flow, and we always have a choice of how to respond to the new eddies and currents of that flow.

We need to check in daily to see where we need to strengthen or nurture ourselves for higher-level wellness. The key is in noticing through that assessment where we are depleted. This brings important awareness about our daily needs, our strengths, and our weaknesses. We must be honest and kind in our assessment—sometimes we just aren't feeling fit, loving, clear or connected. This process teaches us self-acceptance and compassion.

When we accept where we are and set the intention for giving ourselves what is needed, we can let go and let the flow of energy refill the energy "cup" of our wholeness. If we are regularly assessing our wellness in each of the four areas, and if we have a commitment to supporting them on a daily basis, we will be able to soar above the stresses that will inevitably occur in our lives. This takes practice! It is like doing exercises every day to strengthen ourselves for a sport that we want to do. We don't just go out and do it without a foundation of strength. If we want to dance well, we practice the steps until we can flow with the music without thinking about our steps. It is important to design a plan for really taking care of ourselves—physically, emotionally, mentally and spiritually. As my favorite tennis instructor told us: "If you plan your play, you will play your plan!"

Physical. Our physical self-care includes eating, exercise, strength, endurance, movement, and rest. How do you choose to take care of your physical body every day? What goals are you willing to set to improve these components of physical health? You can choose a variety of activities for different days during the week (e.g. yoga twice a week, a dance class once a week, a brisk walk three times a week). It is also important to plan relaxation periods for refilling your energy and decreasing the stress response.

Writing down what you eat and your nutrition goals is very helpful. What about care of your physical body through massage or other bodywork? Maybe you choose this once a month, rather than once a week. But what you do for nurturing yourself on the physical level needs regular planning and commitment.

Emotional. Practice getting in touch with your emotions and embrace your emotions with loving-kindness. Share your emotions with someone you trust. Journal your feelings. Make a list of stress-reduction techniques that work for you. Practice forgiveness, which Carolyn Myss (1987), says is the "most important thing we can do for our healing" (p.18). Welcome humor in your life —lighten up!

It is also important to release emotional issues completely from the energy field to allow for an open heart and free movement of energy in the body (Singer, 2007). This can be done by taking time to allow issues to pass through and not become imbedded and stuck, thereby creating a trigger for future activation.

Mental. Assess your thoughts; listen to your self-talk. It is amazing how many of us are giving ourselves negative messages filled with fear. Let go of "Stinking Thinking"! Choose to see things differently. Is this the thought you are happiest thinking? If not, change your thought! Join a study/support group, or attend a lecture or sermon to help raise your mental vibrations. Practice mindfulness and living in the NOW.

Spiritual. Assess your sense of peace and connection to a greater power. Do you feel supported by the Universe? Make space in your day for meditation, even if you start with 5 or 10 minutes. Take time to "Be", which means quietly being still and connecting to the Divine in your own way. Affirm the goodness of life daily and that you are fully committed to bringing Light, Love, and Balance to this earth. Practice "the attitude of gratitude," which is very helpful for aligning with love and joy.

Techniques

Journaling. The Journal is a significant tool in facilitating wholeness. Writing in a journal can activate healing responses, and various journal techniques have helped clients with self-discovery and empowerment. Journaling is a free form of writing with no rules or obligations. You don't have to journal every day!

The journal becomes a friend who is always there to listen to you with unconditional acceptance. You can cry or scream in your journal without judgments. You can release strong emotions through an "unsent letter." You can dialogue with your body to get guidance on what it needs for healing. You can dialogue with your Higher Self or Inner Healer to learn more about how to support your healing journey.

Alignment and Attunement. A very important daily exercise for healers to raise their energy vibration is the *Hara Alignment*, first described by Barbara Brennan (1993) in *Light Emerging* and taught in Healing Touch Level 3 classes. This exercise connects us to our Hara Line, which holds our life intentions, and allows us to access an incredible flow of wisdom and guidance. Through this alignment, we also attune to our Core Star, which is our Divine Essence.

We are more than our bodies. We are more than our minds and emotions—we are magnificent spiritual beings! By attuning to our true essence, we empower ourselves by connecting to the greatest spiritual source of energy. Spiritually connecting brings a flow of loving energy. When we are in alignment and attunement with that flow, everything falls into place easily. We are one with the divine force and flow. We can let go of effort and allow that flow to be our guide. Practicing the *Hara Alignment* daily will more quickly manifest our intentions, and thus also raise the vibration of our energy dimensions.

We manifest our reality through our power of intention. Remember the energy principle that "Like attracts Like". We will attract the vibration that we are holding within us. If we are in a high vibration, that is what we will also experience around us. If we are angry or upset or sad, (lower vibrations of energy), we will tend to experience more of the same energy patterns.

Energy Vibration. According to David Hawkins (1995) in his book *Power Versus Force*, the highest energy vibration is measured in those who are experiencing Love, Peace, Joy and Enlightenment. Much of our population is experiencing lower vibrations of fear, guilt, shame and sadness. Thus the most important thing we can do as healers is to choose Love over Fear on a moment-to-moment basis. We will be continually challenged with life situations that create angst and pain, but we can choose to see the possibilities for growth and good rather than be depleted by these events. Wayne Dyer (2004) says: "When you change the way you look at things, the things you look at change" (p 183). This leads us to seeing connection rather than separation, which opens us to more harmony and peace in our lives.

Summary

"Healing Touch has changed my life." Over and over I hear these words from Healing Touch students who embrace the practice and path of this work. I believe that the change students profess is related directly to a new energy consciousness; an awareness of an energy dimension and how we can affect that energy with our thoughts and intentions. As we learn to see through "sacred eyes"—seeing the Divine Essence in each other and practicing unconditional love and cooperation—our lives are changed through changes in our perceptions. Living from the heart gives us access to expanded creative intelligence, which opens us to many more possibilities for joy and success on our life journeys. Regular commitment to self-assessment and self-care brings us into harmony from within that extends into all we do. Thus, we will more consistently be living at higher levels of vibration. We will be more resilient with life changes, dancing with the flow and in-tune with a loving energy flow and intention!

Self-Care Between the Beats, Creating Resilience

By Sue Kagel, RN, BSN, HNB-BC, CHTP/I

The heart beats continuously. It rests and restores between the beats, every second or so. Self-care between the beats is a way of being in the world, renewing the self and fitting life elements into a balanced existence in a limited time frame. So often when under stress we feel that there is no time for self-care, usually when it is most needed to create and maintain resilience. Learning to live mindfully, consciously, present in the moment, in alignment with our higher purpose, and with high level awareness are concepts that are life sustaining and evolving, even in times of "no time" for self-care.

The teeter totter of life experiences and emotions tips us in various directions. Our mission is to be aware of the shifting and bring ourselves back to center, keeping the swings smaller and correcting as soon as they are noticed. The body does this automatically in its systems to maintain homeostasis or balance within certain ranges. We can assist this process by assessing and observing ourselves on a continual basis. Our goal is not perfect balance, but flexibility, being as proactive as possible and moving consciously with the swings with small, simple increments of self-care. As practitioners, with our ability to heighten our energy fields, we have additional responsibilities: to be very aware of our energetic and emotional states, to monitor the energy we are exuding at any given time, whether positive or negative, to assess our own energy fields, and to adjust accordingly.

"No Time"

When there is "no time", we can still focus on our way of being. There are myriads of techniques and modalities that support self-care and High Level Wellness, many of which involve a time commitment. What does one do when there is barely enough time to breathe and one has limited options in which to create the time and space for self-care? There is a principle called "Kaizen" that breaks down large situations or projects into bite size pieces and small, manageable steps (Mauer, 2004). Applying this concept can break self-care into simple, moment by moment applications to support balance and calmness and to awaken a sense of inner joy. Variety is the spice of life, so change your self-care practices to keep them fresh.

Quickly Assessing Yourself Daily

There is a quick tool that can be used to assess your status. Create a medicine wheel (circle) with equal size categories for body, mind, spirit, emotion, social and environment. Shade in each section from the center outward, based on the percentage of balance you feel in the moment. This will quickly identify those areas of imbalance and provide direction for filling the depleted areas by means of the little energy boosters described below. This tool can be revisited on a frequent basis to monitor positive changes and further need for adjustment.

Joy and Fulfillment

Self-care can be a long list of activities addressing body, mind, emotion, social, and spiritual aspects, but if these items aren't joyful, you will not want to do them. Consider those things that fill you up, but do not add the feeling of "one more thing" to the "to do" list. Re-evaluate favorite self-care activities enjoyed in the past. Do they need to remain, be re-incorporated, or is it time to try new things to continue evolving? Self-care includes clearing out items (on all levels) that no longer serve you at this time, in all areas of life, including your home and work spaces. Clearing includes removing clutter, releasing unhealthy relationships, and removing the old to make room for the new. Take a few moments each morning to listen internally. Check to see if you need to *do* something for self-care, or just *be*—to rest, rejuvenate, breathe, and come into balance.

Grounding Lowers Anxiety

Returning to our foundational concepts, Rogers states that we are part of a unified field and that we can tap into the greater energy around us, fully embodied, to calm, energize and sustain us. Grounding lovingly into the earth aids in decreasing anxiety and stress while increasing our ability to be present to ourselves and to others. This is a matter of awareness, of noticing ourselves on a regular basis to monitor our grounded status. Being barefoot on the earth or on untreated concrete for 10 min a day may be useful to reset to the earth's energy and connect to the underlying rhythm of life (Oshman, 2008).

According to Dan Benor M.D. (2008), tapping your toes in a gentle, subtle motion, alternating between your feet, also has a calming effect. This stimulates both sides of your brain and tricks it into thinking that you are running away as in the fight or flight response. It seems to have the effect of discharging any trapped energy in the hips and legs, decreasing stress hormones, and focusing on the feet to encourage grounding.

Returning to the Breath

Being present allows us to be the calm eye in the storm of whatever is swirling around us. The simple concept of returning to the breath with awareness aids in returning us to inner calm, focusing in the heart. Teaching ourselves and our clients to note the first place we feel ourselves physically reacting to stress in our bodies, such as: clenching muscles; rapid, shallow or holding breath; increased heart rate; and tight stomach or neck/shoulders, develops an awareness of the body's shift into releasing stress hormones and adrenaline. This awareness allows us to recognize the internal change so that we can mindfully shift back to a relaxation response.

Breathing in a slow, deep, even, and relaxed pattern informs the body that all is well. Visualizing a joyful, peaceful or loving feeling (as in babies, puppies, kittens, bunnies) including evoking the sights, hearing the sounds, smelling the smells and feeling the feelings of the memory, shifts us to the sensory aspect of the brain and heightens the experience. Joyful, peaceful mini-daydreams/visualizations are encouraged.

Using simple cues such as breathing slowly while at a red light, or while walking down the hallway at work, can bring us back to our heart center, and trigger a relaxation response. Pause, breathe out slowly, relax, let go, and allow the body and mind to quiet. Then smile from ear to ear.

Keeping your Fluids Up

Keep your water bottle handy. Keep your heart happy, hydrated and slower, with more time to rest between the beats, by drinking water. You need to replace about 2 liters or 8 glasses of water a day from what is lost through normal activities, such as breathing and sweating, more if you are exercising or out in the heat. Dehydration increases fatigue and can create headaches. If you don't like water, consider substituting herbal teas (such as mint tea) which have relaxing properties. Slices of fruit or cucumber can be added for refreshing alternatives, or try highly diluted energy drinks or coconut water. You can also increase fluids by eating more fruits and vegetables that are 97% water. The best way to tell if you are getting enough fluids is if your urine is clear or a pale yellow color.

Heightening Your Sensory Awareness

The sensory part of the brain encourages the body to relax. Throughout the day, rather than ruminating on stressors, stimulate your sensory aspects of the brain by looking for green nature areas in your environment. Vitamin "G" for green and nature lowers blood pressure and has a calming effect, as does music and art (Groenewegen, van der Berg, de Vries, & Verheij, 2006). Find ways to increase your sensory stimulation by taking a new route, and breaking your routine patterns forcing you to pay attention rather than be on autopilot.

Embracing Change

Change is ongoing, and the more that we can embrace it, the more we can flow with it. When this is done mindfully, in alignment, fully present, connected to source and breath, we can surf the wave of life's changes rather than fight it; we can relax into it and "go with the flow". Even in times of difficulty, keeping our focus on moments of appreciation and gratitude throughout the day will help generate "joyful" neurotransmitters. An attitude of "it is what it is", related to those things over which we have no control, will encourage a less emotionally agitated state. This creates the opportunity for us to be more available for things we enjoy.

Consciously Monitoring the Flow

Observing our outward "giving" flow, in relation to our inward "receiving" flow is paramount to being in balance. There are times when a high flow outward is required due to life circumstances. Take a few moments to analyze this. Are you receiving equal to your giving? How are you filling yourself back up? Do you need to be more open to receive?

Is it necessary to decrease the amount you are giving to bring more balance and to slow the outward flow in order to refill and not burn out?

Sometimes the mountain of stress is larger than the time, energy, and self-care needed to offset it, so evaluation is needed to reduce the mountain in some way. Consider analyzing the mountain and finding ways to chip away at it. Are there areas/items that can be set aside, delegated, reduced, or eliminated? Remember the principle of Kaizen and make small, but more frequent changes to shift your flow.

Optimizing Time

To optimize your time, start the day at bedtime to set the stage for the next day. The first step is to survey the energy of your environment. Clear the clutter as much as possible before going to bed, especially in your sleeping area. Take a few moments to write your list for tomorrow and visualize your day going smoothly and easily, then let it all go. Focus on gratitude and appreciation for several things that occurred in your day, which will trigger relaxation hormones.

Sleep

Restorative sleep is necessary for general health, healing and well-being. Short duration of sleep (Cappuccio, Cooper, d'Elia, Strazzullo, & Miller, 2011) and poor sleep quality including trouble falling asleep and waking earlier than planned increases heart disease risks (Matthews et al., 2013). Sleep and wakefulness are affected by various factors, including light-dark cycles, hormones (e.g. melatonin and cortisol), and brain circuitry (Chellappa & Schmidt, 2010). Janet Mentgen recommended 8 hours of "horizontal time" each day so that whether sleeping or not, your body is flat and resting. She also recommended a short nap as needed (Mentgen, 2000). Be sure to be in bed 7–8 hours before your rising time. Sleep also helps maintain healthy weight (Verhoef, Camps, Gonnissen. Westerterp, & Westerterp-Plantenga, 2013). Suggestions include the following:

- Prepare for sleep with dim lighting, turning off all "screens" and stopping activities earlier in the evening.

- Be in bed by 10 pm and then read awhile, (i.e. a boring book), listen to soft music or Guided Imagery CDs (i.e. CDs for sleep by Belleruth Naparstek, LISW, MA, Steven Gurgevitch PhD, Rubin Naiman PhD) and deep breathe, so that your mind is calm.
- Lights out by 10:30 p.m. Sleep in a cool, darkened room or consider the use of eye shades to optimize natural melatonin formation to aid in sleep.
- Connect spiritually. Turn your issues over to a higher power, whatever that may be for you. If relevant to your belief system, consider saying your prayers, asking your angels to assist you for the highest good of all.

Rising Take Stock

When awaking in the morning, lie in bed, waken slowly, center, breathe into your heart and be grateful for waking up this morning. If you need to use the restroom, do so and return to bed and lie down for a few moments. As you prepare to set your intention for the day, do the following:

- Breathe in for the count of 5 and out for the count of 5, taking slow, even, relaxed breaths with a soft relaxed belly. Do this for 5 cycles while focusing on a loving, joyful feeling/memory. This will create a relaxation response.
- Take a moment and scan yourself from head to toe. How are you physically? Are you rested? How are you emotionally? Are you calm and relaxed? How are you mentally? Are you clear? How are you spiritually? Are you connected? If not, those areas will be your focus for the day to facilitate balance.
- Then check in. What day is it? What needs to be attended to or accomplished today? Review your list in your head or read it over.
- Sit on the side of the bed for a minute to ground, center, set your energy and your intention for the day. Visualize the day. Focus on your intention and see the day as one of ease and grace. See

yourself moving though the day mindfully, intending for this or something greater for the highest good of all.

- Open the curtains to bring in the light, or go outside to bring sunlight through your eyes (no sunglasses for a while), which will stimulate your pituitary gland to produce melatonin for sleep cycle later and may activate serotonin to improve your mood (Crowley, Lee, Tseng, Fogg, & Eastmen, 2003). For those in dark or rainy climates, a full spectrum light box, used daily may be a helpful substitute.

Eating on the Run

Nurturing yourself with healthy food choices is difficult in times of "no time." However, try to eat 3 regular meals, with healthy snacks between meals, to maintain a more stable blood sugar, which will enhance inner calm. Resist those foods, such as sugared foods, simple carbohydrates, and comfort foods, with a high glycemic index (potatoes, processed foods) that may spike your blood sugar and your insulin levels, resulting in a "crash" 30 minutes later. Additionally, you should:

- Avoid caffeinated options (i.e. coffee, tea, soda, chocolate) that may raise your heart rate and create a sense of anxiety. Allow your heart to have more time to rest between the beats.
- Grab an apple a day.
- Cook simple meals in batches or buy pre-made healthy food; freeze in individual portions for quick lunch or dinner.
- Keep power bars, nuts, and protein snacks handy in grab bags for a quick pick up.

Move your Body

Even when you are very busy, it is important to move in some way, even minimally, during the day. Monitor yourself and if tired, slow down or rest. There are ways to sneak in movement. Attempt to get in 30 minutes of movement daily, even if in short intervals. Moderate exercise may help reduce mild to moderate depressive symptoms (Qureshi & Al-Bedah, 2013). A few suggestions include the following:

- Optimize your movement opportunities to get more steps into your day, even if in small increments, as in parking farther away from your destination, walking the aisles of the grocery store, or taking one or more flight of stairs.
- Lift your spirits during routine housework by dancing around to upbeat music.
- Walk meditatively by breathing in for a count of 4 and out for a count of 4 to heighten your senses and focus on the surrounding environment.
- Moving, whether walking, running or swimming, alternates sides of the body and sides of the brain to promote relaxation and deep breathing.

Be Mindful of your Mind

Use the Kaizen principle to keep the mind nourished. Engage your mind in short puzzles and in stimulating conversations or ideas. This can be done by:

- Reading a few pages a day or in the evening before bed. It does not have to be a book or even a chapter, but could be a short magazine article or a page or two.
- Working a crossword or Sudoku puzzle at bedtime, as this can be relaxing and promote letting go of the day.
- Being aware of your mental chatter and self-talk so that it remains positive. In the event that you find yourself rehashing your stressors, return to joyful memories.

Social

Remember that humans don't live in a vacuum, so it is extremely important to connect with other human beings to support the social aspect of balance and the exchange of loving energy. Be open to being present to others and accept offers of assistance and support. Engage in hugs with those you love, including pets, on a daily basis. You don't need to own a pet, you can visit friends or neighbors to play with theirs or stop by a pet store.

Emotions

While it is important to acknowledge your emotions, it is also helpful to "stand on top of the mountain" for a higher perspective and compassionate detachment. Cultivate a response of "isn't that interesting", "curious", "hmmm", "what's that about", without taking it personally. The following suggestions may also be helpful:

- Be present to emotions and allow awareness of them to flow through, coming to acceptance.
- Be an observer and don't get caught in the drama.

Spiritual

Living in heart-centered mindfulness at all times, as mentioned earlier in the chapter, helps you to be aware of your energy and impact on others. The universe has untold lessons for our development but is most concerned with our "joy" of being. This is "it", not tomorrow, not yesterday, but this moment. There are no others.

In times between the beats, simply carrying or wearing a significant artifact or reminder of your spiritual connection may be helpful. This may be a religious object or relic, a piece of jewelry, a symbol of your strength and peace (such as a rock or crystal), or a poem or other writing.

Summary

In summary, all of the above suggestions, applied alone or in combination, attribute to developing a calm, peaceful resilience and higher consciousness in you as a person and as a healer which is a constant, evolving process. This can lead to a more enjoyable, sustainable and healthy existence, even during times of high stress.

Applying Watson's foundational work (Chapter 3), we learned that we must care for ourselves before we can care for others. In the HTI Code of Ethics/Standards of Practice #3 Self Development, we are encouraged to "…integrate self-care practices to enhance our own physical, emotional, mental and spiritual wellbeing." The more we continue to heal ourselves, the more our self-care as practitioners becomes our way of being. Through learning and modeling these behaviors, we create our tool box for client self-care teaching. As we evolve ourselves and our own consciousness, living authentically, we are better able to impart this way of being to our clients, family, and community through energetic entrainment and teaching.

Animals in Healing

By Annis Parker, RN, ADN, DipEd.,CHTP/I

Most of the time, as humans, we tend to think in terms of ourselves only and do not give too much consideration to all the elements of the natural world around us. The planet, the soil, water of all types, weather, animals, plants, birds, and every bug or grub, seen and unseen, are energetic, knowledgeable and communicating beings just like any of us. Our belief that we are somehow superior is not at all helpful or wise. The energy that comes into our total body through active chakras and energy (auric) field actually comes from all of the components of the natural world listed above. The energy is downsized into the nervous system, the bloodstream and ultimately to every cell in our body and is freely given. My request would be that we consciously work with the natural world in awe and gratitude.

Animals, including pets and farm animals, present themselves in many ways. What is important is that you realize that all animals and creatures have chakras and auric fields with physical, emotional, mental and spiritual layers. They also have the ability to understand very complex ideas and from my perspective, spend a great deal of time waiting for humans to catch up.

Brain size has nothing to do with intelligence. A bird can problem solve at a rapid speed. For example, a New Zealand mountain parrot called a Kea, which was researched by *National Geographic* for its problem solving ability, was also found to have a wicked sense of humor. An example is as follows: A Kea landed on a corrugated iron, mountain hut roof. The shepherd inside was suddenly awakened by a tremendous noise of scraping talons and parrot calls as the Kea slid down the roof to the edge. The shepherd leapt out of bed and banged on the roof with a broom. The next moment he saw the Kea hanging upside down looking in through the window, then it flew to the top of the roof and slid down again. Eventually the Kea flew away. The shepherd was awakened again by a sound he knew. But, now there were two! So the game started again, with the Keas sliding down the roof, and the shepherd banging on the ceiling. Then suddenly the shepherd felt the hairs on his neck standing up and looked over his shoulder to see one Kea looking in the window whilst the other one danced and slid down the roof. With a squawk and a final tango on the roof, the pair flew away!

Animal Characteristics

Memory is stored in every cell of the body and, therefore, nothing that has happened to an animal since birth is forgotten. The one thing animals don't do is build on their emotions, like we do. They are much clearer energetically than humans are. We could learn a great deal from this. The horse, cat and dog have undertaken the work of teaching humans to "love without condition"—just as they do continuously. Horses are therapeutically used with the disabled and those with social adjustment problems (such as juvenile delinquents) throughout the world because of the love the horses give without condition and the listening they do as stories are told. Also, when riding, people are sitting on the horse's back heart chakra, which creates a strong, positive energy.

It is interesting to note that all creatures are telepathic, so our continual talking and making a noise can be counter-productive. They have already read our thoughts. Quietness is greatly valued by the natural world, as it encourages humans to observe more carefully and perhaps to hear and suspend all that mental activity which exhausts us. When internal quietness has been achieved, then we can come truly from an open heart, without judgment of any kind, and be aware of how little we really know.

Animals have profound spiritual contacts. Through their feet, the outer layer of their auric field, and their Hara line, animals are aware of what is happening to the land. They know where other animals are and have communication with all living creatures. Their telepathic capacity is also involved in communication. Stress causes their entire auric field and chakras to not function. When their stress rises, injury and dis-ease issues also rise. As humans, we are the greatest stressors to animals and are often unaware of the effects of our thoughts and actions.

The extensive knowledge of living creatures was clearly indicated in the Boxing Day Tsunami in Thailand in 2004. Many animal species were restless and moved to higher ground. For example, elephants broke their leg traces and moved inland in order to avoid being caught in the tsunami. The ability to feel changes in the land through their feet and comprehend what that means is not something we humans remember.

Another example of innate knowledge is seen in the Australian Koala, who eats Eucalyptus or Blue Gum leaves. There are many varieties of these leaves. Over a period of a few hours, the composition of the leaves on one of the varieties of trees changes from tasty and nutritional to poisonous, with the leaves containing enough prussic acid to kill a horse. This is all part of the life cycle of that tree. The koalas stop eating in that tree a few hours before the composition changes and move to another variety. This is but one example of the amazingly intricate natural processes that exist all over the planet in myriads of forms—under the ground, on top of the ground, in the sea and in all water.

In another example, the roots of trees not only anchor the trees and lift nutrition and water upwards into them but also bring up minerals and trace elements to the higher strata of the soil for use by less deeply rooted plants. Worms also live at different levels; some living in the surface layer take leaves and surface vegetation downwards to be broken down, whilst the middle layer worms take some of the upper layers deeper down and bring up elements from the lower levels. It is a complex system of digging that is all done by the worms.

Working with Animals

Working with animals involves contemplating their origins. For example, it is important to know that dogs have a wolf gene buried in their DNA somewhere and that humans, tigers (and all cats) are predators, whereas the deer, gazelle and horse are prey animals. This means these two groups of animals see differently and think differently. These are just some of the things we need to consider with each and every creature, while recognizing that there are many variations. Always, the first question is "What sort of animal is it?" Then we need to become quiet, calm, and have clarity of purpose. It takes time to learn to stay totally out of our emotional fields and stand in our spiritual structure. This is vital, and fear needs to be very firmly under control. This means that all animals are approached as individuals, with all the previous information being considered.

There are so many animal stories worldwide. I will only comment on the very special small dolphin we have here in New Zealand. All dolphins love to play on the bow wave of boats. I watched a mother teaching her calf how to ride the bow wave. She moved in to demonstrate and then moved off to one side to let the calf have a try. She had to increase her speed to keep up with the pressure wave, but a ripple of the muscle was all that was needed. When the calf came off the wave, it leapt in the air with what looked like joy as it twisted and plunged before coming back onto the bow wave. Dolphins are also protective of humans. For example, when swimming underwater in the tropics, it is common knowledge and experience that if there are dolphins around, there will be no sharks about. It has also been proposed that dolphins use sonar to change pain frequencies experienced by women in labor and thus ease a woman's pain. Wouldn't it be great if we knew what those frequencies were and how this all worked? Unfortunately, holding these animals in captivity to research these and other questions creates stress for them.

Working within the Natural Order

One way you can work better with the natural world around you is by just sitting quietly with your animal(s) or alternatively, sitting in a garden focusing gently on a favorite plant. In this meditational mode, keep the mind without thought and just focus on calm breathing, being open to anything which comes to you intuitively.

Everything is about balance, and we know so little. In some languages (i.e. Indonesian), there is no word for "weed" because it is just a plant in a place we do not prefer. Often we don't even know the full range of qualities and the many wonderful attributes that have been found in plants, trees, and algae. Some of these attributes are currently used to assist us with our health. We do, however, often destroy nature without thought or knowledge. This is a dangerous and a very unbalancing practice.

The examples given here are but the smallest portion of something that occurs all over the planet, all the time and everywhere we can possibly look. To be increasingly aware of these complexities will hopefully cause us all to pause, look at, and be awestruck by the natural world. We are interlinked with the natural world, and every aspect of it is about balance. The range of balance is very narrow for all aspects of the planet, but the components of that balance are varied.

The planet is a highly evolved and organized set of systems, many of which have the capacity to help us in so many ways. Healing is just one of those. There are plants which heal and plants which harm. These plants often grow near each other. The stinging nettle grows near the broad leaf dock plant, which when rubbed onto stings will neutralize them. The indigenous cultures of the world have maintained so much more of this knowledge, and we would do well to pay attention and learn.

In another example, sea microbes have managed to clear oil which humans have spilled. However, some things the natural world has not been able to counteract. The seas have had mass quantities of garbage washed or dumped into them. This has also created vast "dumps" of plastic rubbish the size of floating continents. Sea animals consume the rubbish or become ensnared in it. Humans are also carelessly destroying various species of sea creatures. For example, a cruel and unbalanced behavior some humans engage in is chopping off the fins of sharks (who are the garbage disposal units of the sea) and then throwing them back into the water to die. Just because some people want to eat a high priced soup! On a positive note however, many people do relate to sea mammals and to dolphins, in particular.

It is obvious that I have focused on individual examples and on what we as humans could perhaps address. The reason for this is that we can only change our own behavior; we can extend our knowledge and our own view of the world. This must emanate from within us as individuals. It is time to make some very fast changes, cease to be "takers", and work at giving back to this Blue Planet. We need to work very hard at helping to rebalance that which we have critically unbalanced. Manmade "things" will never be able to outstrip the complexity of the natural world, although we try to emulate it.

Therefore, balance, respect, a large degree of awe, and the thought that "just because we can do it—should we?"—This is what I would ask all people to consider. As we explore and learn more and more about energy, how it works, what it does and the complexities of the interrelationships with the natural world, these are things I believe are essential for us to ponder, if we are to continue to live on this planet.

Earth Healing

By Christine Page, MD

If we were able to look over the shoulders of our ancient ancestors, we would see that healing was never attempted without first connecting the patient or client to powerful Earth energies. Indeed, just by strolling through the ruins of sacred healing centers, such as Epidaurus in Greece, it's quickly apparent how much importance was placed upon the medicinal elements of Mother Earth. Such facilities were built in places of natural beauty, where spring waters flowed, food could be gathered from lush soil, and gentle breezes played amongst rolling hills. Compare this scenario with many of our urban hospitals, and it's clear that modern architects grossly underestimate the role the environment plays in the enhancement of well-being.

Traveling even further back in time, we meet Minoan and Mesopotamian physicians who considered the physical body to be an extension of Mother Earth, all facets of which were imbued with divine and creative energy, and hence worthy of worship. Four thousand years later, many people are not only disconnected from the natural world but also from their bodies, often perceiving them as imperfect, non-spiritual, or as an inanimate object similar to a car. Nothing could be further from the truth. As I listen to those who wish to "save the planet," I ask that they first learn to cherish the piece of Earth that they were given to love and nurture, their own bodies. Without such a vibrant and powerful alchemical vessel, the soul is unable to grow or expand in consciousness, and therefore, can never reach true wholeness or healing. If you want to know wellness, first make peace with your body, entering fully into its rich offerings.

Elements of Healing

It is within the physical body, as in Mother Earth, that the four basic building blocks of all life are located. In the past, every student of healing knew how to evoke the four elements—fire, earth, air and water—to restore balance and well-being. When they are synthesized together, they form the light energy of consciousness, also known as ether. All four are represented within the worlds of physicality and consciousness, with earth and water seen as feminine components while fire and air are masculine.

The Elements

When an element is out of balance, it's not uncommon to experience dis-ease. A natural therapist will seek ways to redress the balance by offering suggestions, which may include specific foods to eat, colors to wear or places to visit. For instance, if we experience burnout, the element of fire is out of control. It requires calming down through the ingestion of foods such as watermelon, the wearing of blue clothes or spending more time near or in cool water. At the other extreme, physical or mental stagnation is caused by the excessive presence of the element, earth. A simple remedy is to add a little spice to life through exotic foods, the color red, and some warm sunshine. Finally, everybody instinctively knows how to "lift their spirits" when they are down or depressed through singing, dancing, hiking, laughing, praying, or taking off on an adventure. Unfortunately, these natural cures are often dismissed in preference to the authority given to a prescribed drug.

Signatures of Healing

Over the past few centuries, many of the greatest holistic physicians have taught that healing for all known conditions is to be found within the natural kingdoms. They knew this, not because they had uprooted the plant and dissected it to discover its chemical constituents, but because they recognized its signature. Such recognizable features include a plant's shape, its texture and its environment. Armed with this knowledge, Dr. Edward Bach formulated his flower essences, all originating from trees found in his native England. For instance, there is the proud oak tree with its thick bark. Oak remedy is prescribed for exhaustion in people who tend to push on despite great difficulties and without loss of hope; the classic martyr. On the other hand, we have the bendable, weeping willow tree, usually found growing along river banks. The essence made from this tree is used in those individuals who feel weighed down by sadness from the past, causing them to continually cry embittered tears rather than lifting their heads and moving forward.

Dr. Samuel Hahnemann, the father of homeopathy, also saw signatures of healing throughout Mother Earth. He taught that by observing the natural kingdoms, it's easy to see reflections of disharmonic human behavior, which may manifest as physical disease. When a substance is successively diluted until there is practically no molecular structure remaining, the homeopathic remedy can then be used to reestablish harmony for the individual. For instance, lachesis—created from snake venom—is an excellent remedy for premenstrual syndrome, especially when the woman complains of feeling trapped and wants to spit with frustration, similar to a snake when cornered. Another remedy, which comes from the mineral kingdom, is silicea, found naturally as quartz and sand. Like grains of sand moved by the tide, people who need this remedy can be easily swayed by the opinions of others and often fear taking a stand.

Nature abounds with natural healing gifts:

- The sun shines on us all equally, bringing light and warmth without bias.
- Specific areas of the land are clothed in green, offering places to rest and find calm.
- The moon's monthly phases remind us life exists in cycles with times of fullness and success and times of darkness and introspection, before the new light appears.
- The planet and our body consist of 70% water, reminding us of the importance of connectivity and unconditional love, symbolized by the element of water.
- Everything we need for healing is right in front of us, if only we have the eyes to see, the ears to hear and a heart which is open.

Deva Kingdoms

Some cultures offer that we share this planet with a multitude of energetic beings. Their perceived presence has been recorded throughout history in mythological tales, where they are called fairies, dwarves, elves, nymphs, leprechauns, and sprites. Some are seen to be benevolent while others are decidedly mischievous. They are part of what is believed to be a deva kingdom that evolved alongside humanity with little interbreeding between the two. However, I have certainly met people during my thirty year health care practice who are more comfortable amongst trees and nature and remind me of elves.

Within this belief system, everything in nature has a deva dedicated to its function, including each system of our body. This is one way to honor the natural order of the body. When illness occurs, converse with the deva of the organ to establish what is required to bring the function of the organ back into balance. Sometimes the deva is just overwhelmed by the work it is required to undergo and just needs relief or acknowledgement. I remember talking with the stomach deva of a man who complained of constant indigestion. The deva was proud of its ability to cope with whatever food and drink were ingested, but drew the line when the man's stress levels went extremely high.

Similarly, in our environment, it may be that each rock, plant, and pool of water has a deva who oversees its wellbeing. For example, if mankind moves a stone without asking the rock deva, or fails to speak to the deva before cutting a tree, then we may be asking for problems. It is believed by those who work with the devas and elementals that the deva kingdom is perfectly capable of maintaining abundance on this planet. No one needs to go without clean water or food to eat, if only we would learn to work with these elementals. However, one note of caution, we should not assume the deva kingdom needs humanity, they don't. If we want their cooperation, we need to approach them with humility and grace offering them a gift, song, or dance to attract their attention. In the same way, cursing at or denigrating our body, does little to encourage good relationship and assistance from the devas. Our body is our greatest friend; treat it as such.

Earth Energies

Having discovered the richness that exists upon the planet, it is time to turn our attention to Mother Earth herself. Commonly known as Gaia, she is believed to be a living being, the trees being her lungs, the rivers her blood stream and the mountains her bones. No indigenous person would consider poisoning her circulation with toxic effluent or removing great areas of her lungs until she can't breathe.

Beneath the physical surface, she has the same subtle bodies as are found within the human aura. The first layer, the etheric body, is made up of spirit or ley lines which crisscross the whole planet. Wherever there is a great confluence of ley lines, the ancient people placed sacred temples or stone circles, such as Stonehenge, for they knew it was here that the creative energy of Mother Earth was most powerful. In more recent times, some altars in churches were placed over such meetings of spirit lines, giving power to the priest/minister as he delivered his message.

Ley lines represent the superficial layer of a much more complex grid system which runs throughout the planet. At its deepest level, we meet the heart of Gaia, a place of sublime love. Above, we meet the cyclical wisdom of Gaia, represented in mythological tales as dragon or serpent energy. This profound feminine lava-like energy which feeds our root chakra, situated beneath our feet, honors the cyclical nature of our existence, reminding us there will be times of chaos and death as well as birth, none of which can be controlled by willpower. With the arrival of the patriarchy some 3500 years ago, the leaders decided that such chaos was not acceptable. The dragon/serpent was symbolically slain and humanity became cut off from divine feminine wisdom, leaving just a vestige of such energy in the base chakra; the sleeping kundalini energy.

In time, everything which reflected the feminine face of the divine became denigrated, including the physical body, Mother Earth and women in general. The under-world or hell became known as a place of retribution rather than its early meaning, a place of regeneration. The mass of mankind was warned against entering this place, while this is the only location of spiritual transformation.

Yet, we have reached an impasse when humanity cannot evolve spiritually without embracing the feminine and in particular, the dragon energy beneath our feet. The Earth Mother is reaching out to us, asking us to walk barefoot on her body, float on her waters of love and gather in places of beauty in joy and celebration. She also tells us we are not alone. The bird kingdom is actively flying into our lives to remind us that our spirit is free to soar, and the whales continue to pass along the grid in the oceans, singing new inspiration into the water of our consciousness. Every time you smile at the sight of a duckling, admire a beautiful flower, or listen to birdsong, healing is flowing between you, and all is well.

Chapter Conclusion

Support for healing on all levels, and maintaining a high level of wellness, is a multifocal process. Beginning with a focus in our heart centers to remain calm and peaceful, adding self-care tools to our daily lives to promote health and balance, living respectfully with the animal kingdom, and interacting with awareness in our earthly surroundings creates opportunities to live in harmony and honor the energetic interconnectedness of all things. The more consciously we maintain and enhance harmony and balance, the healthier will be our internal and external environments and quality of life on the earth.

CHAPTER 5

ETHICAL UNDERPINNINGS: RESPECTING AND HONORING THE SOUL

Complementary therapy practitioners often use the qualifier "for the patient's highest good." It is almost impossible to have a discussion about "highest good" without considering ethics, a study of principles and values that charts the course for our personal and professional conduct and provides a framework for action. Being ethical allows us to behave with integrity, best practice, and highest action. The following objectives are explored in this chapter:

1. Review three ethical theories in relation to healing work: Virtue Ethics, Ethics of Care, and Biomedical Ethics.
2. Recognize the importance of using energy for positive change.
3. Increase awareness of ethical issues when conducting healing and intuitive work.
4. Recognize accountability to self, others, and the planet through right relationships.

The Highest Good

By Lisa Anselme, RN, BLS, HN-BC, CHTP/I

Philosophers, spiritual leaders, ethicists, and sages have explored ethical questions throughout the ages. While a number of theories have been put forth to provide an ethical framework for professional practice, several are of particular relevance to a professional health care model: Virtue Ethics, Biomedical Ethics, and Ethics of Care. In addition, it is important that those working within the health care system begin to integrate knowledge of an energetic model of the world into their clinical practice. Although many clinical situations are unique, by taking the best wisdom from each of these models, we can create an ethical framework that establishes a starting point for working towards not only the patient's, but also the global "highest good." Each ethical theory has as its basis, certain ethical principles and rules that assist us in arriving at particular judgments. In addition, spiritual and energetic perspectives allow us to further deepen our conversation of concepts relative to the highest good.

Simon Blackburn (2001) notes that while we are hopefully sensitive to the planetary world that surrounds us as a necessary source for our very survival, we are perhaps less sensitive to the moral and ethical climate, the "climate of ideas about how to live, . . . of what is acceptable or unacceptable, admirable or contemptible . . . of what is due to us and what is due from us, as we relate to others . . . it gives us our standards of behavior . . . it shapes our very identities" (p.1). Blackburn further tells us that

> An ethical climate is a different thing from a moralistic one . . . in our present climate, we care much more about our rights than about our "good", whereas for previous thinkers about ethics, the central concern was the state of one's soul, meaning some personal state of justice or harmony (p.1).

In exploring the "highest good," it appears that one must revisit the concern about the state of one's soul, both as a practitioner and as a patient. People have attempted to arrive at sound ethical decisions through utilizing customs, scientific theories, and religious or metaphysical convictions (deductivism) or through existing social agreements, practices, and norms (inductivism), and each of these have been very changeable through the ages and various cultures. People often contaminate ethics by viewing it through their own filters and lens. The most helpful approach is to view ethics and its theories through a continual testing of the ethical theory itself for adequacy in meeting logic, meaning and coherence. At the same time it is important to guard against the risk of prejudice or simple, intuitive moral judgments. Coherentism, the constant testing of the truth of a theory, is considered to be the soundest way of arriving at reasonable ethical decisions.

As we initiate our exploration of ethics and the highest good, it is helpful for us to first define some commonly used terms. These terms are as defined in *The Principles of Biomedical Ethics* (Beauchamp & Childress, 2009, p. 2–8):

- **Ethics** is the study of principles for appropriate and professional conduct for the clinician, educator and student.
- **Professionals** are usually identified by a commitment to provide important services to clients/patients, along with having advanced training within their specialty. Professionals customarily maintain self-regulating organizations that control entry into occupational roles and formally certify that their candidates have acquired necessary knowledge and skills to meet minimum competency within their specialized field.
- **Medical/Health Care Professionals** provide a service to others and are closely tied to a background of specific education and skills that the client/patient typically lacks. Professionals hold skills that morally must be used to benefit patients/clients and have background knowledge derived from closely supervised training.
- **Professional Codes** represent a framework of the role expectations for members of the profession; in this way, professional standards are distinguished from standards imposed by external bodies. The Professional codes specify rules of etiquette and responsibilities to other members of the profession and relates to ethical behavior. The codes stem from established boundaries, respect for self and clients, business practices, communication skills, high standards of action, and attitudes, technical skills, and competency. Professionalism

originates in attitudes and is made manifest through personal actions.

- **Medical/Health Care Professional Codes** often develop general principles based upon biomedical ethics of do no harm but do good, confidentiality, and patient's rights (respect for autonomy and veracity). Codes also focus on the rights of those receiving services as well as the obligations of the health care professional.

- **Professional Ethics** is about ongoing self-vigilance, self-reflection and self-accountability. As a guide for conduct, professional ethics take into account our values, principles, morals, civil laws and concepts of professionalism. Professional ethics is not about rigid rules and regulations or perfection; instead, it helps us weigh possible courses of action to determine the action of greatest integrity and good for the client, our profession, and society as a whole. The framework provides tools with which to evaluate and consider the effects and consequences of our actions, make appropriate revisions, and correct as necessary.

Ethical Theories Relevant to Healing Work

This section focuses on relevant ethical theories for those involved in the healing arts: Virtue Ethics, Ethics of Care, and Biomedical Ethics. Although there is considerable discussion and statements of theoretical propositions about ethical theories, the focus on these three theories can help guide the practice and conduct of the practitioner.

Virtue Ethics

Advanced by Plato and Aristotle, Virtue Ethics emphasizes socially valued traits of character (Comte-Sponville, 2001; Minch & Weigel, 2012). One's virtue is intimately connected to one's motives. Intentionality is something that has been studied and found to be highly important in energetic therapies. In fact, properly motivated individuals often do not merely follow rules; they also have a morally appropriate desire to act as they do. Typically, the person we trust is not the rule follower who acts out of obligation (but lacks virtue and right motivation), but the person with integrity whose character is generous, caring, compassionate, and sympathetic as well as perhaps courageous, just, fair, prudent, merciful, gentle, loving, and temperate. The virtuous professional is perceived as being compassionate, reliable, stable, discerning, insightful, whole, sensitive, trustworthy, and able to take decisive, appropriate action (Beauchamp & Childress, 2009).

In our modern societies and health care systems, increased specialization, fragmented care, impersonal businesses, loss of intimate contact, and conflicts of interest have contributed to the destruction of trust in professional caregivers. These environments and systems have, in turn, fostered non-virtuous behaviors (e.g. hypocrisy, insincerity, superficiality, self-deception), which then become reflected in the system of health care. As attributed to Aristotle, "We are what we repeatedly do. Excellence then is not an act, but a habit" (Durant, 1926, p. 87).

Ethics of Care

The Ethics of Care originated in Feminist writings (Beauchamp & Childress, 2009). In a relationship-based theory, the emphasis is upon qualities that are valued in intimate relationships, such as sympathy, compassion, fidelity, discernment, and love. The Ethics of Care is based upon a mutual interdependence and role of emotions in relationships with attentiveness to needs, care, and prevention of harm, rather than on rights and obligations. Beauchamp and Childress (2009) write that "insight into the needs of others and considerate alertness to their circumstances often come from the emotions more than reason" (p. 36). From the perspective of "highest good," a measure of attention to relationship is highly valuable.

Our capacity for intimacy is built on deep respect, a presence that allows what is true to express itself, to be discovered. Intimacy can arise in any moment; it is an act of surrender, a gift that excludes nothing (Kornfield, 1993).

Biomedical Ethics

Biomedical Ethics works with four primary principles: autonomy, non-maleficence, beneficence, and justice (Beauchamp & Childress, 2009). The principles are discussed as follows.

Autonomy is concerned with respect for self-governance and authority over one's life; it acknowledges the breathing space and zone of privacy around the body and respects a wish not to be touched, observed, or intruded upon. Respect for autonomy provides the primary reason for rules of disclosure and consent. Consent does not express autonomy unless it is informed. It is important to obtain consent even when we are working with preverbal or non-verbal children and adults. Autonomy requires a respectful attitude AND respectful actions. Using persons as objects or means to an end without regard for their personal goals violates their autonomy. John Stuart Mill, an English philosopher, felt that autonomy does not have priority standing, as it can be overridden by competing moral considerations, such as potential harm to the public or by requiring scarce resources for which no funds are available. The two conditions for autonomy acknowledged in theories are (1) Liberty, or independence from controlling influences, and (2) Agency, the capacity for intentional action. At its core, autonomy requires competence, disclosure, understanding, voluntariness, consent, and a best interest's standard.

Non-maleficence requires that above all, do no harm. It is at the base of the medical Hippocratic Oath. The Nursing code, as per the American Nurses Association, requires safeguarding the public from the "incompetent, unethical or illegal" practices of any person (www.nursingworld.org/codeofethics). Additionally, failure to assist someone when we have the knowledge and means to do so can be as morally reprehensible as doing harm. The concept of non-maleficence supports many other specific moral rules, including do not kill, do not cause pain or suffering to others, do not incapacitate others, do not cause offence to others, and do not deprive others of the goods of life.

Maleficence or harm can be a result of *negligence*, or failure to guard against risk of harm to another (omission) through a breach of duty or departure from the professional standard of care. Maleficence can also come from *malpractice*, the causing of harm through a direct result of one's action (commission) by acting in departure from professional standards.

> Not causing harm requires staying awake. Part of being awake is slowing down enough to notice what we say and do. The more we witness our emotional chain reactions and understand how they work, the easier it is to refrain. It becomes a way of life to stay awake, slow down, and notice. (Chodron, 1997, p.44)

Beneficence is action that is done for the benefit of others. It utilizes the character trait of benevolence, that of being oriented to act for the benefit of others. The Principle of Beneficence implies a moral obligation to act for the benefit of others. The ethics theory of Utilitarianism is primarily based on this principle. Examples of expected standards of beneficence include the following: to protect and defend the rights of others, to prevent harm from occurring to others, to remove conditions that will cause harm to others, to help persons with disabilities, and to rescue persons in danger. The American Nurses Association requires that nursing's primary commitment is to the health, welfare, and safety of the client. Physicians taking the Hippocratic Oath must apply treatments and act for the benefit of the sick, and according to their ability and judgment, keep patients from harm and injustice.

> The great fault of all ethics hitherto has been that they believed themselves to have to deal only with the relations of man to man. In reality, however, the question is what is his attitude to the world and all life that comes within his reach? A man is ethical only when life, as such, is sacred to him, and that of plants and animals as that of his fellow men, and when he devotes himself helpfully to all life that is in need of help. (Schweitzer, 1933, p. 188)

Justice demands fair, equitable distribution of privileges, resources, opportunities, and property in society; as such, this aspect of justice is different from that of criminal justice and retributory justice. Aristotle put forward the concept that equals are to be treated equally although he didn't inform as to how to determine what makes individuals equal or what is equal treatment. He did, however, state that each person deserves an equal share, based on free market exchange, and according to his need, effort, contribution, and merit.

Energetic Framework for Ethical Decision Making and the Highest Good

For centuries, sages from an Eastern spiritual perspective have taught that within each person, at the base of the sacrum, is a core of living, conscious energy, or light. Once awakened, this energy travels up, infuses the energetic core of the person, and initiates the maturational task of achieving mastery, balance, and illumination within each chakra and correlate energy field structure. The goal is that the person enters an enlightened or illuminated state. Once this state is achieved, the person is aware of the inter-connectedness of everything and everyone within the universe and is awakened to a transpersonal sense of purpose and self-knowledge, which is typically missing from our everyday lives. This energetic journey is one taken by the primary nadis as they emerge from and travel up the central vertical energy channel, feminine and masculine energies crossing and separating in bi-directional vertical flow. This causes the chakras to spin, at last merging within the 6th chakra of greater vision and rising as one through the 7th chakra, connecting to the transpersonal point and the chakras beyond. The caduceus, the symbol of medical practice and healing, is modeled after this coiling of core energy and represents the double helix pattern of our genetic DNA, which also replicates this energetic flow.

Within this energetic system, we can note how we grow and mature through the various developmental tasks of each chakra. We can then observe how various wounds and life experiences created obstructions and obscurations within our energetic field and chakras, causing a lack of clarity within that aspect of the field and resulting in an arrested development at that level of function. This can result in some distorted understandings and dysfunctional interactions with the world, as well as difficulties in determining right or highest action.

Beyond the personal field is the transpersonal field. It is comprised of our immediate environment and social mores (which can include family, friends, work, and social media). These all can have profound influence upon our personal field; as a result the transpersonal field may or may not be linked into a higher or greater consciousness. Beyond the transpersonal field is the field of greater consciousness, described by some as the divine mind, the field of pure love, the point of infinite potentiality, the archetype, or oneness. Once we truly have awakened to a "beyond transpersonal" consciousness, we could hypothesize that our thoughts and actions are at last placed into a context of awareness of their effect upon ourselves, other beings, the planet, and cosmos. One would hope that by that point, we might understand what constitutes the "highest good." Accomplishing this type of awareness and consciousness involves diligence and persistence.

Maturation from a Developmental and Energetic Perspective

The American psychologist, Abraham Maslow (1962), looked at this evolutionary task from a developmental perspective, and he created the well-known framework of Maslow's Hierarchy of Needs. By simple virtue of being a hierarchy, people are driven to satisfy their needs in a hierarchical order. When people are unable to place food on the table and their house is in foreclosure, it is challenging to direct a focus toward self-actualization, although these very circumstances may offer an opportunity for a spiritual perspective to emerge.

Of equal importance, the German-born American psychologist, Erik Erikson, described eight psychological stages that an individual passes through and masters to be psychologically healthy and sound (Erikson & Woolfolk, 1967). Both men contributed important theories that can help identify necessary achievements in order for an individual to develop higher order awareness, compassion, and the means by which to achieve a transpersonal, ethical perspective and maturity. Each developmental stage has a task to master, along with a challenge to overcome.

The primary challenge within both systems, as well as in outlining evolution within the energetic system, occurs when we rigidly hold to requiring individuals to complete a single stage prior to moving to the next stage. Rather, if we view these needs or stages as fluid, much like the tide that ebbs and flows, we will be able to better appreciate how we expand, contract, and redirect in consciousness, which is exactly what we do as we move through the energetic system. This fluidity allows us to explain how we can be in extremely dire circumstances, yet able to access transpersonal attributes of compassion, generosity and benevolence, and thus we are able to assist someone who is perhaps in even worse circumstances than ourselves.

Let's review these tasks and their contribution to arriving at a transpersonal perspective by exploring human development through the lens of these two men in relation to the energetic system. We need to keep in mind the fluidity of these stages and the capacity of humans to traverse these stages non-sequentially.

During infancy, a baby is completely dependent upon the caretaker or parent for all of his or her basic biological and physiological needs, along with **safety and security** needs (Maslow). If needs are met with consistency and stability, the infant learns to trust the external world; he or she feels safe and is trusting in future circumstances that may be slightly threatening, thus developing the virtue of hope. If needs are not met, or are managed harshly, the child learns to mistrust the outer world and carries a sense of fear (Erikson). Within the energetic system, the Earth and Root Chakras are involved with our sense of safety and security. When our survival, safety, or security is threatened, these energetic centers and proximal (etheric) layer of the field become compromised or obstructed, and our actions can regress to the level of the infant. Fear then becomes one of our operant behaviors and emotions. People potentially become trapped in a crossroad in which they are unable to let go of old, destructive environments, situations or patterns, and they are unable to enter the world that they desire but fear.

Toddlers begin to assert themselves into the world and if met with support, they develop a sense of **autonomy**. If they are not supported or successful, they begin to develop a sense of shame and self-doubt. Within the energetic system, issues about relationship, balance, power, prosperity, sexuality and creativity are held within the second chakra. Emotional constructs and reactions travel within the energetic field and can cause the field to become significantly congested and stuck, if not channeled into constructive expression. Successful mastery within this task results in the ability to assert power and authority over oneself, maintain essential and appropriate boundaries, prosper financially, create, and have emotionally balanced relationships. If significant challenge and wounding occurs during the toddler stage, there are likely to be subsequent difficulties in finding balance in relationship and power, and one's actions become directed toward obtaining power and control over others and one's environment, while being challenged to develop and respect appropriate boundaries.

Preschool children begin to develop a strong awareness of **self-esteem**, assertion of **power, achievement** and **initiative** over their environment. Their task at this stage is Initiative vs. Guilt (Erikson). If successful and supported, children begin to develop a sense of belongingness and mastery, whereas if reprimanded or unsuccessful, children become ashamed and doubtful of their ability to engage within the world. As they grow, school age children (6–11 years old) work to become **competent and industrious**; failure to accomplish these results in a deepening sense of incompetence and inferiority. Within the 3rd chakra and third layer of the energetic field are ideas, mental constructs, and self-esteem. Our ability to be successful and masterful is reliant upon the openness and health of this chakra and wholeness of the young child. Challenge within this center and associate field results in the adult lacking in self-confidence and self-esteem. This may result in a person seeking these qualities and rewards through external sources in being vulnerable to addictive patterns, behaviors and substances and in being malleable and influenced by others rather than able to self-determine correct courses of action and motivations.

The adolescent and young adult begins to foster an **ego identity and intimacy** through relationships, while developing **cognitive maturity**. The virtuous behavior that is fostered is fidelity and love. If interrupted, unsuccessful or unsupported, the young adult struggles with a sense of role confusion and isolation, and the ability to achieve or sustain intimacy in relationships is diminished and challenging. The 4th chakra and energetic field is focused upon being able to love unconditionally, be compassionate and move from the place of ego into concern for another, while still maintaining a sense of self. Key to this is the ability to forgive and understand others, while disallowing the acceptability of certain behaviors, along with being able to sustain both intimacy and detachment simultaneously. Failure to do so results in behaviors in which one uses individuals as a means to an end and in love that is offered as conditional and based upon the benefits one can receive.

Mature adults begin to gift to the world through the work of their careers, establishing relationships, raising their children, and participating in bettering the larger community. They are **productive, creative,** and appreciative and expressive of the aesthetic. Success at this stage results in the virtue of care. Encompassing the throat, the 5th chakra permits expression of one's authentic self in the world and is critical as the individual attempts to bridge the love and compassion of the heart while developing a clear world view via the 6th chakra. Myss (1996) identifies the inability to bridge and empower the heart with a clear world view as a primary cause of addictive behavior, as even healthy behaviors (exercise, meditation) can become addictive when they are used as a means to "avoid pain or personal insight" (p. 230). Failure to express one's authentic self and gift the world causes the individual to stagnate and feel unproductive and diminished.

The tasks of older adults are to realize and reflect upon their **personal potential**, achievement and self-fulfillment and to continue personal growth and **self-actualization** (Maslow). The virtue gained is wisdom and integrity (Erikson). When older adults feel unresolved guilt about their past, feel unfulfilled, or have not met their life goals, they can spiral down into despair and hopelessness. The healthy brow (6th chakra and correlate energetic field) govern our becoming conscious and clear, detached, and alert, as well as present and far seeing. We are then able to have a world view that is clear, beyond ourselves, and discern all that is within our purview. Congestion and muddiness in the field diminishes our ability to be clear and self-actualized. Lack of resolution of our own actions and their consequences negatively impact our ability to make clear, ethical choices for ourselves and those with whom we work or have been entrusted to our care.

The fully realized adult has the opportunity to act as a *bodhisattva,* or altruistic helping guide to assist others achieve self-actualization and freedom. Individuals work to transcend their limited world view to enter a transpersonal state in which they can act upon the world as well as understand and predict the consequences of their actions.

In his Healing Touch International Conference keynote speech, Evan Hodkins (2012, as transcribed from a recording) described this energetic journey by using a description of paradox. He said, "Paradox is two truths going in opposite directions, so that they cancel each other out, while at the same time inviting us to spring to the next level of consciousness. *Paradox is the Language of God,* [Evan uses the gender free term *Elohim*], and the way that God sports with the world." He notes that in Greek, the word "paradox" means "glory beyond glory" and that "our task is to turn a stumbling block into a stepping stone." Evan believes illness is that stumbling block, an "agent provocateur," or an opportunity to see what seems to be an obstruction as an "open door." In looking more deeply at this concept of paradox, we begin to note how the interplay of health and illness, clarity and confusion, and action and stillness creates a tension within ourselves so that we are forced to enter into the paradox in order to discover truth. Evan notes, "Our task is to know when limitation will heal us and when infinite potentiality will heal us. It is our illness (or we could say our 'woundedness') that makes us tell the truth about our life, and truth is never forgetting exactly who you are."

Throughout our respective life journeys, we are given many opportunities to enter into the energetic fire of transformation. Our life experiences often test us, sometimes wound us, and frequently stretch us through past hurts, losses, betrayals, and seeming injustice. How do we enter the paradox to seek the truth and connect with the highest good? How do we enter the wounds and bring light to the energetic core? It truly is through entering the fire of these experiences, and allowing them to pass through us and ourselves to walk through them, that we discover a great potential for clearing, healing, self-discovery, clarity, growth, self-actualization, and transcendence. Through recognizing the opportunity within the crisis, and seeing the essential humanity in ourselves and even the most wounded of our fellow human beings, we "gain flavor, become nutritious, and mingle with our essential spirit," as Rumi so exquisitely describes (Helminski, 1998, p. 141).

In energetic terms, it is often during such challenging times, times when we have been turned "upside down," that the energetic fire within us begins to activate, ignite, and rise as we seek higher understanding and broader vision. Our energy work contains the invitation to relax deeply and go within, allowing this energy of fire to gently rise, nurture, inform, clear, and transform. Through our own personal work with this energetic fire, we can gather courage to surrender and let go; in this process we can make room within to welcome new growth, new opportunities, greater understanding, and expanding consciousness. This fire also invites us to examine our lives for those things that are no longer life-giving and life-supporting and gives us courage to surrender and let go of those things which no longer serve the "highest good."

Martha Rogers, nurse theorist, described all beings as having the innate urge toward negentropy, or expansion (Meleis, 2012). Essentially, we are hardwired to seek this evolution. And yet, this evolutionary progression does require some active participation on our part. Spiritual teachers talk of an inner path and discipline to awaken this conscious energy. For example, the use of meditation, prayer, and energetic practices can initiate and support this energetic flow through the nadis, chakras, and energetic field, thus supporting a clearing of the internal environment in order to better receive tools for discernment and proper motivation, intention, and action. Practitioners (e.g. nurses, psychotherapists, psychologists, spiritual directors, counselors, physicians) should engage in practices, such as journaling, psychotherapy, and physical activity, to clear the wounds, dysfunction, distress, and misperceptions in our own personalities that interfere with our ability to clearly receive and perceive transpersonal information and perspectives.

Another extremely important means to support this clearing and evolution is through being with those who hold and demonstrate high ethical and spiritual principles, ideals, behaviors, actions, and consciousness. In other words, associate with those who have walked through fire, deeply delved into their own healing, and cleared their muddiness.

Happiness and an Ethical Life

The 14ᵗʰ Dalai Lama (1999) believes that humans who act ethically are happier and more satisfied and that much of the unhappiness we humans endure is self-generated. He believes that the ultimate goal is happiness for every individual and that our very survival depends upon our basic goodness as human beings. Our modern society has created challenges for us through a greater dependence on technology as well as a greater self-independence and autonomy relative to other human beings. This causes us to believe that "others are not important to my happiness and their happiness is not important to me." In addition, in modern, Western medicine, we have elevated scientific principles to an absolute status, without conscious reflection and assessment as to what is right, wrong, good, bad, appropriate, or inappropriate. The challenge here is that neither science nor technology address issues of how to lead an ethical life or how to be happy. The Dalai Lama believes that inner discipline, restraint, proper intent, and motivation give us the means by which to define and motivate positive ethical conduct. He writes, "When the driving force of our actions is wholesome, our actions will tend automatically to contribute to others' well-being. The more this is our habitual state, the less likely we are to react badly when provoked" (p. 32). The Dalai Lama identifies an energetic view of the world in which everything is interconnected. Of course, how we view the world determines our responses and actions. Every one of our actions, deeds, words, and thoughts affects others either positively or negatively. Due to the innate interconnectedness that underlies our reality, what affects you also affects me, and certain actions lead to suffering while others lead to happiness.

According to the Dalai Lama, much of our suffering can be attributed to our "impulsive" approach to happiness. When we think of ourselves only and not of others, we undermine the possibility of lasting happiness. In contrast, the principle characteristic of genuine, lasting happiness is inner peace; it is rooted in *concern for others* and involves a high degree of sensitivity and feeling. If we develop this quality, we will be able to maintain a strong sense of wellbeing, even when meeting life's difficulties.

Non-malevolent vs. Spiritual Acts

There is a distinction between acts that are ethical and non-malevolent, and acts that are spiritual. Acts that are spiritually non-virtuous (thoughts, emotions, or actions caused by selfish and destructive thinking; or projection of characteristics onto things and events beyond what is truly there) undermine our capacity for inner peace. These acts result in anxiety, depression, confusion and stress; they rob us of our discriminative awareness and ability to determine right from wrong and our ability to predict the outcome of our actions. These non-virtuous acts originate from our life "filters" (e.g. karma, life circumstances, needs, confusions, contaminations, pathologies) and reduce our capacity for kindness and compassion. The more of them we have, the less we are able to maintain our inner peace and happiness or resolve our problems.

It is important to cultivate a habit of restraint rather than to deny or suppress these acts and strong emotions. Denial is like closing over an infected wound; it will eventually contaminate all the surrounding "tissue" and cause an overall "toxicity" that corrupts all our actions. As our energetic field holds our thoughts, actions, experiences, and perspectives, it essentially houses and exacerbates any unhealed wounds or experiences and unless resolved, contaminates our future actions.

Energy Therapies and Boundaries

The need for self-awareness, self-vigilance and self-accountability is perhaps higher for those of us practicing energy therapies, in contrast to those practicing standard medical care. When we become fully present and connect energetically with our patients, boundaries may blur, and levels of knowing increase. Just by touching clients, we may have crossed acceptable social norms. As we use gentle touch and unconditional love, many clients are unprepared for the high level of intimacy that occurs within the therapeutic setting of energy work.

Creating an Energetic Ethical Framework

From an energetic perspective, how do we access and cultivate an ethical framework, pathway or guide? How do we developmentally mature within an ethical construct and ethical life? As each chakra has developmental tasks and associated functions, each layer of the energetic field holds constructs and tasks that we must pass through and master in order to access a transpersonal point of view.

To determine and access the greater good, or highest good, we must endeavor to clear the wounds, dysfunction, distress, assumptions and misperceptions in our physical, emotional, mental, spiritual and energetic fields. Throughout time, humans have pursued such clearing through spiritual practice, energetic practice, prayer, meditation, physical conditioning, and study in order to achieve a neutral field to receive tools for discernment so that wisdom and higher consciousness become available to us.

How do we become more discerning? We do so through physical, emotional, mental, and spiritual clearing; by becoming aware of what we put into and how we care for our physical bodies; through becoming cognizant of our spiritually non-virtuous and unskillful emotions and projections; through practicing some form of mindfulness and monitoring of our thoughts, ideas and speech; and through studying and practicing some form of spiritual discipline and evolution. As we continue to evolve the profession of Healing Touch, each one of us has the opportunity to bring forward a model of professionalism, right relationship, high integrity and holistic practice that truly supports the highest good of the client, which, in turn, uplifts all of us who serve humanity through this work.

First and Foremost, Do No Harm: Safety

Our patients and clients have the right to feel and be safe while they are within our care. Through establishing professional boundaries, we create a safe container in which our patients can work fully with us and become whole. Professional boundaries clarify what will happen between the practitioner and patient and define the parameters and container through which we will work. Some examples follow that help delineate appropriate behavior for energy healers as well as represent some common difficulties found in therapeutic relationships. The first scenario provides an example of how to establish appropriate boundaries.

Scenario 1: Certified Practitioner Leanne introduced herself to Mark and invited him into her office, asking him to "Please be seated." Leanne sat down, and she was now face to face and at an equal height with Mark. Leanne explained that everything shared, discovered, or experienced within their session would remain confidential, with the exceptions that information would be shared if Mark was at risk of harming himself or harming someone else or if Mark requested that his health care information be shared with another provider. She asked Mark how she could assist him. She began to gather information from Mark. Upon learning of Mark's challenges and goals of gaining increased mobility following knee surgery, Leanne explained that during the session, she would use light touch on or near the body. She told him that he would be fully clothed and covered with a sheet or blanket, based upon temperature preference, when he was on the massage table or later resting in a hospital bed. Mark could rest or sleep, if he wished, and he should inform her if he became uncomfortable at any time so that they could adjust the session. She explained that this was an equal partnership of care: she would provide energetic support, and they would work at Mark's pace and comfort. She let Mark know that the session would be approximately one hour and that she would start and end the session by sounding a chime. She asked if he would prefer quiet or soft music, and when he chose soft music, she asked him to let her know if he later preferred silence. She confirmed permission to touch and began the session.

During the session, Leanne became centered and calm, did an appropriate energetic assessment, set her entire focus and attention upon Mark's well-being and highest good, determined a plan of care, and remained fully present with her eyes open. She observed Mark for cues regarding his comfort, his response and subsequent shifts in energy flow. She placed her hands carefully, gently and knowledgeably when connecting the energy through stationary hand positions; she made sure that she landmarked her hand location in safe areas (top of thighs near knee) when directing energy near the root and sacral chakras (groin and genitalia). When using hands in motion, she was careful once again to not sweep the physical body with touch but to remain above it, respecting his privacy at all times. At completion of the session, Leanne reassessed Mark's energy field, gently sounded the chime, placed her hands upon his ankles, and assisted him to sit up and dangle his feet along tableside when he was ready. She offered him a glass of water, and helped him off the table.

Boundaries keep us within the limits of our training and safe practice. In order for our clients to feel safe, it is critical that we establish a professional situation by providing clear boundaries and a stable framework of care. Students and practitioners must be aware of the effect of the therapeutic environment upon the client and of any reactive behaviors that are elicited by either the client or the practitioner. When professional boundaries are established and clear, the opportunity for healing is rich. When boundaries are muddied and unclear, the potential for harm is very real. It is important to recognize that **within the therapeutic relationship, the establishment and maintenance of appropriate boundaries, both on and off the table, is always the responsibility of the practitioner.** Inherent in the practitioner/client therapeutic relationship is a power differential. It is implied that the practitioner has greater knowledge and skill in this particular area than the client. This is symbolically demonstrated by the practitioner taking an active role and position within the client's actual physical space, while the client typically is in a reclining position with the practitioner standing over him. In essence, the client's entire being and safety is literally within the practitioner's hands. A critical question regarding this interaction is then, how is the person who has the perceived power managing his/her power? In order to receive, the client has had to relax his/her personal boundaries. It is thus imperative that the practitioner maintain these boundaries by acting with integrity within the structured time and space of the session, respect the client's physical, emotional, mental, and spiritual realms and belief systems, and act in accord with the best interests and well-being of the client. Boundary violations are more likely to occur when the practitioner makes assumptions about the client or situation that are incorrect, when either the practitioner or client have a poor sense of his/her own boundaries, or the client has a history of having been physically, sexually or emotionally abused.

Due to the inherent power differential within the therapeutic relationship, the client may unconsciously recreate a relationship similar to one held with a former authority figure (such as a parent or boss). This is called *transference*. Practitioner-client relationships often recreate the parent-child relationship and may bring up any unresolved issues regarding that relationship. Our utilization of caring touch can potentially accelerate transference, and the result may be that the client rapidly regresses to a childlike and vulnerable state. To further complicate matters, practitioners also carry unresolved needs and issues into the therapeutic relationship and may respond to the client as they responded to someone in the past. This is called *counter-transference* and, if unrecognized and unchecked, can adversely affect the therapeutic relationship and result in diminished efficacy of therapy or even psychological harm to the client.

> **Scenario 2:** Leanne, CHTP, worked with Mark pre and post knee surgery; she saw him both in her office and in the outpatient surgery area. Together, along with the medical and physical therapy team, Mark was able to achieve the mutual goals of comfort, restored range of motion, healing of the surgical site, and successful rehabilitation. Leanne

saw Mark for a total of six sessions. She noticed that she was thinking about him often throughout the day after the 5th session, wondering how he was feeling and whether or not he was comfortable. She wondered if she should call him and check on him, even though that was not her customary practice. She realized that she was beginning to have romantic feelings for Mark. She called her mentor, and she also scheduled an appointment with her counselor. She then saw Mark for a final session and discharged him from her service and into the continued care of his primary care practitioner.

When the practitioner has strong feelings about his or her client, it is time to seek outside help. It is important to note that it is not uncommon for feelings of attraction to arise during sessions. If you are the one experiencing the feeling, the most ethical response to the situation is to first acknowledge the feeling to yourself and next, to refocus your full attention on your *client's* needs. After the session, it is critical that you process your feelings, preferably with a trustworthy colleague or supervisor. When we start wanting to bend boundaries with a client, we need to discuss our feelings with a supervisor or counselor who is an objective, trusted professional with training in human dynamics so that we can keep the relationship focused upon what is best and safest for the client.

If the client is the one experiencing or attempting to act upon an attraction, it is up to you, the practitioner, to ensure the boundaries are intact. Set conditions (restating the goal and plan with option of terminating the therapeutic relationship if the behavior does not stop) and do not hesitate to terminate the session if needed. At the end of the session, it is appropriate to refer your client to a supportive health care professional (e.g. psychotherapist, counselor). Ensure that you document the interaction and referral and seek supervision with a colleague or professional for yourself.

The client has the absolute right to expect that the emotional, psychological and physical environment is safe. There are basic actions that can assist the practitioner in establishing boundaries to ensure safe practice. First and foremost, **be aware and clear of your intentions toward your client.** Romantic and sexual designs or personal involvement before, during or following the treatment session are never appropriate. We don't flirt, date, or engage in romantic or sexual relationships with our clients. We take care of our loneliness, isolation, or boredom elsewhere. Our dress, actions, thoughts, and intentions are non-seductive and modest. Music should avoid provocative lyrics and not reflect music that is typically reserved for amorous situations.

Creating a professional, therapeutic environment is crucial. Practitioners who have their office within their home can take measures to create a professional environment by limiting personal items within the professional space, having a designated workspace (e.g. massage table that is utilized only for therapeutic intervention), and having a separate bathroom facility and private entrance, if possible. Some municipalities require this for an in-home business. It is best to not have a bed in the room unless treating an injured client or bedridden client (e.g. hospice client). It is important to designate at what limited and structured times the space is utilized for clinical practice and adhere to those times so that the practitioner's personal life and professional life do not blend into each other.

The practitioner further provides a secure and safe environmental framework by imparting details of the session plan to the client prior to initiating the treatment (e.g. mutual goals, hands on the body, length of session, fully clothed, permission to touch). Encouraging the client to let you know if he or she is uncomfortable with any portion of the treatment plan or intervention is an absolute necessity and should be reviewed each session. Be mindful and clear about where you place your hands and how you are positioning yourself over the client. Realize that even if your hands are not on his or her body, the client's perception will often be that you are touching him or her. Keep your eyes open! This requires you to remain focused upon the client as opposed to your interior, personal process. Lastly, document your sessions, and seek appropriate professional help as necessary.

Intuitive Information

The next scenario identifies how a practitioner can maintain boundaries by appropriately sharing (or not) information with the client.

> **Scenario 3:** Darla accepts a new client, Claire, who is seeking help for an ongoing migratory physical pain due to an autoimmune disease. A thorough intake interview reveals a medical history of ongoing health challenges since she was a school age child. During the course of the Healing Touch sessions, Darla has a strong intuitive awareness and high sense perception that Claire has experienced significant physical abuse and corporal punishment at the hands of adults and her spouse. Claire has not revealed or said anything to Darla to suggest that this is a valid awareness. Meanwhile, Claire describes making progress during the session and notes she is having decreased symptoms. She says that during the sessions she sees colors and experiences a sensation of floating. Darla **keeps her intuitive knowledge to herself**; she chooses to focus upon clearing the ongoing congestion and to support balancing Claire's energy field. If Claire discloses any awareness about former physical abuse, Darla will continue to clear the field and make any necessary referrals to an appropriate counselor. Meanwhile, she acknowledges Claire's description of her session experience and ensures that she is grounded at the conclusion of the session.

One of the primary ethical constructs is based upon client autonomy—the absolute right to have authority and self-governing choices over their own body, mind, and spirit. Practitioners should access only information that is pertinent to the session at hand and make decisions based upon the clients' own wishes and informed knowledge. Indeed, our premise in Healing Touch of creating a sacred space in order to assist the client to self-heal is based upon the absolute respect for an individual's authority over his or her own being and plan of care. Energetically, the client is the one that is by rights, solely in charge of bringing into conscious awareness what they hold, know, or experience within their being. They have come to the Healing Touch practitioner for assistance in balancing and clearing their energy field in order that they may be assisted to self-heal and become aware and whole.

With regard to consent, Healing Touch is non-invasive and is an approved nursing intervention for the nursing diagnosis of "energy field disturbance." As with other nursing interventions, permission to assist the client is necessary; however, formal written consent is not required, in contrast to that which is typically required with invasive medical/surgical procedures.

Working within the energetic level introduces a different avenue of potential ethical breach of autonomy and privacy akin to energetic voyeurism, the act of looking, investigating, scoping, intuiting, and reading the energetic field and anatomy without express permission on a conscious and soul level. This is the energetic equivalent of a "peeping tom" and, thus, can be a profound breach of boundaries, privacy, and autonomy—if it is without mutual consent, respect and trust.

Recommendations for Managing Information

In an attempt to address these issues, the following are recommendations and guidelines for managing information that has been accessed through the practitioner's high sense perception:

- Access information only with permission of the client's conscious and higher self, whether in a therapeutic or non-therapeutic scenario. Ask verbally and in accordance with your client's chief complaint. In other words, don't probe or snoop in areas that don't relate to what the client is working on or for which the practitioner is not prepared or trained to handle.
- Maintain your center and remain grounded at all times for clarity. This prevents loosening of appropriate boundaries that may occur when you are in a non-ordinary reality (high sense perception) state yourself.
- As a general rule of thumb, keep your awareness and insights to yourself. The vast majority of the time, this information is strictly for us to better assist in moving the client toward wholeness.

The practitioner must be vigilant about his/her motivation of the need to disclose and share information. It is important to determine if it is absolutely necessary or merely serves the purpose of promoting the practitioner's self-importance. In other words, we may notice a tear in the energy field. What is important is that we assist in re-patterning it and sealing it.

- If the client directly asks for information pertinent to the session, we can redirect and ask them to reflect upon what *they* are experiencing. Our primary goal is to re-empower clients and assist them in connecting with *their* higher self and own wisdom, as they alone are the ones who will know the truth for themselves. If the client offers self-awareness, we must remain within *our* legal scope of practice (in other words, if we are not trained in counseling, we are not to be counseling or imposing insights that have the potential of re-enacting trauma).

- When providing any information to the client, all responses should be framed in a factual, positive manner. For example, "I notice that there is congestion of energy over your left temple, where you are experiencing discomfort. I'd like you to take some gentle, full breaths as I begin to smooth this area to assist you to become more comfortable."

- Never offer what could be construed as diagnostic (labeling what is wrong) or prognostic (predicting the outcome or future) advice. To the client, the Healing Touch practitioner represents a skilled expert, and the client will have a tendency to take whatever we communicate as literal, actual, and factual.

By respecting patient autonomy, we acknowledge and support the patient's journey and evolution toward self-actualization. We recognize that we cannot possibly know what is the ultimate destiny and purpose of a particular soul; we can, however, support the healthy exploration of the soul's unfoldment, acknowledging the health continuum as the "agent provocateur" (Hodkins, 2012). This of course requires our ability to be a good, competent, and safe guide.

Mentor – Mentee

The mentor-mentee relationship is one that places the onus of ethical supervision onto the mentor. The following scenario highlights the role of the mentor in maintaining a safe practice for the mentee.

> **Scenario 4:** Upon Suzanne's completion of level 4, Marie agreed to be a mentor for Susanne. Over the next 10 months, Suzanne intermittently contacted Marie by email and phone and forwarded various forms of documentation to her. Marie found her very likeable, but she began to notice that Suzanne would offer advice to her clients (suggesting use of essential oils, herbal supplements, etc.) that would be considered outside of Suzanne's scope of practice. She spoke with her about this, and yet Suzanne continued to make recommendations.

Ultimately, the mentor has to be able to recommend that the mentee has demonstrated safe, competent practice. It is the responsibility of the Mentor to know what that entails and withhold a positive recommendation, if necessary.

Healer Heal Thyself

We know that energy will travel to where it is most needed. It is the practitioner's responsibility to provide the best environment for the client's healing.

> **Scenario 5:** Kristy, CHTP, has had a full and thriving private practice for a number of years. Recently, however, she has had personal health challenges and has experienced a great deal of inflammation, fever, fatigue, and pain, which she manages with narcotics and anti-inflammatories. She recognizes that she is not in her best physical condition and notes that she often feels much better after providing a Healing Touch session.

It is important that the practitioner/provider offers Healing Touch free of any mind altering substances and that he or she does not use the patient to provide the practitioner with energy, instead of the practitioner providing energy to the patient. Kristy needs to seek assistance from a qualified practitioner, address her own health concerns, and avoid seeing clients while taking mind-altering substances.

As always, it is the responsibility of the practitioner to place the highest good of the client over the needs of the practitioner. When there is a question as to what actions accomplishes this, the practitioner should seek consultation from a trusted supervisor.

Chapter Summary

This chapter highlights some of the ethical and developmental aspects of providing energetic healing. There are many more scenarios that could be provided. If you are "not sure" or if you have any doubts about a situation, it is imperative that you seek guidance for an appropriate action. If you observe others acting in a questionable way, it is your responsibility as a Healing Touch practitioner to first clarify the situation by talking with the practitioner in question. If questions still remain, it is important to report your concerns to the Ethics Committee: our goal is always to protect the client and ensure the safety of the public and integrity of our professional work.

There are various times in our lives when we experience challenge; ultimately, this always offers the opportunity for personal growth and expansion. As we support each other in collectively making ethical decisions, we are able to cultivate the highest good for the entire field of practitioners. This further assists us to place our work in a realm of higher and expanding consciousness, and ultimately, to nurture our collective soul.

CHAPTER 6
ENERGY SYSTEM REFLECTED IN PRACTICE

By Sue Kagel, BSN, RN, HNB-BC, CHTP/I;
Diane Wind Wardell, PhD, RN, AHN-BC, CHTP/I;
and Lisa Anselme, BLS, RN, HN-BC, CHTP/I

Human beings have an innate ability to heal by touch (Classen, 2005). This chapter focuses on integrating energy system principles and fundamental concepts from Chapter 3 into a comprehensive Healing Touch session. Information is provided as a guide for developing a deeper awareness of subtle energy and for enhancing individual treatment plans and sessions. Content in this chapter may be of interest for those receiving Healing Touch sessions to further understand the process as well as for both beginning and advanced practitioners. Each practitioner brings his or her own strengths and background to a session.

Healing Touch is an on-going, life-learning process, and each energy session lends insights to the sessions that follow. There is never a set answer or prescription for a healing session. People are unique and their experiences and circumstances manifest as information in their energy field. The challenge as a healer is to learn the "depth" of the work. Learning more and more techniques will not necessarily create a better healer. The joy in Healing Touch is learning simplicity in the midst of complexity, although it is helpful to understand the processes and nature of healing. Therefore, the objectives for this chapter are as follows:

1. Describe an overview of the energy system.
2. Describe the client's "story" of disease.
3. Recognize the influence that disease, story (belief), and environment have on the energy body.
4. Recognize patterns within the energy field during assessment and intervention.
5. Apply referents within a session appropriately.
6. Provide recommendations for sustainability.

This chapter presents information on the energy system in relation to client health issues to assist in deepening the healing work. It is important that the principle of "all healing is self-healing" remains a focal point of the process, while recognizing the practitioner's contribution and learning needed in each individual session.

Overview of the Energy System

Chakras

The word "chakra" is Sanskrit and signifies a wheel. The chakras are wheel-like vortices (or saucer-like depressions) existing on the surface of the energy field or etheric double. They are considered to be the vehicles through which "streams of vitality" flow that keep the body alive (Leadbetter, 1927, p. 3). Chakras originate in the spine and "flower" into the etheric body. According to Leadbetter, they have an increasing number of petals or spokes (of a wheel), ascending from the base, at the root chakra, to the crown, at the top of the head. Each may have qualities that vary from person to person. A secondary force weaves itself under and over the radiating currents of the primary force (spokes). This force also has its own wave-length, which creates a sense of luminosity.

The chakra system has ancient roots in literature. Many references, written over centuries and within various cultures, describe the chakras and their assigned functions and meanings. These references have commonalities; however, they vary according to the source. In the Healing Touch curriculum, Janet Mentgen considered that it was only important to recognize if the chakras were functioning properly (open) or were compromised in some way. An "open" chakra presentation is considered to have a clockwise spin that is about 6 inches in diameter, which can be noted by pendulum or hand assessment. A compromised or blocked chakra presents as any movement other than a clockwise orientation. Ideally, chakras should be about the same diameter throughout the energy system, indicating balance. A more in-depth study through various resources can lead to additional insight and understanding of the individual chakras.

Several references support the Healing Touch International (HTI) Healing Touch Certificate Program curriculum. One modern day healer and author, Rosalyn Bruyere (1994) wrote a single, in-depth book on the root chakra (*Wheels of Life: Chakras, Auras and the Healing Energy of the Body*). Janet Mentgen studied and shared the work of Charles Leadbetter in her advanced classes to provide greater depth of understanding of the chakras. Barbara Brennan, a student of Rosalyn's, provided a review of the chakras and discussed the meaning of the pendulum's spin (vertical, horizontal, elliptical, etc.) in relationship to the chakras in her book, *Hands of Light: A Guide to Healing through the Human Energy Field* (Brennan, 1987). Anodea Judith (1996) wrote a very comprehensive discussion of the chakra system in her book, *Eastern Body/Western Mind*. Cindi Dale (2009) provides another resource with her book the *Complete Book of Chakra Healing*. These sources and others can be reviewed for more comprehensive information.

The chakras are dynamic, rather than static, and can change in an instant. The chakra energy shifts and changes based on internal thoughts, emotions, or health issues and responses to external changes in the environment. Assessing the chakras reflects a snapshot of the energy centers in the moment. Evaluating a chakra requires assessing its activation or size, rate of speed, and directionality. It may also include assessing the color (for those able to see it) as an indicator of clarity and development. The chakras can also vary in brightness, depending on the person's development. Individuals who have higher intuitive ability may have chakras that are perceived as glowing and pulsating with living light as more energy passes through them. The clear and brightened chakras may provide those individuals with additional intuitive faculties. Individuals who are very ill or stressed may exhibit chakras that are compromised, smaller, darkened or "muddy."

Even though assessment of the chakras may be done as objectively as possible (with a pendulum prior to hand scan), interpretation is limited. Therefore, the practitioner should proceed with caution when providing feedback to a person on the status of his or her chakras. The practitioner can share the chakra reading of that moment; however the practitioner should explain that the chakra system is dynamic, and changes often, based on thought, emotion and energy flow.

It is important to look at chakra assessments over time to see if a prevailing pattern emerges. The chakra pattern is available to the practitioner as a piece of information that might facilitate insight into an individual's presenting issues. The pattern may then assist in guiding the healing session. For example, compromised chakras may need to be opened and balanced (use *Chakra Connection*, in Level 1 Student Workbook*)*, be related to one another on the *Spiral Meditation* pathway (in Level 2 Student Workbook), or they may be heavy or blocked and in need of a deep clearing and charging technique (such as *Chelation*, in Level 3 Student Workbook). The Student Workbooks, Levels 1-5, are published by Healing Beyond Borders in Lakewood, CO and are used in the HTI Healing Touch Certificate Program.

Meridians

Meridians are subtle channels through which energy or chi flows throughout the body via a cyclical, 24-hour circulatory pattern. The meridians are also influenced by and influence energy patterns. There are 12 primary meridians, each associated with a specific organ system and element. The meridians were first described fully in the *Huangd Neijing* (*Yellow Emperor's Inner Classic*) and then in a variety of later texts on traditional Chinese medicine and acupuncture (e.g. *An Outline of Chinese Acupuncture* by The Academy of Traditional Chinese Medicine in 1975).

In Healing Touch, as the chakras and energy field are treated, the meridian system is influenced in an indirect manner. Some techniques used in Healing Touch address the meridians specifically, such as the

Scudder Technique (in which the hands glide along and across the meridians to unblock the flow) and *Mind Clearing* (where acupressure points along the meridians on the head are stimulated through the fingertips or palms.

Nadis

The Nadi System is connected to and influences the physical body through the meridian system. The Nadi System is the most subtle of energy channels and forms the chakras. Ancient Eastern texts describe 72,000 nadis throughout the human body, extending from the central channel or vertical energy cord (Dale, 2009). Of these, there are three primary nadis. The *Sushumna* forms the central vertical channel and is the main distributor of energy flow. The *Ida,* which is white and feminine in nature, travels along the left side of the Sushumna. The *Pingala,* which is red and masculine in nature, travels along the right side (Leadbetter, 1927). The remaining thousands of nadis start from the central channel, extend outward, and become thinner. Collectively, they create and comprise the aura or energy field.

Movement and flow along these nadis contributes to the spinning of the chakras. A directional flow around each chakra is complemented by its opposite. As energy flows upward to the right nostril through the Pingala, a downward energy on the other side of the chakra flows through the Ida, which causes the chakras to spin (Judith, 1996). Pingala and Ida meet and unite in the sixth chakra, merging their dual natures with Sushumna, and become transformed and transcended as they rise through the seventh chakra.

Energy Field

Each individual person, animal, plant and object has a *personal* (or individual) energy field (Brennan, 1987). As discussed in Chapter 3, Rogers also describes people as unitary beings with energy fields open to influence from other fields. Individual human energy fields, as with the chakras, vary and are affected by health issues, thoughts, emotions, and external stimuli.

Having an awareness of the instant shifts that can occur in the individual brings more insight into the dynamics of a session. The chakras and energy field may change during the assessment, related to any number of things (e.g. thoughts, feelings, environmental changes). This kind of response is often explored in a Healing Touch Level 1 class: the participant evokes feelings of joy or negative thoughts and the practitioner feels simultaneous shifts and changes in the field. This can be demonstrated to the client during a healing session by assessing the chakras and energy field, having him or her focus on a specific thought or emotion, then reassessing the chakras and energy field to discover the response. Sharing this with clients brings awareness to the immediate effects of thoughts and emotions on their energy field.

Maintaining a more positive, loving demeanor can be demonstrated to show the beneficial effects on the energy system, which then supports wellness. HeartMath research has shown that the emotions of love, joy, and gratitude create a more stable heart rate variability and coherence, which result in a positive influence on stress reduction and health. (See Heartmath Institute website at www.heartmath.org).

With continued development, practitioners (or individuals) may become more sensitive to surrounding external energy fields, both human and environmental. They may find it uncomfortable to be in situations that in the past may not have had a noticeable energetic effect on them, such as crowded, noisy, or high stimulation settings. While avoiding these scenarios may protect the practitioner from discomforting sensations, Janet Mentgen taught that it is important to learn to be present in all situations.

Through conscious awareness and repetition, a practitioner (and individuals) can learn to be mindful of the external environment while maintaining a calm, personal space or field regardless of the external situation (similar to being in the calm eye of a swirling hurricane). It is not recommended, however, to subject one's "field" or self to toxic or difficult environments unnecessarily. The goal is to be able to live and work in any environment and to find a way to create an inner sense of wholeness and completeness, such as one might feel when walking in nature.

A practitioner can develop his or her personal energy field by radiating positive, loving energy in any situation, including in an uncomfortable energy environment. Strengthening the field is accomplished by the practitioner using intention to calm, balance, clear, support and stabilize the environment, and by setting the intention for the "highest good of all." Radiating positive loving energy can be executed in the moment at a particular location. This can also be performed at a distance and combined with an intention, as demonstrated by the research of McTaggert and Schwartz mentioned in Chapter 3.

Rosalyn Bruyere stated in a workshop that "the largest energy field wins." This can be an individual energy field or a collective field made up of many individuals focusing on one intention to increase the impact. For example, Healing Touch International led a worldwide meditation that was offered for Haiti after the earthquake crisis. The intention and focus was set on "peace and calm for the entire area, this or something greater for the highest good of all." A day later, a CNN News correspondent reporting live, was surprised at the peace and calm in the whole area when chaos had been expected.

The Healing Environment

The healing environment consists of the person and the practitioner. This is the *clinical* environment. Within this space, the practitioner maintains an ethical code of conduct, as described in Chapter 5, in order to provide a safe and trusting healing space. The practitioner enhances this environment by his or her ability to maintain a healing presence that is centered, grounded, calm, and focused. A sacredness occurs in the healing environment that must be honored. It is important to recognize that this is a healing environment for both the practitioner and person. The healing environment may occur spontaneously in any setting or be created as a beautiful, peaceful, and comfortable office setting enhanced by the principles of Feng Shui to create an energetically harmonious physical environment.

Planetary Field

Although we often function within a very narrow view of the world, each action is reflected in the *planetary* field. This means that every session both reinforces and builds upon prior sessions and helps to create a healing grid that strengthens the individual. When a change occurs in an individual, it affects the planetary field, shifting interactions consciously or unconsciously. Through more conscious awareness, clarity, and loving focus, the evolution of the healer is also shifting to a higher vibration. Both the client and practitioner are then radiating healing energy into the planetary field. This radiant healing energy ripples outward and influences their families and relationships, extends into their communities, and then out into the world.

Energy Awareness in Healing

Listening from Your Heart—Healer Preparation

The most important aspect of any healing session is a heart-centered connection (as per Tovey in Chapter 4 and nursing theorists Watson and Newman in Chapter 3) and having a positive intention for the highest good of all (as discussed in Chapter 5). A heart-centered connection requires that practitioners focus on unconditional love and acceptance for the person in front of them. This involves "dropping into the heart" or simply into "the moment," a place of compassion where there is no longer any distraction. It includes releasing potential worries and fears, judgments, or comparisons, in order to arrive at a place of acceptance.

From a place of calm, healing presence, the practitioner becomes more open to receive input and can access the limitless exchange of energetic information that is available on multiple levels. Coming through the heart chakra with the intention of helping another, opens one to the world of mystery. The mystery may be engaged through a variety of methods, including simple meditation directed at releasing worries and tensions, chakra balancing, centering, mindfulness training, or a one minute, freeze-frame meditation technique from HeartMath Institute (See website www.heartmath.org). The important denominator in all of these methods is that the worldview is experienced in the moment from a position of reflection and calm. How it "works" is the mystery.

This heart-centering process can be used in any setting to create a sense of peace in the practitioner, a peace which exudes to the person and creates a safe place to facilitate the telling of his or her story—the person's reason for the visit. The practitioner may feel a deep sense of connection with the person's soul, which is the most important focus at this moment. It is indeed a gift and opportunity to assist and observe people in their self-discovery through listening, understanding, and healing.

The "Story"

The story of the illness, distress, or dis–ease is the individual's perception of events, contributing factors and impressions related to his or her issues. It is the recollection of the events as they are patterned into memory. In actuality, perceptions of events are based on unique filters that are influenced by past experiences. Emotional perceptions may create a very different perspective for each person involved. The story is not necessarily an objective observation, which is why accounts can vary from person to person for a single event.

The Gestalt—Looking at the Overall Energetic Picture and Observing for Clues

Activating and heightening the senses as well as the logical mind, and listening while observing for "clues" and subtle nuances enhances the practitioner's ability to create an energetic view of the individual's story and his or her presenting problems. The story begins at the first moment of interaction, which may be a telephone discussion, or during the initial greeting, whether at the door of the treatment space or in a waiting area.

The first task as a practitioner is to observe the individual. If the initial connection is by phone, awareness of tone and pitch of voice, pacing of speech, and mood should be ascertained. If the client is in proximity, notice the manner in which the person is positioned physically in space, in the room or at the door. Observing the client's body language, facial expression, sitting or standing posture, and gait while walking, adds to the picture. A hand shake may reveal degrees of openness and confidence, as well as illness, temperature, and moisture.

Skin color, eye clarity, and focus of sight may yield more information. A person sitting in the back of the room, in a corner, or far from the door, who is slumped and pale with downcast eyes, a weak handshake, and a quiet voice, portrays a very different message and first impression than someone who is standing, pacing, flushed, speaks rapidly and loudly, and has a crushing handshake. While these are two widely differing examples, subtle variations in each client interaction begin to paint an initial energetic impression.

The observation process continues as the practitioner elicits the client's story through a review of the person's physical, mental, emotional, and spiritual history during the intake process. The client's rate, tone and pitch of speech, completion of thoughts or sentences, dryness of mouth, and facial movements, offer clues to his or her level of anxiety, ability to concentrate and focus, and possible medication side effects. From the place of healing presence, the practitioner may perceive the person's energy field during the interview by using a soft gaze and a higher sense perception. It is possible to perceive the person's energy field during the interview and observe it shifting during various topics of conversation, which adds information to the energetic picture.

Understanding the person's story includes observing the way in which he or she relates life events. Every comment has an energetic component that is related to the chakra system and energy field. This adds to the unfolding energetic picture by filling in the details. The pieces begin to come together by asking open ended questions, and observing responses physically, emotionally, mentally, and energetically.

Metaphors or descriptions of sensations, such as "beside myself," "She is a pain in the neck," "It is so heavy," and "I'm tied in knots," may come forth in verbal responses. Additional questions can be asked related to where an issue is felt in the individual's body, to whom or what it may correlate, and what may be needed to release it. This brings the client more awareness and potential insights related to their issues.

Hand movements and gestures may offer clues to the energy disturbances. Observing a client's movement from the starting point, and noting the direction of the gesture, may point exactly to the energetic origin of the issue. The origin of the client's hand movement may be directly on or near a chakra related to the presenting problem.

Often the directionality is demonstrated through hand movements as they pass through other involved areas. For example, the person may move his or her hands in front of the heart, moving in various directions up and out, round in circles, or crushing inward. The client may also describe him or herself with hand movements off to the side of the body or out over the head.

A very expressive person may portray the whole story energetically. The practitioner may observe the entire scenario, while noting the person's body language and drawing the individual's attention to it. For example, "I notice that while you are telling me your story, your hands are at the area of your heart. Might this be where you feel this issue in your body?" "Your hands then move in a downward movement. Have you been trying to hold this down or in?" "You've also mentioned stomach upset. Could these be related?" These questions may open to additional conversation and more conscious awareness for the client. The information can then be incorporated into specific observations in the pre-treatment energetic assessment and the healing session.

Through each comment/response in the interview, the practitioner can consider which chakra may be compromised by the situation presented, and how the situation may affect the shape or congestion in the individual's energy field. The practitioner may then consider what may be occurring as an overall pattern. Clues may come forth that will assist in selecting techniques that might be most effective for the presenting issues. The pre-treatment energetic assessment will reveal more information which can be used in determining the problem statements, mutual goals and choice of appropriate interventions.

Interviewing and Energy Impressions

Eliciting a story is best accomplished in an interview format with a heart-centered exchange. The story unfolds best if the practitioner refers to and asks interview questions from an intake questionnaire to help people tell their story. It is not recommended that the client just fill out a health questionnaire and hand it to the practitioner, as the richness of the information that may be gathered during dialogue is lost in paper form. The important concept is that the practitioner listen for the energetic pattern. This often involves finding information that "resides" in all the layers of the energy field, from the physical layer, through the levels and templates and in the chakras. For example, a physical event may have occurred that resulted in a broken bone or a twisted ankle. Equally important to the physical event are the surrounding circumstances that impact the person emotionally, mentally, and spiritually. In this example, we might notice interactions with life challenges, the ability to stand one's ground, the degree of groundedness, the ability to move forward with flexibility, the pressure of external demands, and possible resistance to change.

The practitioner opens all senses when listening, and learns to expand on what is observed and heard. Information may be received in the form of "knowing" or intuition, and may include sensations, sounds, or vibrations which might be perceived in the practitioner's body and field. Listening continues without judgments or interpretations until the story is complete.

The story is usually multi-focal and involves physical, emotional, mental, and spiritual dimensions. Listening at this level requires a higher degree of sensitivity than simply interpreting the "meaning" of a chakra. It is important that the practitioner recognize the multiple dimensions of healing. The energetic pattern is data for the practitioner to explore in the moment to assist in choosing the Healing Touch techniques that may best facilitate the healing process.

The experienced practitioner links the intake information to the possible energetic disturbances to begin to plan the treatment session. The person's story usually leads to the opening or healing "technique" that is needed. For example: if the story is one of "fracture" or broken bone, the *Chakra Connection* moves through the bones from one joint to the next in the extremities. If there is restriction in the form of breathing, as in asthma, the *Spiral Meditation* can activate and open the centers from the chest outward. *Mind Clearing* quiets a racing mind, creates relaxation, increases focus, and assists with sleep issues.

Pre-Treatment Energetic Assessment— Focus on the Energy System

The practitioner may share the energetic observations with the client while assessing the energy system as a teaching opportunity, and ask if the energetic assessment resonates in any way with the situation. While there are references with suggested relationship to the information held in each chakra, the ultimate interpretation is to ask the client for his or her perspective. Questions might include asking the client what is felt in a compromised area, to determine whether it is a chakra or part of the energy field. This may lead to gathering additional information and to creating possibilities for self-care teaching that can assist in maintaining and enhancing health and well-being.

A hand scan is used to assess the energy field. To deepen this process, the practitioner considers the information gathered in the interview and listens very carefully with the hands over the corresponding areas. The practitioner considers sensations perceived throughout the field that may be related to medications, dietary intake (such as caffeine), or emotional issues. The assessment can then be fine-tuned around the areas discussed in the interview. Key information may be found by paying particular attention to the shape of the energy field and the chakra assessment in relation to the story. For example, a bulge or "dip" over an organ or chakra may indicate distress, or the field may be skewed, which may indicate trauma or emotional issues. This may be the only aspect of the assessment that is distorted. In theory, disturbances tend to manifest in the energy field first, then work their way down into the chakras. Finding the pattern as it is beginning to shift the field, and bringing it back into balance, may provide an element of prevention and energetic health maintenance.

Chakra Patterns

Several sources have explored patterns in the energy field. Brennan (1987) has a Core Energetics basis, and other resources have theories related to certain illnesses or emotional issues. These resources may lend ideas, insights, and trends to the manifestation of a specific issue in the energy system. However, each individual is complex and reflects the impacting issues from his or her own perspective. Observing an individual over time will reveal his or her pattern, which will then change and evolve with repeated energy work.

A pattern in which all the chakras are closed or compromised can indicate a "low-energy" situation (where the person is extremely fatigued). This pattern can occur after an illness, accident, high stress and anxiety, or an emotional trauma. However, it may also manifest as a very expanded and tense field, perhaps with raised areas over a variety of chakras, or a field that is distorted in many directions.

The person may become concerned if all of his or her chakras are compromised. The practitioner can suggest that the healing work will assist in bringing the energy system back into balance. Healing Touch can assist in re-patterning the chakras and energy field to one of balance and wholeness. Laughter can also help to shift open the chakras and field.

Individual chakra compromises may provide information about a person's pattern but should be interpreted in consideration of his or her story. For example, addictions often manifest as disturbances in the solar plexus chakra as one tries to "control" life or create a sense of stability and predictability. However, addictions also manifest in the sacral area as the behavior may have an emotional component or in the head area, if the behavior is to self-medicate or quiet a racing mind.

More complex patterns usually exist for most individuals. Patterns may manifest in "pairs," or in "related" chakras. This pattern is seen in the *Spiral Meditation*, in which the hand balances from one to another (i.e. the sacral and the throat chakras, with emotions/creativity relating to communication/expression). At times, one chakra may compromise all others located above it. For example, the root chakra (one of security and trust) can be damaged by a personal trauma, thus leaving the person unable to form meaningful relationships (sacral), have a poor sense of self-worth (solar), resist loving unconditionally (heart), lack expression (throat), not trust his or her inner knowing (brow), and feel disconnected from a spiritual path (crown).

A compromised root chakra does not always mean the person was traumatized but could simply be a lack of attention to staying grounded and connected to the earth. Janet Mentgen related the story of a healer who was not grounded and had been told she was "no earthly good" by her spiritual teacher. It is best for one to connect to the earth and support all healing through the gifts of the earth as well as through connection to universal consciousness.

Recognizing Energy Field Patterns

Immediate problem patterns can be recognized in the energy field, especially in relation to acute conditions. The sooner one works energetically with a problem, the more likely it is to clear the possibility of lasting or accumulating effects. For example, Healing Touch techniques can be used to decrease swelling, bleeding, and other consequences of an acute injury and activate protective mechanisms within the body. It is also important to recognize the pattern and interaction so that you can prioritize the session appropriately.

Long term or consistent patterns can also be evident in the energy field. Janet's teaching was that "the first compromised is often the last to clear" (Wardell, 2000). For example, if there is a long standing chronic illness that first manifested with joint pain followed by weakness, congestion, and allergies, the last to clear may be the joint pain.

Initially, more frequent sessions will generally assist in holding the newly balanced pattern. Key information can be acquired by watching the pattern evolve over time. Newman (as mentioned in Chapter 3) believed that removing pathology or the disease does not necessarily change the pattern that is in the field. Instead, repeated clearing and balancing support the new patterning needed for health. Selecting homework to support this pattern change is discussed later in the chapter.

Using Referents

A variety of books (referents) can provide guidance on interpretation of both assessments and patterns. Referents are supplemental to Healing Touch and are not required as part of the HTI curriculum. However, outside sources may provide helpful information. Identify those concepts that tend to apply to the client's situation. One way to use referents is to mention select passages from readings to the client. This can be offered as "food for thought" in further exploring their issues and seeing if there is any correlation to the presenting issues. The client should be informed that these are only possibilities and suggestions for their thought process and may not resonate, as there are many ways to look at an issue. Additionally, the practitioner's level of understanding and application of this process will evolve over time as proficiency is gained in energy work. A partial listing of possible authors to consider is as follows:

Barbara Brennan. The author presents more depth on interpretation of the directional swing of the pendulum in her text, *Hands of Light: A Guide to Healing through the Human Energy Field* (Brennan, 1987). The text is based on Brennan's personal experience and may provide additional insights as to the nature of the underlying issue. The detail provided should be evaluated in context of the whole energy system of the person as it is important to reflect on both the story (history) and the relationship to the chakras. For example, she describes a pendulum swing that is horizontal as caused by "holding feelings down to avoid personal interactions" (p. 84). In a later book, *Light Emerging: The Journey of Personal Healing* (Brennan, 1993), she discusses energy field patterns within and between individuals. The illustrations and descriptions can be helpful in identifying repeat patterns of interactions with others. Establishing appropriate boundaries, both personal and energetic, may assist in improving the structure of the field and may be accomplished through regular balancing techniques, such as the *Chakra Connection* (Level 1 Student Workbook) and *Full Body Connection* (Level 4 and 5 Student Workbook) or *Chelation* (Level 3 Student Workbook) with strengthening the 7th level of the energy field.

Louise Hay. Hay first published in 1982 and has since provided a number of texts and supplemental materials that provide insights into healing options. One useful tool is a table found in *Heal Your Body* (Hay, 1988) containing positive affirmations related to possible causes of specific illnesses or injury. For example, for allergies she asks, "What are you allergic to? Denying your power?" and then recommends this affirmation: "The world is safe and friendly. I am safe. I am at peace with life" (p.12). Affirmations can be useful as homework after a session.

Debbie Shapiro. In her two books on *Your Body Speaks Your Mind*

(1997; 2006), Shapiro provides a holistic perspective on the cause of illness. She gives both a disease specific and body specific discussion. For example, she speaks of feet as connecting us to the earth and the reality of the physical world. Therefore, "cold feet" could be due to the person feeling "emotional uncertainty, withdrawal, or resistance to what lies ahead" (Shapiro, 1997, p. 126). This information can be useful in helping to understand the patterns clients may use to deal with life stressors.

Carolyn Myss. In her book, *Anatomy of the Spirit, The Seven Stages of Power and Healing* (1996), Myss looks at chakras in relationship to developmental tasks and to spiritual traditions (archetypes) through demonstrating how emotional and spiritual stressors impact the physical body and human energetics. By exploring this interrelationship, we begin to uncover the root causes of diverse physical illnesses. She correlates the seven chakra system to the spiritual traditions of Hinduism, Christianity and Kabbalah in relation to cultivating one's personal growth and maturity. For example, in looking at the second chakra, she describes its task to be that of finding balance of power in relationships through sex, power, and money, aspects she identifies as the currency of relationships. She describes the second chakra as "literally and symbolically the birth canal....and newborn ideas will fight for survival.....yet fear will often abort a new idea" (p.138). Recognizing this chakra as one that is determined to create, she notes that it is critical that we consider the tenet of "honor one another" (p. 139) as being crucial to our health, wellbeing, and overall balance.

Christine Page. In *Frontiers of Health: How to Heal the Whole Person*, Page (1992) examines the psycho-spiritual meanings and relationships of the seven major chakras in health and disease from the perspective of the soul. Following the theme of exploring the second chakra, Page recognizes the sacral chakra as determining our being "in relationship to" not only people, but also everything within the universe. She notes that "when we stop relating and connecting, we stop growing, which causes great sorrow to the soul." She asks: "What needs to change...the situation or attitude?" She further describes the sacral chakra as being "in relationship to" the base (root) chakra, forming the essence of "who we are" (Page, 1992, p.126). She carries this analogy throughout the life span, beginning with the creative energy of the Virgin, then moving to the Mother, and then to the Crone.

Setting the Intention

At the beginning of a session, intention is always set for the highest good. Anecdotal evidence, as well as the more global research as discussed in Chapter 3, suggests that setting intention for a specific healing for the highest good opens to all possibilities, when one is not attached to the outcome. Frequently a person will come to the session with a specific intention, which becomes a mutual goal. Stating this before the session will begin to move the energy in that direction. Persons who arrive with a clear intention to release something, focus on specific healing, or gain insight, frequently have a more rapid response to their intention. This may be because they have been focusing on the area/problem for a longer period of time, thus setting the energy in motion and manifesting the resolution/healing.

Listening and Assessing during the Interventions

Assessing and "listening" continues during the interventions to deepen the work. When a practitioner pays exquisite attention to the person's facial expression (especially the brow), body position on the table, body movements, muscle tension, breathing pattern, sensations under his or her hands, and any other sensory or higher sense perception, much more energetic information is revealed. The standard Healing Touch curriculum focuses on technique and form. As the practitioner evolves and becomes comfortable with the techniques, he or she realizes a deeper appreciation for the subtleties of energy.

Janet Mentgen taught "follow the energy and let the energy teach you." Under the practitioner's hands, there is an initial sensation and assessment of the area beneath and, perhaps, of the surrounding area. Beginning at the feet, the practitioner can tune in to the energy flow as it moves up the body, sensing the ease of flow up through the feet and noting where it may be impeded or diverted in some way. A focused "listening" with the hands and higher sense perception may pinpoint where the resistance is in the body/field. It can be interesting to reassess the chakras and field after holding the feet for a minute or so, to see what has shifted as the first layers of congestion start to fall away. The chakras may begin to open, the field may become more grounded to the feet, and additional information may be revealed in the energy field shape or congestion that was buried in the thicker initial energy disturbance.

As the practitioner continues up the body, each area that is held will have a specific feel to it. There may be tension, vacancy, temperature changes, or various additional energetic sensations. While the practitioner holds the area, it will generally begin to shift and change. Rather than just staying for a specific time frame, the practitioner allows the hands to remain in place until the shift is completed, the sense of movement ceases, or flow is established. There may be a sense of clearing, or softening and warming, and finally a sense of flow. A sigh (or breathing change) or emotional release may accompany the clearing. If a shift does not occur after several minutes and if appropriate, the person may be invited to bring awareness to the area and breathe into it. If the chakra or area is still not responding well, the blockage may be further up the body, and the session needs to continue. Additionally, this may be as far as the person, who is ultimately pacing the treatment, is able to go in healing that area/issue. Energy therapy is similar to peeling an onion: at times there may be a full release and at times, just a layer clears. A quick reassessment with a hand scan after a release will show how the energy is shifting.

Sensing and watching the flow is fascinating! When the sensation of release occurs in your hands, pay attention to where the flow is moving. There may be a sensation of moving upward, downward, or dissipating. A body part—such as hands, feet, fingers, toes or face—may move, indicating energy just flowed through those areas. This movement may be subtle or a dramatic jump. Sometimes the person will be aware of a movement and comment on it, stating it feels like a "'wave", or while in a peaceful repose, the person may be unaware of such movements. At times a hand or lower arm may "float" up off the table and suspend there for a while, then gently lower. This is just a phenomenon that may occur in deep relaxation, and there is no need to attempt to interpret the event.

Empathetic information, in the form of feeling sensations in the practitioner's body, may be received and can be noted as additional information. The practitioner needs to determine whether the sensations are personal, or are sympathetic to the client. The practitioner can appreciate the information, and then let it clear. Any higher sensory perception information is not to be presented to the client as a psychic reading, but if appropriate, may be used to pose a question such as, "Have you ever noticed or felt something here?" This may bring forth a response or an insight. If the response is a simple "yes", the practitioner can further direct the client with, "You may share or just let it go, if that is okay with you." It is important for the practitioner not to interpret the sensations that may be "seen, heard, or felt", but to allow clients an opportunity to explore for themselves.

Provided the practitioner has training and proficiency, additional concepts may be introduced that encourage the client to have more internal awareness. Specific training techniques, such as guided imagery, interactive guided imagery, breathing into the compromised area, use of metaphors, and dialogue with the body part, are discussed further in Chapter 10 and elsewhere.

Post Treatment Energetic Assessment

After completing a post treatment energetic assessment, the practitioner returns to the pre-treatment energetic assessment data and closely compares it with those areas that were compromised or congested prior to the session. There may be unexpected shifts that have occurred throughout the energy system. If there are any areas remaining that are compromised, additional techniques, such as *Hands in Motion* or *Hands Still* (in Level 1 Student Workbook), can be employed, or the remaining disturbed areas can be added to the plan of care for the next visit.

Evaluation and Follow up

While remembering to not be attached to the outcome, the practitioner examines shifts that may have occurred based on the intake, assessments, and perceptions of the person and practitioner. The evaluation and follow-up section provides the opportunity to determine if the mutual goals have been met or if some other awareness has been revealed. This evaluation will assist in focusing homework and determining referrals to support further energy shifts and in maintaining the new patterns. It is important to convey to the client that energy continues to flow once an area is opened and that healing continues beyond the session. Frequently, individuals will relate continued shifts, new insights, pain relief over time, alterations in consciousness and personal patterns, availability of energy that was absent, mood balancing, spiritual opening, or intentions coming to fruition. Changes can be very subtle or very dramatic.

Supporting and Sustaining a Healthy Pattern

In Chapter 4, self-care activities are discussed that may be applied as homework where they appropriately support healing session issues. When considering homework, it is best to relate it to the original mutual goals, both long and short term, and focus on what may be simple and easy to integrate. Less is more, as always. Applicable homework should support or facilitate a further re-patterning to maintain a health energy system and lifestyle and be specific to the issues and mutual goals.

The practitioner must always recommend that clients seek the approval of their personal medical provider when suggesting new activities or changes that may impact a medical condition. Many health recommendations (for example, dietary and herbal) require specialized knowledge, training or licensing. Such recommendations should be avoided by practitioners, unless they are within their scope of practice.

It is important to appropriately assess the level of potential engagement of the client. Small steps to change work best and are less overwhelming. For example, asking someone to journal who has never written anything since being in school, may present a difficult task. It might be easier to begin by following a structured text or accomplishing a shorter, specific task, such as dialoging with a body part that seems to be creating dis-ease.

Homework is best offered as a few options and possibilities from which to choose, where such options are based on the health issue/problem, chakra(s) or field disturbance, initial insult, time available, and client's skill level and preference. The integration of self-care teaching reinforces the work and encourages the person's empowerment in his or her evolution to wholeness.

Holistically, all aspects of a person's being are interconnected; therefore, focusing on the area most compromised influences other aspects in need of balance. To support a calm, balanced, and open energy system, suggestions might include breathing slowly and evenly, grounding, or attending a meditation class. Those with difficulty grounding may benefit from walking in nature or standing barefoot on the earth for 10 minutes a day. Painting/drawing or doing crafts may be useful for those who wish to enhance creativity or feel that they cannot express themselves well or are healing from traumas. Those with chronic conditions may be taught self-care techniques, such as the *Self Spiral* Meditation (Level 2 Student Workbook), *Self Chakra Connection* (Level 1 Student Workbook), or pain management techniques for daily management.

After a session, clients are returning to a complex environment that may or may not be supportive physically, emotionally, mentally or spiritually of their changes. Once people begin to change (behavior, habits, lifestyle), they begin to influence their environment, which then impacts others in their circle. An example would be a person becoming more expressive of love and gratitude that, in turn, opens a pathway for other family members to be more expressive as well. In contrast, even seemingly positive changes may create disharmony and distress within a relationship in which a person is expected to behave in an established pattern. Others' reactions to changes may reinforce or diminish the person's commitment and ability to sustain a healthy energy system and lifestyle.

Update Sessions—Tracking Energy over Time

The format described for an initial session is utilized in each successive session, and the following sessions now include an update that tracks the energy flow and patterns over time in relation to mutual long and short term goals. The practitioner ascertains that the goals are still applicable, while opening to the possibility for new issues to appear as the energy clears. Homework is reviewed, whether it is being done, at what frequency, any barriers to follow through, and whether it is supporting the healing process.

The interview updates information and is compared to previous findings in the client's energy system. A "quick look" at energy assessment forms from prior sessions provides an opportunity to analyze the progression of the energy patterns and their clearing over time.

Questions to ask the client include the following: "Did the energy system 'hold' the re-patterning since the last session? If so, how long did it hold? If symptoms have returned, was there a gradual or sudden onset? Are the symptoms now different in character?" Based on this information, the practitioner can explore other influences that may pertain to the changes, such as relationships, the surrounding environment (e.g. clutter, noise, work demands), and the planetary field (e.g. earthquakes or hurricanes, group meditations).

Aspects to assess include the following: are the chakras open, is the energy field holding its balanced shape, and are the areas of congestion remaining clear? What does the energetic picture look like now? What has shifted and does the presenting pattern make sense? This information can then be related to choosing an appropriate intervention. For example, if *Chakra Connection* has been used in multiple sessions without any sustainable pattern change, perhaps *Chelation* with upper level techniques would be a better choice for deeper clearing and working within the energetic blueprint. Or, if certain pain techniques were used and the pain didn't change, perhaps a different combination of techniques might work better.

As more congestion clears from the field, other areas of challenge may begin to surface. There now may be more specific techniques that might be used to address these challenges. For example, the practitioner could use direct interventions (e.g. *Ultrasound, Laser*, in the Level 1 Student Workbook) that would follow a specific nerve tract to relieve the person's discomfort that surfaced once the general pain dissipated. Referencing a human anatomy text or pictorial guide may bring more clarity and understanding about the compromised area.

By both the client and the practitioner reinforcing positive changes and patterns, the energy field will be encouraged to "hold" the changes, leading to sustainability of the new pattern. In very select circumstances, it may be helpful to share and review the energy assessment forms with the person. The goal is to provide a better personal understanding of his or her energy field and patterns as well as reinforce improvements related to supporting homework. Areas that may be clearing can be positively pointed out and supported for sustainability. The practitioner continues to observe these patterns as they shift from chaos to higher consciousness over time.

The client is invited to focus on his or her new way of being in the world. This includes the use of regular self-care techniques. The client is encouraged to follow through with appropriate medical referrals and complementary adjunct therapies to further support the healthy re-patterning in all situations.

The ultimate goal is for the client, with the practitioner's support, to shift into a new, balanced and centered pattern. Remember that the pacing of Healing Touch work is at the control of the individual.

There is no prescribed number of visits for an issue. The practitioner can recommend the frequency of sessions, but each session will bring new information to be evaluated in relation to mutual goals. The client will do as much or as little as feels comfortable and appropriate at the time. As the client improves, generally the frequency of sessions can be reduced, and the time between them can be lengthened. Some clients will appear for one session, and then they may not return for quite some time as they integrate the work at their own pace. The practitioner is advised to be wary of developing any personal agendas for the client and to hold true to the mutual goals and the highest good of all while not being attached to the outcome.

Chapter Summary

Each human being has a unique energetic signature that is constantly interacting, engaging, evolving and transforming. Practitioners are to be grand listeners of stories that bear witness to the person's expression of self, be astute detectives of the clues provided, and provide support for the client's journey. Practitioners may recognize that individuals will be called to them, and as part of their own self development, appreciate and honor the opportunity for self-healing and the gift of this therapeutic relationship. Practitioners are called into their best practice and healing presence in order to be facilitators of wholeness.

CHAPTER 7
HEALING TOUCH THROUGH THE LIFE CONTINUUM: CLINICAL APPLICATION

Healing Touch supports the body's ability to self-heal and can be used for a multitude of health issues and conditions. Given modifications for specific situations, Healing Touch has been shown to be safe for all ages throughout the life spectrum—from the newborn to the elderly and from conception to end of life care. In this chapter, we explore and expand upon some of the content in the Healing Touch International (HTI), Healing Touch Certificate Program that is related to specific clinical applications. Certified practitioners and instructors with many years of experience share their perspectives of best practice from their personal anecdotes and evidence-based practices gained from related research. The objectives are as follows:

1. Identify how Healing Touch can be used through the spectrum of life.
2. Recognize the value of Healing Touch for family members/ significant others to further support the patient.

Clinical applications are subject to modification based on presenting issues, age of the individual, and his or her condition. The practitioner assesses patient parameters to determine an appropriate approach, choice of intervention (keeping in mind that "less is more"), duration of the session, and spacing between additional sessions. Details about the techniques presented in this chapter are in the HTI Healing Touch Certificate Program Workbooks Levels 1–5 published by Healing Beyond Borders in Lakewood, CO. Techniques that are described in detail are Healing Touch practitioner developed protocols useful in clinical situations. The descriptions and suggestions presented are not meant to be the only way to address situations, but give a representation of the possibilities from years of practitioners' experiences.

Sensations and Perceptions

Those exploring Healing Touch are frequently curious about the sensations that may be experienced, both by the recipient of the energy work and by the practitioner. Perception of the energetic experience during a session varies among individuals. Sensations may shift and change during the course of the session or be experienced differently in follow up sessions. These variations may be related to the issue being addressed, the condition of the energy system over time, the techniques being used, the individual response, and the practitioner experience. Sensations for both the practitioner and recipient may range from (but are not limited to) tingling, vibration, heat or coolness, pulsation, the presence of an energy wave moving through the body, or a sense of energy breaking up and moving out through the extremities, body, or head. Some recipients describe feeling light or floating; others describe a heavy sensation of sinking into the table. Often both practitioner and recipient feel a sense of clearing of the client's energy, less density in the field or body, or a sense of "lightness." For some, there may be a sense of transcendence, oneness, connectedness, or temporary loss of "self," while feeling connected to something far greater than themselves.

In deeper states of relaxation, some relate descriptions of seeing lights or colors, dream-like snippets, memories briefly surfacing, or the state felt between awake and asleep. As energy clears, the recipient often experiences pain relief and has a less congested, looser, lighter, and more open feeling. Emotions may surface and be released through tears, anger, or laughter. Practitioners may perceive energy through any of the senses (as a sensation in the hands, color, sound, smell, images, taste, or texture) or by intuitive knowing. Each practitioner and each experience is unique, as is each session.

Fertility Issues and Conception
By Sue Kagel, RN, BSN, HNB-BC, CHTP/I

Many anecdotal reports of Healing Touch describe assisting in creating a healthy environment for conception to occur. Women may present for Healing Touch anywhere on the fertility continuum, from trying to conceive on their own, having experienced multiple miscarriages, to having undergone a variety of medical interventions. The suggestions in this section pertain to providing a supportive, calming, and comforting approach for symptom management, and reducing stress and the anxiety that often accompanies infertility treatment.

Conceiving a child, for most, is a normal and natural process. There are situations, however, where medical or surgical interventions are necessary. Women of childbearing age who have delayed starting a family may face age-related issues that often require pharmaceutical or additional intervention. While there may be physical issues with the reproductive system, the emotional component can loom large and unspoken.

The Stress Factor

More women and men today are in high stress work environments and life situations, and stress levels have greatly increased. In many infertility situations, no medical issue is identified. High levels of stress and other emotional issues may play a role in women's choices regarding termination of fertility treatment (Domar, Smith, Conboy, Iannone, & Alper, 2010). The ongoing challenge of conceiving presents significant stress in itself.

Infertility may be related to stress, or depression, that may affect the function of both the ovaries and sperm (Gurhan, Kyuz, Atici, & Kisa, 2009). Mind body techniques may support fertility and conception

(Domar, Rooney et al, 2012). These techniques may work well because both partners learn to reduce their stress and anxiety.

Energetic Approach

Based on the stress effect on reproduction, Healing Touch may assist conception by generating a calm and peaceful relaxation. Opening, clearing and balancing the chakras and the energy field may enhance the energy flow to support conception. The sacral or 2nd chakra is related to physical reproduction and is the logical "suspect" for a blockage. However, congestion or blockages may appear elsewhere in the system.

The sacral chakra is also the seat of emotions. It is not unusual for women to relate a feeling of failure from repeated conception attempts and relate a sense of having failed as a woman. For many women, their greatest wish is to be the mother of their own birthed child. In some, issues of ambivalence may arise from concerns of juggling motherhood with career or giving up her career, fears of childbirth, doubts regarding her ability to be a good mother, or feeling obligated to have her partner's child. Prior sexual abuse, trauma, or unresolved issues related to abortion may arise. Grief from multiple failed pregnancies or miscarriages may be present. The "ticking clock" may be an issue, and each month is seen as "time running out", creating more pressure and stress. With the advent of alternative routes to parenthood, difficult decisions are raised concerning medications, procedures, choosing to use donor egg or sperm, using a surrogate with combinations of parent or donor eggs or sperm, or adoption locally or internationally. These options all bear considerable expense, which further increases the stress load, and may lead to giving up the notion of parenting.

While some of these emotional issues may clear with energy therapy, it may be prudent to recommend counseling so that the woman can work through ambivalences or past traumas, allowing her to be open to conceiving and mothering. Working in collaboration with standard medical care and other holistic therapists may be of benefit. The Healing Touch intervention *Full Body Connection*, with or without *Chelation*, including the area of the ovaries, will assist in deeper clearing.

Impact of Fertility Treatment and Suggested Healing Touch Techniques

During the various types of fertility treatment, there can be levels of anxiety and emotional upheaval related to the intensity of hormones introduced into the body during treatment. The woman and her partner's life may become totally focused on and obsessed with the ovulatory cycle, timing of medications, or need to self-inject hormones. *Modified Mind Clearing*, which tends to be very relaxing, is a wonderful, calming technique that can be used in combination with a full body technique.

When harvesting eggs for InVitro Fertilization (IVF), which increases the number of eggs that are ripening, the abdomen may become very swollen and painful. In addition to *Full Body Connection*, gentle *Hands in Motion* sweeping away from midline of the abdomen and a gentle *Hands Still* or *Pain Drain* to the ovary area can provide relief. Following medical procedures for conception, the anxiety of the woman and partner becomes extremely high with the expectation and worry of whether conception or implantation will occur. This is a time when it is imperative that the anxiety level and stress hormones are low to support the natural hormonal response for implantation. During Healing Touch sessions prior to medical procedures for conception, guided imagery can be used to create a warm, welcoming "nest" for the egg to implant and to intend that the pregnancy carry through to a full term, healthy baby—always setting the intention for the highest good. She can continue this imagery at home.

A woman lives and works in a complex environment that impacts her stress level. Recommending adjustments surrounding the issues in her life that are stressful, including a reduction of outside commitments, may be necessary to support conception and implantation to carry the pregnancy through to full term. This includes suggesting gentle forms of exercise, rather than high intensity aerobics or running, so that adrenaline and other stress hormones are reduced. Quieting activities that evoke a relaxation response throughout the day create a calm internal environment. Encouraging her to let go of fear, relax into the process with breath work, attend regular sessions of Healing Touch, and perform *Self Chakra Connection* at home, are beneficial.

Acupuncture has proven to be effective in supporting conception, and massage as well as other body or energy therapies encourage relaxation and balance. Doing activities such as breathing exercises, meditation, mind-body practices, mindful-based stress reduction, yoga, tai chi, qi gong, guided imagery, cognitive behavioral therapy, and journaling; use of positive affirmations; and omitting consumption of caffeinated beverages (coffee, tea, and soda) and chocolate, combine to support a calmer nervous system.

Pregnancy

By Diane Wind Wardell, PhD, RN, WHNP-BC, AHN-BC, CHTP/I

When conception occurs, a new world of life experiences opens, a world with its own set of energetic needs. The following explores pregnancy, delivery, and postpartum aspects of life using specific Healing Touch interventions to address the bringing of new life. Pregnancy is a time of expansion and growth. It creates a unique opportunity for the practitioner to engage with an intricately combined life force of the mother and baby. Sometimes it is possible to "feel" a difference over (or under) the sacral chakra in early pregnancy that may present as an increased activation, possibly a warmth or tingling or bulge in the field. The provider's purpose is not to either inform of or confirm a pregnancy. However, by using general terms about a change in this area, you may offer an opening for discussion. Do not assume that the possibility of being pregnant is a welcomed occurrence, as there is often a period of adjustment.

Early in pregnancy, the Healing Touch provider's task is to support the woman as the new life (embryo/fetus, which will be referred to as the baby) takes hold and draws on the resources of the environment within the mother. The developing baby will "use" the mother, but it is the perception of this practitioner that the baby energetically remains part of the spiritual dimension by maintaining connection to the divine source or soul's light.

Using general body techniques, such as the *Chakra Connection* and especially, the *Full Body Connection*, can help to balance and support the mother's energetic system, which the developing baby will heavily draw upon. It is best to position the mother on her side (usually left). These techniques, along with pain management techniques for specific discomforts, remain the mainstay throughout pregnancy. In addition, when the hands are over the sacral chakra and the major energy of the baby, gentle loving energy can also be offered to the baby. It can be a delightful option to teach the father, mother, and others to sense this new presence and connect with it using loving energy. For those parents who engage their intuitive natures, a dialogue can occur with the baby at any stage of development. They may ask the baby questions such as "What are you bringing to the family?" or "What do you need"? Simply talking to the baby is also a way to engage and facilitate bonding.

Nausea and vomiting

Nausea and vomiting can tax the mother's reserves, but they also function as a way to ensure that the mother avoids "noxious" elements, such as unhealthy foods or alcohol. Assessing the energy of the food prior to ingestion may help determine if it is the right "match" at the time for the mother's body and baby's needs. Eating simple foods, including simple carbohydrates that are easy to digest, and using one food source (liquid or solid) at a time may also help. Supplemental assistance may also be through using Sea-Band or similar acupressure wrist bands used for motion sickness. Healing Touch techniques that may be helpful include *Magnetic Clearing* and slow and gentle *Hands in Motion* over the abdomen, from midline down and away from the stomach. A calming and balancing technique, such as the *Chakra Connection,* one hour before a meal may be helpful to calm the mother's nausea. Healing Touch techniques offered at closer intervals may have a cumulative affect and may help to decrease symptoms over time. Chelation is generally not recommended during pregnancy. It is best to teach the significant other some of these techniques, so that the techniques can be done daily. It is also best to keep sessions "simple" and focused.

Low back pain

Low back pain can be problematic in pregnancy, and benefits may be gained from simple techniques, such as the *Pain Drain, Hands Still,* and *Ultrasound,* alternating with *Hands in Motion* applied gently to the lower back. Again, the father of the baby or significant others (i.e. grandmother, sibling) can be instructed to provide this support on a daily basis. Healing Touch Level 2 *Back Sequence* can prove to be very helpful, performed with the mother's position modified to a side-lying position for her comfort and for adequate blood supply to the baby.

Edema

Edema or swelling related to retaining fluid, especially in the lower extremities/ankles, can be especially uncomfortable toward the end of pregnancy. Opening the chakras of the feet, ankles and knees, and using *Magnetic Clearing, Hands in Motion, Ultrasound* and *Pain Drain,* can be helpful in relieving some of the pressure and swelling.

Abdominal discomfort

Abdominal discomfort can occur early and late in the pregnancy. Early in pregnancy, this can be due to stretching of the ligaments that hold the uterus in place. In later pregnancy, this is due to the increasing size of the baby that stretches the mother's muscles and skin. Holding the tight areas with *Hands Still* helps the muscles soften and relax.

Preparation for labor

Preparation for labor can be initiated in order to support a relaxed and "open" mother. A general balancing technique, such as the *Chakra Connection,* assists in creating relaxation. Introducing the *Chakra Spread* (once the pregnancy has reached term: 38 weeks) supports the transition from pregnancy into birthing. *Mind Clearing* or *Modified Mind Clearing* may also help relieve anxiety and quiet the mother, enabling her to tap into her innate strength and ability for childbirth. The perception of this practitioner is that, for many mothers, it may be that the baby decides on the day and prepares for the event by coming more fully into his or her body from the spiritual plane. The practitioner may discern a "shift" in the energy of the baby to a more grounded and "earthy" feel.

Preparation for Caesarian delivery (C-section)

Preparation for Caesarian delivery (C-section) can be enhanced by balancing the mother's energy system. A "scheduled" C-section may be necessary for either the safety of the baby (as in breech or twin pregnancies) or be required for health reasons of the mother or baby. Whatever the reason, it is important to support the mother and baby surrounding this form of birthing. Since the mother will be undergoing surgery, the Healing Touch techniques beneficial for pre-operative care (e.g. the *Chakra Connection* for balancing) are important. Healing Touch techniques customarily indicated for post-operative care (e.g. *Magnetic Clearing, Chakra Connection, Magnetic Passes*), and pain management techniques *(e.g. Pain Drain, Sealing a Wound, Ultrasound)* are also extremely helpful in the recovery of the mother so that she can be supportive and available for the baby.

In relation to a C-section birth, this practitioner's perception is that the baby may remain in the spiritual dimension and need some assistance in understanding "where" he or she is and "why," given the abrupt departure from the womb. The baby can be supported on the "earthly path" by a gentle holding of the root and the crown chakras, either touching or hands above the body. Once the baby is comfortable with this hold (noted by the baby's response of calm, warmth, and regular breathing) a short, gentle *Chakra Connection* can be done, using the pad of the index finger instead of the hand. Babies, especially newborns, are very sensitive to energy work, so it is necessary to be very gentle, to tamp down the energy, and to greatly shorten the duration of the session, both for the child and the parents. The Pediatrics section that follows explores this in more depth.

Labor and delivery

Labor and delivery can be supported energetically in a natural birth or when anesthesia (epidural) is used. Pain management techniques, full body techniques, and the *Chakra Spread* during transition all may be helpful or needed at various times. Simply placing a hand on the arm or leg may be all that the laboring mom can tolerate. At times, especially during transition, touch may become intolerable for the mother. In that case, holding space for her with healing presence may continue to be reassuring. The goal is to support the mother's focus on opening and birthing.

Postpartum

Postpartum can offer an excellent opportunity for Healing Touch to help the new mother relax, sleep deeply, and heal and to restore a sense of balance and self. The choice of technique depends on the needs of the mother. *Hands in Motion* can be used for painful or engorged breasts, and energizing an ice pad for the perineum can help those with a tear or repair. These, along with balancing techniques such as *Chakra Connection* or *Full Body Connection* and *Mind Clearing*, can all be beneficial. Pain techniques are useful for these issues as well.

Lactation let down may be encouraged with relaxation techniques, such as *Chakra Connection* or *Hands in Motion* to the entire body, as well as *Hands Still* over the breast area. One lactation specialist found that having the mom hold the baby while seated, using *Hands in Motion* over the mother's full body, including the baby, and *Hands Still* over the breast area relaxed both mom and baby. This encouraged let-down and released the tension that had built up around the inexperience of the new mom and the frustration of the baby.

New mom fatigue from lack of sleep also affects lactation. The above techniques, as well as *Modified Mind Clearing* for calming new mom "brain fog" and *Chakra Spread* for adjusting to motherhood may be helpful. Teaching self-care techniques to the mom that can be done in short time intervals helps her stay present. The baby can be calmed and soothed by gentle *Hands in Motion, Hands Still,* and holding crown and root chakras simultaneously.

In summary, Healing Touch can benefit mothers and babies during pregnancy and postpartum. Healing Touch can be useful in connecting the developing family to each other, providing comfort, and alleviating discomfort as well as supporting the new family.

Growing and Changing Needs of Babies and Children

By LISA THOMPSON, RN, CHTP/I, LMT

As the baby moves through growth and developmental stages into childhood and teens, new situations arise, and adaptations in the Healing Touch work become necessary for both the children and the parents. It is important to be aware that the energy fields of infants, children, and also teens are very different from the energy fields of adults. Children and infants are typically more open, sensitive, and vulnerable. They are integrally connected to the fields of their parents, loved ones, and those in their immediate environment. Besides direct work with the child, working with the parents energetically benefits the child as well.

The treatments for specific issues of children, such as cancer or post-surgical pain, will be the same as they would be for adults; however, less time is spent with an intervention, depending on the child's situation and age. For instance, when using *Magnetic Clearing* for nausea with children, the practitioner needs to be sensitive to the child's energy and stop as soon as the field is sensed as clear. As with adults, a child's energy system craves balance. I have found that given a protected space to relax, children find this balance almost on their own. Their field quickly responds, and most often, the child falls asleep.

Energetic Connection between Child and Parent

According to Barbara Brennan (1988) the chakras of children are not fully protected before the age of 7 years. Children's capacity to shield, filter, and process incoming influences from the universal and collective energy field is more limited than it is for adults. When parents or adult caregivers hold a child, they provide that protective field for the child. For this reason, children are especially vulnerable when their parent(s) are not present, either physically or emotionally.

Care of the Parent

For the parents, choose to employ techniques such as *Mind Clearing* for stress and specific pain techniques. In my role as a nurse and licensed massage therapist, I incorporate gentle massage to the shoulders. Because of the energetic bond between parent and child, the irritable infant or child often falls asleep after the parent's field is calmed. Teach or recommend that parents practice self-care to create a calm, parental field, which may indirectly benefit the child over time. Modalities, such as restorative yoga poses and stretches, aromatherapy, and breath awareness meditation, may be helpful to ground the parents and to support their energy fields.

Care of the Infant

When working with a baby (from 1 day old to 12 months), it is imperative that the practitioner be grounded, present, and sensitive to the infant's field. Healing Touch can be done with the infant in any position; and Healing Touch can be enhanced while a parent is holding the baby. When it comes to length of treatment, less time is more beneficial for infants. A full treatment could last only five to ten minutes. Most Healing Touch Level 1 and 2 techniques are appropriate, except it is not recommended to use *Chelation* with a baby or young child. Begin to assess 6 to 12 inches away from the baby's body and be aware of any signs of discomfort, such as squirming or increased irritability. Respond to any signs of agitation by moving further out in his or her field, until you find the "zone," and the baby is quieter. The primary intervention for almost any compromised assessment at this age is *Magnetic Passes: Hands in Motion/Hands Still*, which can be used with intention to calm and energize the field. Apply gentle, slow *Hands in Motion* movements from head to toe, or do a simple holding of energy using *Hands Still*, with one hand on the root and the other on the crown, either on or off the body, to create a "container." Although *Chakra Connection* is an option, I find that with babies, the former is often as effective, yet takes less time. Once calm, you may notice the baby tracking your movement as you pass through the field, as if the baby is watching the energy of your hands. Many Neonatal Intensive Care (NICU) nurses, without any energy therapy training, intuitively hold babies by the baby's bottom and the top of the head to help soothe their irritability.

Care of the Toddler/Young Child

It can be tricky to approach any toddler, especially in the hospital or after a traumatic event. Healing Touch in this situation is perhaps best received while the child is asleep or at a distance until trust is established. Sometimes using a teddy bear or parent to demonstrate Healing Touch movements in a playful way can capture the child's attention. I hold the intention of calming and balancing the energy of the child as I do this. Many times I have the parent hold the child as I do *Pain Drain, Magnetic Passes: Hands in Motion/Hands Still* or *Chakra Connection*. If the child is receptive, I refer to *Magnetic Clearing* or *Hands in Motion* as a butterfly, helicopter, or airplane and mimic the motion and sounds as I clear, energize, and balance the field. Keep in mind that when a toddler says "no" or "done," the child tends to mean it.

For school age children, inviting them to feel the energy as you do *Ultrasound* on the palm of their hand can intrigue them. I once explained to a 5 year-old boy with a broken leg that when using Healing Touch, the warmth and energy of our hands can help us feel better. He responded to me after some consideration by saying, "Oh I get it, it's like a hug!" I couldn't have explained it better.

Care of the Teen

Perhaps the greatest challenge while working with teenagers is persuading them to put their cell phone or IPad down! It is very difficult for teenagers to receive Healing Touch while they are distracted, fixating on their phone, or obsessing about missing a text or call. Distractions can minimize the effectiveness of the treatment. In the office or in your own home, you can make a requirement to set aside the electronic devices for just a few minutes. Although I cannot fully enforce this in the hospital, I implore the parents to enforce turning off all personal electronic devices, including the parents' own, during the treatment. I also recommend the devices be turned off as much as possible, especially at night, to allow for optimum healing potential. When the teenager feels better, I schedule Healing Touch appointments at a time when these devices can be turned off.

To establish rapport and in alignment with my training, I sometimes offer resistant teens with chronic illness the option of a reflexology treatment or shoulder massage instead of Healing Touch. If they are in need of further sessions, they may be more open to receiving Healing Touch because a relationship has been established. I usually receive requests for energy therapies after the teenager experiences treatments in this way.

Education of the Parents or Caregiver

I teach parents simple Healing Touch techniques. First, I teach them how to ground and center themselves with breath awareness. Then, they learn a grounding visualization, perhaps of a tree with roots growing deep into the earth. Once grounded, I guide them through gentle head to toe energizing, clearing, and then slow *Hands in Motion* and *Hands Still* for specific issues. I remind them that even without official training in Healing Touch, simply by having a focused intention and awareness of the common energy they share with their child, they can influence the child's well-being in a positive way. Infant massage is also a very valuable technique for the caregiver to learn for general wellness, energy balance, and bonding. I encourage interested caregivers to take Healing Touch classes.

Healing Touch can be an invaluable learning tool for children and teens who have never encountered energy therapies. By experiencing positive, pleasant results early in life from healing therapies (such as Healing Touch, massage, yoga, meditation, or acupuncture, etc.), they will more likely make informed health decisions later in life, without being prejudiced by pre-conceived, inaccurate, or biased conclusions regarding integrative modalities of healthcare.

Adult Care Issues

By Sue Kagel, RN, BSN, HNB-BC, CHTP/I

The focus in this section is on the care of the adult. While some of the conditions addressed may occur in children or teens, care will need to be modified for them, as previously described. A holistic approach to adult care encompasses physical, emotional mental and spiritual components, and when working energetically, these are intertwined. When possible, maintaining a whole person approach, while addressing physical issues, assists in the total healing process.

Prevention and Optimal Wellness, Acute and Chronic Care

While the focus of the chapter is on Healing Touch in relation to health issues, the ultimate use of Healing Touch is toward prevention and optimal wellness, while promoting a high quality of life related to all aspects of health and wellness. Stress is an underlying common denominator in acute and chronic health issues. Many health related issues, such as obesity, diabetes, heart disease, and some cancers, especially in the western world, can be prevented through stress reduction, adequate sleep, exercise, and a healthy diet that includes lots of fruits and vegetables (modified as needed for health issues).

Healing Touch sessions focus on maintaining balance, reducing stress and anxiety, and keeping the energy system clear and functioning at a high level. In conjunction with healthy behaviors, Healing Touch may increase immune function, decrease stress related hormones, and create an inner peacefulness, even in the face of adversity or chronic illness (see Chapter 9 on Evidence-based Practice). Using Healing Touch for a periodic "tune up" is supportive of health and wellness for any condition on the life continuum. Teaching individuals to use self-care Healing Touch techniques on a daily basis, such a *Self Chakra Connection* or simply *Magnetic Passes: Hands in Motion, Hands Still,* and providing additional stress reducing self-care options (as mentioned in Chapter 4) assists in supporting their systems between sessions.

Acute Care in the Clinical Setting

Acute care scenarios often involve hospitalization and care giving. In these situations, it is important for family members in caregiver and Healing Touch provider roles to be sure that they are maintaining adequate self-care, including eating and sleeping, and that they are using techniques to keep themselves calm and supported. Stress may become such that it is not in the best interest of the family member/ practitioner to offer Healing Touch, due to high levels of personal exhaustion. Exploring other options, such as through hospital staff (some hospitals have Healing Touch services available), members of the Healing Touch local community, and requests for Distance Healing (described in Chapter 8), may provide additional supportive measures for family members and the patient.

In the busy and noisy environment of critical care units with multiple technical alarms ringing, it can be difficult to perform a complete Healing Touch session without interruption. One staff nurse described her solution as performing a section of the *Chakra Connection* each time she entered the room with the intention of a continuous flow and completion by the end of the shift, or by using pain management techniques with dressing changes or IV starts. For practitioners not on staff or family members, options also include performing the session in sections between hospital personnel visits and procedures, or by simply sitting in the room in "healing mode" and projecting a bubble of healing energy around the patient and the room, attempting to keep as quiet and calm an environment as possible.

After returning home, daily Healing Touch sessions for a few consecutive days will boost the healing process and assist in emotional healing, as well as decrease pain, assist in withdrawal from pain medications, and increase physical energy. The caregiver must continue self-care in this setting as well, as there may not be others to assist in caring for the adult at home. Once the patient has recovered significantly and the caregiver's responsibilities have lessened, healing in the caregiver can begin. This may take a while, depending on the severity, duration, and hyper-vigilance of the caregiving. Exhaustion and recall of the incident(s) may arise. Time for self-care, rest, massage/body care, and Healing Touch, as well as some fun and socialization outside of the care giving role, help facilitate the care giver's recovery. If care giving is prolonged, time away on a regular basis assists in gaining renewed energy and a more positive approach.

In incidents of traumatic injury, there is often an evolution over time as the patient's Healing Touch needs change. As healing occurs, different disruptions show up in the field as layers begin to clear. Beginning in the Emergency Room, the energetic assessments may show the more obvious injuries, and Healing Touch techniques can begin to address these issues. A *Chakra Connection* to open the chakras and balance the energy, followed by specific pain management techniques, can be utilized and worked in around the hospital staff interventions.

The energy field may be very fragile and may change very rapidly as the body reacts to the trauma. Less intervention is a better choice. If additional issues arise as sequelae to the trauma, they will surface in the field and need to be addressed energetically. Each session's assessment may be dramatically different, depending on the severity of the injuries. Gentle shorter sessions may be more appropriate, especially if the energy field is very fragile. As the physical body begins to heal and pain levels recede, the emotional, mental, and spiritual aspects will often surface and need to be addressed. Prolonged hospitalization, especially in critical care areas, may cause temporary mental health issues (ICU psychosis) that can be addressed with calming and supportive energetic care. There may be flashbacks and nightmares that may surface immediately in the hospital or arise on return home. Some medications may intensify these effects. Gentle, slow *Hands in Motion, Chakra Connection, Magnetic Clearing* and *Modified Mind Clearing* may offer relief.

First Aid in the Home and Community Setting

The beauty of Healing Touch is that it can be performed at any time and any place, as the practitioner is the healing environment. Janet Mentgen's dream and vision was to have a Healing Touch trained individual in each family household that could administer Healing Touch preventively as well as for the various health challenges that arise. Her perception was that individuals would be more healthy and balanced, and the world would be a better place as a result. All Healing

Touch techniques can be used for injury, illness, headaches, bug bites, and follow up medical care. Simply learning the techniques offered in the HTI Healing Touch Certificate Program's Level 1 Workshop provides the tools for assisting in healing issues as they arise. Experience has shown that with immediate and frequent energetic intervention, the energy field responds more quickly in returning to a balanced state, and the rate of healing increases.

Continued and Chronic Care

Acute conditions may heal completely, while others may become chronic. Chronic care has different parameters and generally includes the need for lifestyle changes. While some adults may embrace the need for change, it is not always easy to modify life-long patterns or to mentally and emotionally accept restrictions or changes. Family members and caregivers (including practitioners), with the patient's best interests in mind, may insist on enforcing the new patterns; however, the patient may be reluctant or resistant to change. Fear may arise for members regarding consequences of the patient's non-compliance, as well as resentment and concern related to increased care needs and patient deterioration over time. The caregiver may fall into the pattern of neglecting the need for personal self-care.

When patients choose to not change lifestyle patterns or comply with health recommendations, family members and caregivers can be more supportive by accepting that choice and coming to a place of compassion. Creating a loving relationship will be more beneficial than an adversarial one. This will permit the time spent together, even if it becomes shorter, to be positive and caring. Supporting both the person and the frequently overwhelmed caregiver energetically through these challenging times will best support the family unit. Offering Healing Touch to the caregivers, even a brief *Hands in Motion/Hands Still,* will assist in maintaining a healing environment.

Autoimmune and other chronic conditions present a different challenge than working with acute and short term issues that may resolve in just a few sessions. Chronic diseases include but are not limited to: autoimmune illnesses, such as chronic fatigue syndrome, fibromyalgia, diabetes, multiple sclerosis, systemic lupus erythematosis, and rheumatoid arthritis; infections such as Lyme disease and West Nile; heart diseases, hypertension, and kidney disease (including dialysis); gastrointestinal diseases such as Crohn's, ulcerative colitis, and irritable bowel syndrome (IBS); lung diseases such as fibrosis, emphysema, and chronic obstructive pulmonary disease (COPD); cancer as it moves from the acute treatment phase; and other illnesses. All these conditions, hereafter referred to as chronic conditions, present lifelong challenges for the person and family or support members, require regular medical monitoring, and impose a need for diligent self-care routines.

Along with physical changes and challenges, there tends to be an emotional component of grief and loss of the "normal self," which can be accompanied by sadness, depression, anger, and resentment of the illness or condition. These feeling are normal, and acknowledging them is an aspect of healing. It is possible to be "well" in illness, but doing so requires a different paradigm than healthy people are accustomed to experiencing. Routines, regimens and medications can be exhausting and unpleasant, given an already uncomfortable or debilitating physical state. It is important to support standard medical regimens, along with utilization of mental health services, to assist in the adjustment and maintenance of wellness in the face of continued care and chronic illnesses.

Treatment over Time. Chronic situations seem to respond best to frequent Healing Touch treatment sessions over long periods of time. Very frail or weak patients may require shorter sessions, with minimal techniques being used per session. If family and support persons are interested and willing, and the patient is open to receiving Healing Touch from them, it is very beneficial to teach support persons simple pain relieving techniques, or the *Chakra Connection*, so that mini-sessions can be provided between formal Healing Touch sessions. Once the patient is well enough, he or she can be taught daily self-care techniques, such as the *Self Chakra Connection* and pain management techniques (*Ultrasound, Hands in Motion/Hands Still*). The goal is to stabilize the patient and energy field so that healing is supported on all levels. Strengthening the person's coping skills permits him or her to live as fully as possible within limitations or a worsening condition. It is possible to achieve a different sense of wellness and peace while living with chronic illness.

Exploring the Whole Picture. Gathering information regarding the person's physical, emotional, mental, social, and spiritual well-being during the intake interview will create a more complete picture of his or her lifestyle, as many autoimmune and chronic illnesses are triggered by stressful events, life choices, or reactive patterns that may challenge the health issue. Often, those with chronic health issues are overextended and overwhelmed, hard driving, in constant tension, and stressed. Perhaps they are care giving without self-care, not doing self-care in general, or are in crisis. The practitioner during the intake interview can explore the coping mechanisms in place, the external support available, and observe patterns of self-care, or lack thereof, so that these aspects can be used as a "teachable moment" for introducing or affirming self-care activities.

It is important to ascertain the medications being used for treatment and their purpose. Additionally, medications can leave an energetic residue throughout the field that feels very characteristic for specific drugs. Drug congestion may be notably different and spread throughout the field, rather than in a specific area. Prednisone, for example, tends to leave a high, prickly vibration throughout the field. Not all medication is recognizably sensed in the field, but there may be a similarity in the individual's field from session to session. As the rest of the field clears over time, this sensation may remain as long as the person is using the medication. Some drugs remain in the system and may be noted in the field for weeks after being discontinued.

Energy Patterns. Watching energy patterns over time is critical with chronic illness. As the energy system re-patterns, there may be "culprit chakras" that repeatedly block, or specific areas in the energy field that continue to hold congestion. The field shape may distort over certain chakras repeatedly, dropping to a very low level or hiking up to an ungrounded shape, which shows as little energy around the legs and heightened energy in the upper body that may result in very low physical energy and an ungrounded, off balance state. Those who are "ungrounded" tend to be more scattered, have difficulty focusing, and tend to be less aware of their feet, making them more prone to trips and falls as their proprioception, or awareness of where they are in space, becomes distorted. They may also have a more difficult time feeling emotions and connecting to others.

Stressful situations may manifest as a continuing, consistent pattern in the field when symptoms exacerbate or "flare up." Patients have reported that heightened adrenaline and internalized anger seem to aggravate and cause autoimmune diseases to flare (Berne, 1992). As part of self-care teaching, it is beneficial to reflect these emotional patterns to the client. This creates an awareness of the triggers, so the client can recognize what is happening energetically, as well as physically or emotionally, and make lifestyle or coping changes. For example, stressful situations, whether physical or emotional, external or internalized, seem to impact autoimmune and chronic illness fairly substantially. Recognizing and planning for these situations or reactions, and correcting for them immediately after they occur helps to sustain the energy field. Maintaining a balanced lifestyle, while not always possible, facilitates resilience.

When managing chronic illness, it is important to keep the energy demand swings as minimal as possible and to "under-do" activities on the good days. Saving energy up for the end of the day will help rebuild energy for the following day. When stressful events are planned that need more energetic reserve, doing "heavy resting" several days prior to the event will store energy. Doing "heavy resting" again immediately afterward (and sometimes for several days to replenish self) usually results in the ability to "ride" through the event, rather than just pushing through it.

Patients have shared that weather changes, including wide barometric pressure shifts, can also effect symptoms of autoimmune diseases, triggering heightened fatigue, joint issues, and headaches (Berne, 1992). Recognizing that increased symptoms may not be an actual flare up, but are a short lived reaction to a weather change, assists in reducing the anxiety that can accompany increased symptoms. In general, clients report anecdotally that the stronger and more balanced their energy system is, the less it seems to be impacted by stressful internal and external events, including the weather. A strong energy field assists in reducing autoimmune flare up symptoms and creates more resilience to support healing when flares do occur.

Intervention Options. While there have been suggestions for specific techniques in chronic illness, the most important principle is to follow the energy. Integrating intake interview data with the pre-treatment energetic assessment, defining the problem or health issues statement, and creating mutual goals follow the Healing Touch format and lead to the choice of appropriate interventions. A full body technique as an opening, to open the chakras and clear or balance the field, is always important. The choice of technique will depend on the interview and assessment findings.

Specific symptoms that often appear are "brain fog" resulting from certain drugs that can be relieved by *Mind Clearing* or *Modified Mind Clearing*; pain in joints or upper back that may benefit from pain management techniques and *Scudder;* and fatigue that can be reduced by *Chakra Connection* or *Full Body Connection. Magnetic Clearing* can be critical to ameliorate the residue from long term medication use. Fibromyalgia patients have been found in practice to respond to *Hands Still* to the areas of discomfort, with the position held until the area softens. This works especially well for the upper back. Each illness has specific needs and regions to be addressed that are logical to the disease and symptoms. It is important to address these areas specifically, but also to pay attention to what else "shows up" in the energy system, and address these areas by "following the energy."

Influences on Medication. Anecdotal evidence suggests that responses to medications may change with a balancing of the energy system. Individuals with diabetes have reported drops in blood sugar that may be asymptomatic following a session, as the body attempts to come into balance. It is important to inform diabetic clients to test their blood sugar after a session and monitor their glucose levels closely that day. Blood sugar readings may trend downward over time, depending on the disease or response, so it is important to have clients share the readings with their primary health care practitioner. Do not have clients reduce medication on their own, as medication changes should always be prescribed and supervised by appropriate licensed health care professionals who can monitor physiological parameters and side effects. Medication responses may also occur with blood pressure and pain medications, sleep aids, and other medications that may need to be reduced by the medical provider over time. Inform clients of this possibility, and have them consult their primary physician for any dose changes, emphasizing they are not to do this on their own.

Improved Quality of Life. Intentions for chronic conditions revolve around sustainability, stability, balance, improvement, and possible remission. While Healing Touch can assist in stabilizing and balancing the energy field, living with chronic illness depends on life management to improve quality of life. The Healing Touch practitioner, living from a place of awareness, balance and self-care, can model and teach these concepts and refer the client to other providers as appropriate. Review Chapter 4 on Self-Care for optimal wellness suggestions. An excellent resource is *Breaking Eggs: Finding New Meaning in Chronic Illness* by Lucia Amsden (2012). She reflects on many emotional concepts and includes self-care exercises relevant to learning to accept and live with chronic illness.

Lifestyle Modification Recommendations. As mentioned earlier, stress has a huge impact on chronic illness and may be at the root of many of such illnesses. While individuals will be at their own level and place of readiness, the following are some suggestions to improve quality of life, as may be appropriate. The mind is often full of energy, and on a good day, it may want to do more than may be physically appropriate. Disregarding the body's limits can create a setback in energy level for days to weeks, so it is prudent to reinforce self-monitoring.

Consider the disease as a *gift* and an opportunity for change, working to come to a place of acceptance (Amsden, 2012). Have clients pay attention to the sensations in their bodies so that they notice early changes as symptoms shift toward improvement, or the symptoms worsen. This awareness will help clients determine triggers to exercise, food reactions, or stress. Remember that optimal wellness addresses all aspects of life—body, mind, emotion, social and spiritual care—and remember the importance of maintaining balance without pushing to extremes. Journaling can be insightful for those with chronic diseases. Suggest a healthy diet (free of additives and preservatives), adequate sleep, and gentle exercise (perhaps gentle yoga, qi gong, and tai chi).

Remind your clients to take time to feed their souls with things that evoke joy, such as nature, music, and dance—learning to BE rather than DO. Deep breathing, visualization, and guided imagery are useful tools for releasing old emotions and forgiving. Laugher and a positive attitude raises energetic vibrations as well as helps clients to find their connection to a Higher Power, however they see that to be. Have clients focus on learning all that they can from this gift and its many layers, so that they are *grateful and appreciative* of all that is good in life each day. Focusing on a holistic and energetic approach to wellness while living with chronic illness will provide an enhanced quality of life.

Scar Integration

The *Scar Integration* technique was created by Don Stouffer, Marilyn Joyner, and Joan Stouffer in 1998 as a single treatment for subtle "bumps" or ridges in the energy field over scars resulting from accidents, surgery, or dental extractions. The technique evolved from perspectives gained in neural theory and kinesiology (Hunke, 1950,1952). Dr. Stouffer believed that some scars lose their normal electrical potential so that ion flux stops and toxic substances and minerals build up in the cell. The cell becomes unable to heal. A trauma or injury can activate a scar that has been dormant, and even old scars that have been integrated can be activated by a new scar (Dewe & Dewe, 1989). Scar integration may be needed when other corrections are not holding. Stouffer et al. (1998) suggest that scar integration can be achieved by using the *Ultrasound* technique in a figure 8 motion over the scar. They explain this as follows:

> The center line of the figure 8 is determined by holding the pendulum over the scarred region with the intention and guidance for determining the orientation or vector of the figure 8. Since the figure 8 can be traced to left or right when starting at the top, the intention is then set for determining the best direction. The axis of the figure 8 does not always correlate to the direction of the scarring on the skin, since the internal scaring may be oriented in a different direction. The scar may intersect a meridian and alter the direction of integration. Scar

integration is usually completed when the flow of energy from the fingers stops. However, deep scars may require integration on several levels. Thus, it is necessary to re-evaluate the scar (p.6).

There can be a deep internal feeling (perception of one being inside the body) during the treatment that disappears when the scar is integrated. Scar integration usually only requires one treatment; however scars can be re-activated by a trauma or an active scar. Stouffer et al. report that the technique usually takes 5 minutes for simple tooth extractions and about 20 minutes for extensive surgeries.

Transitions and Later Stage of Life

Moving through life brings its many challenges. The wheel of life turns and new opportunities for growth arise, whether welcomed or not. Grief and loss frequently accompany change, whether positive or difficult. As change occurs, there is the letting go of the past, causing a grief response as one moves into the new situation. Healing Touch can be very soothing during any life transition, including events (moving, a job change), relationship challenge or change, or family dynamics (birth, living with health issues, and death). These events can arise at any stage of life. The search for who we are and how we are to be, our mission and our purpose, are frequently questioned during transitional times. Healing Touch provides the space to quietly reflect and listen within.

Palliative Care and End of Life Transitions

BY MARY O'NEILL, RN, CHTP/I

Her breathing was labored and heavy. She was anxious and restless. She had not slept during the night. Following the Healing Touch session her breathing was deeper, less labored. She relaxed, the tension and anxiety was gone from her face. Her hands relaxed and she was able to rest and sleep.

Palliative Care is a specialized medical care for patients dealing with serious illnesses. The focus of the care is to provide relief of the symptoms, pain, and stress of the illness. The goal is to improve the quality of life for patients and their families. This care provides an additional layer of support to the care provided by the medical team. Palliative Care is appropriate for any age and any stage of the disease process, and it can be offered along with curative treatments.

Although the care offered is similar to that of hospice in that both focus on the overall well-being of the patient and family, palliative care differs from hospice in several ways. Palliative Care is appropriate at any stage of the patient's illness, not just at the extreme end of life, and the giving of palliative care is not dependent on a terminal diagnosis. Some of the benefits identified within Palliative Care programs are improved patient care, increased satisfaction from patients, families and physicians, and reduced length of stay in the hospital.

A Palliative Care program was established in a large Midwestern hospital in 2001 to provide additional focused care for the needs of those dealing with serious illness, and Healing Touch played an integral part of the care offered to patients. A *Policy and Procedure for Healing Touch* that provided the framework for offering Healing Touch to patients was established and accepted by the Nursing Council. Patients are referred for Healing Touch through the Palliative Care nurses, Hospice nurses, staff nurses, physician consults, and family or by patient requests.

The session is documented on the patient's electronic health record, and documentation includes the reason for the consult, goal of the session, and the outcome or response. Pain and anxiety levels are measured on a 0–10 analog scale and compared before and after the session. An additional Healing Touch log that lists the patient, room number and reason for the session is maintained. The log contains information that includes diagnosis, pre-treatment energetic assessment, Healing Touch interventions used, post treatment energetic assessment, and patient response and evaluation. The log serves as a tool for the Healing Touch nurses to communicate with one another regarding assessment, the interventions offered, and their effectiveness. The policy provides that Healing Touch can be offered to family members (with their verbal permission). This has been very helpful in reducing the stress and anxiety of those closest to the patient and also aids in maintaining an energetic balance within the environment for the patient. Many times difficult or complex decisions and discussions can take place within the family following a Healing Touch session, when a new perspective and outlook are present. This offers a helpful adjunct to the health care team.

The Palliative Care Team receives a list of patients for each day. The Healing Touch nurses receive an oral report from the Palliative Care nurse and together, they prioritize patients in need of Healing Touch that day. One way to help identify an energetic compromise is for the practitioner to mentally overlay the issues onto the patient's chakra system while reviewing the patient's record (History, Physical, and most recent notes). This can assist in determining the specific chakra or chakras that are compromised and may also assist in setting mutual goals with the patient.

The Healing Touch nurse generally checks in with the nurse caring for the patient for any updates and to see if it is a good time to offer Healing Touch. This practice has provided an excellent working relationship within the staff. A brief verbal report to the nurse after the session, stating the outcome or reduction of discomfort, is also helpful (along with the documentation on the health record). At the beginning of the session, a simple sign is placed on the patient's door stating that a Healing Touch session is in progress and to enter quietly. This allows for staff to be aware of and make a choice if they need to enter or not.

The practitioner provides a simple explanation of the benefits and advantages appropriate to the patient's understanding and need at that time and obtains verbal permission from the patient or family member, if the patient is not able to answer. Depending upon the patient's preference, music can be played. Performing an energy assessment depends on the individual circumstance and preference. For example, the practitioner explains that a pendulum is an assessment tool that provides a visual observation of the movement or flow of energy and demonstrates its use on her own palm chakra. If the patient doesn't want a pendulum assessment, it is not done. The practitioner also explains the hand scan that is used to assess the energy field.

The practitioner may raise the patient's bed to a comfortable level, adjust the equipment and lower side rails for access to the patient (restore the bed as it was at the end of the session). It is always helpful to place a hand on the patient's shoulder and let him or her know when the bed will be adjusted. If contact precautions prevail and protective gloves need to be worn, assessment is done visually, using all senses. However, it is often difficult to obtain a hand scan wearing gloves. The practitioner's attention to the wholeness of the patient can provide a rich assessment. After mutual goals are determined, the session begins. Most sessions are offered for 20 to 30 minutes. In the clinical setting, this is about the amount of time that is available.

The following are some suggestions that have proved helpful in working with Palliative Care patients. If the patient is dealing with respiratory or heart issues, it is helpful to do *Magnetic Passes: Hands Still* at the heart chakra before beginning a full body technique (such as *Chakra Connection*). This allows for the weakened chakra to open and balance before energy is flowing up against the heart. If the chakra is opened first, it can reduce discomfort and pressure the patient might otherwise experience. In addition, sometimes it is most beneficial to use *Hands in Motion* over the back chest area for patients having respiratory issues, prior to using full body techniques on the front of the body.

Gentle touch is very important as many people dealing with serious illness are fragile and weak. Patients appreciate the comfort offered by Healing Touch and will respond with a smile, squeeze of the hand, or a simple "Thank you." By offering Healing Touch in the patient's room, families are shown the importance of touch in the healing process and encouraged to touch or hold their loved one's hand or shoulder.

Healing Touch is frequently requested when a patient is actively dying. It is always an honor and privilege to offer Healing Touch during this very sensitive time. After giving a brief explanation of the comfort that Healing Touch offers, permission is requested from the family. The nurse and the family are invited to remain in the room, if they so choose. For practitioners who are comfortable with prayer, a simple prayer or blessing can be offered at the beginning or end of the session. Praying is optional and at the discretion and discernment of the Healing Touch practitioner. An easy way to approach this is to ask "Would a prayer be comforting for your mother?" "Does she have a particular spiritual practice?" This can give an indicator of the appropriate wording that is within her belief system. Also, a family member might be invited to lead the prayer.

A brief assessment is obtained, and the goal of comfort, peace and relaxation to ease the transition process is established. The ideal technique is *Chakra Spread*, which can be offered slowly and gently so as not to disturb the patient as it is performed without touching. It is a way of honoring the patient and respecting the process that he or she is entering. It is an invitation for the energy field to open and expand. Nothing is ever forced in a *Chakra Spread*, it is always an invitation. This technique can also serve to shift the energy in the room from fear, anxiety, and stress to a more peaceful, serene state. Families may respond with deep reverence for their loved one and the process in which they are engaged. Sometimes when hurt, anger, frustration, fatigue, or stress surfaces in the family, observing a *Chakra Spread* on the dying patient can transform and heal feelings and shift the focus once again onto the patient.

In one instance, after providing Healing Touch to a dying man, his son explained that the patient's wife had died several years before. The son said, "Thank you for what you did for my dad. That is something my mother would have done for him." We are not in charge of the session. The goal of the Healing Touch practitioner is to be 100% present to the patient, open to the flow of healing energy, and allow oneself to be used as the instrument for the peace and comfort of the patient.

Healing Touch has a very special and unique place in the care of patients dealing with serious or life limiting illnesses. It provides opportunities to reduce pain, promote comfort, and ease the stress of dealing with long term illness. For patients at end of life, Healing Touch is a simple, caring means of providing peace and comfort to those in transition. How fortunate we are to have the means to offer such special caring during these tender moments.

Palliative Care Web Resources

Various online sources are available for the practitioner working in palliative care. Resources include the following: International Association for Hospice and Palliative Care, Hospital and Palliative

Nurses Association, National Hospice and Palliative Care Organization, Center to Advance Palliative Care, and Supportive Care Coalition: Pursuing Excellence in Palliative Care.

Working with the Elderly

By Nina Weil, CHTP

Since 2005, I have worked with the elderly and provided Healing Touch to hundreds of long-term and short-term residents at the Jewish Home, a skilled nursing facility in San Francisco, California. My clients have ranged in age from the late 50's to 101, the average age being in the 80's. The receptivity of this population to Healing Touch has been high, with roughly 3 out of 4 residents embracing Healing Touch when referred by physicians, charge nurses, social workers, activities and recreation coordinators, and family members, as well as by referrals originating out of care plan meetings. My clients have been American born as well as immigrants, many of whom do not speak English, who were primarily from Russia, Germany, Poland, Austria, and other eastern European countries.

As a complement to conventional medical care, residents at the Jewish Home receive Healing Touch for pain management, easing of acute and chronic conditions, stress/anxiety reduction, mood enhancement, and compassionate end of life care. Healing Touch has been helpful for residents with a variety of conditions, including Alzheimer's disease, dementia, Parkinson's, Multiple Sclerosis, cancer, and osteoarthritis, as they enjoy the deep relaxation, improved sense of well-being, and pain reduction. Dementia and Alzheimer's patients experience significantly reduced agitation and increased responsiveness. Jen Serafin, a Geriatric Nurse Practitioner employed at the Jewish Home, had the following experience:

> Many of the frail, elderly clients I work with have chronic conditions that modern medicine cannot cure. They deal with severe pain related to these chronic diseases, and the only management tool I can use is strong pain

medications to help them be more comfortable. Of course, these medications have numerous side effects including increased risk for falls, confusion, fatigue, constipation, or loss of appetite that can be burdensome to elderly patients. I have been introducing Healing Touch to many of my patients with chronic painful conditions. They absolutely love their sessions and look forward to the holistic relief that Healing Touch provides. Many tell me how it not only helps their pain, but it also encourages them to relax and have a better quality of life. In some patients, I am even able to reduce medications, which is always a bonus.

Field Assessment and Chakras

In general, when assessing the fields of the elderly, the more frail the elder, the less active physically or socially, and the more negative in spirit, the higher the likelihood is that the field will be small or completely compressed, and the chakras will be compromised or closed. Despite weekly Healing Touch sessions, the expanded field and open chakras achieved during the sessions do not hold for long. Conversely, the more active the elder, and the more positive in spirit, the higher the likelihood is that with regular Healing Touch sessions, the field will remain expanded and the chakras balanced and open.

Areas of Care, Interventions, and Follow-up

Chronic conditions. In treating chronic conditions such as Parkinson's, Multiple Sclerosis, cancer, osteoarthritis and persistent pain (back, joints, abdominal, headaches, etc.), it is useful to begin with *Modified Mind Clearing* for calming and relaxation and *Chakra Connection* or *Chelation* to clear, balance, and align the chakras and expand the field. Specific techniques, such as *Pain Drain, Magnetic Passes: Hands in Motion/Hands Still, Laser,* and *Ultrasound* to specific areas for specific local issues, may be added as needed. *Back techniques* (as appropriate) sometimes need to be done in parts rather than in the full sequence. Technique segments may include *Connecting the Lower Body, Opening Spinal Flow,* or *Spinal Cleansing.* Most often with lower back, hip, and associated leg pain, there is also congestion in the neck that needs to be addressed and cleared. Residents initially receive weekly 45 minute to 1 hour sessions for 4–6 weeks, followed by sessions every other week for 4–8 weeks. They are then placed on an every 1, 2, 3, or 4 week cycle, depending on availability of Healing Touch providers and the degree to which the frequency of sessions impacts their quality of life. Residents as a rule would prefer weekly sessions. I rarely give homework as I have found over time that the assignment will be forgotten from week to week, even if it is written down.

Outcomes. The outcomes will vary, as shown in the following examples of some positive outcomes. A client, who had severe knee pain and limited walking ability when starting Healing Touch sessions, was able to increase her level of activity so that she could enjoy outings with her son and use a walker instead of a wheel chair, even though she had ongoing pain. She also began walking to meals. Another client, who had severe lower back pain, continues to be comfortable and active with significantly reduced pain through Healing Touch and acupuncture sessions. A resident with Parkinson's was in constant pain and had stiffness, particularly in her hips, legs, and neck, that caused sleepless nights. After 2 ½ months of weekly Healing Touch, the pain subsided, sleep improved, and she was able to relax with less stiffness. Healing Touch was particularly helpful as her medications were then reduced, which in turn resulted in the elimination of hallucinations caused by the medications.

Dementia/Alzheimer's Disease

With dementia and Alzheimer's residents, it is helpful to have a few visits of introduction prior to beginning sessions. These visits allow clients to become familiar and comfortable with the Healing Touch provider. When a client is in a highly agitated state, waiting until the agitation decreases is less disruptive. Additionally, it may be less intrusive and more likely to reduce the agitation if the provider works in the field behind the client, off the body, while the client is seated.

As a model, I have used the protocol developed in 1999 for the research study, "Healing Touch on Agitation Levels in Dementia," at

8

Prescott Veteran's Administration Medical Center, Prescott, Arizona by Kris Wang, MSN, RN, CS, CHTP, HNC, and Carol Hermann, MS, CTRS. I believe the protocol works extremely well for dementia and Alzheimer's patients. The protocol includes using *Hands in Motion* (then termed "unruffling" in the study) and *Modified Mind Clearing*, and results show significantly reduced levels of agitation. Additionally, shorter sessions (10–20 minutes) with greater frequency, using *Modified Mind Clearing* (if client tolerates touch) and *Hands in Motion* around the head, work well. Use of these techniques typically opens the chakras, expands the field, and also clears congestion in the head. When an initial hand scan over the body reveals congestion where pain might be felt but cannot be expressed by the client, *Magnetic Passes: Hands in Motion/Hands Still*, *Pain Drain*, *Ultrasound* and *Laser* to the area can be used to reduce possible pain. Consider communicating with the charge nurse if you suspect that the client might be experiencing pain, especially if he or she is unusually agitated. This may result in pain medications being administered for comfort.

A full body technique, such as *Chakra Connection*, might be used, depending on the client, but there may not be tolerance for long sessions. For Alzheimer's patients who wander constantly during waking hours, it is more useful to work with them when they are napping. For clients who are unable to communicate verbally, consider working intuitively to help set specific intentions for what may be needed to release or clear any or all levels—physically, emotionally, mentally, or spiritually.

Depending on the client, the length of sessions for dementia and Alzheimer's patients can range from 10 minutes to 1 hour. With highly agitated residents, the use of short sessions 4–5 times per week brings the best results. Having trained staff, or family or friends, who can utilize Healing Touch as part of daily care practice is highly recommended. In some cases, after a few Healing Touch sessions, agitation will cease completely. Minimum weekly sessions are recommended, if possible.

Outcomes. An example of outcomes includes a resident with Alzheimer's who was continually highly agitated, destructive, and striking out. Healing Touch sessions were initially administered off the body (without touching) and were of short duration. After three months, agitation was intermittent with periods of calm, and the client tolerated touch and extended sessions (including *Chakra Connection)* and was able to indicate areas of pain. Another resident with dementia, Parkinson's, and paranoia tendencies, after receiving Healing Touch weekly for 3–4 weeks, was noted by the unit manager and activity coordinator to no longer exhibit paranoia tendencies.

A very disturbed resident, who cursed, hit, spit, grabbed and was restless, within two weeks of receiving Healing Touch sessions 4–5 times per week became quiet, relaxed and more engaged with staff and family. He also regained his sense of humor. (Note: I recommend ongoing sessions 3–4 times per week to maintain this more relaxed, less agitated state.)

End of Life Care

Healing Touch can play a large part in helping elders through the dying process. Elderly clients are often very realistic regarding death and are very present and in the moment. It is often family members who are reluctant to let their parents go. Healing presence and listening plays an important role in the healing process. Using intuition to better understand the client is important to know what might be most helpful. Simply holding the client might be what is most needed.

When an elderly client is actively dying, consider using *Magnetic Passes: Hands in Motion* to the feet to release grounding, and *Magnetic Passes: Hands Still/Hands in Motion* to the crown chakra to open the crown, followed by the *Chakra Spread*, while quietly speaking words of comfort and encouraging release and letting go. If the client is agitated, it may be useful to start with *Modified Mind Clearing* or *Magnetic Passes: Hands in Motion* to the head to instill calmness. When working with clients in the last months of life, consider useful techniques to support comfort, relaxation, and pain relief, including *Modified Mind Clearing, Chakra Connection, Chelation* (gently, if not frail) or *Pain Drain.*

Outcomes. One resident, while actively dying, had been difficult to calm and quiet even with medication. Immediately following Healing Touch, the resident became quiet and peaceful and passed within 24 hours. Another resident enjoyed weekly Healing Touch sessions in the last three months of her life, particularly the relaxation effect and the human connection. This allowed her to open up and talk about deep seated regrets in her life.

In summary, the use of Healing Touch with the elderly can be very significant in reducing pain, easing acute and chronic conditions, and reducing stress/anxiety. The use of Healing Touch also results in mood enhancement, calming, deep relaxation, and compassionate end of life care. Elders feel a sense of peacefulness on all levels—physically, emotionally, mentally and spiritually—allowing them to be more comfortable in their later years.

Chapter Summary

Healing Touch enhances quality of life from beginning to end. It offers wholeness, support, comfort, coping, pain relief, integration of self-care, stress management and healing in all aspects of life, illness and death. The next chapter expands these areas and addresses specific health issues in more depth.

CHAPTER 8
HEALING TOUCH FOR SPECIFIC HEALTH CARE ISSUES

Healing Touch is supportive for individuals during times of illness and crisis. In this chapter, we expand the foundation given in Chapter 7 and apply Healing Touch to specific health conditions. Application of techniques from the HTI Healing Touch Certificate Program Student Workbooks for Levels 1–5, as well as practitioner developed protocols, are explored in relation to supportive care of cancer patients and donors and recipients in surgical removal of organs and transplantation. We also consider Healing Touch in relation to psychological support, management of trauma, disaster recovery, and distance healing. The objectives are as follows:

1. Explore clinical applications of Healing Touch for specific health care situations.
2. Recognize the complexity of healing patterns.
3. Enhance skills for working with trauma.
4. Explore the benefits of Distance Healing.

Clinical applications are subject to modification depending on the recipient's characteristics, conditions, and situations. The practitioner holistically assesses an individual to determine the appropriate approach, interventions, and duration/spacing of sessions, while keeping in mind that "less is more" in relation to the number of techniques used in any given session. As stated in the previous chapter, these are suggestions for an approach to specific situations; the practitioner always performs a full assessment and determines the correct approach and interventions for each client.

Working with Adults with Cancer

Cancer requires a multi-dimensional perspective in healing. The following sections address varied approaches and focus on different aspects of cancer supportive care as well as transplant treatment.

Healing Touch During Cancer Treatment

By Kathy Turner, RN, NP, CHTP

I had just completed Healing Touch Level 4 and arranged to provide Healing Touch sessions at a local cancer center during my apprenticeship. I remember standing outside the treatment room with a mixture of excitement and nervousness before my first session. As I look back, I realize that all the elements that continue to inform my work today were present in that first session: being of service, non-attachment to outcome, less is more, and trusting my intuition.

My client was a woman my age, who had been recently diagnosed with breast cancer. She spoke of the stresses in her life: her anger at the impersonal medical care she had received, her husband's lack of support, her grief about the loss of her breast, the changes in her body image after surgery and hair loss, fears about finances, and ultimately, coming face to face with her own mortality. As I listened, I felt my anxiety rising, muscles tightening in my neck and jaw, a clenching in my stomach, and my mind going blank. What could I possibly say to her? What if I said the wrong thing? I took a slow, deep breath, and then another. I became aware of my own body in the chair and my feet on the floor. I remembered that I could listen and acknowledge what she was saying— and provide Healing Touch. That was enough.

Service

One of the challenges of working with people dealing with cancer is to navigate through the desire to help them. When confronted with all of their needs—physical, emotional, and logistical—it is a natural impulse to want to help. And that is not our job. Our job is to provide Healing Touch.

Rachel Naomi Remen (1996), a physician and author who has dealt with her own chronic illness, makes the distinction between being of service vs. fixing or helping. She explains that when we fix someone, we see them as broken; when we help someone, we see them as weak. Service, on the other hand, is a relationship between equals. The assumption is that the person we are serving can take responsibility for his or her own experience, including finding appropriate assistance when necessary.

Less is More

In this context, being of service involves being present with the client and doing the work without attachment to outcome. Often cancer patients undergoing treatment have many symptoms, including pain, nausea, fatigue, depression, anxiety, hair loss, lymphedema, constipation/diarrhea, insomnia, brain "fog" or difficulty with concentration, memory loss, and cognitive impairment. Attempting to address each of these in a session with a specific technique is impossible and unnecessary. One of the basic principles of working with clients with cancer is that less is more. One full body technique done slowly with the intention for highest good can be enough. Further work following intuition is more valuable than trying to rush through a laundry list of techniques.

Another place to follow the less is more principle is in regard to the intensity of our energetic work. I generally start out with *Chakra Connection*, as opposed to *Chelation*, particularly when working with a new client. There is no need to amp things up. Sometimes, providers feel the need to come on strong to match the energetic intensity of the disease process and treatment. A gentle approach is more appropriate here and just as effective.

Non-Attachment

It is unrealistic to expect that all of the client's symptoms will decrease in intensity by the end of a session. In fact, some of the symptoms may get worse. This is where not being attached to the outcome is especially relevant. It is important not to establish such an expectation with clients because they can see it as a personal failure if they do not improve right away. I tell clients that it can take several days or more to see the full effect of the work and ask them to take note of the changes over time.

It is also important not to present Healing Touch as a cure for cancer. In the initial session, I talk about the difference between curing and healing: curing is the absence of a disease, and healing is moving to the highest level of wellness and wholeness possible, regardless of what is happening with the course of an illness.

Benefits

In addition to addressing specific symptoms related to cancer treatment, Healing Touch can be a means of providing stress reduction as well as engendering a sense of resilience and hope in the midst of overwhelming circumstances. For some clients, the Healing Touch sessions may be the one place where they can let go, not have to do anything, not have to pretend that they are okay, not have to reassure family and friends, and not have to make any decisions. Over and over again, I have heard from clients how this experience is "priceless."

Practical Issues

Our approach to Healing Touch is, of course, guided by location, timing, length, and frequency. Are the sessions in an in-patient or out-patient setting, in your office, or at the client's home? How much time do you have? Sometimes, a full hour is too long for the client to tolerate. If you are doing a session in the infusion area during a chemotherapy treatment, it can be challenging to carve out enough time, without interfering with the activities of care providers. I have found that negotiating this ahead of time with the nursing staff works well.

People often ask what the optimal timing is for sessions—before or after chemotherapy, radiation treatments, or surgery. There are advantages to each timing scenario. A session before treatment can balance and relax the client and provide receptivity to the beneficial effects of the treatment. A session after treatment can balance the field and clear any non-therapeutic congestion and debris.

Goal-setting for each session is influenced by the number of sessions you will have with the client, and how frequently the sessions are scheduled. It is not unusual for me to see a client one time only. After briefly explaining what Healing Touch is, I ask if he or she has a specific goal for the session, but I make this optional. I might say, "Is there anything you would like me to focus on?" People new to, and sometimes skeptical about, Healing Touch are often not able to formulate a goal. I tell them I will clear and balance their energy field and that there is nothing in particular they need to do or experience. I invite them to breathe and relax and see what they notice. As we all know, the best introduction to the work is to experience it, to literally get on the table.

When working with someone over time, whether for weeks or months, it becomes easier to define short and long-term goals as the client becomes familiar with the effects of energy work. These goals can then serve as a valuable framework for a collaborative relationship. It can be helpful to articulate our ultimate intention that Healing Touch is a complement to conventional medical treatment. It is essential to approach each session as a new experience and do a full assessment, rather than assume that things will follow a predictable course. The assessment includes taking note of cues from a client's affect, body language, and tone as well as performing an energetic assessment. The first step is to receive this information, then let go of the need to respond specifically, and surrender to the flow of the work moving through us in response to all that is present in the moment.

There are some situations that lend themselves to a need for frequent sessions, such as when radiation treatment is administered daily over a period of weeks. Frequent clearing of the field can be beneficial in reducing side effects, such as radiation burn, swelling, and pain. This is a great opportunity to teach *Hands in Motion* to the client, so that he or she can begin to clear his or her field immediately after each treatment.

For fatigue, either teaching the client the *Self Chakra Connection* to use each day, or teaching a family member how to do a *Chakra Connection* for the client on a daily basis, can be beneficial. The latter has the added benefit of providing a family member or friend a tangible way to show caring and support in a situation often characterized by a sense of helplessness for all involved. Different types of chemotherapy and radiation can have a palpable energetic presence in the field. Conversely, the field can be totally contracted in other types of treatment or when someone is extremely debilitated.

Both chemotherapy and radiation are used to destroy cancerous cells. In working with people undergoing these treatments, it is our intention to support the treatment's action against the cancerous cells, while minimizing their effect on healthy cells. It is essential to separate out our personal beliefs about these treatments, particularly if we have a bias against them, and hold intention for the highest good. This can be an opportunity to cultivate a practice of non-judgment, whether it is about a client's treatment choice or his or her decision not to pursue treatment.

A common question among providers concerns the direction of hand movements in *Lymphatic Drain*, particularly when working with breast cancer patients with lymphedema. When patients have physical therapy involving lymphatic drainage massage, the movement is from the extremity in toward the trunk to facilitate the physical flow of the lymph fluid out of the extremity. The movement in the *Lymphatic Drain* energetic technique is in the opposite direction, moving away from the trunk and out the extremities. While seemingly these techniques would be at cross purposes, in practice they are not. They are working in different layers of the field, and the energetic *Lymphatic Drain* is utilizing a principle of moving in the opposite direction to the usual pattern of flow to "backwash" the energy to open and restore flow. In my experience, these techniques complement each other well.

Positioning during a session can be impacted by the client's physical condition. Recent surgery, or the presence of catheters, IV's, tissue expanders or drains, can make it impossible for some to lie on their stomach, side, or even on their back. Work with the client to discover how they can be most comfortable. Sitting in a chair is always an option. I had a client prefer to stand during the session and lean against the side of the table. If clients are unable to turn over onto their stomach because of a medical condition, techniques such as *Lymphatic Drain* and back techniques can be performed while they are lying on their side.

Specific Techniques

A good general rule of thumb is to begin with a full body technique (*Chakra Connection, Spiral Meditation* or *Full Body Connection*), followed by one or two specific techniques. A common sequence used during chemotherapy or radiation treatment is *Chakra Connection* followed by *Magnetic Clearing,* and then by one or more additional techniques based on the energy disturbance, problem statement, and goals. If a client displays a high level of anxiety, often reflected by expansion and congestion in the field around the head, beginning the session with *Mind Clearing* can increase receptivity to the full body technique.

Examples of specific techniques commonly used during cancer treatment are *Wound Sealing, Magnetic Clearing, Hands in Motion, Hands Still, Ultrasound, Laser, Pain Drain, Lymphatic Drain, Etheric Template Clearing,* and *Chakra Spread. Hands Still* over the liver and spleen can be especially beneficial during chemotherapy to balance and energize these organs. The liver processes the waste products of chemotherapy, and the spleen mobilizes more blood cells to replace those destroyed by chemotherapy. When there is pain, inflammation, or swelling in a specific site, *Hands Still* held simultaneously above and below the affected area can be used. *Hands in Motion* over the solar plexus can reduce nausea. Another technique for swelling or lymphedema in an extremity is to hold the hand or foot on the affected side with one hand and your other hand on the client's heart. In receptive clients, teaching *Self-Chakra Connection* and *Hands in Motion* can be a valuable supplement to sessions, both in terms of symptom management and in fostering a sense of autonomy and self-efficacy.

Practitioner Self Care = Self Awareness

In addition to the basic aspects of self-care, grounding and clearing our fields as practitioners before and after sessions, adequate rest and nutrition, and an ongoing spiritual practice, two additional factors are critically important when working with people with a diagnosis of cancer: boundaries and self-awareness. While healthy boundaries in our personal lives can be fluid and flexible, our boundaries in our professional lives need to be clear and consistent. The first step is to have clarity about our role as a practitioner and how it differs from that of a friend. While a friend might provide food, transportation, money, child care or emotional support, our only role as a practitioner is to provide Healing Touch. It is our responsibility to know the difference and to cultivate a state of compassionate non-attachment.

Self-awareness is key. Working with a client diagnosed with cancer can bring up our anxiety about our own mortality or our fear of physical or emotional suffering, or it can activate our need to be a caretaker. It is important to bring these reactions into conscious awareness and hold ourselves with compassion in the process. A place to start is to make a list of what personal needs we are getting met when we do this work. Your list might include the desire to be of service, to use the skills you have learned, or to accumulate sessions for certification. I invite you to look a little deeper. Perhaps there is a desire to feel needed, to be liked, to feel competent, or to be in control.

There is nothing wrong with having needs. What is important is to recognize them and get them met elsewhere, not in a session. If we neglect self-care and become depleted, we are more likely to try to get our needs met in the work. It is important to separate our own needs from the needs of our client. Notice that if you feel pulled to do or say more, or to try to fix or solve something, you should use that as a signal to check and see what need of yours is wanting to get met. Our goal is to be present in each session as a clear channel for energetic flow, while holding the intention for highest good. The service we offer is to listen, to acknowledge, and to provide Healing Touch.

Specific Situations in Cancer Care

For different aspects of care, the following are suggestions for Healing Touch techniques that might be helpful to the person with cancer. The following suggestions are from the Bosom Buddies, Healing Buddies Protocols (2002).

Pre-operative and pre-procedure sessions may include:
- full body techniques to balance and relax client,
- *Mind Clearing* to reduce anxiety, and
- *Hands in Motion* or *Hands Still* to clear and energize the surgical site.

Post-operative and post-procedure sessions may include:
- full body techniques to balance field,
- *Magnetic Clearing* to remove chemical waste products from anesthesia,
- *Hands in Motion* to clear entire field, and
- *Pain Drain, Ultrasound, Hands in Motion, Hands Still, Etheric Template Clearing,* and *Wound Sealing* at surgical site as needed.

Chemotherapy sessions may include:
- before treatment a full body technique to balance and relax the client,
- after treatment a full body technique to balance field,
- *Magnetic Clearing* or *Lymphatic Drain* to clear debris,
- *Hands in Motion* and *Hands Still* over liver and spleen to balance and energize, and a
- *Pain Drain* to refill liver and remove congestion.

Radiation treatment sessions may include:
- before treatment a full body technique to balance and relax the client,
- after treatment a full body technique to balance field,
- *Magnetic Clearing* or *Lymphatic Drain* to clear debris, and
- *Hands in Motion* over radiation sites and congested areas.

For the following conditions, it is recommended to begin with a full body technique, time permitting.

For drain sites suggestions include:
- *Hands in Motion* or *Etheric Template Clearing* to clear field at drainage site, and
- Ultrasound, *Hands Still,* or *Wound Sealing* to seal a drain hole after the drain is removed.

For wound healing suggestions include:
- *Ultrasound,*
- *Hands in Motion,*
- *Etheric Template Clearing, and*
- *Wound Sealing.*

For mouth sores suggestions include:
- *Ultrasound* to break up congestion,
- *Hands in Motion* over face and neck to clear the field,
- *Hands Still* above the face to promote healing,
- *Hands Still* at forehead and throat simultaneously to clear and energize mouth tissue, and *Pain Drain.*

For nausea suggestions include:
- *Hands in Motion* over the solar plexus, and
- *Magnetic Clearing* or *Etheric Template Clearing* to remove debris.

For lymphedema suggestions include:
- *Magnetic Clearing* or *Lymphatic Drain** to remove debris,
- *Ultrasound* and *Hands in Motion* down the affected limb,
- *Hands Still* at top and bottom of limb, and
- if in the arm, hold client's heart and hand.

For soreness/swelling at IV site suggestions include:
- *Ultrasound, Hands in Motion* at site to clear congestion,
- *Etheric Template Clearing* over the site,
- *Hands Still* on limb above and below the site, and over the site.

For fatigue suggestions include:
- *Chakra Connection and*
- *Mind Clearing.*

For emotional crisis (treatment failure, disease progression, body trauma, loss) suggestions include:
- *Spiral Meditation,*
- *Mind Clearing, and*

- *Chakra Spread.*

*If client has a surgical incision, port, drain, tissue expander on the chest or is in pain or very weak, do *Lymphatic Drain* with client lying on side. It can be repeated on the front side with the intention of clearing the back. Do not have client lie on stomach.

A Specific Protocol for the Integrative Use of Healing Touch with Chemoradiation

By: Laura K. Hart PhD, RN, CHTP/I and
Mildred I. Freel, MEd, RN, CHTP/I, Emeritus Professors

This discussion evolves from the research study "Preservation of Immune Function in Cervical Cancer Patients During Chemoradiation Using a Novel Integrative Approach" published in *Brain, Behavior and Immunity* (Lutgendorf et al., 2010). The article describes our observations regarding responses to chemoradiation noted in the patients' energy fields and advances in interpretations, based on our understanding of the literature regarding the biofield. This prospective randomized clinical trial found maintenance of natural killer (NK) cell cytotoxicity and reduction of clinical depression in the Healing Touch group versus a substantial drop in NK cell activity and no change in depression in a relaxation group and a usual care group. Recent research suggests that maintenance of NK cell activity positively impacts cancer survival (Beano et al, 2008; Menard et al., 2009).

Chemoradiation Effects

The study participants received a platinum-based chemotherapy administration once per week and external beam radiation treatments to their pelvic area daily (5 times per week) over the course of approximately 6 weeks. Healing Touch sessions (post-radiation) were integrated into this medical regimen to mitigate side effects, while supporting the mission of eliminating the cancer cell's reproductive capacity. In general, chemotherapy affects cell growth and proliferation by damaging DNA (Seung, 2009). Radiation may cause breakage in one or both chains of the DNA molecule, faulty cross linking, and/or breaking of the hydrogen bond between the two chains. Ionization of the water surrounding the cells results in significant toxic changes that ultimately affect cancer cell survival (Hass, Hogle, Moore-Higgs, & Gosselin–Acomb, 2007).

We noted that the chemotherapy agents appeared to clog the body's energy centers and channels. The energetic flow was reduced, congested, or blocked. The patients often described their response to the chemotherapy with phrases such as: "I feel ill." "I feel toxic." "My head doesn't work." "I have a film over my eyes." "My eyes are blurry." "I can't think or concentrate." "I can't remember things very well."

Radiation appears to shatter and displace patients' energy fields, much like a glass shatters when it is dropped. We found the energy field broken (vacant) at the waist. The upper half of the field was displaced to 24 to 36 inches above (superior) their heads. The lower half was 12 to 24 inches below (inferior) their feet. Within minutes of completion of the radiation treatment, subjects appeared pale with glazed eyes, and they reported difficulty with balance and proprioception.

Healing Touch Session

Healing Touch sessions, which included the techniques described below, were administered on the non-chemotherapy days, four days per week (of 30 minutes each), for the entire duration of the course of chemoradiation. The schedule was designed to minimize interference with the therapeutic effects of the chemotherapy.

Practitioner Preparation. At the beginning of each session, we moved into "therapeutic presence" by directing our awareness inward, becoming centered, grounded, moving into and attuning to the subject's field, and setting the work's intention as the subject's "highest good." According to Dora Kunz (2004a), the heart chakra is the locus where the act of centering is sustained, so that all aspects of the work are expressed through the heart chakra via the human attributes of love and compassion. Intent, a fundamental component of Healing Touch, is thought to be a potent healing force which initiates a flow of subtle energy that directly or indirectly influences desired outcomes (Bartlett, 2007; McTaggart, 2008). Intentions are thought patterns which radiate out from a person in wavelike patterns. The amplitude of the wave depends on the intensity of the pattern and is modulated by the degree of focus or intention (Kunz & Peper, 1985). Further, the effectiveness of a healer is dependent on the "strength and clarity of [the healer's] intentionality" (Kunz, 2004b, p. 201).

Magnetic Clearing. Before we could connect or clear the energy of the patients, their physical bodies and energy fields needed to be reconnected. This was done using the *Magnetic Clearing* technique. It usually took about 10 to 12 passes, starting about 24 to 36 inches above the head and continuing over the body to the feet. The energy below the feet was then raked into or gently pushed back into the physical body. The lower portion usually only took a few passes for it to reconnect. When the reconnection occurred, the energy field was intact around the physical body, color returned to the subjects' faces, their eyes became brighter, and proprioception returned (as evidenced by their ability to tell where their feet were without looking at them). Many would comment, "I am back." We then continued *Magnetic Clearing* for at least 30 passes to clear the subject's field of emotional and physical debris.

The most energetically congested area was the pelvis, the cervical area receiving radiation. Although congestion was usually also felt in the chest and abdomen areas, it was not felt to be as dense as that in the pelvis. Our pre-treatment energy assessment of the chakras with a pendulum always found the second chakra energy still, and commonly the energy of the third chakra, the solar plexus, was also still. These observations are consistent with 1) the impact of pelvic radiation on the sacral area (second chakra), and 2) the transforming function of the solar plexus (third chakra) of converting prana into the body's vital energy (Kunz, 2004c). The increased energy demands to repair damaged tissue, and the inflammatory response initiated by the chemoradiation cell damage, could be expected to increase demand on the energy transforming function of the third chakra, thus challenging its function.

Chakra Connection. The next task addressed was reconnecting the body's energy centers, or chakras. When the chakras connected, the patient usually became relaxed. Relaxation tends to expand a person's energy field in all directions as it becomes more energized, balanced and harmonized, allowing one's energy to move more freely (Workman, 2010). Initially it was thought that this technique should be done first. However, the minor chakras of the foot and ankle were not able, or were very slow to connect, when the energy field and the physical body were not integrated. Thus, we found that it was necessary to do *Magnetic Clearing* first.

Energetic siphon (Liver Drain). Since most chemotherapy agents are excreted through the liver, an energetic siphon (*Pain Drain*) was used to accelerate the exit of chemotherapy drugs from the liver. The liver meridian was also drained between the first two toes of the right foot.

Mind Clearing. The subject's cranial and spinal energetic flow was reconnected and rebalanced with the *Mind Clearing* technique. This technique alters the energy flow inside the head, interrupts negative thought patterns, helps refocus the mind, and with the emergence of more positive emotions, promotes relaxation and mental focus. According to Dora Kunz (2004a), opening the energy at the base of the head to the spinal energy flow evokes an immediate relaxation response throughout the entire body, facilitating immune system function and healing. The points at the base of the occipital bones consistently took the longest to open of the 11 sequential *Mind Clearing* positions.

Patients receiving chemotherapy frequently report (1) changes in cognitive function, such as reduced ability to concentrate, memory loss, and difficulty learning new information, and (2) changes in vision, to the extent that they think they need new glasses (Workman, 2010). It was noted that when points just above the ears and up along both sides of the head were opened (energy felt symmetrically pulsing), the subjects reported that their head "cleared" and their ability to think improved. When the energy flow was re-established in points around the eyes, especially the points lateral to the eye, participants usually reported that their vision cleared, and the film in front of their eyes disappeared. According to the Ayurvedic system, points around the eyes specifically influence eye function (Chapman, 1937; Tuwaru, 1995).

Supplemental Techniques

It was noted, in the core energy complexes of all patients, that the Tan Tiens (described below) were congested. In addition, the Hara Line (described below) was interrupted or broken.

Clearing the Tan Tiens. In addition to the more peripheral energy centers, the chakras, there are centralized, or core, energy centers, which are thought to both generate and store life energy (chi or Qi). These centers are referred to as *Tan Tiens* (or *Dantian*). The *Tan Tiens* are thought to be connected to the meridian channels, particularly the eighth Extra-channel (MacRitchie, 1993). When toxins enter the *Tan Tiens*, they need to be cleared in order that energy can flow easily in and out of these centers to support organs and their energy systems. The *Tan Tiens* are thought to act like energy reservoirs and when needed, propel life energy throughout the body, like a pump. The *Tan Tiens*, according to most systems, are located at the navel, the lower abdomen and center of the head (Chia & Chia, 1990; Guorui, 1986; MacRitchie, 1993). Cohen (1997) identifies an additional one in the chest (near the heart area). The microcosmic orbit, composed of the conception (functional) channel (meridian) joined to the governor channel, links these core energy centers with all the vital organs of the body. A fifth energy area connected with the microcosmic orbit is the pole star point located above the head (Chia, 1983). *Etheric Template Clearing* technique was used to clear debris from these five areas.

Hara Line Repair. The second energy complex found disrupted in all patients after their radiation sessions was the *Hara Line*. The *Hara Line*, which originates in a point 3 ½ feet above the head and extends through the center of the body deep into the center of the earth, is thought to be the vibratory life source (Brennan, 1993). This line was always found disrupted in the area which had been radiated. Other sections of the line were frequently disturbed as well. Using *Hand Still* and *Hands in Motion* in a manner developed by Kathy Sinnet (2004), the disrupted areas were held and energized until completion or a settling was felt (usually took less than half of a minute). Flow was then encouraged along the *Hara Line* with *Hands in Motion*.

Techniques to minimize/neutralize iatrogenic effects

The synergistic interaction between chemotherapy agents and radiation therapy results in an enhanced radiation effect. Chemotherapy agents can interfere with some of the enzymes and synthetic mechanisms needed to rejuvenate radiation damaged cells. Although the synergistic effect of radio-chemotherapy is exploited therapeutically, resulting in enhanced disease-free survival, this improvement can inadvertently cause undesirable reactions in healthy tissues, such as the skin, gastrointestinal tract, nerves, lymphoid tissue, and bone marrow (Seung, 2009). When a participant experienced iatrogenic effects, the Healing Touch techniques described below were included in the sessions.

To assist with the reduction of the gastrointestinal (GI) symptoms, Hovland's (2003) *Laser* technique was used to relax the esophageal sphincter, pyloric valve, and/or ileocecal valve until these areas softened and were no longer tender. The patients reported that this changed or muted the GI distress, if not immediately, then within the next few hours.

Neuropathy resulting from chemotherapy most commonly presents in the fingers and toes (Workman, 2010). When participants experienced neuropathy, it was found that the energetic fields of their limbs were not integrated with their physical bodies. Most often the energetic field was in front of the limb. Reconnection was accomplished by gently pushing or raking the energetic field of the appendage back into the physical body. Once reconnected, to reduce neuropathy, the affected areas were drained using the *Pain Drain* technique. Then, using the Healing Touch *Etheric Template Clearing* technique, the areas above the affected part(s) were combed with our fingers until congestion was no longer noted. The patient was also asked to picture the affected body parts as covered with a rose light (rose mitten, rose socks). We also visualized rose light surrounding the affected parts and the nerves innervating those body parts. The rose-colored ray has been proposed as particularly relevant for the nervous system. According to Leadbeater (1927), when nerves are not fully supplied with rose light, the vibration of the nerve becomes intensely irritated.

Two techniques were used to assist those experiencing hot flashes. One was Hovland's (2003) technique called *Endocrine Balance and*

Timing. This technique is similar to the *Chakra Connection*, only it is applied to the endocrine system. The purpose of this technique is to energize, balance, and harmonize the endocrine glands in the body with the master glands (pituitary/hypothalamus). The second technique used was to *Laser* the pituitary reflexology point on the thumb.

Cutaneous sensitivity was minimized by using *Magnetic Clearing* and *Etheric Template Clearing* to remove debris out of the 7 energy layers and core energy centers. Frequently, energy leaks were found in the area that had been radiated. These leaks were repaired using the *Wound Sealing* technique. The *Chakra Connection* could then re-establish the energetic flow to support the health of this organ, the skin.

General clearing and re-energizing techniques supported normal blood cell counts. In addition, when congestion was noted in the spleen area, the *Magnetic* and *Etheric Template Clearing* techniques were used to clear the field above the spleen.

Conclusion

For Healing Touch sessions to become a practical application in a health care setting, we tried to limit the sessions to a relatively brief time frame, while still being able to deliver efficacious results. Therefore, the majority of the sessions were done as a team effort, with two experienced practitioners. This assisted in maintaining a high level of energetic vibration and facilitated quick movement of the energy. The team approach also allowed for techniques such as *Mind Clearing* and the *Pain Drain* to be done simultaneously. Working together facilitated delivery of the *Etheric Template Clearing* activities. Techniques which elicit deep relaxation were done early in the session to facilitate energy movement. The intensive administration (4 times/week post radiation treatments) coupled with immediacy (sessions usually occurred within 10 minutes of completion of the radiation session) allowed for quick correction and re-establishment of normal energy flow before a new pattern of congestion, interruption, and blockages could become established. This may explain why the sessions took less time (moving from an average of 30 minutes to 20 minutes) as the course of the chemo–radiation treatment progressed.

The use of complementary or integrative modalities can help nursing mature in its practice mission, expanding its scope of practice, all of which enhances, rather than conflicts, with professional holistic nursing practice (Hart, Freel, Haylock, & Lutgendorf, 2011). Appropriate integration of complementary care modalities has the potential to enhance the impact of conventional health care, as Florence Nightingale advised, by placing the patient in the best condition for nature to act upon the patient (Nightingale & Barnum, 1992).

Organ Removal and Surgical Transplantation

BY LISA ANSELME, RN, BLS, HN-BC, CHTP/I

The medical specialty of solid organ (for end stage organ disease) and bone marrow/stem cell (used in the treatment of leukemia and blood disorders) transplantation brings the use of Healing Touch concepts of energetic balance, non-attachment, wholeness, and connection into the immediate foreground. These concepts can also apply to other surgeries that remove organs (e.g. hysterectomy) and surgeries that use cadaver tissue (e.g. repair of torn ligaments in the shoulder and knee).

Since the first successful kidney transplant between identical twins in 1954, the means by which transplant recipients achieve balance and acceptance of a solid organ graft or tolerance of bone marrow or stem cell grafts have played a critical role in life expectancy. Donor organs and cells can be gifted by either a living person who is a family member (live-related), friend or stranger (live non-related) or by someone who has died (cadaver). Solid organ living donors can gift one of their kidneys or portions of their livers, lungs, intestines or pancreas. If there is no available living donor, then the default option is cadaver donation.

The patient is referred to a transplant center for medical and psychological evaluation and preparedness. If determined to be a candidate for organ transplantation, the patient is added to the national waiting list. Some sobering facts from the United Network Organ Sharing database are as follows: in the USA alone, one person is listed for transplant every 11 minutes (120 each day), 75 people on the average receive organ transplants each day, and 19 people die each day waiting for a transplant (See United Network Organ Sharing at www. UNOS.org).

Blood and Tissue Typing

In a healthy state, our bodies react and attack foreign objects that are introduced. Our immune system perceives an organ transplant as a foreign object containing "antigens". As a result, we produce "anti" bodies to reject these organs. Thus, the first step in preparing for organ transplantation is the identification and matching of donor and recipient for blood, tissue and immune system components to minimize rejection of the organ and tissue disagreement between donor organ and recipient. Energetically, this is notable in the energy field as the recipient goes on alert and mounts an energetic response through the root (safety and security) and throat (immune system oversight) chakras.

The need for an organ or bone marrow/stem cell transplant occurs when there is a life challenging illness, as in when the patient is receiving artificial life supportive therapy (e.g. dialysis for kidney failure or a Left Ventricular Assist Device for cardiac failure). This is a time of both high anxiety and hope for both the recipient and living donor. Simple full body balancing and *Mind Clearing* techniques are helpful for both potential donor and recipient (and often times a family member), as these techniques support the overall physical, emotional, mental, and spiritual aspects of each person.

Solid Organ Transplant

Live Donor Preparation. My experience in this area is the result of working in the transplant setting for 20 years as an RN Certified Clinical Transplant Coordinator and as a Certified Healing Touch Practitioner. During this time, I developed an understanding of the energetics of this complex situation and learned which interventions would best serve the transplant population. My approach includes working with the donor and recipient as well as with the organs/cells.

Once it has been determined that there is a potential match and a willing live-related or non-related donor (and the green light has been given to proceed with transplantation), the energetic preparation can become more specific. The recommended techniques to prepare the donor for surgery include full body techniques (*Chakra Connection, Magnetic Clearing*) that serve to balance, clear, support and calm, and *Mind Clearing* to quiet the mind. These techniques are particularly helpful, especially immediately prior to the surgery in which the organ or cells will be harvested.

During the Healing Touch session, the donor organ is isolated (if kidney) or cells (if liver, lung, intestines or pancreas), and if appropriate, the donor can be supported in having an internal "conversation" or visualization experience with the organ or cells. The donor can express appreciation for the amazingly beautiful strength and support that the organ or cells provided and tell them that now they will be given the opportunity to gift life and support for a future recipient. The organ or cells are invited to come into a consciousness of service and harmony as they will be integrated into a collegial relationship with their recipient's cells and tissues and provide the gift of life to this new person.

In addition, I energetically hold the organ or cells to clear any antigen-producing virus, bacteria, or aversive memory, so that they come in "clean" with intention to avoid introduction of further challenge to the recipient. Through intention, I place this work into future time, so that this energetic clearing occurs after organ harvest and prior to introduction into the recipient's body (often during a time of flushing the organ and walking it across the hall to the next operating room).

Along with patient education related to post-operative care, I often teach the donor a centering visualization, transforming and relaxed breathing, and *Pain Drain* to assist in pain management following surgery. I reassure the donor that along with standard medical care, we will be working to support the flow of energy and comfort post-operatively and provide energetic support to facilitate healing and recovery. Of note is that in many cases, the recipient frequently feels greatly improved post-operatively with the newly functioning organ, whereas the donor's recovery often carries some grieving for the loss of the organ/tissue and often involves a more extensive surgery.

Cadaver Donor Preparation. With the exception of connective tissue donation (e.g. ocular, bone, skin) that can be harvested, preserved, and banked, solid organ donation is generally from someone who has died due to a sudden trauma, such as an automobile accident, that resulted in irreversible brain death. In the process of preparing the organ for donation, there is acknowledgment of physical and energetic shock to the donor and organs.

Upon learning that the recipient has been called in to begin preparation for transplantation, I initiate distance work upon the cadaver donor. In this process I ask permission of the donor from my spirit to his or her spirit to work energetically, and await consent which I perceive as a sense or feeling of it being okay, rather than a sense of resistance. Upon achieving consent, I set a *hara line* and come into the highest vibration I am capable of through *spinning my chakras* at a very high frequency and *expanding my core star* to the fullest. I then begin to work with the donor, inviting all the available energies to assist in this process and surround this donor with infinite love. My intention is to offer and assist in clearing the traumatic event, as well as the donor's disorientation and suffering, ensuring throughout this time that I am coming from a place of deep compassion and honor. I thank the donor for the gift of life, and acknowledge that his or her spirit is entrusted to the care of guides and Source. I invite his or her precious heart to deeply forgive any injury that has occurred throughout life. I then direct my attention to the individual organs and tissues; acknowledge them, hold them energetically, and offer clearing of any antigen—producing virus, bacteria, or aversive memory as described above, while sharing that he/she is being given the opportunity to continue life for others.

Recipient Preparation. Immediately prior to transplant surgery, the best techniques for Healing Touch sessions include preparatory full body techniques that balance, clear, energize, and calm. I then invite the recipient to dialogue with his or her physical body, informing the body that it will be welcoming a new collection of cells that are being gifted to assume the workload of the diseased organ. We engage a consciousness of deep gratitude and compassion for the donor and the new organ, whether from a living or cadaver source. I encourage the recipient to remain open to receive all support through the surgery and beyond, such that the recipient/body enters into a new relationship and harmony with the donor's healthy organ. Then together, we invite the wisdom of the cells to enter into a balance of perfect vigilance within the immune system and give protection against harm through external threats (e.g. infectious agents), while coming into harmony with the donor cells.

Post-operative: Living Donor. If possible, I continue to work energetically with the donor within the recovery room or upon admission to either the Surgical Intensive Care Unit (SICU) or surgical unit. The donor, having just undergone major surgery with general anesthesia, will need acute post-operative care, including pain management (address any *Pain Ridge* or *Spike* exiting from the surgical area), detox and clearing of anesthesia (*Magnetic Clearing*), suturing and sealing the surgical area (*Ultrasound, Laser, Sealing a Wound*), and then balancing and energizing the energy centers and field (*Chakra Connection*). In addition, even though an organ or component of an organ is now absent, the energetic organ remains in the energetic blueprint. *Pain Drain* over the fully or partially dissected organ assists in reducing inflammation, while *Hands Still* serves to support and energize it and encourage regeneration. I then make sure that the organ is linked up with the surrounding energy centers within the energetic blueprint, which seems to significantly reduce the pain associated with the donor organ removal and appears to support healing of the remaining tissue. Follow-up sessions address any ongoing pain issues, and overall balancing and support assists in enhancing recovery and reducing risks of complications (such as infection).

Post-operative: Recipient. The recipient has also undergone surgery with general anesthesia. If possible, I continue to work with him or her within the recovery room or upon admission to the intensive care unit. I also move into the energetic blueprint and weave the donor organ/tissue into the blueprint matrix and connect it to the rest of the field. In addition to needing acute post-operative care (as described above), the recipient's cells now must begin to enter into harmony with the transplanted organ cells. By optimizing the recipient's energy system, we can hopefully optimize the utilization of necessary anti-rejection medications, while minimizing their side effects and risks of immunosuppression (infection).

Bone Marrow or Stem Cell Transplant

Pre-transplant. In a healthy person, bone marrow makes young cells (called stem cells) that differentiate into mature white blood cells to fight infection, red blood cells to carry oxygen to other cells, or platelets to help the blood to clot. Stem cell transplant or bone marrow transplant (BMT) is utilized when a disease state causes the bone marrow to fail to produce blood cells, to produce excess blood cells, or to produce too many immature cells. BMT is also used to rescue cancer patients who have been treated with aggressive doses of chemotherapy that have destroyed their bone marrow. Some diseases that may be treated with BMT include leukemia, aplastic anemia, Hodgkin or non-Hodgkin lymphoma, or multiple myeloma.

Of note is that in a BMT, the situation of rejection and attack is the opposite of what occurs in a solid organ transplant. New bone marrow or stem cells are infused into the recipient, and these donor cells are capable of mounting an immunologic attack against the recipient's body. The energetic and immunologic task here, then, is for the new bone marrow to recognize the recipient as non-threatening and enter into harmony with it.

Pre-transplant Recipient. In order to prepare for BMT, the recipient will be tissue and blood typed to determine potential donors. Prior to transplant, the recipient undergoes a process called "conditioning" and receives a high or moderate dose of chemotherapy to either destroy cancer cells (in patients with cancer) or to disarm the immune system (in people with autoimmune or marrow related diseases). This results in the recipient being unable to form new blood cells or mount an immune response to outside threats. If the person is elderly or fragile, he or she may only receive low dose conditioning, which will weaken the bone marrow and immune system but will not destroy it.

Energy work at this point necessitates supporting the recipient's energetic boundaries (reinforcing the 7th layer of the field), as the immune system no longer has the means to mount a response to any external threat. Also important is the strengthening, balancing and energizing of the energy centers and field. At this point, I utilize gentle, full body techniques, such as *Magnetic Passes: Hands in Motion/Hands Still* and *Chakra Connection* along with pain management techniques.

Pre-transplant Donor at Harvest. The donor source may be from the patient (self-autologous transplant), in which the patient receives stem cell mobilization/collection or bone marrow harvesting to preserve his or her own marrow prior to receiving conditioning. In this case, there is not a risk of rejection of one's own reintroduced marrow following transplant.

The donor source may also be from a related donor (often a sibling) or non-related donor. The closer the match is, the better the chance of a successful transplant, and less the risk of the new bone marrow cells attacking the recipient host (known as graft vs. host disease).

There are two options for donating the bone marrow or stem cells. Either blood stem cells are non-surgically removed from the blood via a needle in their arm, or under anesthesia, a needle is inserted into the back of the pelvic bone and liquid marrow is withdrawn. Support during the process of donation includes pain management techniques, sealing of the needle site, clearing of anesthesia (*Magnetic Clearing*) if a bone marrow donation, and *Chakra Connection* to support replenishment of the immune system marrow cells.

Recipient in a Post Bone Marrow or Stem Cell Transplant. The recipient receives the bone marrow or stem cell transplant through a central or peripheral IV within several days after conditioning. It typically takes 2–4 weeks for the cells to populate and grow within the bone marrow ("engraftment") and allow the bone marrow and immune system to recover. During this time, the recipient remains vulnerable to infection and in the case of an allogenic (other than self) transplant, is vulnerable to the new bone marrow cells attacking the recipient's organs. Energetically, the task once again is for harmonic balance to support the successful engraftment of new transplant cells into the bone marrow and for the recipient or host's physical and energetic body to tolerate the new cells. This can be assisted through some of the techniques used in solid organ transplantation, as described above, and include having conversation with the transplant cells prior to their introduction. The conversation can include informing the transferred cells of their new task of successfully carrying oxygen, assisting with clotting, and warding off external threats outside this new physical body. I energetically work to have the recipient come into a "neutral" energetic state, one that is non-threatening to the new transplant cells. From a soul level, this is akin to the recipient entering into a state of calm disarmament, while the donor transplant cells enter a state of high level discernment. As we set intention for the highest good, we hold space for this unique tolerance and for a truly blended human being to emerge and thrive.

Conclusion

Working with individuals undergoing the process of transplantation affords us a rich opportunity to witness firsthand how balance, harmony, cooperative relationships, and clarity are necessary for life itself. This is true at the most basic micro cellular level, as the transplanted cells must enter into harmony with the recipient cells to sustain life, and at the macro level, as we must find those same qualities throughout our body, mind, emotions, and spiritual levels and in our relationships with others and the planet itself. As we work with these principles and qualities, we are given the opportunity to examine and strive for greater embodiment and expression of these qualities within ourselves and to appreciate this precious gift of life.

Emotional/Mental Health Issues

While all aspects of healing involve an emotional component, as noted in the above scenarios, psychological issues can be predominant conditions requiring modified treatment, careful boundaries, and additional training. The use of Healing Touch with patients who have debilitating emotional or mental health issues must be carefully considered for the client's health and safety.

Healing Touch in Psychiatric or Psychological Issues

BY MARY SZCZEPANSKI, BSN, MS, HN-BC, CHTP/I

Healing Touch is a supportive approach for many individuals with psychiatric diagnoses or other psychological issues, but Healing Touch interventions should be used with caution. Offering techniques for general comfort and relief of pain and anxiety are generally useful for clients with depression, anxiety, trauma, addictions, insomnia, grief, and physical pain. In some cases, it may be necessary to develop a trusting relationship before introducing Healing Touch. While Healing Touch may help prevent individuals from getting upset and losing control, patients who are acutely angry, manic, or agitated are not good candidates. In those cases, the individuals may have difficulty hearing or understanding an explanation of Healing Touch. Physical closeness might escalate the agitation; those who are psychotic, with disorganized thinking and delusions, may be at risk for misinterpreting the actions of the Healing Touch practitioner. For example, the Healing Touch experience could be incorporated into the patient's paranoid delusion and interpreted as something malicious.

My personal experience using Healing Touch in the psychiatric setting provides a variety of situations for its use in clinical application. I am providing some examples that demonstrate the versatility of the work.

A patient hospitalized on the Mental Health Unit had anxiety and pain from physical injuries to her neck. She had experienced massage and several types of energy work in the past. She requested Healing Touch for pain relief, although she also had many concerns about her hospitalization and issues that were related to moving to a new location. On assessment, her field was uneven and depleted in places. She described being frustrated about her situation. I began with a *Mind Clearing* to ease her tensions. She relaxed as her field readily absorbed the energy. Next I did a *Chakra Connection*; followed by *Ultrasound*, *Laser*, and *Pain Drain* to the neck. Her pain level was reduced by several points on the pain scale. Her voice was calmer; she was able to smile and express gratitude.

I met with another individual at my private practice office. For various reasons, she missed the first 3 appointments that she had set up. She wanted Healing Touch for knee surgery that had been performed several weeks previous. I used *Mind Clearing*, *Chakra Connection* (hands on with her permission), and pain relief techniques for the knee. During the session, it was difficult for her to rest quietly. Her speech was somewhat pressured as she described scenarios of dysfunctional relationships, making it clear to me that she had periods of mental instability. She eventually revealed that she had been diagnosed with Bipolar Disorder. She came to my office for one additional session, after several more cancellations. She reported some pain relief in her knee and had minimal relaxation by the end of each session.

The next time I saw her was on the Mental Health Unit. She had been admitted to the hospital in an agitated, manic state and was verbally abusive to staff. She was surprised to see me working on this unit and asked to receive Healing Touch. When we discussed it, I told her it would be better to wait until she was more stable. Due to her mania, she had set up many complicated and entangled communications with various staff members, some of which seemed manipulative. I did not want to have Healing Touch become part of her system of dysfunctional interactions.

Weeks later, after assessing that her behavior had slowed down and she was able to sit in one place for a short interval, I agreed to give her a brief Healing Touch treatment. This time, I used *Magnetic Passes/Hands in Motion* with the patient sitting in the chair. The session duration was about 10 minutes, while I carefully evaluated how she tolerated it. I kept a clear boundary, since she was still not completely stabilized. I did this by explaining we would only have a brief session, minimizing touch, having her sit in a chair, and encouraging her to focus on positive thoughts and releasing upsetting memories. The only physical contact was holding her shoulders to ground her at the end. She was grateful for the treatment and rested on her bed afterward.

Following this hospitalization, she called me to ask if she could take Healing Touch classes. I told her that giving energy treatments to others required having the discipline to stay grounded and to be able to focus on the needs of another person. I invited her to take any introductory classes I teach, but to focus on her own healing.

Addictions

There are many possible applications for Healing Touch when working with clients with addictions. Initially, Healing Touch can help relieve the physical withdrawal symptoms of alcohol and drugs, as well as decrease fear and anxiety. Some types of drugs, such as benzodiazepines, can take weeks to detoxify from the body. Even as patients are leaving the detox unit and entering the next phase of their treatment, the effect of withdrawal may persist. As treatment progresses, Healing Touch can help manage the stress of re-entering life without the use of addictive substances. Additionally, some individuals have physical pain, and they may or may not be able to continue using pain medications.

One evening a volunteer joined me in giving treatments to young women who came for a special women's recovery program. Three women requested treatments, mostly for stress or pain. They all left with relief of their symptoms, and reported feeling more whole.

Holistic Healing Groups

Both on the Mental Health Unit and in the Substance Abuse Treatment Program, holistic healing groups provide an opportunity for teaching self-care, such as setting intentions, breathing exercises for relaxation, using guided imagery tapes, and the *Self Chakra Connection*. The group setting can provide self-care teaching to a greater number of recipients than might otherwise have access to treatments.

Trauma Informed Care

The Center for Mental Health Services National Center for Trauma Informed Care has indicated that there is a near universal prevalence of trauma in individuals seeking services in the public health system. Professionals serving this population are encouraged to address trauma issues regardless of the cause. These issues could include, for example, child abuse or neglect, domestic violence, sexual assault, war, terrorism, or natural disasters. Trauma survivors experience a wide range of symptoms, including flashbacks, mood and cognitive disruptions, physical pain, relationship disturbances, and spiritual disconnection. They may have physical problems resulting from injuries or illnesses, such as fibromyalgia and immune disorders, related to cumulative, long term stress.

Many of these survivors are treated by multiple care practitioners who offer a host of approaches, yet the survivor may still suffer. Healing Touch provides an excellent adjunct to medical treatments or psychotherapy and can often release the energy of traumatic experiences without re-traumatizing the client. Caution should be taken to establish a trusting relationship, and practitioners should observe closely how a client is tolerating the treatment. Short treatments with non-contact techniques may work best at first.

Case Example. I had re-connected with an old friend who I had not seen in years. As I described my Healing Touch work, she was interested in receiving a treatment. I began with a *Chakra Connection*. As I came to the major chakras, she began to sob. I checked in with her to be sure she was tolerating this, and she wanted to continue with the treatment. She then proceeded to describe different memories of abuse that surfaced and were released at each chakra. She cried loudly, as if each event was being repeated. I held each chakra until she was finished releasing the painful emotions held there. I marveled at how she stayed in control of the session and directed me to continue. When the session was completed, she felt relaxed and appreciated the release of these memories.

Healing Touch can provide relaxation and relief of some symptoms for appropriately chosen clients suffering with psychiatric conditions or psychological problems. It is also rewarding for practitioners to be able to offer a comforting approach when individuals might feel stressed and desperate.

Depression

By Rosalie Van Aken, RN, PhD, CHTP/I

In 2004, I completed a study on the experience of Healing Touch for people with moderate depression (Van Aken, 2004). I used the self-administered Beck Depression Inventory (BDI) to establish the presence of moderate depression, which is assessed as between 20 and 30 points. Although the purpose of this research was not intended to prove that there would be a reduction in depressive symptoms, it was interesting to note that all of the participants demonstrated a reduced BDI score at the completion of the research, and it is important to note the changes. The largest change was 27 points, and the smallest was 10 points. The energy patterns presented, particularly in the energy field, were also very interesting. In the early sessions, all energy fields were absent around the body, except for a mushroom type formation at the top of the head. This began to change around the third session (Van Aken & Taylor, 2010). I will outline the experience of one of the participants from the study as an example of working with a client with moderate depression.

Jasmine was 35 years old at the time of data collection and worked on a casual basis in the retail industry. At a festival where I was demonstrating Healing Touch, she stated her reason for volunteering to receive a session was to gain "insight into and healing of my depression." She found some relief in just this one demonstration session of Healing Touch.

The most recent significant event for Jasmine was the ending of a relationship prior to the study. On a physical level, she shared that some of her health issues were fairly frequent infections, pain in the joints, and lack of regular exercise. She liked reading channeled spiritual books and listening to guided visualizations; she had recently enjoyed a 10 day Vipassana meditation course. She reported feeling very little trust since her best friend died and her partner left her, but she said she has experienced the presence of God through the beauty of nature. Jasmine looked tired and thin. Her hair was lank and a little greasy, and she showed very little facial expression. She scored 29 on the BDI. She said she felt totally stressed, out of body, and was looking forward to Healing Touch.

When assessed with the pendulum, the legs, root and sacral chakras were horizontal, and the solar plexus and throat were elliptical. The energy field around the body was absent, with a large field over the head (Van Aken, 2004, p. 117) until the shoulders and then large over the head (a common pattern with all participants of the study). There was also coolness noted over the liver, spleen, heart and throat. The techniques in the first session were *Chakra Connection, Magnetic Clearing,* and *Hands Still* over liver/spleen and heart/throat. After the session, all chakras were open, and the energy field was a more regular shape. Jasmine stated that she felt more relaxed and grounded, with a slight increase in energy.

At the next session, Jasmine still looked tired and somewhat disheveled. She said she felt worried, upset, fearful, and very angry. All chakras were horizontal. The energy field was absent to the shoulders, as in the first session. A coolness was noted over the chest and tingling over the abdomen and legs that appeared to be related to the energy beginning to move. *Hands Still* technique on the feet was followed by *Magnetic Clearing. Hands in Motion* over the whole body and *Modified Mind Clearing* were done to balance the chakras and clear the field. All chakras were open, and the field was clear. Jasmine said she felt quiet.

Although Jasmine still looked tired, her grooming was much improved at the third session. She said she felt unemotional, thoughtful, and task-oriented. In the pendulum assessment, the sacral, solar plexus, heart, and throat were horizontal. The energy field remained absent to the shoulder. There was some thick energy over the abdomen, with tingling over the legs noted from the hand scan. *Hands Still* on the feet, followed by *Chakra Connection, Magnetic Clearing* and *Modified Mind Clearing,* were completed again to balance the chakras and clear the field. The chakras were open, and the energy field was clear with a much improved shape. Jasmine said she felt peaceful and open, with more relaxation and balance. This seemed to be the turning point for Jasmine.

At the fourth session, Jasmine looked much brighter but said that she still felt scattered. She was pleased that she had commenced Aikido classes. I noticed that her energy was much stronger. The solar plexus and heart chakras assessed by pendulum were horizontal, with some tingling in the upper chest, and I also felt a tear in the energy field at the back of the heart chakra. During the hand scan, Jasmine said that she felt a "black hole." *Hands Still* on the feet, *Chakra Connection* on the front, and *Magnetic Clearing* on the back were completed. I felt a very big energy shift, and before the session was completed, Jasmine sat up and said, "I feel like a butterfly." All chakras were open, and the field was clearer. Jasmine said she felt slightly out of body, but calm.

Jasmine looked bright and had a bounce in her step at her fifth session and said she felt peaceful and calm. All the chakras were open, with some tingling over the throat. *Hands Still* on feet, *Chakra Connection, Magnetic Clearing,* and *Hands Still* over the high heart and throat were the techniques used to balance the chakras and clear the field. All chakras were still open, and the field was clear. Jasmine stated she felt joyful for the first time in a long time and felt like her mind was clear, with a shift to deeper consciousness.

At the final interview two weeks later, Jasmine looked happy and glowing as she entered the room. Her reassessment with the BDI showed a score of 4, a significant improvement (25 points). Jasmine pinpointed the change to be in session 4, where she felt she had been to the "Temple of the Moon," and she was aware of making a reconnection at that time. She felt that the *Magnetic Clearing* and *Modified Mind Clearing* were the most calming and nurturing techniques as they helped her to find "space in between the chatter." When I saw Jasmine casually a year later, she looked wonderful with a wide smile, flowing movements, and a very attractive outfit.

The research I did taught me much about the energetic pattern found in moderate depression. What I noticed was the distinct pattern in the shape of the energy field being nonexistent around the feet, close to the body until the shoulders or above the head, and then a mushroom shape. This seemed to be a disconnection with the earth, others, spirit, and oneself created by this pattern. Healing Touch Level 1 techniques were used to assist participants to reconnect. The sequence of techniques was guided by the assessment. *Modified Mind Clearing* was initially chosen intuitively over *Mind Clearing* as being the most beneficial. During the study, I noted that the participants seemed to relax into *Modified Mind Clearing.* One participant, Hermes, particularly enjoyed *Modified Mind Clearing* and commented the experience was like "resting on a cloud of loving fingertips" and "lying on a marshmallow mattress" (Van Aken, 2004, p.121).

The Effects of Disasters and Physical Trauma on the Energy System

While physical and mental health issues and medical procedures can cause trauma and disruption of the energy system, external forces, such as natural or manmade disasters, and physical traumas, create a different scenario energetically. These situations affect not only those who are directly impacted but also first responders, family members, the surrounding community, and depending on the severity, may have global impact that compromises the earth, resources, and the plant and animal kingdoms. These external force issues are explored in the following section.

For those who feel drawn to the site of a disaster to offer your services, it is recommended that as a practitioner, you have a connection and training through a first responder agency in order to have clearance to be there (and so not add to the chaos). Many well-meaning and enthusiastic practitioners and volunteers have been turned away from a disaster area because they were not part of a system and "in the way." Being farther afield from the disaster site, or linking with other groups, may be better received. Distance Healing (explained at the end of this chapter) may be employed as well.

When working closely within traumatic situations, the practitioner must be aware of the potential for "compassion fatigue" or burn out. When hearing the stories of other's trauma, the same neurotransmitters running in the body of the client can be triggered in the practitioner. This is similar to how visualization works to create relaxation, but has the opposite effect. Re-telling the trauma may be useful initially, but repeating the story can be re-traumatizing for the client. Caution must be used in these situations, and practitioners must allow the energy session to do the work.

Healing Touch in Times of Natural and Other Disasters

By Mary J. Frost, RN, BSN, MS, HNB-BC, CHTP/I

There are a variety of subtle and powerful natural and human events happening daily on this planet that affect not only the personal biofields of individuals but also those of multiple kingdoms, including animal, insect, and plant. Ultimately the effects ripple throughout the bodies of water, rocks, and minerals; man-made and geologic structures; and across the globe. These "disastrous" events have far-reaching impact on us as individuals, families, communities, regions, and countries. This is not unusual, as we are all connected energetically, and our systems are inevitably intertwined. How many of us have been personally affected—or known someone who has been—by a flood, fire, hurricane, typhoon, earthquake, cyclone, tornado, loss of power, shooting, bombing or other large-scale or single incident? We can even be gravely affected by watching or listening to news reports or stories of such events. Even though our resulting individual energetic patterns will change and vary depending on many variables and our individual relationships to each of these events, we all can be or are influenced in some way.

There are also collective emotional responses to these events in varying degrees, such as shock, sadness, fear, loss, depression, hopelessness, and unsettled dreams or moods. The root chakra is often disturbed and compromised to some degree when we feel threatened, our safety is at risk, or our personal lives are turned upside down, the world as we knew it is no more, and the future is full of unknowns. The entire chakra system can go out of balance, become misaligned, shut down, or have widely diverse swings. Our energy fields may become drained or depleted, compressed, twisted, or even shattered. Many of the changes to the energy system and fields remain long after the event has passed (Slater, 2004).

280

Reflections of Hurricane Katrina and the Power of Healing Touch

On August 29, 2005, my world did turn upside down. I was living in Waveland, Mississippi, a quiet, small town on the southern United States' coast, just two blocks from the Gulf of Mexico beach. Hurricane Katrina had formed to a Category 5 velocity and was on a course that would bring it straight to the border area between Mississippi (MS) and Louisiana (LA). Since Waveland is low and is the first beach town adjacent to this area of direct hit, we suffered a 32 foot surge of sea water, or tsunami, which caused an almost complete annihilation of all structures and infrastructure, with much loss of life. The entire Gulf Coast area was affected up to 250 miles inland. The New Orleans levee system failed, and the city filled with flood waters; 1,500 persons lost their lives from the surge and winds, and many more died from secondary effects in the weeks and months that followed. The destruction was vast and unprecedented. We watched the aftermath in horror on TV at a motel where we had evacuated to safety. Immediately, I was in a state of disbelief at the enormity of the destruction, yet I held out the hope that my house was still standing, that our friends who stayed behind were safe, and that our cat had survived. I had begun the initial stages of the grief process while witnessing the loss of my greater community of New Orleans, where I had worked and lived in years past and still had many friends. Media focus was on New Orleans and the tragedy unfolding there, and as no news came in from the MS gulf coast initially, I could be in denial. Later as the truth became apparent, we realized we could not go home. We had no home, no jobs, and precious few belongings—only those we had in a suitcase or thrown hurriedly into the car prior to the quick departure.

The lessons I had learned and integrated throughout 15 years of studying and teaching Healing Touch, receiving Healing Touch sessions, reading diligently from the Healing Touch reading list and beyond, and most especially, developing close relationships with other Healing Touch practitioners, were invaluable to me at the time of this life-changing experience. The depth of understanding and knowledge absorbed during those years guided me. For this I am eternally grateful.

I discovered I had developed a source of resilience from all aspects of my Healing Touch experience as well as my spiritual life, and I turned to my Healing Touch community in time of need.

When we left the motel after a few days, we landed in Baton Rouge, LA, where I spent almost six months at the homes of two dear Healing Touch friends and colleagues. I attended the Healing Touch International Conference in the midst of the sheltering tall pines of Breckenridge, Colorado and was lifted up by and floated in the healing energy of these loving souls who came together at the annual gathering. I could be vulnerable and cry and be cared for, a balm for my grieving and aching Spirit. My cellular phone was inoperable, signal towers were all downed, and I had no news of my best friend and neighbors who stayed behind. Unsettled but safe, the lesson of impermanence and the lesson of being in the moment I had read about had come home to me to be practiced and lived.

Core Concept: Cultivating Resilience

"We have many ways of overcoming adversity. Resilience is the capacity to adapt successfully in the face of threats or disaster. People can improve their capacity for resilience at any time of life." This quote comes from the transcript of The Public Broadcasting Service (PBS) documentary, *This Emotional Life*, presented in 2009. Ways to contribute to resilience included the following: maintaining close relationships with family and friends, having a positive view of self and confidence in our strengths and abilities, having the ability to manage strong feelings and impulses, developing good problem-solving and communication skills, feeling in control, seeking help and resources, seeing self as resilient (rather than as a victim), coping with stress in healthy ways and avoiding harmful coping strategies (such as substance abuse), helping others, and finding positive meaning in life despite difficult or traumatic events.

I realized that Healing Touch as a therapy and practice provides a source to develop these qualities and is a brilliant path to empowerment. The Healing Beyond Borders (Healing Touch International, Inc.) Core Values of integrity, heart-centeredness, respect for self and others, service, community, and unconditional love are woven within the strong character fabric offered in the PBS documentary list of factors. These core values provided me with a perspective to build on an intrinsic inner strength gained by following Healing Touch self-care, *Self Chakra Connection*, and other practices, such as *Hara Alignment* and *Hara Alignment Meditation,* on a daily basis. The conference *Resilience: Strength Through Compassion and Connection* sponsored by the Tulane University School of Social Work that was held in New Orleans, LA in May of 2013, hosted His Holiness, The XIV Dalai Lama. He offered many words of wisdom and insight, including these: "When we meet real tragedy in life, we can react in two ways—either by losing hope and falling into self-destructive habits, or by using the challenge to find our inner strength." A strong lesson had been provided when I was instantly relieved of material belongings, community, jobs, friends, and all obligations except survival.

Post Katrina, I signed on to become a paid Stress Management Provider within the Greater Baton Rouge Community through a grant from the Federal Emergency Management Agency (FEMA). However, I was temporarily weakened and energetically disabled from multiple losses and grief; my immune system was compromised, and I became ill. I was unable to practice my Healing Touch work. I learned I needed to receive care for myself from my peers, who held a framework of hope and compassion for me. This assisted me to reconnect to and regain that which dwelled within me. As a result, I am stronger and more resilient, and I am a better therapeutic practitioner. I now insist on time to balance myself and participate only in social events that bring joy, happiness, and meaning. I do not value "things" so much, but people and relationships are most important, as is the natural world and serving others.

Healing Touch Practitioners: Working within the Community Post Katrina

Many lessons were learned about the delivery of care from this catastrophe. In the weeks that followed Hurricane Katrina, as well as the advent of a second hurricane, Rita, that struck less than a month later and disabled and flooded several southwestern LA parishes, even more citizens were displaced and homeless or suffered countless losses and needs. The Red Cross and FEMA had been mobilized to provide for basic needs, and citizens from across the country and the world arrived with aid, sent care packages, and gave construction and cleanup assistance. They were still coming eight years later. We needed everyone for conditions so drastic. The new normal was—there was no normal. That was our catch phrase. If you saw something that needed to be done, there was no one to give you permission; you just did it. Leaders spontaneously arose on every block. If you had, you gave.

Michal Curry, Certified Healing Touch Practitioner and her friend, Jo Hanna, massage therapist, garnered a massage table and days after the hurricane showed up at the evacuee shelter in Gonzales, LA, a large center that housed hundreds of displaced persons from New Orleans. They set up outside the building under a pecan tree, procured a couple of folding chairs from inside the shelter, and announced that they were providing free treatments. They worked for several hours and moved the table to follow the shade, as the summer heat was still quite intense. Michal describes the resulting activity as follows:

> The first several weeks only children came out to see what we were doing. As they waited for the massage, I asked them if they would like to "relax and let go." If they said "yes," I did the *Amygdala Connection* with them. The *Amygdala Connection* is a helpful energy technique for people who have experienced trauma. The children were very receptive and open to this energy work. It took about 5 minutes to do this technique, whereas with an adult it took about 15 minutes. Then about the third week, the older children and young adults (12–25) came out to us. It wasn't until the fourth or fifth week that the older adults and parents were even able to come outside and receive a treatment. I found the *Amygdala Connection* perfect to use with each person because it facilitated bringing people back into their bodies and grounding them. It

could also aid in releasing stress or trauma from the hurricane experience, and it didn't take long to do.

I have found that this technique follows the neuro-pathways of the "fight-or-flight" response in the body-mind. It begins to "reset" the amygdala gland, which is where this response originates. [See later in this chapter for a full description of the technique.] It can create a deep sense of calm, peace, and grounding. I have been using this in my trauma clinic—and it is usually the first technique that I use on a client—because I discovered it opens up all chakras immediately to allow for deeper healing to occur. I teach this to my clients so they can use it on themselves.

Another volunteer project that began out of a perceived need was organized by some massage therapists, Healing Touch practitioners, and other energy workers. They arrived on a regular basis at the headquarters for emergency first responders at the end of both 12-hour shifts (7 a.m. and 7 p.m. daily) to offer a variety of treatments in massage chairs to the men and women on the "front lines" of the search, rescue, and recovery operations. This was very well-received by grateful and exhausted men and women. About six weeks out from the hurricane events, FEMA awarded grant money to the Louisiana Department of Health and Hospitals and the Office of Behavioral Health to begin a project named, Louisiana Spirit Hurricane Recovery Program, soon nicknamed "Louisiana Spirit". One of the large service providers for this project in the Greater Baton Rouge and Greater New Orleans areas was the Volunteers of America (VOA). One role of the VOA was to provide care in the form of stress management for first and second responders to prevent burnout and compassion fatigue. Several Healing Touch Practitioners and complimentary care providers were hired to provide Healing Touch, massage, aromatherapy, and other modalities in several locations to social workers, counselors, fire fighters, Red Cross staff, and National Guard soldiers.

A nurse who helped to oversee the practitioners taught the *Amygdala Connection* to use as the first energy treatment approach with anyone who practitioners deemed to need it. I introduced this technique to the local area at a conference to raise awareness about delivering care for returning military personnel deployed in the middle-east war zones.

Jill Laroussini, RN, nursing instructor, and student of Healing Touch, tells a story of being with her public health nursing students in the lobby of a Lafayette, Louisiana hotel, where she was showing them how to do simple Healing Touch techniques on a group of evacuees housed there. She made this a part of their class unit on nursing care with the homeless population. She says, "They were able to get quite a different kind of clinical experience that year."

Sue Heldenbrand, CHTP, related that she provided Healing Touch services for a year with the VOA and worked with the *Amygdala Connection* and other Healing Touch techniques, such as *Magnetic Clearing* and *Hands in Motion* for many of all ages who were responders: emergency medical technicians, medical personnel, and church volunteers. Stress was the big presenting challenge for all, and she recalls that some had very "hot" fields. The one situation that she remembers "like it was yesterday," because it really touched her heart, was a case manager who came to her with a special request. She related the following:

> There was a man in his 70's or 80's who was alone in the shelter [Cajun Dome], with no family or friends and no belongings to speak of; his entire domain was a mattress on the floor. He had not been able to sleep for days, and I was asked if I could help him. I helped him get comfortable and performed the Healing Touch technique, *Mind Clearing*, for him and he fell asleep. What a gift I could give him.

Sue also mentioned that she saw many National Guardsmen in their 20's who were greatly affected by what they experienced, but they hesitated to talk with the counselors. However, they would readily get on the tables for Healing Touch and massage. The Lafayette group of healers called their work a "Ministry of Presence."

Another experienced CHTP, Bessie Sennette, resisted becoming involved with the thousands of homeless survivors at the Cajun Dome.

Strong memories of her work during the aftermath of Hurricane Andrew 10 years prior were still too fresh. She found other ways to be a part of the ministry at the Cajun Dome and employed some novel approaches derived from her Healing Touch training. She says, "I declined going to the dome but agreed to do remote work (distance healing) from home. I worked for two hours visualizing an energy grid surrounding the dome and a light column through the center of the grid to anchor it." Bessie then was requested to use her Healing Touch skills taking another approach, by working energetically with the donated bottled water for the survivors. She shares, "Water was stacked from floor to ceiling three rows deep in a room the size of a small warehouse. I placed my hands on each stack one at a time, concentrating on infusing each bottle with energy of peace and calm."

Bessie went on later to become part of the Spirit of Louisiana stress management team and worked 40–50 hours a week for nine months with crisis counselors and first and second responders. One of the most interesting things she reports is as follows:

> I began to notice a pattern developing in the energy field of each crisis counselor that concerned me. The transpersonal point above the crown chakra was separating from the energy body. I find the usual distance between the crown chakra and the transpersonal point is between 12–18 inches. Our clients were presenting with a distance of 3–4 feet between these energy centers. When I was convinced that it was occurring in all of these workers after a period of a month, give or take a few days, I surmised that it was resulting from the ongoing vicarious trauma they were experiencing.

She also noticed that they were presenting with more rapid, shallow breathing patterns, and had begun to neglect themselves as well. In the light of these developments, she began to employ the *Amygdala Connection* technique, but it did not seem to provide long term benefit. Bessie states the following:

I began to develop a technique to reconnect the human biofield to the transpersonal point. After using this process for several weeks the individuals . . . were more aware of their body's needs, and I observed that their breathing was returning to normal rhythms.

Over time it seems that Healing Touch practitioners develop the ability to serve in new and creative ways. This can mean discovering and using "in the moment" energy mediating techniques based in the foundational work of Healing Touch.

Earthquake: Christchurch, New Zealand

In February of 2011, a 6.3 magnitude (Richter Scale) earthquake struck the South Island of New Zealand at Christchurch, right under the center of the city. The disaster claimed 185 lives and severely damaged this second most populated city in the country. Just six months prior, on September 4, 2010, the Canterbury Earthquake (magnitude 7.4) struck nearby and weakened infrastructure and buildings, which then toppled in the subsequent quake. The powerful aftershocks following both of these major quakes continually interrupted recovery efforts and kept the stress level high in the entire population. The aftershocks have continued since that time, with over 2,500 aftershocks being recorded. Certified Healing Touch Practitioner and Instructor, Annis Parker of Christchurch, has this to relate about these events:

> Healing Touch was done but in very different ways. Clearly it wasn't offered or done for many weeks, and in some cases months, due to the death and destruction and the absolute shock. People had nowhere to live, and terror was common due to the continuous aftershocks. However, Healing Touch was done wherever and whenever it was appropriate. For example, I basically balanced the nurses giving chemotherapy in the Oncology Department who were back at work within days, although the hospital was damaged and their own lives a shambles in so many different ways. If one has hands, then I believe it is mandatory to use them in whatever way possible—if this is appropriate for the individual. Just a calming, fast chakra balance was all

one had the time for. To get some part of the energy system "up and running" was vital to assist these people to function at all.

We ultimately had a massive "Heal Christchurch", where we were part of a full weekend event. Many practitioners offered various types of treatments to almost 200 people. We ultimately needed to choose appropriate techniques quickly, as time was of the essence, and we were working in chairs. We Healing Touch folks found ourselves working "flat-out" because no one else was doing energy work, and we were "picking up the pieces" for so many. Many times upon assessment, there were absolutely no active auric/ energy field, active chakras, or functional Hara Line. Therefore, some energy treatment strategies were to open and "drain" the root chakra and use *Full Body Connection* and *Hara Line Connecting* to help hold the subtle structures. *Ultrasound* was also brought into use, along with the occasional *Hands in Motion,* but not until the very end of the session.

For a long time after the big quake, grounding people and taking them into voice guided meditation was the best thing to do—along with listening, listening, and listening again. Helping persons identify what was most important in life also became a crucial component of everything we did. To ground and connect people to the core of the planet helps them to be able to function when they don't trust the earth at all and disconnect with every aftershock.

We are now nearly three years out from the major quake, and the citizenry of Christchurch is still suffering from post-stress. People are turning up in our clinics in droves now.

Conclusion

There are many ways to serve with Healing Touch when a disaster strikes a community or region. It is necessary that the practitioners are taken care of and have what they need to recharge, rest, and replenish nutritionally in order to stay strongly grounded and maintain higher frequency energies to help stabilize others.

If traveling into a disaster area, volunteers must be self-contained with portable accommodations, vehicles, fuel, food, water, etc. and not depend on locals to supply needs. Agencies that are experienced and equipped to handle organizational needs can offer the best means through which to work and become integrative partners for a sustained period. Practitioners must assess client needs quickly, provide simple, effective treatment, adapt to the environment, and refer those who require basic survival needs to others. There is room for all groups and individuals to provide care in many capacities, and I saw and felt many miracles take place post Katrina through presence and caring. Hand-made quilts from the church ladies in Montana were a hit in my community and provided a source of softly radiant security during long, dark nights in temporary housing.

The Mobile, Alabama Society for the Prevention of Cruelty to Animals (SPCA) came to my town of Waveland and provided pet food, carry cages, and animal rescues for many traumatized four-legged survivors. They reunited many pets with their owners and filled many hearts with joy and healing. My own grief turned into ecstatic happiness when my beloved cat was returned to me two weeks after the hurricane broke our house into bits and washed it over the landscape. My "White Kitty" and I had a loving, healing energy treatment exchange, softer and sweeter and more "purrfect" than any other!

Healing Touch in Disasters

By Diane Wind Wardell PhD, RN, WHNP-BC

A variety of natural and human events can affect the environmental and personal field of individuals, families, and communities. Disasters also affect multiple kingdoms, including animal, insect, and plant.

Since all can be influenced, the resulting energetic patterns can vary, depending on individual relationships to each of these. There can also be a collective response to these events, such as a disturbance in the root chakra, as many natural events—floods (water), hurricanes, tornados (wind), and fires—threaten our safety (Slater, 2004).

Practitioners should recognize also that temporary congestion or disturbance in the body or environment can also benefit from thorough cleansing and bringing the energy field back into harmony. This can be most clearly seen in the wake of a forest fire, which through heat stimulates the bursting of dormant seeds into life.

The chakra system can be interpreted in a variety of ways. Rosalyn Bruyere (1989) offers an in-depth explanation on the importance of the root chakra in *Wheels of Light,* including a discussion of its meaning and purpose, and she also gives a brief description of the other chakras. The root is the chakra primarily responsible for our sense of safety and belonging, as it relates to the physical component of our manifestation on earth. The root chakra is elementally related to fire, and it also resonates with the earth. It is responsible for dealing with movement of vital energy (both in and out) and is directly related to our breathing. Observe your clients. How are they breathing? Is it shallow (decreased exchange of life force) or is it deep and sustaining that shows one is fully alive.

The sacral chakra is the emotional chakra and related to water. The overabundance of water that occurs with floods may result in a disturbance of this chakra, with resultant emotionality. Tears that cannot be stopped would be one indication that this chakra has been "flooded" or compromised.

The solar plexus chakra is related to the element of air. In working with those affected by tornados, Slater (2004) found that not only was the root chakra not functioning well, but that many clients complained of feeling dizzy or not being able to get things done; some felt that they were "going in circles." On assessment, it was noticed that there was "rapidly spiraling energy flow, much like the winds of a tornado . . . primarily over the bladder, lungs, sinuses and ventricles in the head" (p.87).

The heart chakra is elementally related to the earth. When the

291

heart is the primary target of disturbance, the sense of loss can be overwhelming. The heart chakra is responsible for transmutation of thoughts and feelings connecting to the throat chakra, where they become words and concepts. Earthquakes create confusion or "shake us up," so that we are left without words to express the dissidence we feel. Repeated quakes de-stabilize further, and can alter not only thoughts but also the functioning of the lower three chakras.

Management

Working with those affected by disasters requires gentleness and conscious, excellent personal grounding. When we have adequate "fire power" from the root, others feel safe in our presence and have enough energy to serve (Bruyere, 1989, p. 169). Basic techniques that create harmony and balance, such as the *Chakra Connection*, can be used in this situation. Additionally, providing support to the affected chakra with *Hands Still* either above, or one *hand above and the other below*, can be helpful. Additionally, it might prove beneficial to connect all the chakras to the root (or problem chakra), both front and back (Slater, 2004). The hara line, which Brennan (1993) describes in *Light Emerging* as being related to intentionality and our soul's purpose, can also be affected. She describes it as a line that runs along the spine, above the head, and deep into the earth. There are several different techniques to repair the hara line. One is described here. If two experienced practitioners are available, repairing the hara line, as stated in Janet Mentgen's unpublished writings, can be implemented as follows (Italicized words have been added to provide clarity):

> Perform the *Chelation* technique (as taught in Level 3) <u>together</u> through the first four layers of the energy field. Then do any specific intervention work needed, *then continue with* the 6th level intervention *simultaneously by both standing together at the head*, holding *the intention of* unconditional love, letting the guides and the higher source complete the healing process. *When this feels complete*, one person continues to hold the hands above the 3rd eye center, (6th chakra) while the second person moves to the feet with

hands moving (drawing) above the body in an egg shape arc to the feet. Again, hold this position until there is *a sense of* completion. Then move to the golden *7th* layer by having one person hold *the cord-like energy of the hara line* off the soles of the feet and one *hold the cord-like energy* off the crown of the head. It is like holding a rope and pulling from each end. This is a golden cord, and it needs to be taut. It takes considerable work and strength to hold this cord. Do not let up and keep yourself very grounded during this process. Hold until there is no longer a sense of pressure and all becomes smooth and easy. Then move to each side *of the person* and hold the edges of the egg shaped *energy field* until there is no longer any pressure or pulling, and all is smooth. End with the usual blessing and release.

Man-Made Disasters

As with natural disasters, the root chakra is often involved in man-made disasters, such as terrorist attacks, mass shootings, and war. The solar plexus, the chakra of "air" and mental quality, can also be involved, as well as the heart, as a function of transformation from throat to thoughts into words and then into actions. People can feel as if they have been "hit hard" by the event (solar plexus metaphor of having no air to breathe), and they also find themselves questioning the reasoning for someone's intention to commit harm. During the Healing Touch session, techniques similar to those used in natural disasters can be used to restore harmony and balance.

Traumatic events can leave long term changes in the personal auric/energetic field if not addressed, and early intervention is helpful. Practitioners are cautioned to recognize the necessity for referral to mental health providers for those with psychological trauma and to offer appropriately guided homework and self-care to support the person's healing. It is not necessary to recreate the scene or event, which in itself can create harm (Naparstek & Scaer, 2004). Instead, one can focus on re-establishing harmony and balance that assists in the healing, and use multiple sessions as necessary.

Amygdala Connection

BY MARTY RATHER, REV., BFA, CHTP/I AND BONNIE
JOHNSON, RN, MS, AHN-BC, CHTP/I

The *Amygdala Connection* technique was created by Marty Rather and Bonnie Johnson, who were inspired by the PBS series presented in 2002, *The Secret Life of the Brain*. This technique, which can be used alone for self-care or administered by a practitioner, is useful for calming chronic anxiety and fear. Its purpose is to de-activate stuck reactive patterns to perceived life-threatening situations. It may be useful for persons with post-traumatic stress syndrome, chronic patterns of fear, or panic and anxiety. The *Amygdala Connection* assists in shifting one out of fear-based energetic patterns by opening energetic pathways for a new response of calm and compassion. It may provide long-lasting changes in one session (Johnson, 2008). How the *Amygdala Connection* works, as described by Rather and Johnson, is as follows:

The Brain Anatomy

Begin by reviewing the relevant anatomical structures in the following drawing. Identify the location of the amygdala, the brain stem, the pre-frontal cortex in the brain, the adrenal glands under the last ribs on the back, and the root chakra.

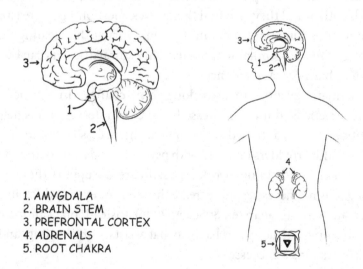

1. AMYGDALA
2. BRAIN STEM
3. PREFRONTAL CORTEX
4. ADRENALS
5. ROOT CHAKRA

The **amygdala**, located just above the brain stem in the middle brain, consists of 2 almond shaped glands and is part of the limbic system, which is the emotional center in the brain. This brain area is part of the first alert response to danger. When danger is perceived, before the person has any conscious awareness of danger, the amygdala has detected and alerted the brain stem to react (fight or flee).

The **brain stem**, located at the base of the brain, is the instinctual, automatic lower brain. We live as long as this part of the brain is functioning. The brain stem controls heart beating and respiratory function as well as automatic muscular reactions. It is the brain stem that sends the message to your leg to stop mid-step in the case of danger.

The **pre-frontal cortex** is the newest, evolutionary and development wise, part of the brain. Often called the upper or higher brain, it processes high intellectual and complex discernment processes. For example, the pre-frontal cortex helps us to differentiate a stick from a snake.

The **adrenal glands** produce the biochemical adrenaline, also known as the fight-or-flight hormone. When the brain stem receives the message of danger from the amygdala, it sends a message to the adrenals to produce and send adrenaline to the body, particularly the muscles, so that the physical body can fight or flee. It takes an increased heart rate, deeper, more rapid breathing, increased blood sugar, and muscle power to fight or flee.

The **root chakra**, or 1st energy center, connects, grounds, and roots us to the energies of the planet earth. The earth has a powerful electro-magnetic field that feeds and nourishes us continuously. The energies that we experience and know as strength, protection, plugged-in, safety, security, aliveness, vitality, and a sure trust in our own abilities and in our environment, are processed by the root chakra. It encodes messages that help us to detect and avoid danger. In the human energy model, the root chakra detects the possible danger first, before the physical body does. The root chakra's job is to ensure that the physical body continues to stay alive.

The Amygdala Connection Technique

The procedure described below is for use on the self. It is easily translated to use by a practitioner on a client. Hold each one of the positions for 1 to 5 minutes.

Preparation

Now that you recognize and understand the anatomy, prepare yourself for giving and receiving the healing energy by eliminating distractions. Quiet yourself. Ask yourself what you would like to receive in this healing. Set the intention for the Highest Good for yourself and the whole universe. Then focus your attention on the healing process.

Procedure

1. Place the fingers of one hand so that tips of fingers point through back portion of top of head toward the **amygdala** in the center of the brain. Make contact with and become aware of the energy of the amygdala by saying **"I am now contacting the amygdala."** Continue for 1 to 5 minutes to allow the healing energies to restore the energies of the amygdala to a harmonious, balanced, soft golden radiance.

2. Keeping **fingers on the amygdala**, place the **other hand on the brain stem** (fingers at base of skull and pointing into and toward the brain). Hold this position until the amygdala and brain stem are quiet and easily **"communicating"** (which may be perceived initially as resistance that then melts away into a sense of calmness).

3. Keeping **fingers on the amygdala**, place the **other hand on the pre-frontal cerebral cortex** (palm of hand at front part of top of head and edge of brow). Hold this position until the amygdala and cerebral cortex are quiet and easily **"communicating."**

4. Keeping **fingers on the amygdala,** move the other hand from the prefrontal cerebral cortex to **one adrenal gland**. Hold this

position until the amygdala and adrenal gland are quiet and easily **"communicating."**

5. **Repeat with the other adrenal gland.**
6. Connect **one adrenal** with **the root chakra**. (Place the hand at the knee area, aiming towards the root chakra. Hands are never placed at the private area of the pelvic floor with clients). Hold this position until the adrenal and root are quiet and easily, **"communicating."**
7. **Repeat with the other adrenal gland.**
8. Leave your hand aimed at the **root chakra** and return fingers of the other hand to the **amygdala.** Hold this position until the amygdala and root are quiet and easily **"communicating."**
9. **Rest both hands on the heart**. Sit quietly until ready to resume normal activities. If working with a female client, keep hands slightly above the body to respect this private area.
10. Be sure to **ground.** When working with clients hold their feet, allowing them to return to a more alert state.

Follow up

The *Amygdala Connection* may be repeated as needed. The energetic healing changes last from one session to next. Each subsequent session starts from the new energetic state, not from the same place as the first session. This healing intervention increases the radiance of compassionate energy (even in previously or logically perceived life-threatening situations). It helps move us out of reacting from our first three chakras and into communicating with the love energy of the heart chakra.

Trauma: When Patterns Are Shattered

By Terry Sparks, JD, MDiv, CHTP/I

As a staff chaplain at the Oklahoma City Veterans Affairs Medical Center in the United States, I offer Healing Touch as part of my chaplain duties. Over the years I have worked with several clients who have post-traumatic stress disorder (PTSD) and other traumatic injuries or who have experienced sexual trauma. Some are veterans of the war in Iraq or the war in Afghanistan and have experienced traumatic brain injury (TBI), the United States military's term for closed head injury (usually from a blast). My purpose here is to share what I have learned in doing Healing Touch with these clients from the perspective of what may have been shattered energetically by trauma. I am not addressing how the brain processes these events or how to approach trauma from a psychological standpoint.

The sense of physical safety often shatters as a result of a major trauma. Patterns of life that were reliable, consistent, and allowed the person to feel in control of a situation have suddenly vanished, or they have become a source of potential danger. Because of this, it is important that the client have as much control as possible over the treatment room environment. Creating the environment, such as to whether the door is open or closed, whether he or she is sitting or lying down, whether the session is with music or quiet, is a client decision. Tell the client about possible background noises, because he or she may startle easily. Give the client specific permission to stop the session at any time. Accommodate client desires as much as possible.

When the client's sense of emotional safety is shattered by trauma, he or she probably has set up internal barriers around the traumatizing memories. Do not try to "see" through these barriers or penetrate them energetically. Prying behind these barriers may lead to the person being re-traumatized. The Healing Touch practitioner does not need to know the details of the trauma in order to use Healing Touch. Part of the client's healing process is to let these barriers dissolve in his or her own time.

Do not perform Healing Touch if the person is actively re-experiencing the trauma (flashback), but help the person ground and come back to the present time. Have some strategies at hand so that you can ground the client quickly in case traumatic memories or distress begin to activate during the Healing Touch treatment. Belleruth Naparstek (2007) of Health Journeys Inc. and an expert in guided imagery, suggests four approaches for quick de-activation and grounding (Naparstek & Scaer, 2004; B. Naparstek, personal communication, May 2012):

1. *Notice Boundary Contact* by inviting the client to be aware of:
   - where his/her body contacts the table/chair,
   - the feel of her/his own weight on the table/chair,
   - the feeling of support against his/her back, and
   - the sensation of his/her feet touching the floor.

2. *Body Scan – Head Down to Feet* (always move down the body for grounding) by inviting the client to
   - begin at the head and become aware of what it feels like in the head, and then
   - move down to the neck and just notice what it feels like there, and so on
   - down the body.

3. *Counting the Breath* is done by inviting the client to
   - take a few deep breaths, just noticing what this feels like,
   - then ask the client to begin counting "one...two...three" on each inhale, and
   - count "one...two...three" on each exhale.

4. *Anchoring Imagery* is done before the session
   - by asking the client to choose an image, memory, wish or fantasy of comfort, safety, and calm; and
   - suggesting to the client that in the unlikely event he/she experiences distress during the session, he/she can come back to this imagery quickly.

The sense of spiritual connection often shatters with trauma. Before the traumatic event, the person may have had a sense of God/Higher Power's protection, of fitting into a religious or spiritual group, of the world being a good place that God/Higher Power created, of God/Higher Power being in control, and so forth. Some or all of these may have been shattered in the trauma. Just when the person most needs connection with God/Higher Power, and to experience love and support from his or her spiritual community, these avenues may be blocked, resulting in feeling abandoned or betrayed.

The traumatic experience may have shattered the client's physical energy field (etheric field), so that memories, emotions, thought forms, and other aspects of the trauma may have become embedded in the client's physical body (somatization). Touching, or being in the energy field near a traumatized area, may trigger both physical and emotional pain. For example, touching the hip chakra on the side of the hip of a person who has been sexually traumatized may bring back a flood of memories. Working with a painful shoulder might reactivate the trauma of being shot by a sniper during war. Before beginning the session, ask the client if there are areas he or she does not want touched. Find out how far out from the body the person is comfortable with you working; literally put your hands at various distances from the body, asking if that is comfortable for the client.

The energetic grid structure of the field may have been shattered in the trauma, particularly in blast injuries, such as those resulting in TBI. The field simply may be missing over one side of the head, or there may be a large hole in the field at the site of the injury. Victoria Slater, RN, PhD, CHTP/I, who has a great deal of experience with TBI clients, recommends checking for damage to the field when assessing these clients. If there is damage, she recommends occasionally holding the client's feet with the intention that the repair to the field is spread throughout the body, not localized in one place. It may take a few or many sessions for the grid to be restored. Where there is a gap in the energy field from the traumatic injury, I use *Wound Sealing* to repair the gap. Vicki suggests moving longitudinally down the area of a missing limb in the case of an amputation to repair damage to the field of the missing limb. In cases of TBI, she recommends either not working directly at the head or doing so with the intention of just being present, rather than directing or sending any energy (V. Slater, personal communication, May, 2012).

Because the usual boundaries that keep mental and emotional patterns within the client's field may be seriously weakened, a Healing Touch practitioner may be confronted with the traumatic experience in some way. Working to resolve any trauma in the practitioner's life can help the practitioner be more resistant to secondary traumatization. If the practitioner is not comfortable with a particular client, it is best to refer that person to another Healing Touch practitioner, and use this awareness as an opportunity to seek personal help.

Any level of Healing Touch training is helpful in working with this population. Often the techniques in Level 1 are very appropriate for working with trauma. Use what you know. Janet Mentgen's Trauma Release technique, taught in the Energy Wisdom and Practice class in Healing Beyond Border's Professional Development Series, can help. If the client needs work that the practitioner is not yet able to provide due to lack of training, refer to a Healing Touch practitioner who can do this work.

I am coming to think of Healing Touch as the bass line in the healing song of the client's life. The bass line in music is the foundation for the piece and often sets the rhythm. Once the field is repaired, and the person has been able to release some of the trauma through Healing Touch, he or she may be more able to process it verbally or in other ways. Guided Imagery, Energy Psychology techniques, somatic releasing techniques, mindfulness meditation, other spiritual or religious practices, and traditional Western psychotherapy can all help build the melody and harmony in the person's healing song. Healing Touch can help when used alone, but it is also useful in a synergistic way when integrated in combination with other approaches.

Working with trauma using Healing Touch may seem daunting initially, but can yield great rewards. Suggestions for working with this population include the following: Learn all that is possible about how the body/mind/spirit/emotions store and process trauma. Compile a list of professionals with whom to both refer and consult. Become proficient in helping a client ground quickly. Remember that all of us have experienced some level of trauma, so we can feel empathy and compassion for traumatized clients. As a practitioner, it is necessary to work through personal traumas so they do not interact with the client's issues. Refer to another Healing Touch practitioner if you are not feeling comfortable in this arena. The practitioner's compassion and the energy directed through the heart may be of great help in evoking another person's healing song.

Phantom Limb Pain

By Janet Mentgen BSN, CHTP/I, as compiled by Diane Wind Wardell, PhD, RN, WHNP-BC, AHN-BC, CHTP/I from personal communication received on December 5, 2001

This section gives Janet Mentgen's suggestions for working with phantom limb pain. Following an amputation, either surgically or traumatically, the area where the limb is no longer present continues to experience phantom pain. Many returning veterans are experiencing multiple amputations that may be both traumatically or surgically caused. Diabetics and patients with peripheral vascular disease may also undergo amputations that may require revisions for non-healing, such as amputating higher on the leg. The information that follows is from Janet's own thoughts and words:

> I have had a number of experiences with patients with phantom pain, each one being unique, so there must be multiple variables. What I have consistently done is: *Chakra Connection*, holding the area where the limb would be as if it was there. *Magnetic Unruffling* [*Magnetic Clearing*] of the energy field and *Etheric Unruffling* [*Etheric Template Clearing*] are also very useful interventions.
>
> One particular case was with a man who had a previous amputation, with significant phantom pain following the surgery. I recall that he was diabetic and developed gangrene in the second foot. The idea of another amputation was not to his liking. However, we worked with him pre-operatively (pre-op) to prepare and he eventually felt he could do it. His second postoperative (post-op) experience was totally different from the first. He healed rapidly without developing phantom pain.
>
> My idea would be to do Healing Touch pre-op and post-op. Second, would be to work with an old amputee

with residual phantom pain on a weekly basis for a set number of weeks (for example, 6 weeks). The time frame may vary from one to more sessions or so, while carefully measuring outcome and change and using a variety of techniques related to the energetic response. This takes an experienced practitioner who knows how to follow the energy rather than technique. Being flexible is important.

Janet also suggested using *Hands in Motion*, smoothing down the extremity, from above the level of amputation down and off at the level of where the limb would have ended, to bring it back into straight alignment. The theory is that during trauma, the extremity may have been left at an unusual angle or position prior to being surgically removed. Returning the energy of the extremity to its normal position seems to assist in decreasing phantom pain as well.

Distance Healing

Sue Kagel, BSN, RN, HNB-BC, CHTP/I

Healing Touch Practitioners are not always able to be physically present with those requesting or in need of healing energy. *Distance Healing* may seem like a "far-fetched" (pun intended) approach to healing, however it can be very effective in sending the intention and healing energy for the highest good. In Chapter 3, research studies performed by Lynn McTaggart and Dr. Gary E. Schwartz, in conjunction with the Healing Touch International Annual Conference attendees, were reviewed that used distance healing to focus on individuals, groups, situations, or locations.

Permission

Distance Healing is offered to individuals with their consent. Not everyone is open to receiving healing energy, and this boundary must be honored, even when family members or friends are requesting it for the client. When unable to receive permission directly from the individual due to his or her inability to communicate, it is possible to sense energetically whether that person is open to receiving the healing energy. For example, imagine hugging someone. When the person is open to receiving the hug, the response may range from a friendly shoulder hug to a full embrace. This is similar to the sensation practitioners energetically feel when offering healing energy to someone open to receive it. Conversely, if the person is not receptive to a hug (or energy session), there is a sense of "push back" or resistance. Honor this sensation, recognize this boundary, and withdraw the offer *for Distance Healing.*

Approaches for Distance Healing— Simple to Full Sessions

Distance Healing can be performed for just a few minutes or for up to an hour in a more detailed session. The practitioner begins with a very simple approach; the person is held in positive thought or in an image of a bubble of white light. The practitioner focuses on offering unconditional love and healing energy for the highest good of all, while envisioning that the energy is received at a time when it is suitable and convenient to be assimilated in whatever way it is needed. More specific intentions, such as pain management techniques, may be added. Those receiving distant healing may describe a feeling of the energy coming through to them, followed by a sense of calmness, relaxation, and warmth or a sense of radiating support. Interestingly, when a number of practitioners are sending healing energy (group distance healing), "rolling" the energy through times zones around the globe, recipients mention feeling "waves" of energy coming through at various times throughout the day and night.

Practitioners may also use a teddy bear or similar object to act as a surrogate and perform the interventions on the surrogate. One practitioner uses this format every few days at bedtime to support her elderly mother who lives several states away. She reports that a distance *Chakra Connection* has helped to maintain their loving connection and that her mother feels the sessions support her energy level and reduce her pain.

Some clients have shared that after having received a Healing Touch session, they can evoke the sensations and calming effect through visualizing that they are in a session, lying on the massage table, and receiving healing energy from the practitioner. The calming, balancing effects are felt, and the energy field responds from the "imprinting" connection that remains in the field.

Full Sessions at a Distance

The Healing Touch Sequence for distance work is as follows:

1. **The Intake Interview** is used to gather pertinent information to focus on for the session. The intake interview can take place by a conversation either immediately before a session, or at some time prior to the session using available technologies.

2. **Practitioner Preparation** for the session begins by grounding, centering and intention setting.

3. **The Pre-Treatment Energetic Assessment** is performed by either imagining the person or using a surrogate (another person or object). For example, a shirt and pants may be placed on the massage table or other surface as a reference for the body, or a surrogate (teddy bear, etc.) could be used as in the simple version above. Energetically, and again with permission, the practitioner asks through intention to be shown the energy field/system of the recipient in order to sense it. A full energetic assessment including pendulum, hand scan, and defining the shape of the energy field can then be performed. Practitioners often report perceiving areas of disturbance in the energy field correlating to the injury or problem area, even when they have not been completely informed of the situation.

4. **The Problem Statement** can be identified from the information obtained in the intake and energetic assessment.

5. **Mutual Goals** set prior to the session may not be able to be modified or discussed with the recipient unless there is available communication. Goals may include pain relief, calming, support during illness, healing from surgery, support during cancer treatments, or ease in the dying process.

6. **Interventions** are then performed on the energetic image of the person specific to the issues and the energy assessment. It is possible for sensations to be experienced by the practitioner and the person simultaneously during the distance healing session.

7. **The Post Treatment Energetic Assessment** is then performed to re-assess the energy field impression and can be documented to note any changes in the energy system.

8. **Ground** the person's energy image and release it with the intention that the healing session flow to the recipient gently and easily for the highest good, at the appropriate time.

9. **Evaluation** may take place electronically immediately or later, depending on the circumstances. Feedback may also be provided by someone present with the person. If the practitioner identifies something specific, notes the time, and has asked the person to do the same, it can be very interesting to compare the findings.

As with any Healing Touch session, early energy intervention tends to facilitate a more rapid healing response in whatever way it is needed. *Distance Healing* can provide an opportunity for early response.

Distance Healing with Groups

Group *Distance Healing* can be done by several practitioners gathered in one place (support group) or with multiple practitioners in different locations focusing on a person or situation, either simultaneously or at different times. In a simple format, practitioners gather in a circle, imagine the person's image is present, and send loving energy for the highest good. Adding another dimension, a massage table or chair may be used to hold the energetic image. The practitioners, having grounded, centered and set intention, each allow their hands to be "drawn" to a place in need of healing and allow the energy to flow.

A full session done in a group distance situation includes the Healing Touch Sequence steps listed above. The Pre-Treatment Energetic Assessment can be completed by one or two practitioners, and the findings presented to the group. Based on the presenting issues and energetic findings, the group chooses specific interventions, which can then be done gently and simultaneously by several practitioners who verbally communicate their findings, impressions, and sensations as they attend to specific areas. The session is completed as usual.

An example of this group work involved an elderly woman, who was attacked by two dogs and had multiple severe injuries, emotional trauma, and intense pain. This information, without much detail, was shared with a group of practitioners at a support group. The energy assessment conducted by two of the practitioners revealed the location of the injuries. Interventions were chosen accordingly. One of the practitioners "sensed" that the elderly woman experienced an emotional release while being treated. The injured woman told the practitioner who was with her that the painful areas were diminishing significantly; the practitioner reported that she had been tearful. The pre-treatment assessment identification of injuries was also verified by the person in attendance. At the time the session was completed, the injured woman reportedly fell into a deep and restful sleep.

Global Approach

Distance Healing can be provided by individual practitioners or in groups during times of crises and disasters (natural and man-made). The session begins with an open, loving heart setting the intention for the highest good of all. In this situation, permission cannot be individually granted, but the intention can be set so that anyone who is in need of the healing energy, and is open to receiving it for the highest good, can easily receive it, either consciously or subconsciously. Supportive energy can also be sent to the first responders and health care practitioners who are working locally. Additionally, individuals who are affected emotionally by the situation and those injured, dying or in sudden transition can be provided with energetic loving and healing support. Many groups (e.g. sound healers, Reiki, meditation) use this approach as well.

A more generic approach involves sending healing energy to the entire planet on a set date and time (e.g. on a specific day, 12 noon in each time zone for a 24 hour period), with practitioners joining in worldwide. The healing energy is sent around the globe and continues through the multiple time zones, creating a wave and blanket of loving, healing energy for all who may be open to receiving it. These group energy healing sessions are often initiated through the Internet.

Spreading Healing Support Worldwide through Distance Healing

Distance Healing can be used in a variety of settings and at any distance to support or facilitate healing. Sometimes this process is even easier to accomplish, as the information is not processed through our usual interpretive mechanisms of sight and touch. Instead, the energetic field is accessed directly for information and for healing. *Distance Healing* increases the opportunity for practitioners, working alone or in groups, to assist in spreading healing support worldwide from wherever they are located, and whenever it is needed. The *Distance Healing* process also increases the number of people and situations that may benefit from healing work.

Chapter Conclusion

Healing Touch across the life continuum offers comfort, soothing, and peace for all involved. The clearing and balancing effects of full body techniques used in general, in conjunction with pain techniques for specific conditions, are supportive of healing, even in the dying process. The recommendations presented throughout this chapter come from years of practitioner experience as well as research, and serve as guidelines to enhance healing. As practitioners continue to work in a wide range of areas, more recommendations and research will arise that will continue the evolution of evidence-based best practices.

CHAPTER 9

EVIDENCE-BASED PRACTICE
By Joel G. Anderson, PhD, HTI-P and
Mary Erickson Megel, PhD, RN, CHTP

This chapter provides an overview of evidence and evidence-based practice (EBP), describes processes for evaluating evidence and applying research results to practice, reviews selected best evidence in Healing Touch, and provides suggestions for research methods and future studies in Healing Touch. The objectives of this chapter are as follows.

1. Recognize the importance of evidence-based practice components in applying findings from Healing Touch research.
2. Utilize a variety of sources for assessing Healing Touch research.
3. Identify current research strategies used within Healing Touch.

Evidence-Based Practice

As health workers, Healing Touch practitioners are held to ethical standards that mandate continual development of skills and expertise through life-long learning and, above all, doing no harm to our clients as identified in the *International Code of Ethics/Standards of Practice for Healing Touch Practitioners* (Healing Touch International, 1996, 2014). To fulfill this mandate, our practice needs to be based on sound evidence of what works best.

Why do we need to know how to apply principles of EBP to the practice of Healing Touch? Spurred by such groups as the *Institute of Medicine*

(IOM), the *Agency for Healthcare Research and Quality* (AHRQ), and the *Institute for Healthcare Improvement* (IHI), the EBP movement was born. All health care providers are expected to use evidence to support the care provided if the needs of our clients are to be truly met (Malloch & Grady, 2010). This expectation also pertains to Healing Touch practitioners.

Definitions

According to Melnyk and Fineout-Overholt (2011), *evidence* involves believable facts or data. *Evidence* also has a legal connotation as it can be used as proof of the value of something (Hendrix, 2012). In health care, *evidence* is used to support (or refute) the use of medications, laboratory studies, or regimens of care from lifestyle behaviors to sophisticated medical and surgical treatments. EBP, then, is the use of results of sound, rigorous research in the provision of care to clients.

Most authors attribute the definition of evidence-based medicine by Sackett, Richardson, Rosenberg, and Haynes (1997) as the modern-day starting point of the movement toward EBP in health care. The original definition integrated two major components: use of best clinical research and the expertise of clinical practitioners. More recently, a third major component was added to the definition of EBP: patient or consumer preferences and values (Melnyk & Fineout-Overholt, 2006). This component is of critical importance as health care consumers become more and more skillful in accessing health care information electronically. Consumers know how to locate information about health care and often seek out what they wish to receive from health care providers (Melnyk & Fineout-Overholt, 2011).

Healing Touch practitioners and other care providers should be aware of what constitutes good quality in research so they may more accurately understand research reports and use research results to support practice and health care recommendations provided to clients. This means that Healing Touch providers need to understand the EBP process, which is in line with the standards of practice of Healing Beyond Borders (HBB) with regard to scope of practice, communication and education, and quality care. Consumers who wish to receive Healing Touch, as well as Healing Touch practitioners, can access current research from the website (www.healingbeyondborders.org).

Process of EBP

According to Hopp and Rittenmeyer (2012), the EBP process is a decision-making process consisting of the following five steps:

1. Ask a clinical question.
2. Acquire relevant evidence.
3. Appraise the level and quality of the evidence.
4. Apply results in practice.
5. Assess the effectiveness of the change in practice.

Asking the clinical question typically involves development of a *PICO* question, with *P* referring to the population or patient group of interest, *I* to the intervention of interest, *C* to a comparison intervention or "usual care," and *O* to the desired outcome(s). The time-frame (T) is needed for the desired outcomes to be manifested or remain in evidence. However, not all clinical questions require the time-frame. An example of a PICO question is as follows: In women being treated for gynecological and breast cancer (P), what is the effect of noninvasive interventions such as Healing Touch (I) compared to usual care (C) on quality of life (O)?

After asking the PICO(T) question, the health care provider searches the literature to acquire all relevant research evidence. Each piece of relevant literature must then be read and appraised for the level and quality of evidence. The *level* of evidence identifies each type of evidence found. The article may be a formal study, a systematic review of research in the area of interest, or a clinical practice guideline outlining best practice in the area of interest. All evidence is not of equal *quality*, and most providers practicing EBP use a framework to help them determine the level. While there are several frameworks available, most are similar and are hierarchical in nature with the most rigorous scientific work at the top. Level 1 evidence usually consists of systematic reviews with or without meta-analyses of randomized controlled trials. Level 2 evidence typically includes individual randomized controlled trials: research in which subjects are randomly assigned to experimental and control groups, and the intervention being tested is given to the experimental group only. Level 3 evidence is often quasi-experimental or nonrandomized research. Level 4 involves studies that do not have an experimental design, such as correlational, cohort, or case-control designs. Level 5 includes descriptive or qualitative research, and Level 6 includes expert opinion articles. Clinical practice guidelines usually fall into the hierarchy close to the top, but the ranking really depends on the level and quality of the evidence used to develop the guideline. These hierarchies are the initial step in determining quality of research studies; the reader also needs to consider how well the study reflects current practice as well as whether or not the client will accept the treatment. However, it is important to point out that all levels of evidence in research are essential in building the evidence base to support future research and inform practice.

To continue with the previous example, in searching the literature to answer our PICO question about the use of noninvasive interventions such as Healing Touch with women having radiation therapy for gynecological and breast cancer, a relevant study by Cook, Guerrerio, and Slater (2004) was found. Based on the hierarchy outlined above, this particular study's level of evidence would be Level 2 as the study is a randomized controlled trial.

Once the evidence has been found, the reader must read all of it to determine the level of each piece of evidence and the overall quality of the body of evidence found, looking to see if the research warrants application of results in practice. Research containing serious methodological flaws that call the results into question would be removed from the body of evidence being reviewed. Research can be difficult to evaluate without knowledge in the sciences and practice. Members of the HBB Research Committee can assist Healing Touch practitioners who seek to understand research studies.

In general, research studies fall into two broad categories, quantitative and qualitative research. Criteria for the appraisal of these types of studies follow, with examples to assist in answering our PICO question.

Quality Criteria in Quantitative Research

Quantitative research (Level 2, 3, and 4 evidence) is designed to find answers to problems through the gathering of numerical data analyzed using statistical methods. In all research, quality is determined by how well the researcher demonstrates that the methods are rigorous, the findings are accurate, and the intervention being studied most likely is responsible for the results. In quantitative research, this means the study methods and results have *validity* and *reliability*. However, to complete the EBP process, the results also must demonstrate that the intervention is appropriate and helpful for those served, meets the desire for the intervention, and if the expertise and resources needed to provide the intervention are available.

In quantitative studies, validity is supported by randomly assigning subjects to groups, so that experimental and control groups are as similar as possible on characteristics that could affect the study results at the beginning of the study. The sample size of the experimental and control groups needs to be adequate to detect differences between groups, and statistically determined using a power analysis prior to beginning data collection (Melnyk & Fineout-Overholt, 2011). Instruments used to collect data, such as questionnaires and laboratory equipment, preferably should have previously determined *reliability* (consistency in measuring the variables of interest) and *validity* (accuracy). The researcher also must be clear and thorough in describing the methods of the study, including a description of anything that could affect results. The reader should be able to determine if the study meets quality criteria or should be discarded (Hopp & Rittenmeyer, 2012; Melnyk & Fineout-Overholt, 2011).

In the example study by Cook and colleagues (2004), 78 subjects were randomly assigned to study groups (experimental group = 44 subjects; control group = 34 subjects). The experimental group received six Healing Touch treatments: the control group received six mock Healing Touch treatments. The authors indicate this number of subjects was the maximum that could be feasibly enrolled given the researchers' resources. At the end of the study, 16 had dropped out (10 in the experimental group = 22.7%; six in the control group = 17.6%). This drop-out rate should catch the attention of the reader. The greater the drop-out rate, the smaller the remaining sample of study participants. This can increase the possibility of bias or error in results.

Instruments used for data collection included a 4-item self-administered questionnaire developed for the study that measured attitudes toward Healing Touch at the beginning of the study (baseline). Statistical testing showed that this questionnaire had adequate internal consistency (*reliability*) and face *validity*, which was established through pilot testing. The instrument used to measure quality of life (QOL) was the well-established SF-36. Adequate test-retest *reliability* was reported. These measures revealed that at baseline, subjects in both groups were similar. Additional strengths of the study were the meticulous description of methods, and designing the study so that subjects were not aware to which group (Healing Touch or mock Healing Touch) they were assigned. Furthermore, the study coordinator was not aware of which type of treatment the practitioner provided (blinded).

Data analysis was accomplished using an intent-to-treat analysis, which means that subjects' data were analyzed in the groups to which they were initially assigned. The *t*-test statistic was used for analysis of the SF-36 results; this is appropriate as the test determines differences between two groups. Because of the drop-out rate, the authors did not pursue more advanced statistical analysis (use of covariates), which is an appropriate decision.

Overall results revealed higher SF-36 (QOL) results for the Healing Touch group in comparison to the mock Healing Touch group (MT), but results were not statistically significant ($p = 0.06$). However, scores for three SF-36 subscales (pain, vitality, and physical functioning) were statistically higher for the Healing Touch group versus the MT group, and overall SF-36 scores were significantly improved over time for the Healing Touch group, but not for the mock Healing Touch group.

The authors appropriately addressed study limitations. No fatal flaws were found which would disqualify this quantitative study from retention in our body of evidence to answer our PICO question.

Quality Criteria in Qualitative Research

Criteria to determine quality of qualitative studies (Level 5 evidence) are similar to quantitative research (*reliability* and *validity* considerations); however, the terminology used to describe study rigor is quite different from that used with quantitative studies. Creswell (1994), an early author of qualitative methods, provided guidance for readers of qualitative research that is still useful today. An updated evaluation standard by Creswell (2013) is supported by other authors. Different approaches to determining rigor or *trustworthiness* can be found, but the closest framework to quantitative research criteria is that of Lincoln and Guba (1985). The criteria these authors developed include four components: credibility (truth or *validity)*, dependability *(reliability)*, transferability (relevance of results to other populations), and confirmability (researcher objectivity).

No published qualitative studies involving Healing Touch were found that related to our specific PICO question. However, an unpublished study by Eschiti and Baker (2012) was found that examined the experience of women who received Healing Touch following mastectomy for breast cancer. This study involved five participants who had been diagnosed with breast cancer and experienced a partial or full mastectomy within eight months of their one-hour telephone interview. All had received Healing Touch within six months of surgery. The purpose of the study was to seek an understanding of the women's experiences to develop and strengthen services to improve their QOL (e.g. Healing Touch).

Credibility was provided by allowing the women to tell their own stories in their own words. Potential participants were contacted through fliers about the study so that they would not feel pressured by the Healing Touch practitioner. The authors indicated that data saturation was not obtained (more information may still have been forthcoming if additional participants had been recruited); therefore, this study was regarded as a pilot study.

Dependability was supported by using the same open-ended questions and outlining procedures so that another researcher could have followed the authors' approach. Transferability of findings to women being treated for other forms of cancer seems supported by the women's description of general feelings: feeling relaxed, comfortable, and/or supported. Objectivity was supported by the use of an interview guide. All interviews were recorded, which could allow an outside person to review them for potential bias.

Because qualitative and quantitative studies yield such different types of results, more studies are being conducted using "mixed methods," in which quantitative and qualitative methods are combined. This can enhance the strength of the evidence (Polit & Beck, 2006).

Assessing Overall Strength of Evidence

Once all the relevant, good quality evidence has been reviewed, the reader should come to a conclusion about the overall strength of the body of work. A helpful resource in this determination is the *Oncology Nursing Society's* (ONS) *Putting Evidence into Practice* (PEP) recommendation format. This format provides the reader with the levels of evidence and consistency of results that are necessary to arrive at a recommendation for practice, or not. ONS categories of recommendations include recommended for practice, likely to be effective, benefits balanced with harm, effectiveness not established, effectiveness unlikely, or not recommended for practice. On the basis of consistency of results in the two articles reviewed for our PICO question, we might decide that the evidence shows that Healing Touch is likely to be effective in improving the QOL of women being treated for cancer. Additional evidence reviewed would need to support that conclusion.

Final EBP Steps

If the evidence is good enough to apply to practice, then the final steps are application and evaluation of how well it works with the practitioner's own clients. For example, at Stanford University Medical Center, the *Healing Partners Program* was developed to provide Healing Touch to patients with breast cancer. Outcomes were measured, including affect, QOL, and energy level. After six months, 76 participants reported positive affect, 65.2% reported reduced depression, 63% reported reduced anxiety, 80% reported improved QOL, and 75% reported feeling more energetic (Turner, 2005).

Evidence in Healing Touch Research

To date, most published research on the use of biofield therapies, including Healing Touch, in clinical settings and studies has been among cancer, pain and palliative care patients (Jain & Mills, 2010). In the course of conducting a previous systematic review (Level 1 evidence) of the clinical effectiveness of Healing Touch in randomized, controlled trials, Anderson and Taylor (2011) found 17 potential randomized, controlled trials for review. However, 12 studies were excluded because these studies did not meet the inclusion criteria established for the systematic review, which required Level 2 evidence. What follows is a summary of the best evidence of Healing Touch research (Level 2), which includes the most recent, valid, reliable, and well-designed studies following the hierarchy outlined in this chapter. Given this system of evaluation, the scope of the Level 2 studies reviewed was limited to patients with cancer or cardiovascular disease. In addition, Healing Touch studies from peer-reviewed publications, including case reports, are summarized in Table 1.

Cancer. In a randomized, controlled trial in patients with cervical cancer, Lutgendorf and colleagues (2010) reported a significant preservation of natural killer cell activity (representing immune function) over time following chemo-radiation treatment in those individuals receiving Healing Touch versus relaxation therapy or usual care. Those individuals in the Healing Touch group experienced a significant decrease in depressive symptoms and depressed mood compared to the relaxation therapy and usual care groups. Jain and colleagues (2012) conducted a randomized, controlled trial of "Chelation," as defined by Rev. Rosalyn L. Bruyere, in a sample of fatigued breast cancer survivors. A significant decrease in total fatigue was observed in those individuals receiving "Chelation" or mock treatment versus controls. Cortisol levels were significantly decreased in the treatment group versus the mock treatment and control groups.

Post-White and colleagues (2003) examined the effects of therapeutic massage, Healing Touch, and presence in patients with cancer. A significant decrease in current pain was observed following the Healing Touch intervention. As described earlier, Cook and colleagues (2004) conducted a study with two groups, Healing Touch and mock Healing Touch. A significant increase in overall functional score, emotional role functioning, mental health, and health transition in the Healing Touch group was reported. There was a significant increase in health transition and physical functioning in the mock Healing Touch group as well.

Cardiovascular Disease. In a randomized, controlled trial in first-time elective and non-emergent inpatients who had undergone coronary artery bypass graft surgery, Healing Touch significantly decreased the length of stay (120% greater chance of length of stay ≤ 6 days) and decreased anxiety levels, versus a group receiving visitation or usual care alone (MacIntyre et al., 2008). Seskevich, Crater, Lane, and Krucoff (2004) used a randomized, controlled design to examine the effects of four noetic therapies, including Healing Touch, on mood in patients undergoing percutaneous coronary intervention. Noetic therapies are defined as treatments involving no tangible drug or medical device (Krucoff, Crater, Gallup, et al., 2005). Healing Touch significantly decreased feelings of worry and increased feelings of satisfaction compared to standard care alone. This pilot study gave rise to additional studies at multiple sites using combinations of noetic therapy interventions, including Healing Touch, in patients with cardiovascular disease, with similar positive results on quality of life indicators, though no significant results from Healing Touch alone were observed.

Krucoff and colleagues (Krucoff, Crater, Green, et al., 2001) conducted a study with five intervention groups, including usual care alone, imagery, Healing Touch, stress-relaxation therapy, or off-site intercessory prayer in a sample of patients scheduled to undergo percutaneous coronary intervention. A 25% to 30% reduction in adverse cardiovascular endpoints (defined as death, myocardial infarction, congestive heart failure, urgent repeat of the procedure, or bypass surgery) was observed following all of the noetic therapy interventions; however, no significant results from Healing Touch alone were reported.

Developing Healing Touch Research

Based on the available published evidence, as well as following the recommendations of other authors, studies of Healing Touch could be improved by reporting clear methodology, describing any randomization procedures and blinding used, and reporting attrition rates of participants (i.e., those individuals who withdraw from the study). With regard to recruitment and randomization of study participants, this can be a problematic issue because of the beliefs, practices and preferences of potential participants (Verhoef, Casebeer, & Hilsden, 2002). In studies of Healing Touch, a selection bias in recruiting may be encountered because some people may be more or less inclined to participate (Warber, Gordon, Gillespie, Olson, & Assefi, 2003). This is particularly important given that research studies of complementary therapies like Healing Touch often suffer from small sample sizes. To detect smaller effects, such as those encountered in studies of Healing Touch, larger samples sizes are required. Therefore, it may be appropriate to plan for detecting the smallest effect that would be clinically significant during small studies.

Study Intervention

There is great debate in the area of complementary and alternative medicine (CAM) research regarding appropriate study interventions and controls. In a typical randomized, controlled trial, the study intervention is standardized, meaning that each participant receives the exact same treatment. Moreover, control groups are usually easier in studies of new drugs because placebo treatments that look, taste, and feel like the actual treatment can be used. Many believe that CAM research must use the same standardized types of treatments to provide the most convincing evidence, following the model of the randomized, controlled trial. But CAM therapies do not necessarily lend themselves to such designs, particularly those types of therapies that involve a practitioner, such as Healing Touch, in which it is believed that the person's field can also influence the outcome.

Even beyond fields interacting, practitioners often view the relationship with their client as an important part of the treatment itself. This, too, is something that is not included in the randomized, controlled trial paradigm in research of new drug therapies. However, these same issues are faced by anyone conducting research with a behavioral intervention, such as a weight-loss program or diabetes management, where the patient is interacting with a person delivering the intervention. While some practitioners may describe the intervention and techniques used as an art form, biomedical scientists insist upon standardized treatments that follow a particular protocol that can be replicated. Indeed, being able to replicate the studies and results of others is a hallmark of scientific research.

Practitioners involved in Healing Touch research must weigh these seemingly opposing viewpoints carefully when designing research interventions. The Healing Touch curriculum with its standardized techniques lends itself to research in that the techniques and interventions are replicable. However, in a real-world setting, practitioners modify the sequence and types of techniques they use to suit the client's needs based on an energy field assessment. Sound arguments can be made for using or eschewing standardized Healing Touch interventions in the research setting. What is essential is that the intervention remains true to the tenets and philosophy of Healing Touch while providing the most rigorous scientific research methods possible. This may allow for the evidence-based data needed for the use of Healing Touch in the real-world clinical setting.

The choice of comparison groups or controls used to create a blinded study is probably the most challenging issue in designing trials of Healing Touch. In general, the use of an untreated control group might allow the researcher to assess whether the addition of Healing Touch is more effective than no treatment at all, and controls for the natural history of the illness. The comparison of Healing Touch with usual care for a particular condition is helpful in determining if Healing Touch offers any advantages in terms of efficacy, side effects, or patient preference (Warber et al., 2003).

Clinical trials also must take into account the qualifications of a practitioner and his/her competency (Warber et al, 2003). Several practitioners who meet the same standards of training and practice should be used to avoid measuring the effects of a single individual. The practitioner's intention is a hallmark of Healing Touch that must be taken into account (Forgues, 2009). Having placebo Healing Touch-naïve practitioners cognitively engaged in mathematical calculations is believed to avoid energy interaction and to be an effective placebo (So, Jiang, & Qin, 2008); however, this tactic may not be adequate in preventing field interchange.

Assessments and Measures

Previous studies of Healing Touch have not used all types of outcomes, including the collection of physiological, psychological, and descriptive data. Studies would be greatly enhanced by the addition of functional measures or biomarkers relevant to the condition or disease being studied. Not to be discounted, descriptive data may prove vital in understanding the uniqueness of the perceived effects of Healing Touch versus other interventions. Following the lead of the nursing science field, the use of the "mixed methods" approach described earlier would provide a more complete assessment of Healing Touch (Verhoef, et al., 2002; Wilkinson, et al., 2002). Also, because mood, expectations, and state of relaxation can influence symptoms, it is important to collect data on subjects' psychological states and the anticipation of benefits from treatment before the intervention begins (Warber et al., 2003).

Subjective measures. Subjective symptom measures that are validated and reliable for use in clinical research will allow for better comparison between Healing Touch studies, studies of other integrative therapies, and conventional care studies using drugs or devices. The issue of comparison is one that is encountered in all clinical research studies generally, and the issue has become even more relevant in the current climate of EBP in conventional health care. Table 2 outlines a set of measures for use, as appropriate, in Healing Touch research to assess stress, depressed mood, anxiety, fatigue, pain, sleep disturbances, and quality of life —symptoms that commonly cluster together. These instruments are frequently used throughout clinical research and are reliable, valid tools for assessing subjective health outcomes. An important note to remember when designing and conducting a research study is that of study participant burden. While it is essential to collect appropriate and adequate data, burdening the study participant with too many questionnaires should be avoided.

This table of measures is not all inclusive. Indeed, given that symptom scales may not capture all of the potential positive and negative effects of the Healing Touch intervention (Verhoef et al, 2002), study participants and practitioners could answer several open-ended questions at the conclusion of a study to capture descriptive, qualitative data regarding individual experiences. Few studies of energy therapies have measured the participants' beliefs about the efficacy of the treatment or about group assignment (Rexilius, Mundt, Megel, & Agrawal, 2002). These data are important given that a participant's beliefs are closely related to his/her expectations about the intervention and may have an impact on study results (McDonough-Means, Kreitzer, & Bell, 2004).

Physiological measures. Like other biofield therapies, Healing Touch is most demonstrable when used to treat symptoms associated with QOL. Relaxation, decreased anxiety and stress, and improved mood are the most common effects and hallmarks of Healing Touch and frequently have been reported in various study populations (Jain & Mills, 2010; Lutgendorf et al., 2010). However, the inclusion of appropriate physiological measurements in Healing Touch research will allow for a better understanding of the various physiological mechanisms involved. In an editorial, Mills and Jain (2010) wrote that "the study of... 'energy therapies' might be found to be fruitful in better understanding... mechanisms that drive healing responses" (p. 1230). The authors liken the state of the science regarding energy therapies to research involving meditation about two decades ago, when such research was gaining momentum. Given that energy therapies still remain controversial in many circles, the inclusion of physiological measures may not only support EBP but also provide continued opportunities for Healing Touch research.

Healing Touch has been shown to decrease salivary cortisol (Wang & Hermann, 2006; Wilkinson et al., 2002), the so-called "stress hormone." Additional reports of studies measuring physiological parameters of Healing Touch reflect positive changes in heart rate, blood pressure, respiratory rate (Post-White et al., 2003), and heart rate variability (Kemper, Fletcher, Hamilton, & McLean, 2009), suggesting effects of Healing Touch are reflected by changes in the response of the nervous system. Healing Touch has been reported to increase salivary IgA (Wilkinson et al., 2002) and increase the activity of natural killer cells (Lutgendorf et al., 2010), both indicators of immune function.

Study Analysis and Presentation of Results

Previous studies of Healing Touch and other biofield therapies have had issues related to statistical analysis, including the lack of assessment or use of covariates, omission of information concerning effect sizes related to clinical relevance, and inappropriate control for statistical errors (Jain & Mills, 2010). Additionally, it is important for publication in peer-reviewed journals to present results of Healing Touch research in a standardized, systematic way so that it can be clearly interpreted and replicated by the research community. One such way that is currently being recommended is the *Consolidated Standards of Reporting Trials* (CONSORT) statement developed by researchers and journal editors to provide a systematic framework for reporting and presenting research studies. The CONSORT statement provides a checklist and flowchart that can be used when developing a research study and in writing manuscripts of the findings for publication. While originally designed for randomized controlled trials, use of the CONSORT statement in all clinical research studies is encouraged. In fact, many peer-reviewed journals require the use of the CONSORT guidelines for publication. The statement and associated documentation can be accessed online (www.consort-statement.org).

Chapter Summary

Though biofield therapies are among the most ancient of healing practices, scientific research into the mechanisms and effectiveness of Healing Touch remains to be explored. The current lack of high-level studies needed to influence EBP provides an opportunity for Healing Touch researchers to develop sound research that will demonstrate both the effectiveness and the therapeutic potential of Healing Touch. Recent reviews and meta-analyses have found many biofield studies to be inadequate in design, such as appropriate controls, blinding, and adequate sample size, but promising enough to warrant further research (>80% of CONSORT criteria) (Pierce, 2007). However, proper integration of biofield therapies such as Healing Touch into the health care system requires scientific justification equal to more conventional therapies (Forgues, 2009) provided in peer-reviewed publications. The authors hope this chapter may serve as a guide toward designing and implementing the trials needed to address these research method issues, filling the gaps in knowledge and moving the field of Healing Touch research forward.

Table 1. Peer-reviewed Healing Touch Publications

Reference	Type of study	Sample condition	Main results	Level of Evidence
Wetzel, 1993	Case report	Wound infection	Anecdotal report	Level 5
Wardell, 2000	Qualitative methods	Healthy subjects	Descriptive study of the instruction and experience of the "Trauma Release" technique	Level 5
Krucoff et al., 2001	Randomized controlled trial	Percutaneous coronary intervention	No significant results from HT alone	Level 2
Taylor, 2001	Mixed methods	Healthy subjects	No significant results from HT on coping ability, self-esteem and general health	Level 3
Wardell, 2001	Mixed methods	Healthy subjects	Significant increase in the sense of spiritual awareness with increasing levels of HT training	Level 3
Rexilius et al., 2002	Quasi-experimental repeated measures	Caregivers of patients with cancer	Non-significant decrease in anxiety and depression, and increase in fatigue and subjective burden	Level 3
Wilkinson et al., 2002	Quasi-experimental repeated measures	Healthy subjects	Significant increase in secretory salivary IgA	Level 3

Reference	Type of study	Sample condition	Main results	Level of Evidence
Post-White et al., 2003	Randomized controlled trial; cross-over design	Cancer	Significant decrease in respiratory rate, heart rate, blood pressure, current pain, total mood disturbance, and fatigue	Level 2
Ziembroski et al., 2003	Randomized controlled trial	End-of-life hospice patients	Non-significant increase in relaxation, relief of pain, spiritual benefit, calmness and improved breathing	Level 2
Cook et al., 2004	Randomized controlled trial	Gynecological or breast cancer	Significant increase in overall functional score, emotional role functioning, mental health, and health transition	Level 2
Forbes et al., 2004	Case study	Healthy subject	Testing of surface electromyography as a device for detection of physiological changes during HT	Level 5
Seskevich et al., 2004	Randomized controlled trial	Percutaneous coronary intervention	Significant decrease in worry and significant increase in satisfaction	Level 2
Wardell & Weymouth, 2004	Review	Various populations	Descriptive review of HT studies	Level 4

Reference	Type of study	Sample condition	Main results	Level of Evidence
Krucoff et al., 2005	Randomized controlled trial	Percutaneous coronary intervention	No significant results from Healing Touch alone	Level 2
Kissinger and Kaczmarek, 2006	Case report	Fertility	Client reported deep relaxation and calming	Level 5
Wang and Hermann, 2006	Cohort study	Dementia	Significant decrease in agitation levels with HT	Level 4
Wardell et al., 2006	Quasi-experimental	Neuropathic pain in spinal cord injury	Significant improvement on one item of the Brief Pain Inventory	Level 3
Dowd et al., 2007	Randomized controlled trial	Healthy subjects	Non-significant decrease in stress	Level 2
Engebretson & Wardell, 2007	Review	Various populations	Descriptive review of energy-based modalities	Level 4
Danhauer et al., 2008	Cohort study	Acute leukemia	Significant improvements in fatigue and nausea, and non-significant improvements in distress and pain	Level 4
MacIntyre et al., 2008	Randomized controlled trial	Coronary artery bypass graft surgery	Significant decrease in mean length of stay and mean anxiety scores	Level 2
Maville et al., 2008	Cohort study	Healthy subjects	Increased relaxation	Level 4

Reference	Type of study	Sample condition	Main results	Level of Evidence
Wardell et al., 2008	Secondary analysis	Neuropathic pain in spinal cord injury	Qualitative method to describe experience of clients	Level 5
Kemper et al., 2009	Cohort study	Pediatric leukemia	Significant decrease in stress and heart rate variability versus rest alone	Level 4
Jain & Mills, 2010	Systematic review	Clinical studies with mixed populations	Reviews clinical studies of HT, Reiki and Therapeutic Touch, ranking the level of evidence	Level 1
Lutgendorf et al., 2010	Randomized controlled trial	Cervical cancer	Significant preservation of natural killer cell activity with HT over time, and a significant decrease in depressive symptoms and depressed mood versus relaxation therapy or usual care	Level 2
Tang et al., 2010	Cohort study	Nurse leaders	Significant improvement in self-reported stress, depression, anxiety, relaxation, well-being, sleep, and autonomic function as measured by heart rate variability	Level 4

Reference	Type of study	Sample condition	Main results	Level of Evidence
Anderson & Taylor, 2011	Systematic review	Clinical studies with mixed populations	Reviews randomized clinical studies of HT	Level 1
Curtis et al., 2011	Case report	Intractable neuropathic itch	Clinically significant decrease in severity of itch	Level 5
Decker et al., 2012	Quasi-experimental	Older adults with persistent pain	Non-significant decrease in pain, improvement in activities of daily living, and increase in quality of life	Level 3
Jain et al., 2012	Randomized controlled trial	Breast cancer survivors	Significant decrease in total fatigue and cortisol using "Chelation"	Level 2
Wardell & Engebretson, 2012	Secondary analysis	Older adults with persistent pain	Qualitative method to describe experience of clients	Level 5
Jain et al., 2012	Randomized controlled trial	Active duty military with post-traumatic stress disorder (PTSD)	Significant improvements in PTSD symptoms, depression, mental quality of life and cynicism using Healing Touch combined with guided imagery	Level 2

Table 2. Suggested Subjective Patient Outcome Measures for Healing Touch Research

Instrument	Measure
Numeric Rating Scale (NRS)	A simple, yet sensitive measure of subjective phenomena that has been used successfully in various research studies.
Visual Analog Scale (VAS)	A simple measure that has been widely used for capturing subjective ratings and that may be more compatible with the altered state experienced during a Healing Touch session.
Perceived Stress Scale (PSS)	A 10-item scale that asks individuals to rate how often they have felt or thought a certain way.
Beck Depression Inventory (BDI)	An instrument with 21 questions that is the most widely used for measuring the self-report of depressive symptoms.
State-Trait Anxiety Inventory (STAI)	A standard instrument to assess anxiety and measures feelings of apprehension, tension, nervousness and worry.
Lee's Fatigue Inventory (LFI)	An 18-item scale that assesses fatigue and energy using numeric rating scales.
McGill Pain Questionnaire-Short Form (MPQ-SF)	A 15-item scale that measures aspects of pain using sensory and affective descriptors.
Pittsburgh Sleep Quality Index (PSQI)	A 19-item scale that generates seven subscale scores related to subjective sleep quality, the sum of which yields one total score.
Short Form Health Status (SF-36)	A questionnaire that relies on 36 items to assess aspects of quality life including functional health and well-being, and has proven useful in both general and distinct patient populations.
Tellegen Absorption Scale	A validated means of quantifying the personality characteristic of increased focus, which is associated with greater usage of complementary modalities delivered by a practitioner and may be indicative of the effect of a healing presence.

CHAPTER 10
INTEGRATING HEALING TOUCH

The versatility of Healing Touch, with its options of short and simple techniques to full sessions, facilitates its collaboration with diverse systems and modalities and integration into a wide range of settings. Healing Touch can be integrated as part of a professional practice, enhance personal growth, and bring a transformative approach to life. Students and practitioners who incorporate basic tenants of Healing Touch into their lives often find that their way of being changes to that of a calm, healing presence at any time, in any role, and in any situation. This way of being creates the possibility for a healthier, richer, and a more self-aware approach to life, one that ripples out to influence family, the work environment, the community, and the world.

Healing Touch is complementary to both standard and indigenous medical health care systems. Using a holistic and integrative approach, coupled with an energetic world view, it can stand alone or weave well with other therapies and modalities, potentiating each to create a greater effect than the individual treatments. Because Healing Touch stimulates self-healing by clearing and balancing the energy system, it works well in combination or in conjunction with any situation related to the health care continuum and general well-being. Examples of Healing Touch integration worldwide were shared in Chapter 1, and its use with specific health care specialties was discussed in Chapter 8. While this chapter explores several integrative options, it is not meant to be all inclusive. The objectives are as follows:

1. Apply Healing Touch principles in daily life and professional role.
2. Identify ways to integrate Healing Touch with other modalities.
3. Describe collaborative and integrative approaches with other health care providers and systems.

Integrating from Self to Family, Community, and the World

BY SUE KAGEL, RN, BSN, HNB-BC, CHTP/I AND
LISA ANSELME, BLS, RN, HN-BC, CHTP/I

Integrating Healing Touch begins with the individual student/practitioner bringing the principles of Healing Touch and self-care into daily awareness and viewing healing presence as a way of being in life. From this way of being present, Healing Touch can be shared through assisting family and friends during times of need in all areas—physically, emotionally, mentally and spiritually. As providers reach out beyond family, they may volunteer in their community through a cancer support group or church group clinic, or they may offer co-worker support in a corporate setting. Others integrate Healing Touch into their careers, service projects, or service organizations, which may be local or may provide opportunities to bring Healing Touch out into the world.

Healing Touch moves organically, where individuals are drawn to introduce it, and capitalizes upon each individual's skills, sphere of influence and broader relationships. The possibilities for using Healing Touch are endless, and flow from the creative inspiration and openness of students and practitioners exploring situations where they can be of service. A requirement for the HTI Healing Touch Certificate Program involves providing and documenting sessions. Students may complete this practicum through participating and working in a myriad of situations. Frequently, these sessions lead to further Healing Touch opportunities based on the setting and the connections made. Another course requirement includes a community project in which students introduce and offer Healing Touch to their communities in some way (e.g. presentation, health fair, work place event, working with an underserved population) to bring Healing Touch where they feel they can make a difference, or where the opportunity presents itself. These community projects frequently result in the development of a service project or may become an employment opportunity. Projects may evolve into becoming part of the culture of a health care institution, providing training for staff in several or all departments, or projects may grow and expand to create the need for multiple Healing Touch providers.

Several community projects have grown to provide Healing Touch to large health care systems, regions of a city, or state. In 1991, the first model for providing Healing Touch to hospital in-patients originated at a 500 bed acute tertiary medical center, Queen's Hospital in Honolulu, Hawaii. The program was brought into the hospital through the efforts of Hob Osterlund RN, MS, Nurse Manager of the Pain Clinic (now retired). In this new service, nursing staff were initially trained as providers. Later, volunteers trained in Healing Touch provided sessions to in-patients throughout this health care system. This service continues today.

Subsequently, in 1999, a collaboration of a 12 woman advisory council of Healing Touch students, practitioners and instructors representing Queen's Medical Center, Wilcox Memorial Hospital, Kaiser Permanente, Kapli'olani Medical Center, Healing Touch Hawaii, and the Healing Arts Center established *Bosom Buddies of Hawaii, (BBoH)*. *Bosom Buddies* was the first national Healing Touch Community Service Project to offer free Healing Touch partnerships for one year with women in Hawaii who were diagnosed and undergoing treatment for breast cancer. In this program, Healing Touch students and practitioners underwent further training to address the needs of this patient population.

In 2002, this service program was launched in the Denver, Colorado area by Anne Day, MS, RN, CHTP/I, Sandy Priester BSA, MBA, CHTP, several others from QuaLife Wellness Community, and Lisa Anselme RN, BLS, HN-BC, CHTP/I and Janet Mentgen, BSN, RN, CHTP/I from Healing Touch International, Inc. Established as Healing Buddies this program was re-incorporated as *LifeSpark Cancer Resources* in 2005 to continue this endeavor. In keeping with an expanded mission of *BBoH*, *LifeSpark* trained volunteers to provide Healing Touch to individuals with all forms of cancer, in collaboration with health care facilities throughout the Denver and front-range area.

Healing Partners grew out of a student's volunteer sessions and community project at Stanford University Medical Center in California. Based upon the previous two models, Kathy Turner, RN, NP, CHTP and Elizabeth Helms, RN, MA, CHTP, another student, created the Stanford-based program in 2005 to serve hundreds of women located in the San Francisco Bay area and peninsula region undergoing treatment for breast cancer. A large number of students and practitioners volunteered for three month rotations to provide Healing Touch during the course of medical treatment. The program has been expanded to work with anyone undergoing cancer treatment. *Healing Touch Buddies*, a similar project, located in Jupiter, Florida, was established in 2004 through the efforts of Judy Lynn Ray, MS, LMT, CHTP/I and Betty Ann Baker, LMT, CHTP. Many communities have Healing Touch service programs integrated with cancer treatment and other health related issues in hospitals, hospice centers, clinics and community health settings.

According to the publication *Healing Touch and Health Care Integration* (2007), Healing Touch programs have been integrated as a hospital-based volunteer approach, and some programs have evolved into paid positions for both nursing staff and non-medical persons. Other settings where Healing Touch has been integrated include outpatient clinics, hospice, and long term care facilities. Additionally, Healing Touch may be provided by medical employees in their course of duty. Other models include the development of individual private practice businesses or group practices integrating Healing Touch practice with other healing arts providers. Another format is the creation of integrative clinics, where Healing Touch is included with wellness classes and other healing arts or medical modalities that use a holistic approach. Further, church-related health and spiritual ministry departments have integrated Healing Touch into their services by providing sessions for house-bound or hospitalized parishioners. Churches also offer clinics for parishioners and the public. Some request a donation to a scholarship fund to provide training for additional practitioners.

Although the HTI Healing Touch Certificate Program curriculum is a continuing education offering, it has been integrated into community college and private and public university systems. Integration has occurred in both traditional allied health training and advanced training for holistic health professionals.

Healing Touch is ground breaking, bringing the work to where it is needed by those who are drawn to provide it. Jobs are not created for the practitioners, but arise from students and practitioners tapping into creative possibilities, following the energy, and working within their skill sets and networks to bring forth this healing work. The practitioners' charge is to find or create their niche. Janet Mentgen frequently stated that with every step she took, she was bringing light to the earth and working to transform the world. Where are your steps leading you in your journey?

Holistic care encourages the study and proficiency of a variety of modalities to address the totality of client's needs—physically, emotionally, mentally, and spiritually. Healing Touch practitioners may integrate multiple modalities into their sessions, and practitioners of other modalities may integrate Healing Touch into their professional modality. While practitioners may not have all the training or credentialing needed to practice multiple modalities, they are encouraged to be knowledgeable of available resources and refer their clients to other modalities as necessary.

Integrating Healing Touch with other Health Care and Healing Arts Roles

Health care providers are held to their highest credentialing, licensure, and scope of practice when integrating Healing Touch into their work. Nurses can and do integrate Healing Touch into most aspects of their practice, and many techniques are short and specifically created for that purpose. As identified through a poll of State Boards of Nursing in the United States, the addition of Healing Touch to standard nursing care is within the nurse's legal scope of practice when the nurse is trained in Healing Touch. This holds true in many other countries, although it may vary by each country's nursing regulatory agencies. Healing Touch is also considered to be an independent and autonomous nursing function. It is suggested that Healing Touch be administrated through the policy and procedure of the nurse's facility or agency.

Massage therapists can also integrate Healing Touch into their professional body work practice. Healing Touch is offered by allowing the loving energy to flow through their hands while massaging—perhaps starting with a *Chakra Connection* to enhance relaxation, using *Mind Clearing* to create a quiet mind, and incorporating specific pain relieving techniques to further loosen muscles and deepen their work. Physical and Occupational Therapists working within their scope of practice may include specific Healing Touch pain relief and relaxation techniques with their patients.

Healing arts providers offering other energy therapies—such as Reiki, Cranial Sacral Therapy, acupuncture, spiritual direction, or coaching—must work within their legal scope of practice when offering Healing Touch services. If qualified, they can integrate Healing Touch techniques to better approach the person's presenting issues. As Healing Touch is open to all with an interest in healing, providers are encouraged to know the legal parameters in their areas of residence and in their professional fields regarding license to touch, and then practice accordingly. In the United States, a growing number of states have passed a Health Freedom Act that allows non-licensed practitioners to practice those healing arts for which they are trained, with provision of full disclosure to the public of their training and practicing within the scope of practice of that training.

Integrating with Other Modalities

Because Healing Touch is a "stand alone" collection of techniques developed to facilitate another's healing, other techniques or procedures are usually not needed to accomplish mutual goals with the client. However, with training and development, a practitioner may find that adding other modalities for which they have acquired training and credentialing, may facilitate the movement of energy in a different or unique way that enhances healing.

Optimally, practitioners should have a strong base in Healing Touch and its techniques before integrating other modalities into a session.

Likewise, practitioners should have adequate training in the therapy to be integrated. This allows practitioners to have a working knowledge of the unique response to each therapy and the possible additive benefits. However, integrating multiple techniques in a single session is not the ideal. A common misunderstanding is that "more is better," whereas working at a deeper level often requires less intervention. When Healing Touch is used alone, the recommendation is that "less is more" in terms of the number of Healing Touch techniques used, while carefully ensuring individual needs are addressed, and this applies to the inclusion of additional modalities as well.

Careful selection of clients is necessary for integrative work. Informing the client and obtaining consent for any additional techniques is imperative whether the practitioner is adding Healing Touch techniques to a session (massage or other therapies) or a Healing Touch provider is including additional modalities. Practitioners should also explain their qualifications/ training in the additional modality and any implications it may have for care.

Some examples of integrating Healing Touch with other techniques follow. Guided imagery is an example of one modality that can be Integrated with Healing Touch, and BioScalar Healing is another. The BioScalar technique was gifted to Rauni Prittinen King and Anne Day by Dr. Valerie Hunt and was presented at the Healing Touch International conference in 2007 and gifted to the organization.

Guided Imagery

By Diane Wind Wardell, PhD, RN, WHNP, AHN-BC, CHTP/I

Guided imagery techniques have been integrated into Healing Touch for approximately two decades. Through the guidance of her spiritual mentor, Claire Etheridge, a psychologist, Janet Mentgen introduced the reading of "scripts" while doing Healing Touch in the early 1990's. This technique was then taught by Myra Tovey, RN, a nurse and Healing Touch colleague.

Two studies, one by Jain and colleagues (2012) and the other as a Healing Touch initiative at University of Arizona (See http://drc.arizona.edu/spotlight/20) have used Healing Touch along with guided imagery audio-recordings. The audio recordings were developed by a psychologist and guided imagery expert, Belleruth Naparstek, LISW, MA, for veterans experiencing post-traumatic stress disorder (PTSD). Naparstek's presentation at the 13th Annual Healing Touch International, Inc. Conference in Tucson, Arizona in 2009 demonstrated the importance of creating peacefulness and calm and of not recreating trauma. Her recordings cover a variety of situations, including healthful sleep, stress relief, weight loss, healing grief, trauma, cancer, and general well-being.

One study, published in *Military Medicine* in 2012 by Shamini Jain and others, showed a significant reduction in PTSD symptoms, depression, and improvements in mental quality of life in returning combat veterans. Treatment included a combination of Healing Touch, administered twice a week for 3 weeks, and listening to guided imagery recordings daily. The study done in 2011 as a Healing Touch initiative with returning veterans who were students at the University of Arizona also reported preliminary findings in the reduction of depression and improvement of symptoms.

Using guided imagery recordings or reading scripts while performing Healing Touch techniques can be a powerful way to supplement Healing Touch work. Skill is required for selecting those individuals who would most benefit, and training is needed in how to select and integrate the appropriate material. Delivery, in the case of reading scripts, also needs to be practiced in order to get the proper voice cadence in relation to hand placement. This also needs to be done in the appropriate sequence to match the story being told in the imagery or script.

The outcome can be an energetic "matching" of words (mental) with physical touch (body) that moves through the healing process in a more gentle and holistic fashion. The client has an opportunity to re-integrate at a more complex and complete level using these matched vibrations.

BioScalar Healing

By RAUNI PRITTINEN KING, RN, BSN, MIH, HNB-BC, CHTPI, BASED ON THE WORK, WRITINGS, AND INTERVIEWS OF DR. VALERIE HUNT

Before applying the *BioScalar Technique* in an energy session, it is helpful to understand its underpinnings. Since health is the ideal state of a constantly self-healing organism, Dr. Valerie Hunt renowned author, researcher and Professor in Physiological Science (retired) at the University of California at Los Angeles, identifies two key responsibilities for self-healing: (1) remove conditions known to lower our human resistance, including lifestyle choices; and (2) assume primary responsibility for health through our attitudes, practices, and meditative skills. She further defines health as a self-organizing biofield that allows for successful evolutionary adaptation. The mark of health is a constantly self-healing field that has a coherent flexible relationship with a person's self and the world. Health is also beyond any single state of consciousness, but is a continuum of consciousness (Hunt, 1997).

Dr. Hunt found that some energy frequencies are tied to disease and some to the emotions behind the disease or to one's behavior, interests, and motivation. In her laboratory, she observed that cancer patients who had no red color vibrations in their energy fields—which are related to the lower electromagnetic spectrum—more often succumbed to the illness. Those patients, who had these lower field vibrations and the color red in their fields, had good prognosis, remission, or cure. Therefore, if practitioners could see red in the energy field of the patients with cancer, or if the patients could experience it in their bodies, their healing capacity was accelerated. According to Dr. Hunt, the energy of the cancer field is present even if the cancer is in remission. She feels that the energy of the cancer field must be changed for the cancer to be permanently healed. Dr. Hunt does not agree with the premise that the cancer creates a lower energy frequency and that the vibrations of the person need to be raised to treat it. She believes people with cancer have frequencies that are too high and need to be grounded. The patient may need the lower frequencies to sustain them physically (the red root chakra is related to grounding and physical energy). Sometimes the cancer field is trying to stimulate the color red to increase the lower vibrations; therefore, it is important to keep the lower chakras active. She observed that when human body frequencies become complex, coherent and flowing, the body's physiology operates at maximum efficiency, and health is then insured.

For that reason, it is important for healers to understand the concepts of self-healing for themselves and their clients. We know that electromagnetic environments in which we live powerfully affect our biological fields (Hunt, 1995). Each disease, perhaps, has its own energy field which must be reversed or shifted before healing can occur. For example, in looking at healing the soul, some healers believe that "forgetting who you are" on a soul level is the source of the illness. Most importantly, a person's will to recover stimulates the body's natural healing response to overcome the imbalance. Medicine frequently refers to those healings as spontaneous remissions.

From her 40 years of studying bioenergy fields, Dr. Valerie Hunt postulated the concept of a static scalar or a standing wave. Through her research and observations of psychic healers, who could open and close the body with no bleeding and scars, she became aware of a profoundly different energy state used by the healers, unlike any she had experienced before. During these surgeries, she found that there was no electromagnetic wave action; but rather "a standing" or "stationary" wave was noted during the psychic healing state. She termed this BioScalar energy. She believes that it is essentially the electromagnetic phenomena of all healing techniques.

BioScalar energy is different from electromagnetic energy in that it has no frequency; it is static, stationery, a "standing" energy. Dr. Hunt explained that this is a powerful, passive energy that can be directed to anywhere in the body to heal trauma, remove inflammation, eliminate pain, and cure disease. She believes scalar waves are the electromagnetic phenomena of all effective healing techniques. As part of the electromagnetic field of the universe, scalar waves are organized in a unique form at the level of the atom. Scalar waves are created when two waves of equal frequency meet head on at 180 degrees. Instead of another wave, the frequencies cancel out and this creates a "glob" of energy that is a standing wave. These scalar waves can be directed to expand in all directions within the body and can be used with a clear intention for healing (Hunt, 1995).

BioScalar Technique

The *BioScalar Technique* is a full body technique developed by Dr. Hunt for the purpose of accelerating the healing process of tissue congestion or edema by removing physical, mental, emotional, and spiritual debris and enhancing the optimal circulation of the lymphatic system. The *BioScalar Technique* is used specifically for working with individuals who have cancer and for before, during, and after surgery, although it can be used for any healing as its purpose is to expand the healing vibrations in the body. Dr. Hunt taught the technique to Anne Day and Rauni Prittinen King in April, 2006 in her Southern California home.

Setting the intent for healing is important and can be done with the client. Intent creates emotion, which creates major changes in the fields. It is important that the healer emotionally care about the intention, since intent is emotional versus intellectual. The amount of emotional energy and focus put into the intention will create more scalar energy. Proceed by allowing the energy to do the work, and letting go of any attachment to the outcome. The technique can be done on the self or on another, as explained below (V. Hunt, personal communication, April, 2006):

Self-Healing with the BioScalar Technique

1. Relax by using the breath and spinning your chakras to open your field.
2. Visualize your entire body as a container that draws in electromagnetic energy with each inhalation.
3. Begin by breathing into your body from side-to-side, or from top-to-bottom. It may help to visualize a color vibration coming into your body and meeting head-on with the wave from the other side at 180 degrees. This begins to form a scalar standing wave in the center of the body. Continue this breathing in and visualization until there is a feeling of fullness. You have created a powerful quantity of energy within you.
4. Begin to let this energy "wavelike glob" expand outward through all the cells of your body as it gradually moves to the body's surface. It is like a pool of moisture moving outward on a paper towel. As this scalar wave expands, it affects the fluids of the body. This energy works to dissipate tension in the body by loosening tight muscles and connective tissue and expanding

the space between the cells. This allows the lymphatic system to flow more freely, thus facilitating healing.

5. Direct this energy to go to wherever you need extra healing at this time—use your intention with emotion! Notice how the body begins to feel lighter, larger, and more resilient.

BioScalar Technique with Others

1. Set your intention for healing (as described above).
2. Place hands or intent to the opposite sides of the body—side to side, or top to bottom. If two healers are working together, use the same vibrational frequency (agree on the same color). Allow energy vibration to come from opposite sides (180 degrees) to create the scalar energy, which is a standing wave within the body.
3. Breathe in energy; it comes into our hands in a stream. Do not break or breathe out this energy. The collection of standing energy gets bigger and bigger and creates a powerful quantity of energy in the center of the body (it feels full).
4. Send this scalar energy to the area to be healed in the client. Tell it what to do. See the organ as healthy instead of with disease. Affirm that the healing is taking place and completing the process.

The scalar wave is believed to work on the atomic level, unlike electromagnetic energy that works through connective tissue. As the scalar wave expands out in all directions, the cellular tissues become less compressed and all fluids flow more freely, including lymphatic circulation. Painful, tight areas become lighter and less congested. This results in accelerated healing of the tissues.

Healing Touch through Appropriate Languaging and Frame of Reference

One of the Healing Beyond Borders (HBB) Code of Ethics/ Standards of Practice is to explain Healing Touch to individuals in a way that they can understand the process. A simple explanation is best, informing clients or patients as to what they might experience, adding information as needed. It is important to "meet them where they are." For example, engineers use the paradigm of systems and mechanics and medical professionals refer to science and research studies. The scientific minded often want to explore the underlying mechanisms of energy, while spiritual communities or church groups are more likely to explore Healing Touch from their individual perspectives. It is important to know the audience, their culture, frame of reference, and "languaging." This permits interfacing in a matching manner that facilitates understanding and communication and opens the possibility of integrating Healing Touch into that paradigm. The following section is an example of this concept.

The Interface between Healing Touch and Religion

By Terry Ann Sparks, JD, MDiv, CHTP/I

One of the really great things about Healing Touch is that it is an easily accessible method for helping people open to the depth and breadth of what it means to be a fully alive human being. During Healing Touch sessions, people often experience an expanded consciousness and spiritual depths they may not have experienced previously. They may feel surrounded by love from any number of sources. They may feel peace and joy. Many of these experiences and emotions parallel religious experiences and emotions. Because of the similarity in experience, clients, and sometimes practitioners, can come away with the thought that Healing Touch is a religious practice. Healing Touch is not a religious practice and does not ascribe to a particular spiritual belief system, but it can be used by all people, whatever their religious and/or spiritual orientation.

As an ordained United Methodist clergy (Christian Protestant denomination), I have been a Staff Chaplain within the United States Veterans Affairs Hospital System for a number of years. I practice Healing Touch as part of my chaplain duties. I find that some scientifically oriented medical and mental health personnel often are "put off" if they perceive that Healing Touch has religious or "New Age" overtones. Similarly, conservative religious people often are opposed to Healing Touch if it appears religious, their concern being it may not match the tenants of their particular religious practice.

In the United States it is mandated that health care professionals and systems must acknowledge a patient's spiritual belief system. Yet, medical and mental health professionals are scientifically oriented in their professional life. Whatever their personal belief system, they often do not want to put something that appears religious into their medical or mental health practice. Some of them are becoming more open to integrating spirituality into their practice, and may talk about ultimate reality, if not religion. Yet many want to maintain science and religion as separate, and for some, even science and spirituality. Calling Healing Touch a "spiritual path", talking about angels and guides in conjunction with Healing Touch, or putting it into a religious context can be alienating. These health professionals see themselves as looking out for the best interests of their patients and of the medical/mental health system as a whole.

It takes an open mind to challenge an existing worldview by looking at the scientific grounding in cellular biology and quantum physics that supports Healing Touch. Some may not be willing to make changes in their own worldview as it may be too dissonant with their belief system, while others will use a "let's see" approach. Still others will embrace this new way of thinking about the quantum universe and seek further scientific evidence.

For most Christians and people of other religious faiths, Healing Touch's scientific basis is an adequate explanation. However, if Healing Touch is presented in religious or even spiritual terms, it may alienate people with conservative religious views. Their belief may be that if

Healing Touch is permitted within their particular religious system, it would actively call on Jesus, G_d, Allah, Buddha, Krishna, Great Spirit or whatever the person's tradition calls the Higher Power. For this reason, conservative religious people may respond to Healing Touch as healing "through a false god." Some label Healing Touch as "New Age" as a way of talking about a religious system that their beliefs do not sanction. They are responding out of their worldview, their belief system, or to what they see as prohibited religious practice.

A way does exist to talk about Healing Touch that is sensitive to these concerns, making Healing Touch more accessible for many people. The energy grid and the energy itself is simply what exists, and this appears to some physicists to be the way the universe is structured. There are no Hindu quarks, Jewish photons, Christian electrons, Islamic quantum waves, or Buddhist neutrinos. I have no doubt that these all participate in Ultimate Reality in their own way, but probably not in a way that closely resembles human religious practice. Religious systems generally have particular ways of understanding God/Higher Power, expectations of behavior, loyalty to the religious community, and so forth. In a way, religious systems are a way of understanding how our lives integrate with the energy and with the grid, but the energy itself is not defined by our religious conceptions.

When I talk with religious people about Healing Touch, I share my belief that the energy system is simply part of what God put into Creation. I allow them to draw their own conclusions about the presence of the energy system in the created world, how it got there, and what purpose it serves without trying to persuade them of anything. This is one reason Healing Touch is not religiously based. The energy is beyond all our religious conceptions. It simply exists. I happily discuss any biblical or other references, either for or against the idea of energy, angels, spiritual beings, and so forth that the person may bring up as a concern. I want the person to receive Healing Touch standing in their own integrity. If they believe Healing Touch is not a comfortable fit with their belief system, they have the choice not to receive it.

For those people who have Christian religious objections and questions, one common concern is that receiving Healing Touch will open a person to unwanted spiritual influences. At that point I might remind them of the overwhelming and protective power of the resurrected Christ whom they follow. Sometimes people will say that their friend or their pastor says Healing Touch is not Christian. I invite the person to think about her or his own experience of God or Higher Power, and consider whether Healing Touch is congruent with that. Sometimes the idea of the energy as love itself, or disinterested "agape" love, is helpful to a person with these concerns. Because Healing Touch is not religiously based, it does not contain any religious concepts— unless people add them. This encourages thinking for oneself.

The simplest approach is for the Healing Touch practitioner to simply be in connection with the source of unconditional love and compassion and support the client's spiritual belief system. Another option is to offer to teach the person how to do Healing Touch on him or herself, and in that way the person controls the framework for the session, and can use Healing Touch according to his or her own belief system. Healing Touch does not contain religious content, but it can be added by the person who chooses to see it through a particular religious worldview. For example, the person can begin their energy session with a prayer, either quietly or audibly, to set the intention for the session.

Healing Touch does help us connect with and experience what is most deeply human within us, the things we generally think of when we think about spirituality. One way to describe spirituality is that it is about three relationships: relationship with self, with other people, and with the person's Higher Power/God. From the tradition of Alcoholics Anonymous, the "Higher Power" is that which is greater than the self, so that a person can experience this in a way that is meaningful to him or her. In this way of looking at spirituality, each person's spiritual connection is unique because we all experience these relationships differently. Healing Touch can help us connect with this deep level of experience and can help us communicate from a place of connection and universality. Coming from a place of greater awareness, Healing Touch allows us to recognize the commonality we all share in the depths of human experience.

Healing Touch is based on the energy itself, and the energetic structures it forms; something that simply exists. Healing Touch also helps us connect with the deeply human, deeply spiritual center of ourselves, where we can find commonality with other people. Together, this forms a strong foundation for Healing Touch, one that makes it available to everyone, whatever their worldview.

Once people understand that the foundation for Healing Touch *is not religiously based*, they can choose to place their own religious/spiritual/worldview framework on top of it, if they so desire, to understand Healing Touch in their own way. A person, who sees life through a worldview of science, can understand Healing Touch as a way of working with the particles and waves of the field. A person, who sees human life as an outgrowth of God's love and practices a particular religion, may view Healing Touch as a form of laying-on-of-hands healing, or as a physical form of prayer. Someone, whose worldview includes angels and guides involved in our lives, can understand them as helping with Healing Touch work. If we present Healing Touch as having a non-religious foundation, open to being used by people of all worldviews and all religious frameworks, it will be much more available to everyone. This way of practicing Healing Touch is radically inclusive, and allows Healing Beyond Borders to be an open, welcoming and inclusive community of healers.

Creating a Venue for Healing Touch—Preparing for Integration

By Sue Kagel, BSN, RN, HNB-BC, CHTP/I

Whether setting up a small Healing Touch venue or entertaining a larger creative vision, there are some preparatory steps to consider. It is important to know what you bring to the table. Listing your skill-set on paper will give you a better sense of what you have to offer and allow you to capitalize on your unique skills in your presentations and conversations. Evaluate your own skills and strengths and allow them to lead you to where you are best suited. Consider your area of training, career path, experience, and expertise.

Connections, networking, and circles of influence may assist in opening doors, so note where you have influence and acknowledgement for what you do. There is a saying "grow where you are planted," and it is apropos in this situation. Integrating Healing Touch into a new area works best when you have that area of expertise and have connections within that area. Set up your venue where you have the background, experience and acknowledgment from those around you. Walking into an arena where you have none of the above is generally not successful. However, teaming up and collaborating with someone who does have the necessary background, expertise, credentials, sphere of influence, and "insider" positioning, does significantly enhance and optimize the potential for a successful endeavor.

Remember these points: 1) know yourself, 2) know your clients 3) find where you insert, and 4) develop a holistic plan and approach that shows the benefits of Healing Touch to those who will be the end users. Although all of these points are recommended for successful integration, they may not be weighted equally, depending on the situation.

Approaching Integration from the Inside

While it is exciting to bring Healing Touch into new settings, experience has shown that introducing Healing Touch into existing settings works best when brought forward by practitioners who are already employed by or work in conjunction with the facility. Collaborating with immediate supervisors who can support the practitioner and introducing Healing Touch concepts to the administration is a good strategy, as a team approach has been found to be very effective. It is best to proceed within the institutional system in a gentle and loving manner, creating a scenario that incorporates the right timing, right place, and right people. The following segments are personal accounts of the experience of integrating Healing Touch and provide wonderful examples of the far reaching effects that are possible as Healing Touch ripples out into a system.

Integrating Healing Touch into Healthcare Organizations

By Rauni Prittinen King, RN, MIH, BSN, HNB-BC, CHTPI

Scripps Health is a large, prestigious health care system in Southern California with over 13,500 employees and some 2,700 affiliated physicians. Scripps Health has five hospitals and many outpatient clinics, which are distributed around San Diego County. Scripps Clinic is the largest multi-specialty clinic with approximately 400 physicians. Scripps Clinic and Green Hospital are only a parking lot away from the Scripps Center for Integrative Medicine (SCIM) in La Jolla, overlooking the Torrey Pines Golf Course and the Pacific Ocean.

What follows is my story of how Healing Touch was integrated within Scripps and where it is today. I introduced Healing Touch in 1993 while I was working in the intensive care unit (ICU) at Scripps Memorial Hospital in La Jolla. I had attended a weekend retreat and, as a side offering, learned about energy healing. This retreat changed my entire life and took my career path in a direction of health and healing. I was determined to bring this newly found way of healing to patients who were so sick in my unit. Although I was already using tools that modern medicine offered, I knew something was missing, but I did not know what it was. After giving and receiving Healing Touch, I felt that I had found what I had been looking for but could not identify—healing. I did not focus on the fact that the health care system was conservative and that the energy system was not part of medical and nursing education at that time. My vision was to make healing available for all Scripps patients, and I was ultimately successful in this mission.

I was fascinated with the simple hands on healing and how it made a difference to my patients. Many of them were trauma patients, and not only were they physically traumatized, but they also suffered emotional, mental, and spiritual traumas as well. It did not take much time for our trauma and open heart surgeons to recognize that the patients who received Healing Touch were calmer and often able to move out of ICU sooner than other patients.

My fellow nurses observed this healing work and saw the benefits. I convinced them to take the Healing Touch Level 1 class offered in San Diego. I invited 10 of my colleagues to take that daring step into the unknown and learn about the human energy system. Healing Touch was so unlike the hemodynamics and other biometrics that were on top of our daily work list. One nurse went to her religious services on a Sunday morning concerned that Healing Touch was not aligned with the teachings of her faith. She became one of the biggest supporters of Healing Touch.

Little did we know that this healing modality was going to spread throughout the Scripps system and become one of the healing treatments for both in-patients and out-patients. I coordinated all Scripps Healing Touch classes until I became a Certified Healing Touch Instructor. Forty participants enrolled in the first two classes. The momentum of Healing Touch took off. Since then there have been hundreds of Healing Touch classes at Scripps, which has resulted in over 2000 trained personnel (mostly nurses).

My career slowly took me away from critical care to holistic healing. Around the mid 1990's, when we started the Dr. Dean Ornish Program for Reversing Heart Disease multi-center heart trial, I met Dr. Mimi Guarneri, a Scripps Clinic Interventional cardiologist. The Ornish program studied the impact of vegetarian diet, yoga, meditation, group support, and exercise on sick patients with cardiovascular disease and focused on the power of lifestyle change. We realized that there was a need to do more and as a result, our vision evolved to create Scripps Center for Integrative Medicine (SCIM), which is now nationally and internationally known.

No matter what job description I have had, Healing Touch has always been a very important part of my work. While working as the Director of Programs and Planning, I had the opportunity to implement Healing Touch in various forms at Scripps. My goal was to create a full time, paid position for a nurse to provide Healing Touch to patients. I wrote a proposal for this position in 1999, which was immediately approved. The position was implemented at the SCIM and Scripps Green Hospital. We started a Nurse Appreciation Day annual event at SCIM at that time, and Healing Touch was introduced to the nurses as one of the offerings.

One of my objectives has been to conduct Healing Touch research. This is an important priority since the healthcare community frequently wants evidence-based practice. We have conducted several protocols using Healing Touch with cardiac surgery and bilateral knee replacement patients. Recently we published a study in the journal *Military Medicine* on post-traumatic stress disorder (PTSD) using Healing Touch and Guided Imagery with returning active duty military personnel (Jain et al., 2012).

Currently at Scripps Memorial Hospital in La Jolla, Patricia Wragg, RN, CCRN, CHTP/I, administers Healing Touch for three different departments in her role as a critical care nurse and CHTP. She provides daily treatments in all three ICUs and PCU based on referrals from the intensivists, nursing staff, patients, and families. She also offers Healing Touch to family members of critically ill patients. One day per week she works for Palliative Care and provides Healing Touch for symptom management. The new "LVad program" has a mandatory referral for Palliative Care, and patients report liking Healing Touch "very much". One day per week, she works at the Cardiac Treatment Center, where Healing Touch is offered to patients and staff members.

Elizabeth "Liz" Fraser, BSN, CHTP/I, is at SCIM and Scripps Green Hospital as the Healing Modalities Coordinator. She provides Healing Touch with Guided Imagery CDs to the cardiac surgery patients pre and post-operatively. She implemented this same protocol for plastic surgery patients as well as liver and kidney transplant patients. She also provides Healing Touch to bone marrow transplant patients, cancer patients, orthopedic patients and others for pain management, relaxation and stress reduction, depending on referrals. The requests can be from the patient, patient family members, nurses and/or physicians. The treatments are given for approximately 20 minutes, charted in the patient record, and provided without fee. She provides Healing Touch with music and sometimes incorporates guided imagery or aromatherapy. At SCIM, Liz provides Healing Touch for out-patients and charges a fee for service. She also participates in research protocols as a healer when it involves Healing Touch and Guided Imagery. Liz coordinates bringing in Healing Touch students and volunteer practitioners to provide Healing Touch at various Scripps events, such as nursing and medical conferences. This is great way to bring awareness of Healing Touch and light to the medical providers.

Mary Jane Aswegan, RN, CHTP/I, at Scripps Encinitas is a nurse educator who was asked in 2004 to coordinate and start a Healing Touch program there. Her goal has been to teach nurses and staff to incorporate Healing Touch into their routine nursing care. Healing Touch is listed in their charting as an option, along with pain medication, and has been incorporated into the "Relaxing Care Team", which offers Healing Touch from 4–8 pm. During a recent realignment of Nursing Education, Mary Jane moved into the Center for Learning and Innovation. Currently she teaches Healing Touch Classes at Scripps Encinitas, Scripps Mercy, and Scripps Chula Vista. She also facilitates a monthly Healing Touch support group. Scripps Encinitas Rehabilitation Center also uses Healing Touch in their Brain Injury Program.

Donna Cahill, RN, CNS, CHTP, at Scripps Mercy Hospital and Scripps Chula Vista Hospital and a Clinical Nurse Specialist for Pain and Palliative Care, spear-headed Healing Touch, which began to grow with dedicated interest in April 2009. I have seen before that it takes a champion, preferably someone who is an insider, to bring Healing Touch into a new setting. Donna wanted patients and families to have an improved sense of well-being through care and compassion. Current ways that Healing Touch have been integrated into the hospital activities and events include supporting a healthy work environment for staff, direct offerings of Healing Touch to patients and families, and education for staff, physicians, and the community. Donna is now engaged in teaching Healing Touch at the new graduate RN training program. One aspect of Donna's role is to bring complementary modalities to the patient's bedside as needed. Pain and Palliative Care receives direct physicians' orders for Healing Touch and other complementary modalities for anxiety and pain.

Healing Touch is part of "department specific team building" events to enhance a healthy work environment. Healing Touch is also requested during times of high morale distress and fatigue in areas such as the Emergency Department, Intensive Care Unit, and Trauma Unit. Since 2009, over 200 staff members have been provided with Healing Touch. Virtual healing rooms have been set up to ensure easy access for staff.

Individual units have designated healing rooms with additional healing spaces in the Outpatient Behavioral Health and Medical Surgical units. Practice groups are being established to provide Healing Touch on a weekly basis to staff on dedicated days and times.

Healing Touch is now in most of the major medical centers in the San Diego area and has a very prominent role in community organizations and events, such as the annual San Diego Heart Walk and Stand Down for Homeless Veterans. I am working to expand Healing Touch integration to other healthcare organizations in the USA and abroad, including the United States Veterans Administration Hospitals. I am proud to "do this work," as Janet Mentgen often said. I was fortunate to have Janet as my teacher and mentor. I will continue her mission and work by teaching and giving presentations in various venues and conferences throughout the world, as well as providing Healing Touch treatments and education in hospitals and in the community—Spreading Healing Light Worldwide.

Integrating Healing Touch in a Health Resort Environment

By Sue Kagel, BSN, RN, HNB-BC, CHTP/I

As a nurse, I have always been interested in wellness and holistic approaches. I had joined the American Holistic Nurses' Association (AHNA), taken a Therapeutic Touch course, and read everything I could find on the subject well before my first Healing Touch class. In 1991, I was very excited to begin working at Canyon Ranch Health Resort in Tucson, Arizona, a holistic mecca with an international clientele that embodies an integrative approach. Services include preventive and standard western medicine and a mini urgent care. Additional consultations provide nutrition, exercise physiology, life management, oriental medicine, bodywork, energy modalities, meditation, yoga, breathing, spirituality, and much more. This setting contains all aspects of what I had been studying, and I felt I was "home."

My hands were "calling me" to work with them through some

form of healing arts. I explored many options and in the process, I was introduced to Healing Touch by Donna Gilson, RN, who had studied with Janet Mentgen. I was drawn to Healing Touch because it is born out of nursing and has a certification credential to lend academic credibility, which was very important to me and later aided in opening many doors. I began my studies in Healing Touch shortly after my employment at Canyon Ranch and was rapidly convinced of its effectiveness in my personal healing experience with chronic fatigue syndrome.

As an eager student of Healing Touch, I offered Healing Touch sessions to staff members during my lunch hour. One of these was an area supervisor who was feeling very ill as a side effect from radiation treatment for cancer. He responded with an immediate reduction in nausea and fatigue. In the ensuing follow-up conversation, I was asked what I wanted to do with this work. I replied that my dream was to bring Healing Touch as a service within the medical department that would be performed by certified nurses. I was told to "Hold on to that dream."

My dream became a shared dream as I continued to discuss and practice Healing Touch with staff members and encouraged other nurses to learn Healing Touch. As Assistant Nursing Manager, I had relationships with all levels of administration. I provided administrators with in-services and gave Healing Touch sessions—which they loved. As I continued my studies, I was encouraged to submit a proposal to bring Healing Touch to Canyon Ranch. Credentialing is an important component at Canyon Ranch when offering services. When I completed the Healing Touch Certificate Program, then offered through the AHNA, the proposal was accepted, and I was granted permission to begin creating the service. My dream had come true.

We had laid the groundwork over the two year period while I was continuing my studies, working as a team with the support and assistance of the Nurse Manager, Nancy Arbas, BSN, RN, HNB-BC. During this time we met with each department to inform them of our new service, discussed concerns, and garnered support throughout the facility, which was not an easy task as we were breaking new ground. Simultaneously, Nancy and I also completed our holistic nursing training, which included a practicum for creating the vision of a Healing Touch Practice that integrated foundational concepts of holistic nursing and Jean Watson's Theory of Human Caring. We launched this Healing Touch model as a Canyon Ranch offering in September 1996, after I submitted my application for HTI Healing Touch Certification and for Holistic Nursing Certification to the American Holistic Nurses Credentialing Corporation (AHNCC). This original Healing Touch model of practice has been shared and incorporated into other teaching programs and settings.

Two other nurse co-workers, Herschella Horton, RN, BAM, CHTP and Connie Kosky, RN, were not far behind me in their training and began sharing and demonstrating Healing Touch around Canyon Ranch, as well as creating lectures to inform the guests. Healing Touch caught on rapidly and spread by client word of mouth as well as through our marketing strategies, lectures, program advisors, medical/nursing members, and staff members in other departments. Our Healing Touch department grew over the years as I coordinated classes, mentored students, became an instructor, and taught Healing Touch locally as well as internationally to train other Healing Touch providers.

Another door opened, thanks to the Healing Touch Certification credential. In 2001, I was invited to be an instructor, and a year later, the lead instructor of a team creating and teaching an Energy Medicine online module and residential workshops for the University of Arizona Center for Integrative Medicine initiated by Andrew Weil, M.D. The initial residential weeks were held at Canyon Ranch, and I was invited to present a Healing Touch lecture/workshop; many were to follow over the years. The Healing Touch work continued to ripple around the world into medical communities as I sat at my computer in dialogue with the international Integrative Medicine fellows, or provided hands on workshops as the fellows explored integrating alternative and complementary services, such as Healing Touch, for their practices and institutions.

Our number of Certified Healing Touch Practitioners (CHTPs) increased over time as we included nurses Kathie Stogsdill, Claudia Halsell, Ruth Hanon, and Lisa Stone, all who contributed to the early success of Healing Touch in providing healing sessions to our guests. The Healing Touch service spread to the Canyon Ranch, Lenox, Massachusetts facility through Joan Berry, RN. Each Healing Touch practitioner contributed his or her time, energy, and passion to increase the awareness and growth of the service. These efforts led to Healing Touch being offered on the Queen Mary cruise ship. It also permitted one of our CHTPs, Ruth Hanon, RN, MA to create a Healing Touch volunteer service within the newly formed Sunstone Cancer Retreat Center that was affiliated with Canyon Ranch. Tucson students were able to be of service while working on their program and certification requirements, and many of their community projects lead to creating related satellite outreach program offerings around the city.

Canyon Ranch is rewarding for both the "guests" and practitioners. It offers the ability to refer to multiple modalities in one setting that might be needed, and it supports collaborative and synergistic endeavors with the other departments for the betterment of the guests. Healing Touch sessions usually include relaxing music and may integrate guided imagery or breathing and relaxation techniques, but they do not add in other modalities. While Healing Touch is a service located in the medical department, medical issues are not the only focus. Because the Healing Touch service was created with a holistic and integrative approach, it addresses physical, emotional, mental, and spiritual issues that one would not normally consider available at a spa. While a healthy vacation is an option at Canyon Ranch, many are utilizing it as an integrative approach to health and healing.

On the physical level, Healing Touch is provided for a wide range of issues, including acute and chronic health conditions, pre and post-surgery, cancer supportive care, orthopedic post injury and trauma rehabilitation, migraines and unexplained headaches, fertility issues, stress manifesting in the body, and more. The medical staff has respect for Healing Touch and often requests sessions for guests, including those with puzzling diagnoses, in order to explore the energy component. In addition, a variety of services are available for referral after Healing Touch sessions, including medical follow up, nutritional guidance, proper exercise modification, chiropractic adjustments, and physical therapy. We may also work in conjunction with other service providers over several sessions, depending on the length of the guest's stay.

Emotionally, as many guests are high level executives and under tremendous stress, the issues of anxiety, depression, racing mind, relationship and family issues, sleep disturbance, and other stress related symptoms are often encountered. Many come to Canyon Ranch for the sanctuary it provides during times of acute grief, loss, or times of transition that may be minor or all encompassing. They may continue their recovery programs, explore their patterns, or work through weight and eating issues. Guests frequently ask to be "cleared out, unblocked, centered, and grounded." The calming effect of Healing Touch on the mind and body can be enhanced through referrals to breathing class, yoga, tai chi or qi gong, sessions in life management, or various massages. Healing Touch related self-care techniques may be taught during sessions or lectures.

For some, Healing Touch is a spiritual exploration, a seeking or clarifying of mission and purpose, or going inward to hear the quiet voice within. Guests report a feeling of peace that they have not experienced in a long time, if ever. Often guests state on return that they felt their sessions were life changing, creating a sense of lightness, a feeling of being settled back in their bodies, a quieting of their minds, or a release of old patterns. Artists, writers and others in the creative arts find that blocks to their creativity open, and they are once again able to express themselves, sometimes with even more clarity than previously.

Several generations of guests have now come through our Healing Touch service; the guests bring their parents, siblings, adult children, and other relatives. Some frequent guests have received more than 100 sessions over the years. Our practitioners combined have provided 50,000 sessions or more, spreading healing light to our international clientele. As a destination resort, we see guests sometimes only once, perhaps a few times in one stay, frequently every year, or intermittently over many years. Many guests state that they return for Healing Touch as they love the feeling and seek it for specific health issues, especially for relieving emotional stress. We offer Healing Touch referral information so that treatment can continue at home. Several guests have even gone on to study and become certified in Healing Touch.

Lectures on Healing Touch are offered to our guests weekly and include the experiential teaching of *Self Chakra Connection*, breathing, grounding, and a holistic approach to wellness. The Healing Beyond Borders website is given as a resource so that local Healing Touch providers and classes are available to support the guests, their families and friends. All helps to continue spreading the healing light of Healing Touch worldwide.

Personal, Professional, and Institutional Integration

By Deborah Larrimore, BSN, RN, LMBT, CHTP/I

I have been a nurse for 37 years. One might ask how a scientific nurse who at the time was a Head Nurse of an Intensive Care Unit within a major medical university found her way into a non-traditional arena of care. And I ask, "How is it that medicine ever came to a place that this did not exist? How is it that medicine became so advanced that we went backwards?"

Healing Touch ignited a spark within me that has grown into an endless flame. I believe that same spark ignites within each person who finds his or her way into a Healing Touch classroom. I believe the spark soon becomes a light, which illuminates his or her path. And with each passing course and each passing moment that each person extends Healing Touch to another human being, the road becomes a little longer and the mapping better defined.

In my beginning, 20 years ago now (1992), there were no clear directions—only what you might describe as headlights, which helped guide me a short distance. My work in Healing Touch has been a faith walk, not necessarily in a religious way but in a way that acknowledged I was to faithfully walk a path of service.

Healing Touch did not have a formal presence in my area, a southern conservative community in North Carolina. My early task was to not only work personally towards becoming a CHTP, but to raise awareness about Healing Touch in the community.

It was a difficult, personal journey as colleagues, family members and friends scoffed at my study of energy medicine. Of course there were strangers who joined in as well, and so I dealt with lots of "eye rolling," snickers, and comments of skepticism—comments such as "Don't let that woman touch you. We don't know where she gets her power." I knew I was dealing with people's fear of the unknown. And in the kindest of ways, I believe I was dealing with simple ignorance. People simply didn't know, and what they didn't know, scared them.

And what I knew was that I had no greater power than they did. Some people would say to me, "You have *the gift*. You are a healer." For a moment I wondered if I did, or if I was, but my ordinary-self thought not. In the deepest part of me I knew we could all, each and every one, do this work. I decided I must teach, so I set out to do so.

My nursing career continued to unfold. After 15 years of critical care nursing, I left the institution of hospital-based nursing and worked as the Nurse Educator for our local Hospice, which covered the city and county. At the same time my life paralleled with the study of Healing Touch. Many people continued their skepticism and would mockingly ask, "Are you going to take that laying-on of hands course?" I would smile and simply say, "Yes, I guess that I am." I tried not to defend my intrigue or hide my passion. And at the very same time, others would come up to me and ask if I could alleviate their headache or bring comfort to their dying patient.

I dealt with ridicule and judgment from those who did not understand and at the same time, I witnessed miracles of healing. Not miracles of curing, because I was a Hospice Nurse and people were dying. But somehow, Healing Touch was alleviating their suffering, calming their anxiety, and bringing a sense of wholeness to their spirit. I came to know that this was my life's work. If I could bring calm and ease to the dying process for just one person, then I felt my work on this earth was complete. Patient after patient, loved one after loved one, affected me so deeply that my humanness filled with tears and with gratitude. And as this happened, I became more determined to educate not only my community, but in grandiosity, the world.

As a matter of fact, in the wee hours of a morning in 1997, I awoke with a poem that I called "Intention." Simultaneously the thought came into my head that I should send it to the biggest voice I knew at the time, to one who could take this message out into the world. The next morning I went to the mailbox, and with great humbleness thought,

"Who do you think you are?" And with that question, I dropped the poem into the mail to Oprah. It's been 15 years since then. I still wait.

So without a large audience, I set off on foot, to pioneer the land. I opened a private practice, which I maintained for the next 15 years. And it seemed that one person would know another and with the momentum of what at the time seemed like molasses, things eventually began to flow. There were miraculous healings of all sorts and of course those people would tell their neighbors. There were documentaries, local newspaper writings, and then stories about Healing Touch began to emerge on the evening news. People called me a Healer and I called myself a "Healing Presence." I believed I could be present to another person in his or her journey and that presence alone could facilitate the healing process.

Over time my reputation began to build, and over time I was building a community of awareness. I began to educate others and brought Healing Touch classes into the area. Soon there were other "Me's," healers and people who understood energy and who were passionately awakened. In the deepest parts of myself, perhaps in the recesses of my soul, I could see that ancient healing was re-emerging in the modern world of medicine. I knew that to heal with the use of our hands, the use of our hearts, our compassion and our intentions of goodwill . . . was innate.

This was not new age but some of the oldest ways known to mankind. I became convinced that to save the world, to save humankind, I—no, actually We—must help people remember. I believed that people already knew this, but somehow it had been forgotten. Perhaps the increase of Alzheimer's was simply a reflection of what was in existence. The knowledge was within. Now the task was to help people remember.

Either by chance or probably better said, in divine order, my path crossed with a physician who also believed in the effects of energy, human touch and compassion. And as fate would have it, she was on faculty at my previous place of employment, Wake Forest University Baptist Medical Center, those beginning 15 years of critical care. So we teamed up and began teaching second year medical students some of the basic principles of energy, the effects of touch, and the importance of thought or intention. We offered lectures and seminars together in Washington, DC and across the nation.

I also began to revisit old colleagues within the medical center, knocking on doors and bringing in volunteers from the Healing Touch Community to assist in giving free sessions of Healing Touch within the hospital. Weekly we gave free Healing Touch sessions to exhausted parents of children within Brenner, the pediatric hospital. We called it "Tenderly Touching Your Tuesdays." We gave Healing Touch sessions away at health fairs, malls, and churches. We opened a monthly free clinic to the public. We served.

I began to receive small grants and funding through the Integrative Medicine Program at Wake Forest University Baptist Medical Center. I was a huge advocate that the monies be allocated for Healing Touch education, with the thought of educate, educate, educate. I set out to teach Healing Touch to nurses within the hospital and within their specific units, on all shifts from 6 am to midnight and back at 4 am. I brought them coffee and doughnuts, and I brought them human care. I gave Healing Touch to nurses, doctors, unit secretaries, and housekeeping. I believed, and believe, the only way to have Healing Touch accepted was to de-mystify the illusion of "This is a gift I or only a few have." My goal was to teach them that we all have the capacity to promote healing.

Simultaneously, I began to teach Healing Touch in the community, the state, the surrounding states, the nation, and around the world. And with each lecture, each opportunity, I never ended a talk without giving the audience an experience in Healing Touch.

I believe no one truly learns Healing Touch from his or her head. It is not assimilated in the left-brain or through logic. It is knowledge that comes from a deeper place, which defies our current scientific evidence and yet magnifies our spiritual wisdom.

I truly did not know how to reach the multitudes, so I simply reached the ones and twos before me. My hope came from the *100th Monkey Theory*. The story as told by Lyall Watson (1976) is that scientists for over 20 years studied monkeys that lived on an island off the coast of Japan and watched them eat wild sweet potatoes, *dirt and all*. One day, a monkey dug up a potato, went down to the seashore, and washed the dirt off before he ate the potato. Shortly after, another monkey who saw this behavior did the same, and then another and another, all washing their potatoes before eating them. The whole group of monkeys began to change their behavior, because of this one monkey (the exact number of monkeys is not known, so the number 100 is symbolic.) The story goes that when the 100th monkey dug up a potato and took it down to the shore to wash it that within an hour's time, monkeys on two other widely separated islands, who were also being observed by researchers, began to take their potatoes down to the seashore to wash them, although they had not witnessed the new behavior. Prior to this, they ate their potatoes, dirt and all. Class after class, I passed out potatoes. No matter where in the world I went, I would stop and buy potatoes. I was convinced that if I could place a potato in other's hands and they could clasp their hands around it while I told them the 100th Monkey Story, then they could grasp their minds around how "one person at a time, we can change our world." Whether you call it the *100th Monkey Theory*, the tipping point, or critical mass, I knew this teaching was raising human consciousness.

I felt if I could help others realize that when they go back to their homes, their families, their workplace, and the strangers in their own lives, and extend goodwill, kindness and compassion…that when there was enough of us, that somewhere on an island far away…in other countries or within the dark places within our own, human behavior would be changed. I was convinced that one person at a time, we could change the world.

It has now been twenty years and thousands of potatoes later, and I see beautiful hands reaching out to touch others and bring comfort, reaching to hold them and say, "There, there, I am with you. I see your pain. I wish it was not there. I am sorry for your suffering."

My mission then and my mission now remains the same. Let me teach you how to do this work, for your hands work as good as mine. I simply have learned how to use them. I have learned the value of human compassion, goodwill, and unconditional love, extended through the human heart and touch.

My work has expanded from a single nurse offering Healing Touch at the bedside to a community of healers who offer Healing Touch in all sorts of ways—in hospitals, in cancer centers, in health clinics, in Hospices, in schools and in individual homes. The ripple effect continues.

I have coordinated efforts to bring Healing Touch research into major medical centers and have been thrilled to see scientific evidence come forth to support the benefits and effects of Healing Touch. Personally, I did not need the evidence, for time after time it was lying beneath my hands or in the gentle face of a sleeping soul, who moments before had been writhing in pain. Those who don't understand, say "prove it to me" in the laboratory with cells, plants or mice. Show me the changes in the lab values.

And I say, come with me for a moment in time and see the infant who suddenly quits crying, witness the calming of anxiety, see depression lifted in the eyes of another as she looks deeply into your soul with gratitude. So maybe you can understand that I have not cared so much about the evidence as I have the results. And yet I value the importance and acknowledge the necessity of your inquiry.

Give me a moment in your day to teach you and my work is done. I am the instructor, but it's the experience that's the teacher.

In 2008, I returned to my roots and early beginnings, stepping back into the institution of modern medicine. Not as a novice nurse, but this time as a nurse of 37 years who has been on a journey into energy medicine, which has greatly influenced and directed my path. I had traveled the world, teaching from the villages of India and across the canals of Amsterdam to the major cities within the United States.

I currently hold a position in nursing education and research. My responsibilities are to educate our nearly 3000 nurses in the concepts of Healing Touch, to participate in Healing Touch research, and to coordinate the newly launched Healing Touch Consult Service. Through the consult service, Healing Touch is available to all patients and is free. It is a nursing measure, which does not require a physician's order. We have a nursing policy and procedure as well as computerized nursing specialty flow-sheets, designated to the art of Healing Touch. Healing Touch, the ancient art of healing, has found its way around the world and back and now resides in the hallways of my early beginnings. We are an 800 bed tertiary medical center with a Magnet award from the American Awarded Credentialing Center. Our medical institution acknowledges, accepts and values the art of healing.

The thing that supports my work now is the thing that supported it long ago. It is the effects of human touch with a compassionate heart. My work is summarized best in the poem I wrote nearly two decades ago.

Intent

It is with Intent
That you touch the human soul
It is with compassion
That you touch and that you hold
It is with a listening ear that you hear another's heart
It is in the being that you feel what might impart.

Bring your focus to the Spirit
That lies beneath your hands
And allow that part of you to know
What the head can't understand
In the space and in the moment
A sacred time is spent
As love transcends the essence
Of what is called Intent.

©1997

As I age with a lifetime of study and of practice, may my work reveal a small glimpse into healing and the effects that we as human beings can have on one another. May I offer understanding of compassion and intention and may I set aglow within others the desire to carry forth kindness, teaching them how to become a Healing Presence.

"And if I walk this earth but once, may I inspire others to shine so brightly from their being that they illuminate the path of my soul."
—*Deborah*

Chapter Summary

This chapter provided some examples of how Healing Touch can be integrated into one's personal and professional life, integrated with other therapies, and brought into various systems. Through each story, the ripple effect from self to family, to community, and out into the world repeats, each following the energy and moving with the flow to bring Healing Touch into the world in an integrative fashion. The possibilities are endless, and the journey unfolds to bring opportunities to be of service in Healing Touch work.

CHAPTER 11
EVOLUTION OF THE
SELF INTO SERVICE

This final chapter provides a deeper understanding of the nature and foundation of energy work from an expanded focus. It moves from personal creative transformation and transition to ways of being in the world, being of service, evolving our practice, visioning, and manifesting in our lives and for the world. We are scientifically a unified field; how we are and what we do affects everything. Using this information consciously on a personal and professional level and in focused, loving community groups creates the possibility for deep, collective, and collaborative energetic transformation. The objectives for this chapter are as follows:

1. Explore ways for personal enrichment and transformation.
2. Develop a greater degree of conscious awareness in yourself and your healing practice.
3. Recognize ways to contribute by expanding your role of service for your personal mission or purpose.
4. Recognize the principle of energetic connection in working globally.
5. Reflect on the future evolution and possibilities of healing work.

Personal Enrichment and Transformation

By Sue Kagel, BSN, RN, HNB-BC, CHTP/I

Healing Touch has the potential to facilitate personal transformation. For some, a single session may be life changing. As the energy shifts into a balanced state, the person quiets, perhaps receives insight, and feels lighter and more connected to the self and beyond. A client expressed her experience by journaling it poetically the day after a session.

Awakening

I am waking up to this new day
Arising to a new ME
I feel liberated, Shiny, radiant and free
Feeling as if a ton of weight has been lifted from my
    back and heart.
I am light. I am radiant love and joy.
Delighted with myself and this new day.
The cage that held me hostage has been removed and
    I am dancing and twirling in my new light body.
The stillness within is glowing like never before.
I am feeling so inspired and grateful.

by Mika Fly

Another client described the Healing Touch journey in this way:

Work on the self is an ongoing process. It brings me joy, inner peace, unity and connectedness. It reawakens the inner child and brings me to a place of light and playfulness. The sense of wholeness invites others to that place. I feel a shift to joy and laughter to sustain me.

From a global perspective, another client offered that he felt "connected to everything beyond myself—spiritually to all things." Others have shared experiences, such as the following: "I'm walking much lighter on my feet. I feel lighter in my body as I move." "It moves me through the journey from my head to my heart." "It has increased my intuitive abilities and the confidence to follow my inner guidance." "In my desperation and emptiness, you have given me hope! Please know you helped change a life and path in someone in need. I will never forget."

A group of students attending a Healing Touch Level 2 workshop shared that they had committed to working on their personal healing after attending a Healing Touch Level 1 class a few months prior. Sharing their personal transformation experiences resulting from use of the self-care techniques for personal health and development, the students noted the following: "It awakens inner joy, and a mindfulness of what fills you up." "I moved to a place of higher personal integrity; more loving and compassionate, better boundaries." "Healing Presence, it becomes how you live your life. It becomes who you are, how you show up in the world." They also reported that it was a process. "Peace with who I am, allowing the process, moving through the journey, alignment with self, increased energy and cognitive function." Another shared an experience of "Shifting in work, not clear, but able to allow, accept, release, not attached." There was also a sense of being embodied, grounded, and balanced. Students reported moving out of chaos or toxic situations, making changes in their jobs and relationships as well as changing their environment by clearing clutter, releasing things that no longer served, and eliminating material items.

Creativity

Creativity often awakens and is enhanced through Healing Touch, which tends to heighten the possibility of inspiration, both personally and professionally. Writer's block may open, and artistic abilities may heighten to be expressed through art, photography, or other artistic media. Specific techniques may be useful. For example, using the *Spiral Meditation* technique can assist in enhancing creativity as it connects the seat of creativity (2nd chakra/sacral) and the seat of creative expression/communication (5th chakra/throat); it opens energy flow for creativity to be fully expressed. This can be a very effective technique in releasing blocked creativity and can be taught as a meditative self-care technique for continued creative opening.

Several artists have shared their thoughts. An artist and Healing Touch Practitioner Apprentice, Sharon Wolpoff, offered the following:

> It is my desire to find a way of being in this world that illuminates others. Healing Touch and art-making both share the root principle of working with the hands through the heart. Both are lifetime studies through which one learns how to listen inside then act on what is "heard." Both rely on the mysterious intelligence possessed by the hands themselves.
>
> I am deeply committed to both disciplines so it was with great wonder that I realized how these two seemingly different activities are able to weave into one another, connecting and supporting one another. Each practice informs the other, creating the opportunity for cross-training. The experience of cross-training enhances my perception, sometimes accelerating it, sometimes slowing it down. It keeps me honest and attentive and anchored in integrity, as both disciplines serve to cross-check one another, merging into a larger system of inner guidance.
>
> This experience shows in my paintings, which appear to be more fully realized now, and it brings new confidence to my practice of Healing Touch. Most importantly it helps me to feel renewed, filled with energy and resources that can easily be shared. In a world where people are often overfed and undernourished on many levels, the capacity for renewal emerges as a true gift and a welcomed way of life.

Another artist, Susu Meyer, from Houston, Texas, had not been painting for a while when she came to receive a Healing Touch session. The practitioner felt "bubbles" inside the client during the session and shared this sensation with her. Healing Touch sometimes has an immediate response, and at times it may be more delayed and unfolding. Some weeks later, Susu emailed her practitioner and shared the following:

> I think your vision of bubbles is becoming something—I feel them now. After I saw you, I took a quick road trip out to New Mexico with a friend. We went past Santa Fe up to "O'Keeffe Country." I kept looking at that landscape, which I have grown to love so much over the years, and was commenting about an artist I've always admired as we were rounding a curve which overlooks the Chama River. I asked to stop, to look, and to snap some pictures. Got out of the car, and there was a hand painted sign there, "Louisa McElwain 1953–2013," the same artist I had just been describing. I couldn't believe it. I came home and thought and felt so much. Her passing hit me hard. I'd always so enjoyed the way she painted—so physical, so free—and seemingly fearless. I decided to mimic her—did a smallish painting using only a palette knife—it was so freeing. Then I painted over something using the same technique, and it became something totally different, but really interesting, and sculptural. I never met McElwain. But she has touched me . . . as an artist and has given me permission to take another step. I am now home and working on a triptych using palette knives, sticks, q-tips, and brushes. The surfaces are so much more alive. I have bubbles within me—exciting ones—and am anxious to work now. I have to admit when I left your place a couple of weeks ago I was miffed—a bit dulled out. But now I feel very inspired and eager.

Evolving the Self and the Practice

As we continue in our healing work, the expectation is that we continue our self-growth and professional development. With awareness, we have the opportunity to pay attention to our own patterns and work to heal ourselves. One of the patterns is that of the co-dependent triangle, which includes a rescuer/martyr, victim, and perpetrator. The role of the healer is that of facilitator and support person, rather than that of a rescuer or fixer. It is important to be clear on these roles. There are many resources for gaining a better understanding of this dynamic. Some specific tools for change can be found in *Boundaries and Relationships* (Whitfield, 1993) and in *Kitchen Table Wisdom* (Remen, 1996).

Another awareness to develop as healers is that of discernment; viewing situations from multiple aspects. One can listen to the words, observe the actions to see if they match, and observe and sense the energy in situations and relationships. Moving to the place of "observer" may assist in releasing emotional attachment, achieving the clarity needed to sense and see the whole picture from a different vantage point, and noting areas that match up or are out of alignment. As we develop self-awareness and clear ourselves, we are better able to serve through modeling, entrainment, and our global energetic connection of entanglement.

Paying Attention

By John Shukwit, MA, LPC

There's an old Zen story. A student said to Master Ichu, "Please write for me something of great wisdom." Master Ichu picked up his brush and wrote one word: Attention. The student said, "Is that all?" The master wrote, "Attention Attention" (Beck & Smith, 1994).

We are conscious beings, we know that we know, it is our greatest gift. Consciousness simply exists, it contains no judgment. Consciousness is what we are. It allows us to know that we are having an experience. Consciousness is like the air we breathe. Without consciousness, there is no awareness. Consciousness can also be directed, and that's where awareness (attention) comes in. When we focus our attention on something, we become more aware of it. Our awareness engages the senses and we become more cognizant of our direct experience. We find that our direct experience is through the senses, be it seeing, hearing, tasting, touching, or smelling. We then tend to qualify our experience by judging it as "this is good," "this is bad," "this is right," "this is wrong," "I like this," or "I don't like that." What we add to our direct experience is the source of either happiness or suffering.

Present Moment

It's really quite simple. What complicates the ability to pay attention is that much of the time we are either thinking about the past or thinking about the future. That being the case, we are not present, and if we are not present, we are being driven by habit. Habit contains no awareness. If we view habit as the disease, the antidote is awareness, and the only time we can be aware is now. If we are not in the present moment, we cannot access the options, possibilities and resources available only in the present moment. If you have any doubts about this, take a minute and observe what is going on in your mind—interesting, isn't it! The past can be a millisecond ago or 30 years ago, and the future can be two seconds from now or six months from now.

Understanding the Brain

Paying attention to what is going on between our ears is quite useful, and it helps to have some general understanding of how the brain works. Consider that there is a negative bias in the brain, which means that we tend to remember the negative and minimize the positive—this is how the brain is wired. The limbic system, part of our nervous system which has evolved over millions of years, is our early warning system that helps alert us to possible dangers. This early warning system is commonly known as the "fight or flight" response. When we are fearful or distress arises, this engages the amygdala, a portion of the brain that generates internal emotional states and the external expression of them. If there is a perceived threat, the limbic system overrides the cortex, or higher level thinking. Since the limbic system favors speed over accuracy, the connections that are made can be quite loose, and mistakes can be made. For example, if you are walking in the desert and a situation arises as to whether you are seeing an object as a snake or a stick, the limbic system kicks in automatically, triggering the fight or flight response, and your reaction is to move away. The limbic system makes an immediate judgment that it is better to be safe than sorry. The limbic system can be influenced by previous life experiences. It is obviously better to mistake a stick for a snake than a snake for a stick!

Hanson and Mendius (2009) in the book *Buddha's Brain: The Practical Neuroscience of Happiness, Love, and Wisdom*, use the analogy that we have Velcro for negative experiences and Teflon for positive ones. Think about it, someone gives us a compliment, and we tend to dismiss it. But if someone says something that irritates or upsets us, we latch onto it for an hour, perhaps all day, or maybe longer.

To make the situation even more interesting, Hebb's axiom, a well-known theory in neuroscience which is also mentioned in *Buddha's Brain,* states that neurons that fire together wire together, meaning that the more we hear something repeated, the more we believe it, and the more we believe it, the more we see it. Every time we act out of habit, the response gets stronger over time and harder to change. Looking at this from a stress management perspective, stress is simply the response to a stimulus, internal or external.

Distress

Distress results from a combination of our perception of what the outcome of a given situation should be, and the actual limits with which we have to work. For instance, there are five things on your "to-do" list, and realistically you can accomplish only three. Thinking you *should* complete all five items creates distress, which can then get in the way of completing anything. Distress does not and cannot come from anything external to us; it comes from within our mind. This pattern of thinking can become a habit and create continual distress. As mentioned earlier, habit contains no awareness. So by focusing attention on the present moment and that which can be realistically accomplished, we reduce our distress and can access the resources at hand.

Self-Judgment

Having an understanding of how the brain works (e.g. Hebb's axiom, flight/flight response, negative bias) helps to normalize our situation, regardless of what it is. This may reduce the tendency to self-judgment, which is what we usually do when we find ourselves doing something we think we shouldn't. Experience has probably shown you that judging is not helpful, but actually makes things worse—the image of throwing gas on a fire comes to mind!

Breaking Habits

How do we break the cycle of habit, judging, and strengthening the pattern? Cultivating non-judgmental awareness is the key. As Master Ichu wrote, we need to pay attention. This is not only important, it is vital to the evolution of our consciousness.

Resistance

And the day came when the risk to remain tight in a bud
was more painful than the risk it took to blossom. ~ Anais Nin (1967)

Since consciousness is, and we have the ability to focus it by paying attention, it is necessary to look at what gets in the way of being aware. Resistance becomes our teacher in this realm. The fight/flight response and our conditioning teach us to move away from the source of our distress. By moving away, we lose the opportunity to learn from our resistance. There is nothing wrong with resistance and feeling and experiencing negative emotions. By their very nature, these feelings inform us of what is getting in the way of being present in our direct experience. They are telling us to "LOOK HERE!" and to determine where the resistance is coming from. As mentioned earlier, the resistance is not coming from anything external to us; rather, it is coming from our desire to have things be other than the way they are.

Pain versus Suffering

As we become more familiar with resistance, we come to see it as a useful tool to work with difficult situations. We also discern the difference between pain and suffering, which is an important distinction to make. Pain is something we all experience as a part of being human. Suffering, however, is always self-induced, because we want things to be other than they are. With practice, and practice is imperative, we come into a different relationship with resistance, and it becomes a tool that can be used in any situation we choose rather than a roadblock. As mentioned earlier, if we are in the present moment, we have access to the resources available in the present moment. If we are resisting, we are not in the present moment, because we want things to be other than the way they are. Resisting brings us back into habitual patterns.

Expectations

There is nothing wrong with expectations if they are flexible enough to accommodate the situation. What gets in the way are unrealistic expectations. What makes expectations unrealistic is that they have nothing to do with reality. Unrealistic expectations are the source of our suffering. For example, you are late for an appointment and upset with yourself because you are late. This might be a recurring pattern. Judging yourself for being late is the suffering and won't change the situation, it will only keep you stuck in that pattern. Moving to a place of non-judgmental awareness frees us to look at other options (leaving earlier, prioritizing, etc.) and brings the focus to what you can do in the future, rather than on what you can't change. So in that regard, what we see here is that the suffering doesn't come from the situation, but from our reaction to it. As we practice non-judgmental awareness, the disparity between the facts as they are, and how we want the situation to be, becomes more balanced. We reduce our suffering and become more self-aware.

Acceptance

Acceptance is the quality that enables us to notice resistance and unrealistic expectations. It does not imply agreement or approval. Acceptance implies no judgment at all. It simply means seeing things as they are. If there is acceptance there is no suffering, if there is suffering, then we have not come to a place of acceptance. This does not imply passivity; it actually encourages us to take full responsibility for that which we can be responsible.

Awareness

Cultivating awareness can also lead to a "lightness" in the way we view our lives. Recently, I was driving to work and noticed ruminations about some pending issues that were causing distress. Without particularly intending it, a thought arose, "If I knew I was dying this afternoon, would those things be important?" Instantly I began to laugh and the "spell" was broken. Paying attention and being aware allows us to wear our lives lightly, to not take ourselves too seriously, and to help us prioritize what is really important.

Stillness

Being aware and quieting ourselves brings us to a point of stillness. We come to understand that stillness is our inherent nature. From the point of stillness comes clarity. Clarity brings the possibility of being more responsive, rather than reactive. Imagine a jar with dirt and water. As we shake it, there is cloudiness. As we set it down, the dirt settles, the water clarifies, and stillness prevails. The same occurs when we come to that point of stillness and clarity. Our awareness and knowing can then increase.

Knowing

The implication of self-awareness is that we move from our heads to our hearts, from thinking to being. Opening to a place of "being" brings us to our place of "knowing." The more we are in this place of "knowing," the more we can begin to trust it. As we trust our own "knowingness," our actions come out of our place of being, rather than doing. By being present, we become more aware of our inherent nature that does not change, just as the clouds obscuring the sun don't diminish its inherent brilliance.

From the place of stillness, our perception changes and we begin to notice that we are so much more than we think we are. We may come to see that our experiences bring us opportunities to grow, that this planet is a training ground, and everything that happens becomes an opportunity to become more awake and aware. As we take that opportunity to become more awake and aware, we become a vehicle for the manifestation of that understanding.

Cultivating our self-awareness connects with the Healing Touch practice. As the practitioner evolves to a higher level of consciousness and a more clear energy field, the clients are then assisted in clearing their energy systems. This may support the evolution from the ego/mind to the heart through quieting of the client's mind, which can create a shift to stillness. Healing Touch helps to remove the barriers to the recognition of our inherent nature. As the barriers are removed, we have the opportunity to open to our knowingness. We can free ourselves from suffering and simply open to life as it unfolds.

4 Concepts

(1) We are doing the best we can (2) in the situation we find ourselves (3) with the information available (4) right now. This is a true statement; however, the variables are constantly changing. If you notice any resistance, it is coming from an assumption that things should be other than the way they are.

Taking Responsibility

There are three areas related to taking responsibility for ourselves. These are (1) recognizing our limits (which could be physical, mental, or emotional) and understanding what we can and cannot control, (2) communicating those limits without blame, and (3) recognizing the roadblocks. The roadblocks to our limits and assertive communications are the unrealistic expectations. These might be the "shoulds" and the "what ifs" as well as self-doubts and old negative tapes. There is no need to judge, just notice. We don't have to do anything. If we just notice, they will pass. This process breaks the thought/feeling/behavior loop pattern.

Taking responsibility for those things for which you can be responsible has an influence on those around us and allows others to do the same. We do have to keep in mind that which we can't control. Relative to others, we have no control over what anyone else will do or say, think or feel. This does not imply passivity; it actually encourages us to take full responsibility for that which we can be responsible.

Trusting our own knowingness leads to discernment which allows us to notice our resistance and work with it responsively. This leads to clarity which allows us to remove the roadblocks to self-awareness. As self-awareness increases, we come to know that we are that which is "the source of all that is."

A Deeper Look: Three Levels of Work and Wisdom within the Healing Touch Experience

By Jonathan Ellerby, PhD

Every healing art and science has its own unique worldview and spectrum of innate experiences. Each health and healing discipline offers its own gifts and challenges, and calls forth distinct constellations of characters and qualities. We have all been conscious at one time or another of the stereotypes found in various types of nursing, medicine, surgery, psychology, and energy healing traditions. Of course, not every practitioner fits the stereotype of his or her profession and not every practitioner walks through each and every experience or stage of development available to him or her. Nevertheless, the ultimate personal and practical success of most practitioners lies not in their skill or understanding, but in how they navigate and mature through the spontaneous and unplanned encounters within their work.

Stress, trauma, transference, projection, disappointment, loss, sexual arousal, romantic feelings, and emotional attachment are just a short list of the many experiences that may arise in the life and work of a Healing Touch practitioner or other energy modality practitioner. Preparation to face the range and depth of human distractions, setbacks, and advances seeded within healing work is an essential point of departure for this text. Most specifically, it is necessary to face the spiritual and existential dimensions that offer to enrich and test each practitioner of this extraordinary craft.

The World of Energy and the Energy of the World

Healing Touch is built entirely on a worldview that assumes that every human being is comprised of something more than what the medical model readily accepts. Innate to the work is the study and sensing of the human energy field—its channels, currents, blocks and balances. Contrary to what many practitioners may have been taught as young adults, the awareness of energy is both at odds with mainstream thinking, and yet in keeping with the intuitive experience of most people, especially as children. When followed with appropriate rigor, the understanding of the human energy field integrates easily within the Western medical model and simply arises as a deeper knowledge of the subtle qualities of the physiological and psychological anatomy.

When learning Healing Touch, there is no need to embrace a new religious worldview, or to surrender existing ones; there is no need to adopt a radical philosophy of energy and spirit as the foundation of life, though it may be implied. In fact, it is easy enough to remain within a dominantly allopathic approach while using the intuitive and esoteric skills of Healing Touch. A basic level of holistic thinking is required, but not in any extreme form, and spiritual growth is not a forced or obligated topic of study or development.

The challenge within Healing Touch, however, is that the very practice itself is so deeply rooted within a profoundly holistic, even holographic reality that it inevitably tests and challenges the practitioner as much as it is designed to empower and heal the client. To know this is to have the power to embrace this and make the most of it, a path which, in my opinion, infuses and enhances the therapeutic work. In fact, to be a long term or serious Healing Touch practitioner and not consider the personal, spiritual and cosmological implications is perhaps to miss the secret power and gift that lies within the discipline.

Technique versus Experience

By definition, when a person cultivates an awareness of energy and a strong sense of intuition, it is the nature of energy to draw a person into a psychic realm of color, sensation, imagery and a felt sense that accompanies most subtle phenomena. In fact, the human practitioner becomes the tool of diagnosis, the radar, the ultrasound, the CAT-scan; the human practitioner is directly affected by the very techniques used to impact the client. Most Healing Touch practitioners fall into a meditative or focused, trance-like, but grounded state during their work, especially once the techniques have been mastered.

In a state of heightened "listening," and meditative awareness, the practitioner is not only attuned to the client, but to all matters of subtle energy and information. Many practitioners may experience guiding voices, premonitions, angelic and energy "beings," and even the presence of God—or an Ultimate Source Energy.

Healing Touch is not a religion or a sacred technique for achieving enlightenment or spiritual awakening, and yet, it is critical for the mental and emotional health of each practitioner to be aware that life changing insights, spiritual experiences and an encounter with the sacred is commonplace in the work. It is helpful to think of the depth of spiritual experience and spiritual orientation as defined in three levels or layers of the Healing Touch practice. This spectrum can prepare practitioners to both self-assess and monitor their own development within a conceptual framework that normalizes the extremes of experience they may encounter.

Three Levels of Work

To more clearly understand the nature of healing work and how it affects the practitioner, it is possible to identify three dominant modes or approaches to the work. Each of these levels is necessary and also reflects a state or stage of personal development and relationship to the work. The levels are Externally Oriented, Internally Oriented, and Eternally Oriented.

External orientation. The Externally Oriented approach to Healing Touch is one in which the practitioner has a strong relationship to the exact technical form that is taught in each Healing Touch level. These practitioners also have a strong sense of boundaries, a strong sense of delivering a solution/treatment for a symptom or problem presented, and they relate to the professional role and the work as a powerful treatment tool. This is typically an effective, client-centered approach; the role of sacred or spiritual forces is not seen as essential, and the role of personal development is important only as far as it ensures an ethical, quality practice. Intuition is a critical yet focused tool. The mental, emotional and spiritual dimensions are all viewed as a part of the healing process, yet are addressed as required. Externally oriented practitioners may begin their relationship to Healing Touch viewing their work, themselves, and their clients through a more conventional lens based on a dualistic worldview.

Internal orientation. The Internal Oriented approach takes the notion of holism much deeper, and the role of the practitioner shifts to a much more subjectively driven one. All symptoms and sources of disease or imbalance are seen as reflections of the mental, emotional, spiritual, and physical dimensions, with an emphasis on a rich and layered understanding of energy and spirituality. The universe is seen as an intelligent energy system, and the approach to care is always soul-centered, placing great emphasis on the practitioners' personal relationship to their own sense of soul and their ability to connect with the same in their clients. Prayerfulness, intuition and the caregiver's spiritual life all become viewed as top priority and critical to a successful practice. The internally motivated Healing Touch practitioners work because of a sense of calling and trust that their own intuitive and inner knowing is equally as important as any clinical conversation, client story, or prescribed technique.

The notion of a soul-level dialogue or mutual exchange of information, wisdom, and healing emerges. Though Healing Touch is innately a compassionate and holistic therapy, this approach shows a much more horizontal relationship between practitioner and client and requires an on-going exploration of self-awareness, personal healing, and spiritual intervention. The Internal Approach recognizes that the consciousness of the practitioners is the primary foundation to the success of any technique and that their sense of spiritual connection is integral to the development of their intuition and capacity to direct clean, clear, and balanced energy.

The internal approach is also one in which spiritual realities, such as angels, Light Beings, and even God, become more apparent during treatments and personal healing experiences. These dimensions of energy and life become more "real" though they may remain more personal, more private and shared with some caution. The approach to each client is more practitioner-centered, not as a replacement to the client focus, but as an access point to the best care of the client.

Eternal orientation. The Eternal Orientation occurs when the experience of the spiritual world becomes integrated into the daily life and work of a practitioner. The practitioner is open emotionally and mentally to guidance from the spiritual world and the direct experience of the spiritual world. An ultimate Source Energy—God, Divine Origin, Creator Spirit—becomes the central focus of both personal development and quality care. Mystical experiences of divine energy, a feeling of oneness and a sense of the united nature of all life emerges as the foundational reality and reference point.

Handle with Care: The Limits of the Levels

Practitioners who feel mostly rooted in an *External Orientation,* should be careful not to become too technical in their work nor too ridged in their self-concept as a healer and caregiver. They should also remain open to the unexpected and unconventional when in the work experience, and consider complementary studies in philosophies and healing traditions that they find personally enriching.

Internally Oriented practitioners should take care to maintain professional standards, while exploring their own natural passion for personal growth and energy awareness. It will eventually be very important and helpful to choose only one or two traditions of healing and spirituality to explore in depth and not simply allow their intuition to "pick and choose" the lessons and teachers they follow. A heightened spirituality and sense of intuition is often served best by a supportive structure and not only free thought and exploration.

People who embrace an *Eternal Orientation* should be careful not to dismiss the importance of the other two levels of care: professional standards, boundaries, and ethics are still relevant and important; personal growth and self-knowledge are still key filters and facilitate effective energy work; and neither negate an attitude of ultimate trust, surrender, and the cultivation of a mystical way of being. The true gift of the *Eternal Orientation* is the deep sense that all experiences, suffering, and imbalance are ultimately empty of value or importance. All things are precious, all things are passing; all life experiences are powerful and emotionally real, and yet are insubstantial and mere expressions of impersonal energetic movements in the universe.

Summary

Taken first as a conceptual map of potential views and approaches, and then as a personal course for development and integration, the three states and stages outlined in this section can serve to both inspire and anchor a wise and skillful practitioner. What this picture of development reminds us, is that anyone who relates to the human energy field on a regular basis is, by transitive properties, relating to the much broader universe of subtle energy, including profoundly spiritual and sacred domains.

To provide a healing talent to another is in itself precious and honorable, but to realize that it is also a pathway to personally come into a new and profound relationship to the world is a sacred gift. When we open ourselves to the true potential in ourselves, as revealed by a craft such as Healing Touch, we begin to understand the world differently. When we allow the energy we conduct to communicate freely within our own hearts and minds, we learn that no one is separate or alone; we are all healers and in need of healing; we live in a vibrant living energy universe; and if we want to see real change in the world, we must become the medicine we seek to provide.

On Living in the World

DIANE WIND WARDELL, PhD, RN, CHTP/I

I have forgotten what I know. As a child I knew how to fly. Where did that knowledge go? Each of us comes to this planet to learn and to grow, forgetting much of what we knew in our child's mind along the way. Healing work gives us a chance to enter into that mystery once again by flying above our fears and dancing with the stars by offering love to another. For it is our deepest yearning to be connected to the divine essence that makes us who we are. So that all healing becomes self-healing, moving from giver to receiver and back again.

We share a path of healing with many souls. They are here to offer you an opportunity to learn so that expansion is always possible. All lessons are not always easy. Having to give up something that you have attached meaning to, whether it be a trinket or a person through loss or distance, is hard. The important thing is to be reflective and allow the search for meaning to continue within. Each hardship lends us a hand on the healing path for it is always a blessing to have cared deeply for another. It is important to honor that gift with generosity and caring for others. Each step is not forward, for we are not perfect. Just remember to come back to your soul's purpose to learn and grow here on planet Earth.

The journey can be hard and difficult. Hard because of circumstances and of who we are. No matter how hard you try you will make a mistake along the way. Acknowledge your mistakes, the "not nice" parts of yourself, for only in doing so can you change. But, conversely, no need to hold on to them either. In this way we can let light enter to heal the old wounds that were created.

Do not be afraid to ask for help. I remember getting lost on a trail outside our conference in the mountains of Breckenridge, Colorado. I ended up in a housing development not in sight of the hotel. I had always been reluctant to ask for help for anything or of anyone thinking I was totally self-sufficient. Fear gripped me, I would miss my plane home, disappoint others, and all this would reflect badly on me (or so I thought) so I asked for help from my guides. Just then a car (I had not seen any to this point) rounded the corner and a man stepped out unheeded by word or gesture and literally walked me to the path I needed to take. When I turned around he was gone, no car, no anything except a sense of divine presence. Today, I am learning to ask not just from my guides but from my family, friends, and strangers as I experience the limitations of Parkinson's disease. Ask for help on the physical, emotional, mental and spiritual planes. No matter. Your guidance is your connection to the divine.

Connect with others in a mentoring group, whether as a student of Healing Touch or in a mastermind or spiritual group that offers regular support and accountability. It also provides an opportunity to share and most importantly to combine healing energies for the greatest good. And by asking others to hold the intention for whatever the need might be, seeing it as done and giving thanks for this or something greater gives a boost of supportive energy as well.

We stand on the shoulders of many healers. It is through the heart that we live and practice as healers. And in doing the energetic work of healing the work goes on. We don't take personal credit for healing, nor do we limit its potential. It is our task to empower others. Remember you are not alone as other souls have joined you in your mission and purpose in this life.

Acknowledge the divine in all persons with a simple smile or nod as you walk through you day. As you radiate loving energy your positive energy field influences others, even in the grocery store or mall. It is good to have a conscious awareness of this, to enhance your field throughout your day, thus enhancing the fields of others.

Some principles that have been shared by many spiritual leaders are to live life simply and in joy. Recognize the importance you place on your surroundings and detach from the meaning you place on items in your possession. Find the essence of holding an energetic space which supports and nourishes you and recognize that it changes. Hold within your heart the essence of joy, a smile, a delight, a caress of the true person you are. Honor and care for that being.

Each of us, student, teacher, patient spread the work. Each gift of healing puts a spark of light from one to the other and that other to another. I am and I am all those healers who have blessed me by putting their hands on me and offered me a Noel's Mind Clearing, a Chakra Connection, or a Chelation, to name a few. You also sparkle with the light of your children, babies, partner, colleagues, and/or students and countless others. Therefore, it is important that you recognize the gifts others bring to your learning. Be humble, generous, and kind.

We are responsible for learning and growing. It is not just about learning new techniques. Our task is to recognize the subtle path of connectedness that is established in the healing moment and to remain open and in our hearts for that healing to manifest. It is this divine light that shines out into the universe. Our work is not just for ourselves but for mother Earth, our universe, the cosmos. We are beams of light.

In summary, the principles that healers may use as they walk on earth are: all healing is self-healing, others provide an opportunity for us to grow, acknowledge all aspects of yourself, you are not alone, ask for help, be humble and kind, remain heart-centered, take care of the self, live simply, be joyful, offer gratitude for the gifts you have been given, learning is continuous so study hard and well, recognize your soul's purpose, and you are part of the whole. Always live in and from the heart. In your work among others, be free of expectations and be gentle in your healing arts. You are an exquisite part of the mystery unfolding.

Being of Service

SUE KAGEL RN BSN, HNB-BC, CHTP/I;
DIANE WIND WARDELL, PhD, RN, WHNP-BC, AHN-BC, CHTP/I
AND LISA ANSELME RN, BLS, HN-BC, CHTP/I

Opportunities for being of service can present in multiple forms. Janet Mentgen emphasized that Healing Touch is about being of service, showing up when needed, being present, and always working for the highest good of all. She also stressed the importance of "giving away" the work. This does not preclude an energetic exchange of some sort, whether in trade or in fee for service, but that we are available energetically from a heart-centered place to be of service.

We may feel called or guided to be of service in a variety of ways, from small acts that are responsive to immediate circumstances to long term commitments for a notable mission and purpose. Any of these situations can require working either solo or collectively. Being of service does require the need for energetic balance and re-filling your personal well. When manifesting your work, consider the energy of being in service for the highest good of all, and remember to include *your* highest good as well. Carolyn Myss (2002) in her book *Sacred Contracts: Awakening Your Divine Potential*, discusses the servant archetype. She states that this archetype is lived in a healthy manner only if the servant is simultaneously able to be of service to the self. Without strength to maintain his or her wellbeing, the servant archetype becomes consumed by the needs of those around it and loses all focus and the value of his or her life.

Laws of Service

Susan Trout (1997) identifies service as following certain laws. The laws include the *law of synchronicity* in that our minds are joined: when one needs help there is someone/thing there to offer service. The *law of dharma* occurs when we follow our duty and function, our higher purpose. The *law of omnipresence* recognizes that everything we do is service, either serving or being served. As we move through integrating all aspects of self in our physical, emotional, mental, and spiritual beingness, our lower desires give rise to higher ones, so that our inner state determines the quality of our service in the *law of evolution*. This law also can function for the group as well.

Further, according to Trout's *law of receiving*, we receive what we have given, and the law demands that what we receive be given away, so that our vessel is always available. Whatever we give is given to humanity as well as reflected by the *law of uniformity*. The *law of extension* offers that we "naturally become healers of that which we ourselves have healed" (p. 22). The *law of agreement* is that prior to incarnation, our soul, or group of souls, may agree to play a particular role in someone else's life. The *law of transmutation* involves the capability of negative events to offer learning in a completely new way than it occurred, so that learning and growth can manifest. The final law, the *law of transcendence*, assures us that we are "served at the level of the soul that goes beyond our human understanding" (p. 25).

Expanding Service

The Dalai Lama (1999) speaks of evolving our level of consciousness to that of citizens of the universe—as a global consciousness. From that place, there is an expectation of stewardship and service. When working with others, animals, or the planet itself, all are dynamic fields with their own blue print. We serve by clearing their congested energy and allowing the earth energy to flow through. As practitioners, we need to work with our own energy fields as clear as possible and come from a heart-centered place—respectful, and not from ego or a personal agenda.

Some situations may directly "call" for us to show up, respond to what presents itself, and be actively involved in the work or healing, while other situations may feel like it isn't our place to deeply assist. Certainly we can send love, peace, and compassion to an area or situation.

At times we may feel called to work with a specific area of the earth. From a very energetically clear place in ourselves, we may feel a sense of "permission" to serve and be present as a lightning rod to re-align the energy of a particular area or grid, much like we might work with a human being. When called in this fashion, the purpose is often unclear and requires presence, selfless service, and heart-centered work. The Dalai Lama (1999) reminds us to be very cautious and conscious in these actions: "Unless you can see all the repercussions of your assistance, you might want to not mettle: just be in compassion."

Whatever we choose to do needs to be done consciously from a place of loving, healing energy as our vibration and our way of being affects the whole. We are a global unified field in which we are interconnected, and our actions and way of being have the potential to impact everyone and everything from an energetic perspective. We then have a responsibility, whether in a healing session or in our lives, to be mindful of the condition and clarity of our personal energy fields and be as clear as possible, so that on a daily basis, we add to the clarity and loving energy rather than contribute confusion or chaos.

There is a ripple effect from our personal energy fields connecting to the world in a very direct way. Whatever you do for yourself, you are already doing for the world. You influence individuals, who influence their families, communities and their nations, and ultimately the world. In the quantum world, there is instantaneous shifting through entrainment and being present. Your clear energy can be useful in working from wherever you are in the moment, using intention, healing thoughts, and visualizing a new outcome for the highest good of all.

Communitas—Working in Sacred Community

Communitas is where our hearts are shaped by the deep heart of true fellowship (Hodkins, 2002). Those in community elevate beyond ego-related agendas and connect at a higher, a more sacred level of the heart. Through the mutuality of our suffering and our personal wounds, we become united in compassion. In order to arrive at this place, we begin by healing the self to bring our body, mind, emotion, and spirit into best alignment. It can be difficult at times to determine when we may be stuck in our own issues. *Communitas* may provide individuals within the group who can assist as quality, heart-centered "mirrors" that reflect and process rough spots within us.

Forgiveness for self and others frees the self to be more heart-centered. When we take offense, we create the same offence that was given to us. Rather, we must transform and transmute our own energy fields to be the energy we wish to share with others. When we find this sense of community and harmony within the self, including self-compassion, we can heal ourselves, radiate that energy outward, and share it in community—*communitas*.

It is important to be aware of the energetic boundaries of ourselves and others and be respectful of others' need for personal space. The area of residence often influences personal space/energetic boundaries. Those from high density areas, such as large cities, tend to have smaller, contracted energy fields from close interaction with others, while those from less dense or sprawling areas are conditioned to a more expanded personal space. This can also apply to the housing conditions in which people live alone or with families, and how they respond to their personal space and energy comfort levels.

The world is rapidly changing, and it is of utmost importance to create greater stability and resilience within the self, have the spiritual maturity to gather to the self, to perceive through the density of the earth energy, to observe what is occurring, and to notice spirit at work. Moving to a place of "observer mode," rising up to imagine looking down at the situation rather than being embroiled in it, offers an opportunity for clarity and a new perspective. Situations can be perceived as opportunities for growth that may be taken up with both hands by participants, or avoided. As this approach becomes more integrated, we can recognize that these are all great paths of Spirit and recognize that there is nothing to fear. People are living their choices, with or without awareness, which brings us the opportunity to just observe and accept them, and then consciously and proactively choose our responses and interactions.

When life on earth is experienced in this way, we can have compassion for those who may not share this awareness and for those moving through turbulent times, both internally and from external situations. Living on the earth becomes easier and easier when you can see where you can be loving and compassionate, and notice how your love can change the world.

Collective Work—Evolving and Raising the Vibration

Working collectively can take the form of being in *communitas* and in group communication, while simultaneously focusing healing energy on a person, animal, situation, or area. Collective work may also be done individually, with a unified focus, during daily meditation. Working in a group can raise the collective vibration of the healing opportunity (Sawyer, 2007). This technique can be used for setting intention for self, projects, group collaboration or master-minding to magnify individual efforts. Consider including in the intention statement "this or something greater for the highest good of all." Practice not being attached to the outcome, because we do not always know what the highest good is, and this approach helps to release a specific agenda and to be open to a wider range of possibilities.

Energy follows thought. We observe this in a classroom activity in which the instructor guides a group of students to think of and feel specific situations, while another group assesses their energy fields and notes an instant change in response. We can use this also in creative manifestation to shift the energy to a more positive outcome. Janet Mentgen, in a taped presentation in June 2005, recommended that we "Focus energy on what you want to happen rather than focus on the negative, as this overlays a new pattern on the matrix of energy and changes it." We do not have full control; however, with the addition of the statement "this or something greater for the highest good of all" and not being attached to the outcome, we are open to possibilities that may appear differently than we are intending.

Working Globally

Distance healing techniques for a global perspective were discussed in Chapter 8. These can be enhanced by setting intention and "visioning" that which may be helpful for the highest good. Work may be done as mentioned above with natural disasters or for general peace and healing in the world. While many practitioners avoid watching the news to stay in a positive frame of mind, one practitioner has a different approach. She chooses to be of service and in healing mode while watching the news. Thus, she is informed of world events, notes areas with difficulty or need, and then sends energy for the highest and best healing—rather than being emotionally impacted and feeling helpless.

Vision of Optimum Wellness for the Planet

We have explored the contributions that the practice of Healing Touch can make on those in all walks of life. Looking to the future, we have the opportunity to contribute to a healthier world, addressing the health of ourselves and our world's human inhabitants, animals, plants and trees, water, air quality, and the earth itself. Our vision and goals lead us to where we place our "energy" related to self-healing, when working with our family and friends, our communities and our world. The overarching focus is on enhancing and improving the quality of our lives and those around us.

As Healing Touch and holistic practitioners, we have the opportunity to offset the many preventable chronic conditions in ourselves and in others through our chosen expression of healing work. Stress and lifestyle choices are an underlying common denominator in chronic, preventable health issues. Along with clearing and balancing the energy system, self-care practices can be taught and reinforced to specifically address stress, and referrals made to other modalities for decreasing physiological reactions in the body. Chronic diseases may be supported or improved with Healing Touch, which may decrease their impact on longevity and health care costs.

While we have addressed best practice in the use of Healing Touch related to these issues, prevention is the better way to manage these health issues. Healing Touch has been shown to assist in general well-being. With concomitant lifestyle changes, Healing Touch can support optimum health, even when clients are living with chronic disease conditions. As practitioners, we have the opportunity to model and promote healthy energy fields and behaviors.

Taking it into the Future—7 Generations Forward

The vision Janet Mentgen received for Healing Touch is that it "go forth until the 7th generation", which means perpetually. Everything we influence and the choices we make continue to roll forward from where we are in time, and we must always consider the greater impact on the planet and all beings on it. This philosophy comes from the Great Law of the Iroquois Confederacy in the United States, which states we are to always live mindfully and consider future generations in how we live our lives and in our decision-making (Vecsey & Venables, 1980). There is no end point.

Mission and Purpose

Many people feel called to a sense of mission or purpose, to be of service and make a difference in the world. This may come to them through dreams, visions, an inner knowing, or an external event that triggers the awareness of a need to be fulfilled. Often the sense of mission and purpose is not clear as to what it is, what it looks like, or where to find it. Some feel a sense of urgency around it and become frustrated that they are not able to move forward. Janet Mentgen recommended to "sit and be quiet, let it come forth from your heart center and you will know . . . Go broader to infinite possibilities." The answer lies in your heart, although you may hear it in your head. Life experiences may lead you and create openings, and the past may be woven together with the present to create something new to be brought into the future. Allow yourself to be led into it as you meditate on it daily. Then take it into your circle, being authentic to who you are and what you do in your area of expertise and your network.

Meditation

The following meditation is offered as a way to move forward. With the breath, connect with the universality of all things, follow the breath down to the crystalline core at the center of the earth, connecting throughout the universe. Breathe "groundedness" into all your cells and all beings, plants, and animals. Be connected to the ground and feel the nurturance that is coming from there and beyond. Breathe up into higher consciousness and infinite wisdom. Let that shower down upon yourself and on all beings and creatures, breathing down into the center of your heart. Raise your vibration with feelings of joyful memories, love and appreciation, for the highest good of all. Imagine yourself in a place of beauty, where all is already created and you just have to listen in your heart for the answers for the highest and most loving and joyful good of all. Sit in silence, rest and listen in your heart. Ask to be in alignment with your vision and mission. Listen.

The Questions

How are you contributing by consciously being in the world? Where do you see yourself in one year, five to ten years? What are you doing? What would you like to be doing to contribute to the betterment of the world? What tools do you need? What tools and skills do you have to share? In what ways are you willing to step up and stretch yourself?

What other things just come up without thinking? Write these thoughts down now and meditate with this concept often. The more you focus your attention on these thoughts, the more you open up to what is possible. When the mission, purpose and service become clear, be open to the energy flow and manifest it. See all that you need in support of your mission or purpose coming together effortlessly and easily, in divine timing. See it as done and give thanks for it, this concept coming to fruition or something greater for the highest good of all, and then see yourself courageously step into it.

Together as collaborative and collective genius, and in sacred community, *communitas*, we create new possibilities. We plant seeds, and flow with their germination, growth, blossoming, blooming, and harvest—as we catch the trade winds in full sail. Or, as attributed to Mark Twain: *"Twenty years from now, you will be more disappointed by the things you didn't do than the ones you did do. So throw off the bowlines. Sail away from the safe harbor. Catch the trade winds in your sails. Dream. Discover."*

Evolution

This book represents an evolution in energy healing. We have journeyed through the early days of Healing Touch and noted the energy as it flowed across the globe, energy that continues to widen and deepen as we move forward in time. We have explored theories that are foundational. The research to facilitate the understanding of the mechanisms of energy therapies continues to unfold, as well as inform best practices through clinical research. Self-care, and the teaching of self-care to others, has an impact on the health and wellness of our self and others, decreasing the impact of stress-related disease processes and enhancing well-being. The ethics of energy continues to unfold, and the depth of our understanding of the energy system increases.

Every day new applications for this work surface in combination with other techniques or modalities for an even richer integrative and holistic approach to healing. The future evolves through our personal commitment to growth and development, raising our consciousness, our way of being on the planet, and our intention for the highest and best healing for all. We continue to be open, to allow the energy to flow and lead us to the next levels of this work as it continues to unfold to support global healing and wholeness.

NAME UPDATE AND CHAPTER 1 REFERENCES

Anderson, J., Anselme, L.& Hart, L. (2017). *Foundations and Practice of Healing Touch*. Lakewood, CO: Healing Beyond Borders.

Carlson, R. & Shields, B. (Eds.). (1976). *Healers on healing*. New York, NY: J. P. Tarcher/Putnam.

Dass, R. (1976). The intuitive heart. In R. Carlson & B. Shields (Eds.), *Healers on healing (pp. 171-172)*. New York, NY: J. P. Tarcher/Putnam.

Fontaine, K. (2000). *Healing practices: Alternative therapies for nursing*. Upper Saddle River, NJ: Prentice Hall.

Keegan, L. (2001). *Healing with complementary and alternative therapies*. Albany, NY: Delmar Thomson Learning. Krippner, S. (1989). Touchstones of the healing process. In R. Carlson & B. Shields (Eds.), *Healers on healing* (pp. 111-114). New York, NY: J. P. Tarcher/Putnam.

Randall, B. (2003). *Songman: The story of an aboriginal elder*. Sydney, Australia: Australian Broadcasting Commission.

CHAPTER 2 REFERENCES

ANA's Committee for the Study of Credentialing in Nursing. (1979). Credentialing in nursing: A new approach. *American Journal of Nursing*, April, 674-683.

ANCC Report to 2013 ANA Membership Assembly, American Nurses Credentialing Center. Retrieved from http://www.nursingworld. org/ancc

Barrett, E.A.M. (1990). *Visions of Rogers' science-based nursing*. New York, NY: National League of Nursing.

Brown, B.J. (1975). A nurse views credentialing. *Journal of Nursing Administration*, Oct, 34–37.

Byrne, M., Delarose, T., King, C.A., Leske, J., Sapnas, K.G., & Schroeter, K. (2007). Continued professional competence and portfolios. *Journal of Trauma Nursing, 14*(1), 24–31.

Carpenito, L J. (1984). *Nursing diagnosis: Application to clinical practice*. Philadelphia. PA: J B Lippincott.

Dossey, L. (1993). *Healing words: The power of prayer and the practice of medicine*. San Francisco, CA: Harper Collins.

Hanley, MA. (2008). Therapeutic touch with preterm infants: Composing a treatment. *Explore: The Journal of Science and Healing, 4*(4), 249–58.

Healing Beyond Borders. (1997). Vision and Mission Statement. Retrieved from http://healingtouchinternational.or/index. php?option=com_content&view=article&id=333&Itemid=250

Iowa Board of Nursing. (1998, December). *Role of the registered nurse in providing massage therapy and therapeutic touch*. Des Moines, IA: Iowa Board of Nursing [Memorandum].

McDonough-Means, S., Aicken, M., & Bell, I. (2006, May). *A novel assessment model of non-specific placebo effects: An assessment framework and pre-post study questionnaire data on caregiver attitudes and beliefs about an energy healing modality*. Poster session presented at the North American Research Conference on Complementary and Integrative Medicine, Edmonton, Alberta.

Monsen, R.B. (Ed.). (2005). *Genetics nursing portfolios: A new model for credentialing*. Silver Springs, MD: American Nurses Association.

National Institute of Health. (1994). *Alternative medicine: Expanding medical horizons. A report to the National Institute of Health on alternative medical systems and practices in the United States prepared under the auspices of the Workshop on Alternative Medicine.* NIH Pub No. 94-066. Washington, D.C.: U.S. Government Printing Office.

Nemeth, L. (Ed.). (2012). The value of certification. *AHNA Beginnings, 12*(1), 3–27.

Nightengale, F. (1969). *Notes on nursing: What it is, and what it is not.* New York, NY: Dover Publications.

Styles, M.M. (1986). *Credentialing in nursing: Contemporary developments and trends U.S.A. Within a world view.* ANA Credentialing Monograph Series. Silver Springs, MD: American Nurses Credentialing Center.

Wardell, D.W., Decker, S., & Engebretson, J. (2012). Healing Touch for older adults with persistent pain. *Holistic Nursing Practice, 26*(4), 194–202.

CHAPTER 3 REFERENCES

Ahn, A.C., Nahin, R.L., Calabrese, C., Folkman, S., Kimbrough, E., Shoham, J. & Haramati, A. (2010). Applying principles from complex systems to studying the efficacy of CAM therapies. *The Journal of Alternative and Complementary Medicine, 16*(9), 1015–1022.

Becker, R., & Selden, G. (1985). *The body electric: Electromagnetism and the foundation of life.* New York, NY: Quill.

Benson, H., & Klipper, M. Z. (2000). *The relaxation response.* New York, NY: Harper Collins.

Bohm, D. (1983). *Wholeness and the implicate order.* London, England: ARK Paperbacks.

Brennan, B.A. (1988). *Hands of light: A guide to healing through the human energy field. A new paradigm for the human being in health, relationship, and disease.* New York, NY: Bantam Books.

Chapman, E. (2004). *Radical loving care.* Nashville, TN: Baptist Healing Hospital Trust.

Dossey, L. (1982). *Space, time, and medicine.* Boston, MA: New Science Library.

Einstein, A. (2010). *The Theory of Relativity and other essays.* New York, NY: Philosophical Library.

Engebretson, J., & Hickey, J. (2011). Complexity science and complex adaptive systems. In J. B. Butts & K. L. Rich (Eds.), *Philosophies and theories for advanced nursing practice.* Sudbury, MA: Jones & Bartlett.

Engebretson, J., & Wardell, D. (2012). Energy therapies: Focus on spirituality. *Explore: The Journal of Science and Healing, 8*(6), 353–359.

Gadwig, G.B, & Wardell, D.W. (2011). Disturbed energy field. In B. Ackley & G. Gadwig. (Eds.), *Nursing diagnosis handbook: An evidence-based guide to planning care* (9th ed.). (pp. 345–349). St Louis, MO: Mosby.

Garber, D. (1978). Science and certainty in Descartes. In M. Hooker (Ed.), *Descartes.* Baltimore, MY: Johns Hopkins University Press.

Jacobson, E. (1929). *Progressive relaxation.* Chicago, IL: U. of Chicago Press.

Joy, B. (1979). *Joy's way: A map for a transformational journey.* New York, NY: J. P. Tarcher. Knowles, J.H. (1977). The responsibility of the individual, *Daedalus, 106,* 57–80.

Lindberg, C., Nash, S., & Lindberg, C. (2008). *On the edge: Nursing in the age of complexity.* Bordentown, NJ: Plexus Press.

Lindley, D. (2008). *Uncertainty: Einstein, Heisenberg, Bohr, and the struggle for the soul of science.* New York, NY: Anchor Books.

McTaggert, L. (2001/2008). *The field: The quest for the secret force of the universe.* New York, NY: Harper.

Newman, M.A. (1990). Newman's theory of health as praxis. *Nursing Science Quarterly, 3*(1), 37–41.

Newman, M. A. (1994). *Health as expanding consciousness* (2nd ed.). New York, NY: National League of Nursing Press.

Newman, M. A. (2008). *Transforming presence: The difference that nursing makes.* Philadelphia, PA: F. A. Davis.

Oschman, J. L. (2000). *Energy Medicine: The scientific basis.* New York, NY: Churchill Livingstone.

Osler, W. (1932). *Aequanimitas* (3rd ed.). New York, NY: McGraw Hill.

Palmer, P. (2000). *Let your life speak: Listening for the voice of vocation.* San Francisco, CA: Jossey-Bass.

Pert, C. (1999). *Molecules of emotion.* New York, NY: Touchstone.

Quinn, J. (1992). Holding sacred space: The nurse as healing environment. *Holistic Nursing Practice, 6*(4), 26–36.

Rogers, M. E. (1986). Energy fields. In V. M. Malinski (Ed.), *Exploration on Martha Rogers' science of unitary human beings* (pp. 3-8). Norwalk, CT: Appleton-Century-Crofts.

Schwartz, G. E. (2007). Conference intention experiment yields best results yet. *HTI's Perspectives in Healing, 4,* 10.

Schwartz, G. E. (2009). Can distant group healing intentions affect patterns of cosmic rays? *HTI's Perspectives in Healing, 6*, 22–25.

Schwartz, G.E., & Kagel, S. (2011). HTI intention experiments with Gary Schwartz. Review of Tucson and St. Louis results. *HTI's Perspectives in Healing, 2*, 22–23.

Schwartz, G. E., & Kagel, S. (2011). Intention experiment: Hawaii 2011. *HTI's Perspectives in Healing, 4*, 22–23.

Selhub, E. (2009). *The love response.* New York, NY: Ballantine Books.

Shealy, C. N (2011*). Energy Medicine: Practical applications and scientific proof* (4th ed.). Virginia Beach, VA: Dimension Press.

Sisken, B.F., & Walker, J. (1995). Therapeutic aspects of electromagnetic fields for soft-tissue healing. In M. Blank (Ed.), *Electromagnetic field: Biological interactions and mechanisms, Advances in Chemistry Series 250* (pp. 277-285). Washington, DC: American Cancer Society.

Society of Rogerian Scholars. (2008). *Martha Rogers: A short biography.* Retrieved from http://www.societyofrogerianscholars.org/biography_mer.html

Stacy, R. (2001). *Complex responsive processes in organizations.* New York, NY: Routledge.

Stanfield, B. (2000). Is US health really the best in the world? *Journal of the American Medical Association,* 284(4), 483–485.

Suchman, A. (2006). A new theoretical foundation for relationship-centered care: Complex responsive process of relating. *Journal of General Internal Medicine, 21,* 0–44.

Van der Waerden, B. L. (1967). *Sources of quantum mechanics.* Amsterdam, Holland: North-Holland Publishing.

Verhoef, M.J., & Mulkins, A. (2012). The Healing experience. How can we capture it? *Explore: The Journal of Science and Healing, 8*(4), 231–236.

Waechter, R. L. & Sergio, L. (2002). Manipulation of the electromagnetic spectrum via fields projected from human hands: A qi energy connection? *Subtle Energies and Energy Medicine, 13*(3), 233–246.

Wardell, D.W. (2001). Unfolding transpersonal caring-healing through story. *The International Journal for Human Caring, 6*(1), 18–24.

Watson, J. (1985). *Nursing: Human science and human care: A theory of nursing.* Norwalk, CT: Appleton-Century-Crofts.

Watson, J. (1988). *Nursing: Human science and human care: A theory of nursing.* New York, NY: National League of Nursing.

Watson, J. (1999). *Postmodern nursing and beyond.* New York, NY: Churchhill Livingstone.

Watson, J. (2005). *Caring science as sacred science.* Philadelphia, PA: F.A. Davis.

Watson, J. (1989). Watson's philosophy and theory of human caring. In J. Riehl-Sisa (Ed.), *Conceptual models for nursing practice* (3rd ed.). (pp. 219–236). Norwalk, CT: Appleton and Lange.

Zimmerman, B., Lindberg, C. & Plsek, P. (1998). *Edgeware: Lessons for complexity science for health care leaders.* Bordentown, NJ: Plexus Press.

Zimmerman, J. (2000) Laying-on-of-hands healing and therapeutic touch: A testable theory. In J. L. Oschman (Ed.), *Energy medicine: The scientific basis* (pp.76–79). New York, NY: Churchill Livingstone.

CHAPTER 4 REFERENCES

Benor, D. (2008). *7 minutes to natural pain relief.* Santa Rosa, CA: Energy Psychology Press.

Brennan, B. (1993). *Light emerging: The journey of personal healing.* New York, NY: Random House.

Cajochen C., Chellappa S., & Schmidt C. (2010). What keeps us awake? The role of clocks and hourglasses, light, and melatonin. *International Review of Neurobiology, 93,* 57–90. doi:10.1016/S0074-7742(10)93003-1.18

Cappuccio, F.D., Cooper, D., D'Elia, L., Strazzullo, P., & Miller, M.A. (2011). Sleep duration predicts cardiovascular outcomes: A systematic review and meta-analysis of prospective studies. *European Heart Journal, 32*(12), 1484–1492. doi:10.1093/eurheartj/ehr007

Crowley, S.J., Lee, C., Tseng, C.Y., Fogg, L.F., & Eastman, C.I. (2003). Combinations of bright light, scheduled dark, sunglasses, and melatonin to facilitate circadian entrainment to night shift work. *Journal of Biological Rhythms,18*(6), 513–23.

Dyer, W. (2004). *The power of intention.* Carlsbad, CA: Hay House.

Groenewegen, P. P., van den Berg, A., de Vries, S., & Verheij, R.A. (2006). Vitamin G: Effects of green space on health, well-being, and social safety. *BMC Public Health, 6,*149. doi:10.1186/1471-2458-6-149

Hawkins, D. (1995). *Power vs. force.* Carlsbad, CA: Hay House.

Institute of HeartMath. *Quick coherence technique.* Retrieved from www.heartmath.org.

Joy, B. (1979). *Joy's way: A map for a transformational journey.* New York, NY: J. P. Tarcher.

Matthews, K.A., Everson-Rose, S.A., Kravitz, H.M., Lee, L., Janssen, I., & Sutton-Tyrrell, K. (2013). Do reports of sleep disturbance relate to coronary and aortic calcification in healthy middle-aged women? Study of women's health across the nation. *Sleep Medicine, 14*(3), 282–287. doi:10.1016/j.sleep.2012.11.016

Mauer, R. (2004). *One small step can change your life: The Kaizen Way.* New York, NY: Workman Publishing Co.

Mentgen, J. (2000). *Right rhythmic living.* Address presented at Australia Healing Touch Conference, Sydney, Australia.

Myss, C. (1997). Why people don't heal and how they can. New York, NY: Harmony Books.

Oshmann, J. (2008, June). *Renewing Health Care: A journey to new heights.* Panel on Subtle Energies presented at The American Holistic Nurses Association 28th Annual Conference. Bretton Woods, NH.

Qureshi, N.A, & Al-Bedah, A.M. (2013). Mood disorders and complementary and alternative medicine: A literature review. *Neuropsychiatric Disease and Treatment, 9,* 639–658. doi:10.2147/NDT.S43419

Singer, M.A. (2007). Untethered soul: The journey beyond yourself. Oakland, CA: New Harbinger Press.

Tovey, M. (2007). *Meditations from the Heart* [CD]. Colorado Springs, CO: Heart Center.

Tovey, M. (2002). *Yes, I will.* New Orleans, LA: Morgana Publishing Co.

Verhoef, S.P., Camps, S.G., Gonnissen, H.K., Westerterp, K.R., & Westerterp-Plantenga, M.S. (2013). Concomitant changes in sleep duration and body weight and body composition during weight loss and 3-month weight maintenance. *American Journal of Clinical Nutrition, 98*(1), 25–31.

CHAPTER 5 REFERENCES

Blackburn, S. (2001). *Being good.* New York, NY: Oxford University Press.

Beauchamp, T., & Childress, J. (2009). *Principles of biomedical ethics* (7th Ed.). New York, NY: Oxford University Press.

Chodron, P. (1997), *When things fall apart.* Boston, MA: Shambhala Publications.

Comte-Sponville, A. (2001). *A small treatise on the great virtues.* New York, NY: Henry Holt.

Dalai Lama. (1999). *Ethics for a new millennium.* New York, NY: Berkeley Publishing Group.

Durant, W. (1926). *The story of philosophy.* New York, NY: Pocket Books: Simon & Schuster.

Erikson, E., & Woolfolk, A.E. (1987). *Educational psychology* (3rd ed.). Parsippany, NJ: Simon & Schuster, Inc.

Helminski, K. (1998). *The Rumi collection.* Boston, MA: Shambhala Publications.

Hodkins, E. (2012, September). From Keynote address presented at the 15th Annual Healing Touch International Conference in Westminster, CO. Portland, OR: Backcountry Recording.

Kornfield, J. (1993). *A path with heart: A guide through the perils and promises of spiritual life.* New York, NY: Bantam Books.

Maslow, A. H. (1962). *Towards a Psychology of Being.* Princeton, NJ: D. Van Nostrand.

Meleis, A. (2012). *Theoretical nursing development and progress* (5th ed.). New York, NY: Lippincott Williams & Wilkins.

Minch, M., & Weigel, C. (2012). *Living ethics, an introduction* (2nd ed.). Boston, MA: Cengage Learning.

Myss, C. (1996). *Anatomy of the spirit. The seven stages of power and healing.* New York, NY: Crown.

Schweitzer, A. (1933). *Out of my life and thought, An autobiography* (C. T. Campion, Trans). New York, NY: Henry Holt.

CHAPTER 6 REFERENCES

Academy of Traditional Chinese Medicine (1975). *An outline of Chinese acupuncture.* Peking, China: Foreign Language Press.

Brennan, B. (1987). *Hands of light: A guide to healing through the human energy field.* New York, NY: Bantam Books.

Brennan, B. (1993). *Light emerging: The journey of personal healing.* New York, NY: Random House.

Bruyere, R. (1989/1994). *Wheels of light: Chakras, auras and the healing energy of the body.* New York, NY: Fireside Books, Simon & Schuster.

Classen, C., (2005) *The book of touch.* New York, NY: Oxford Press.

Dale, C. (2009) *The complete book of chakra healing* (2nd ed.). Woodbury, MN: Llewellyn.

Hay, L. (1988), *Heal your body.* London, England: Hay House.

Judith, A. (1996). *Eastern Body, Western Mind. Psychology and the chakra system as a path to self.* Berkeley, CA: Celestial Arts.

Leadbetter, C. W. (1927/1980). *The chakras*. Wheaton, IL: Theosophical Publishing House.

Myss, C. (1996) *Anatomy of the spirit: The seven stages of power and healing*. NY, New York: Crowne.

Page, C. (1992/2000). *Frontiers of health. How to heal the whole person*. Sydney, Australia: Random House.

Shapiro, D. (1997). *Your body speaks your mind: How your thoughts and emotions affect your health*. Freedom, CA: The Crossings Press.

Shapiro, D. (2006) *Your body speaks your mind*. Boulder, CO: Sounds True.

Wardell, D. (2000). White shadow: Walking with Janet Mentgen. Lakewood, CO: Colorado Center for Healing Touch.

CHAPTER 7 REFERENCES

Amsden, L. (2012). *Breaking eggs: Finding new meaning with chronic illness*. Retrieved from www.outskirtspress.com

Berne, K. (1992). *Running on empty: Living with chronic fatigue immune dysfunction syndrome*. Alameda, CA: Hunter House.

Brennan, B. A. (1988). *Hands of light: Study of the human energy field*. New York, NY: Bantam Books.

Domar, A.D., Smith, K., Conboy, L., Iannone, M., & Alper, M. (2010). A prospective investigation into the reasons why insured United States patients drop out of in vitro fertilization treatment. *Fertility and Sterility*, 95, 1457–1459.

Domar, A.D., Rooney, K.L., Wiegand, B., Orav, E. J.,Alper, M.M., Berger, B.M., & Kikolovski, J. (2012). Impact of a group mind/

body intervention on pregnancy rates in IVG patients. *Fertility and Sterility, 95*(7), 2269–2273.

Dewe, B., & Dewe, J. (1989). *Professional kinesiology practice.* Queensland, Australia: International College of Specialized Kinesiology and Natural Therapies.

Gurhan, N., AKyuz, A. Atici, D., & Kisa, S. (2009). Association of depression and anxiety with oocyte and sperm numbers and pregnancy outcomes during in vitro fertilization treatment. *Psychological Reports, 104,* 796–806.

Huneke, F. (1950). In ARGE d.w.-dtsch. Aerziekammern Methoden. desHerdnachweises, Stuttgart, Germany: Hippokrates Marquardt & Cie.

Huneke, F. (1952). Impietoitheradie, Stuttgart: Germany: Hippokrates Marquardt & Cie.

Maizes, V. (2013). Can meditation relieve infertility ? Retrieved from http://www.alternativemedicine.com/balance/mind-body-connection/can-meditation-relieve-infertility.

Stouffer, D., Joyner, M., & Stouffer, J. (1998). A Healing Touch approach to scar integration. *Healing Touch Newsletter, 9*(4), p.6.

Wang K., Hermann C (1999). Healing Touch on agitation levels to dementia. *Healing Touch Newsletter, 9*(3), p.3.

CHAPTER 8 REFERENCES

Bartlett, R. (2007). *Matrix energetics: The science and art of transformation.* Hillsboro, OR: Beyond Words.

Beano, K. A., Signorino, E., Evangelista, A., Brusa, D., Mistrangelo, M., Polimeni, M. A.,. . . Matera, L. (2008). Correlation between NK function and response to trastuzimab in metastatic breast cancer patients. *Journal of Translational Medicine, 6,* 25–35.

Brennan, B. A. (1993). *Light emerging: The journey of personal healing.* New York, NY: Bantam Books.

Bruyere, R.L. (1989). *Wheels of light.* New York, NY: Simon & Schuster.

Champman, F. (1937/1969). *An endocrine interpretation of Chapman's reflexes.* Carmel, CA: Academy of Applied Osteopathy.

Chia, M. (1983). *Awaken healing energy through the Tao.* Santa Fe, NM: Aurora Press.

Chia, M., & Chia, M. (1990). *Chi nei tsang: Internal organs chi massage.* Huntington, NY: Healing Tao Books.

Cohen, K. S. (1997). *The way of qigong: The art and science of Chinese energy healing.* New York, NY: Ballantine Books.

Guorui, J. (1986). *QiGong essentials for health promotion.* Beijing, China: Fujian People's Press.

Hart, L.K., Freel, M.I., Haylock, P.S., & Lutgendorf, S.K. (2011). The use of Healing Touch in integrative oncology. *Clinical Journal of Oncology Nursing, 15*(5), 519–525.

Hass, M. L., Hogle, W. P., Moore-Higgs, G. J., & Gosselin-Acomb, T. K. (2007). *Radiation therapy: A guide to patient care.* St. Louis, MO: Mosby.

Hovland, S. (2003). *Experiential anatomy & physiology for healers: An energetic approach—Level 1 class notebook.* Denver, CO: Healing Therapies.

Johnson, B (2008). *Three turns of the kaleidoscope: Healing the victim within.* Kingston Springs, TN: Westview.

Kunz, D. (2004). Beneficial influences on the chakras. In D. Kunz & D. Krieger (Eds.), *The spiritual dimensions of therapeutic touch. Rochester* (pp. 149-155). Rochester, VT: Bear & Company.

Kunz, D. (2004). Chakras and the therapeutic touch process—Introductory comments. In D. Kunz & D. Krieger (Eds.), *The spiritual dimensions of therapeutic touch* (pp. 132–133). Rochester, VT: Bear & Company.

Kunz, D. (2004). Therapeutic touch—Questions and answers. In D. Kunz & D. Krieger (Eds.), *The spiritual dimensions of therapeutic touch* (pp. 201–205). Rochester, VT: Bear & Company.

Kunz, D., & Peper, E. (1985). Fields and their clinical implications. In D. Kunz (Ed.), *Spiritual aspects of the healing arts* (pp. 213–261). Wheaton, Ill: The Theosophical Publishing House.

Leadbeater, C.W. (1927/1979). *The chakras: A monograph.* Wheaton, Ill: The Theosophical Publishing House.

Lutgendorf, S. K., Mullen-Houser, E., Russell, D., DeGeest, K., Jacobson, G., Hart, L., . . . Lubaroff, D.M. (2010). Preservation of immune function in cervical cancer patients during chemoradiation using a novel integrative approach. *Brain, Behavior, and Immunity, 24,* 1231–1240.

MacRitchie, J. (1993). *Chi Kung: Cultivating personal energy.* Rockport, MA: Element Books.

McTaggart, L. (2008). *The field: The quest for the secret force of the universe.* New York, NY: Harper Collins.

Menard, C., Blay, J.Y., Borg, C., Michiels, S., Ghiringhelli, F., Robert, C., . . .Zitvogel, L. (2009). Natural killer cell IFN-gamma levels predict long-term survival with imatinib mesylate therapy in gastrointestinal stromal tumor-bearing patients. *Cancer Research, 69,* 3563–3569.

Naparstek, B. (2007). Counting the breath; body scan. In *Guided meditations for help with panic attacks*. Akron, OH: Health Journeys.

Naparstek, B., & Scaer, R. (2004). *Invisible heroes: Survivors of trauma and how they heal*. New York, NY: Bantam Books.

Nightengale, F., & Barnum, B. S. (1992). *Notes on nursing: What it is, and what it is not*. Philadelphia, PA: Lippincott-Raven.

Public Broadcasting Service. (2001). *The secret life of the brain*. Retrieved from http://www.PBS.org/wnet/brain/

Public Broadcasting Service & Vulcan Productions. (2009). *This emotional life: In search of ourselves and happiness*. PBS Home Video. Available from www.PBS.org

Remen, R.N. (1996). In the service of life. *Noetic Sciences Review, 37,* 24–25.

Seung, A. M. (2009). Adverse effects of chemotherapy and targeted agents. In M. A. Koda-Kimble, L. Y. Young, B. K. Alldredge, R. L. Corelli, B. J. Giuglielmo, W. A. Kradjan, & B. R. Williams (Eds.), *Applied therapeutics* (9th ed.) (pp. 89-1–89-39). Philadelphia, PA: Lippincott & Wilkins.

Sinnett, K. (2004). *Energetic transformation*. Troy, MI: Advanced Energy Works.

Slater, V. (2004). Human holistic and energetic responses following a tornado. *Journal of Holistic Nursing, 22* (85), 85–92. doi:10.1177/0898010103261119

Tuwaru, M. (1995). *Ayurveda: Secrets of healing*. Twin Lakes, WI: Lotus Press.

Van Aken, R. (2004). *Emerging from depression: The experiential process of Healing Touch explored through grounded theory and case study* (Unpublished thesis). Southern Cross University, Lismore, Australia.

Van Aken, R., & Taylor, B. (2010). Emerging from depression: The experiential process of Healing Touch explored through grounded theory and case study. *Complementary Therapies in Clinical Practice, 16,* 132–137.

Workman, M. L. (2010). Care of patients with cancer. In D. D. Ignatuvicius & M. L. Workman (Eds.), *Medical-surgical nursing: Patient centered collaborative care* (pp. 414–439). St. Louis, MO: Saunders.

CHAPTER 9 RESEARCH REFERENCES

Anderson, J. G., & Taylor, A. G. (2011). Effects of Healing Touch in clinical practice: A systematic review of randomized clinical trials. *Journal of Holistic Nursing, 29,* 221–228.

Cook, C. A. L., Guerriorio, J. G., & Slater, V. E. (2004). Healing Touch and quality of life in women receiving radiation treatment for cancer: A randomized controlled trial. *Alternate Therapy Health Medicine, 10*(3), 34–41.

Creswell, J. (1994). *Research design. Qualitative & quantitative approaches.* Thousand Oaks, CA: Sage.

Creswell, J. (2013). *Qualitative inquiry & research design* (3rd ed.). Los Angeles, CA: Sage.

Curtis, A. R., Tegeler, C., Burdette, J., & Yosipovitch, G. (2011). Holistic approach to treatment of intractable neuropathic itch. *Journal of the American Academy of Dermatology, 64*(5), 955–959.

Danhauer, S. C., Tooze, J. A., Holder, P., Miller, C., & Jesse, M. T. (2008). Healing touch as a supportive intervention for adult acute leukemia patients: A pilot investigation of effects on distress and symptoms. *Journal of the Society for Integrative Oncology, 6*(3), 89–97.

Decker, S., Wardell, D.W., & Cron, S.G. (2012, June). Using a Healing Touch intervention in older adults with persistent pain. *Journal of Holistic Nursing, 30*(3), 205–213. doi:10.1177/0898010112440884

Dowd, T., Kolcaba, K, Steiner, R. & Fashinpaur, D. (2007). Comparison of a Healing Touch, coaching, and a combined intervention on comfort and stress in younger college students. *Holistic Nursing Practice, 21*(4), 194–202.

Engebretson, J., & Wardell, D.W. (2007). Energy-based modalities. *Nursing Clinics of North America, 42,* 243-259.

Eschiti, V. S., & Baker, B. A. (2012). The lived experience of postoperative mastectomy patients receiving Healing Touch. Healing Touch International Research Survey (13th ed.). Retrieved from healingtouchinternational.org.

Forbes, M. A., Rust, R., & Becker, G. J. (2004). Surface Electromyography (EMG) Apparatus as a measurement device for biofield research: Results from a single case. *Journal of Alternative and Complementary Medicine, 10*(4), 617–626.

Forgues, E. (2009). Methodological issues pertaining to the evaluation of the effectiveness of energy-based therapies, avenues for a methodological guide. *Journal of Complementary and Integrative Medicine, 6*(1), 1–17.

Healing Touch International (1996, 2014). International Code of Ethics/ Standards of Practice for Healing Touch practitioners. Available at http://www.healingtouchinternational.org

Hendrix, I. (2012). Evidence. In J. Giddens (Ed.), *Concepts for nursing practice* (pp. 453–461). St. Louis, MO: Elsevier/Mosby.

Hopp, L., & Rittenmeyer, L. (2012). *Introduction to evidence-based practice. A practical guide for nurses.* Philadelphia, PA: F. A. Davis.

Jain, S. McMahon, G.F., Hasen, P., Kozub, M.P., Porter, V, King, R., & Guarneri, E.M. (2012). Healing Touch with guided imagery for PTSD in returning active duty military: A randomized controlled trial. *Military Medicine, 177, 9*, 1015–1021.

Jain, S., & Mills, P. J. (2010). Biofield therapies: Helpful or full of hype? A best evidence synthesis. *International Journal of Behavioral Medicine, 17*(1), 1–16.

Jain, S., Pavlik, D., Distefan, J., Bruyere, R. L., Acer, J., Garcia, R., . . . Mills, P. J. (2012). Complementary medicine for fatigue and cortisol variability in breast cancer survivors. *Cancer, 118*, 777–787.

Kemper, K. J., Fletcher, N. B., Hamilton, C. A., & McLean, T. W. (2009). Impact of healing touch on pediatric oncology outpatients: Pilot study. *Journal of the Society for Integrative Oncology, 7*(1), 12–18.

Kissinger, J. & Kaczmarek, L. (2006) Healing Touch and fertility: A case report. *The Journal of Perinatal Education, 15*(2), 13-20.

Krucoff, M. W., Crater, S. W., Gallup, D., Blankenship, J. C., Cuffe, M., Guarneri, M., . . . Lee, K. L. (2005). Music, imagery, touch, and prayer as adjuncts to interventional cardiac care: The monitoring and actualization of noetic trainings (MANTRA) II randomized study. *Lancet, 366*(9481), 211–217.

Krucoff, M. W., Crater, S. W., Green, C. L., Maas, A. C., Seskevich, J. E., & Lane, J. D. (2001). Integrative noetic therapies as adjuncts to percutaneous intervention during unstable coronary syndromes: The monitoring and actualization of noetic trainings (MANTRA) feasibility pilot. *American Heart Journal, 142*(5), 760–769.

Lincoln, Y.S., & Guba, E.G. (1985). *Naturalistic inquiry*. Newbury Park, CA: Sage.

Lutgendorf, S.K., Mullen-Houser, E., Russell, D., DeGeest, K., Jacobson, G., Hart, L., . . . Lubaroff, D.M. (2010). Preservation of immune function in cervical cancer patients during chemoradiation using a novel integrative approach. *Brain, Behavior, and Immunity 24*(8), 1231–1240.

MacIntyre, B., Hamilton, J., Fricke, T., Ma, W., Mehle, S., & Michel, M. (2008). The efficacy of healing touch in coronary artery bypass surgery recovery: A randomized clinical trial. *Alternative Therapies in Health and Medicine, 14*(4), 24–32.

Maville, J. A., Bowen, J. E., & Benham, G. (2008). Effect of healing touch on stress perception and biological correlates. *Holistic Nursing Practice, 22*(2), 103–110.

McDonough-Means, S. I., Kreitzer, M. J., & Bell, I. R. (2004). Fostering a healing presence and investigating its mediators. *Journal of Alternative and Complementary Medicine, 10*, S25-S41.

Mallock, K., & Grady, T. *Introduction to evidence-based practice in nursing and health care.* Sudbury, MA: Jones and Bartlett.

Melnyk, B., & Fineout-Overholt, E. (2011). *Evidence-based practice in nursing & healthcare. A guide to best practice* (2nd ed.). Philadelphia: Wolters Kluwer/Lippincott Williams & Wilkins.

Melnyk, B., & Fineout-Overholt, E. (2006). Consumer preferences and values as an integral key to evidence-based practice. *Nursing Administration Quarterly, 30*(2), 123–127.

Mills, P.J., & Jain, S. (2010). Biofield therapies and psychoneuroimmunology. *Brain, Behavior, and Immunity, 24*, 1229–1230.

Pierce, B. (2007). The use of biofield therapies in cancer care. *Clinical Journal of Oncology Nursing, 11*(2), 253–258.

Polit, D. F. & Beck, C. T. (2006). *Essentials of nursing research. Methods, appraisal, and utilization* (6th ed.). Philadelphia, PA: Lippincott Williams & Wilkins.

Post-White, J., Kinney, M. E., Savik, K., Gau, J. B., Wilcox, C., & Lerner, I. (2003). Therapeutic massage and healing touch improve symptoms in cancer. *Integrative Cancer Therapies, 2*(4), 332–344.

Rexilius, S. J., Mundt, C. A., Megel, M. E., & Agrawal, S. (2002). Therapeutic effects of massage therapy and Healing Touch on caregivers of patients undergoing autologous hematopoietic stem cell transplant. *Oncology Nursing Forum, 29*(3), 1–14.

Sackett, D., Richardson, W. S., Rosenberg, W., & Haynes, R. B. (1997). *Evidence based medicine. How to practice and teach EBM.* New York, NY: Churchill Livingstone.

Seskevich, J. E., Crater, S. W., Lane, J. D., & Krucof, M. W. (2004). Beneficial effects of noetic therapies on mood before percutaneous intervention for unstable coronary syndromes. *Nursing Research, 53*(2), 116–121.

So, P. S., Jiang, Y., & Qin, Y. (2008). Touch therapies for pain relief in adults. *Cochrane Database of Systematic Reviews,* (4) doi:10.1002/14651858. CD006535.pub2

Tang, R., Tegeler, C., Larrimore, D., Cowgill, S., & Kemper, K. J. (2010). Improving the well-being of nursing leaders through Healing Touch training. *Journal of Alternative and Complementary Medicine, 16*(8), 837–841.

Taylor, B. (2001). The effects of Healing Touch on the coping ability, self-esteem and general health of undergraduate nursing students. *Complementary Therapies in Nursing and Midwifery, 7*(2) 34–42.

Turner, K. (2005). Healing Touch for breast cancer patients. *Stanford Nurse, 25*(2), 8–10.

Verhoef, M. J., Casebeer, A. L., & Hilsden, R. J. (2002). Assessing efficacy of complementary medicine: Adding qualitative research methods to the "gold standard." *Journal of Alternative and Complementary Medicine, 8,* 275–281.

Wang, K.L., & Hermann, C. (2006). Pilot study to test the effectiveness of Healing Touch on agitation in people with dementia. *Geriatric Nursing, 27*(1), 34–40.

Warber, S. L., Gordon, A., Gillespie, B. W., Olson, M., & Assefi, N. (2003). Standards for conducting clinical biofield energy healing research. *Alternative Therapies in Health and Medicine, 9,* A54–A64.

Wardell, D.W. (2000). The trauma release technique: How it is taught and experienced in Healing Touch. *Alternative and Complementary Therapies, 6*(1), 20–27.

Wardell, D.W. (2001). Spirituality of Healing Touch participants. *Journal of Holistic Nursing, 19,* 71–86.

Wardell, D.W., & Engebretson, J.C. (2012). Healing Touch for older adults with persistent pain. *Holistic Nursing Practice, 26*(4), 194–202.

Wardell, D., Rintala, D. & Tan, G. (2008). Study descriptions of healing touch with veterans experiencing chronic neuropathic pain from spinal cord injury. *Explore, 4*(3), 187–195.

Wardell, D., Rintala, D.,Tan, G., & Duan, Z. (2006). Pilot study of Healing Touch and progressive relaxation for chronic neuropathic pain in persons with spinal cord injury. *Journal of Holistic Nursing, 24*(4), 231–240.

Wardell, D.W. & Weymouth, K. (2004). Review of studies of Healing Touch. *Journal of Nursing Scholarship: Image, 36*(2), 147–154.

Wetzel, W. (1993). Healing Touch as a nursing intervention: Wound infection following cesarean birth: An anecdotal case study. *Journal of Holistic Nursing, 11*(3), 277–285.

Wilkinson, D. S., Knox, P. L., Chatman, J. E., Johnson, T. L., Barbour, N., Myles, Y., & Reel, A. (2002). The clinical effectiveness of healing touch. *Journal of Alternative and Complementary Medicine 8*(1), 33–47.

Ziembroski J, Gilbert, N., Bossarte, R., & Guldberg, G. (2003). Healing Touch and hospice care: Examining outcomes at the end of life. *Alternative & Complementary Therapies, 9*(3), 146–151.

CHAPTER 10 REFERENCES

Anselme, L., (2007) Healing Touch and Health Care Integration,Healing Touch International, Inc. Lakewood, CO.

Jain, S. McMahon, G.F., Hasen, P., Kozub, M.P., Porter, V, King, R., & Guarneri, E.M. (2012). Healing Touch with guided imagery for PTSD in returning active duty military: A randomized controlled trial. *Military Medicine, 177*(9), 1015–1021.

Hunt, V.V. (1995). *Infinite mind, Science of the human vibrations.* Malibu, Ca: Malibu Publishing.

Hunt, V.V. (1997). *Mind mastery meditations: A workbook for the "Infinite Mind."* Malibu, CA: Malibu Publishing.

Watson, L. (1976). Introduction. In B. Lawrence (Ed.). *Rhythms of vision: The changing patterning of belief.* New York, NY: Schocken Books.

CHAPTER 11 REFERENCES

Beck, C.J. & Smith, S. (1994). *Nothing special: Living Zen.* New York, NY. Harper Collins Publishing.

Dalai Lama. (1999). *Ethics of a new millennium.* New York, NY: Riverhead Press.

Hanson, R. & Mendius, R. (2009). *Buddha's brain: The practical neuroscience of happiness, love, and wisdom.* Oakland, CA: New Harbinger Publications.

Hodkins, E. (2002). The school of heartbreak, *The Alchemist, 2* (3), 1–3.

Myss, C. (2002). *Sacred contracts: Awakening your divine potential.* New York, NY: Three River Press.

Nin, A. & Stahlmann, G. (Eds.). (1967). *The diary of Anais Nin, Volume 2 1934–1939.* Orlando, FL: Hartcourt Brace.

Remen, R. (1996). Kitchen table wisdom. New York, NY: Riverhead Books.

Sawyer, K. (2007). *Group genesis: The creative power of collaboration.* New York, NY: Basic Books.

Trout, S. (1997). *Born to Serve: The evolution of the soul through service.* Alexandria, VA: Three Roses Press.

Vecsey C., & Venables R.W. (1980). *American Indian environments: Ecological issues in Native American history.* New York, NY: Syracuse University Press.

Whitfied, C. (1993). *Boundaries and relationships: Knowing, enjoying, and protecting the self.* Deerfield Beach, FL: Health Communications Inc.

Index

G

Germany, Healing Touch energy
therapy in, 32
Green, Dr. Elmer, 94
Group vibration, 131
Guided imagery, 337–338

H

Habits, breaking, 375
Hahnemann, Dr. Samuel, 155
Hands in Motion, 206, 215, 251, 269–270
Hands Still, 206, 215, 268, 269–270, 277
Happiness, 173
Hara Line repair, 261
Harmony
    heart-centeredness, 120–124
    living in, 119–158
Hawkins, David, 137–138
Hay, Louise, 202
HBB. *See* Healing Beyond Borders
Healing. *See also* Health care; Illness
    about, 75
    animals in, 148–153
    chakras and, 128–130
    complexity science and, 113–118
    versus curing, 64
    distance, 303–308, 392
    earth, 153–158
    electromagnetic field and, 111–112
    electromagnetic induction and,
        110–111
    energy awareness in, 194–210
    environment, 193
    ethical theories relevant to, 162–167
    evolution of, 395
    foundational aspects of, 75–118
    healer preparation, 194–195
    providing service, 130
    relationship between healer and
        patient, 4–5
    self and, 184–185
    spiritual aspect of, 4

story and, 195
Healing arts, integrating with Healing
    Touch, 335–336
Healing Beyond Borders (HBB), 65–67,
    343
    Code of Ethics/Standards of
        Practice, 66–67, 343
    credentialing, 67–73
    Scope of Practice statement, 66
Healing Buddies, 333
Healing Partners Program, 316, 334
Healing Touch, 93. *See also* Amygdala
    Connection treatment; Chakra
    Connection; Etheric Template
    Clearing technique; Hara
    Line repair; Laser technique;
    Magnetic Clearing technique;
    Magnetic Passes technique;
    Mind Clearing technique; Pain
    Drain; Self; Wound Sealing
    technique
    application of, 83–84
    art and practice of, 64–67
    becoming a practitioner, 65
    being of service, 387–395
    benefits of, 250
    challenges and benefits of, 26
    credentialing, 67–73, 354
    description of, 63
    in disasters, 290–293
    education and certification, 63–73
    eternal orientation, 383
    evolution of, 395
    external orientation, 382
    generations forward, 393
    healing arts roles and, 335–336
    healthcare organizations and,
        349–353
    in a health resort environment,
        353–358
    integrating, 331–365
    integrative use of chemoradiation
        and, 257–264
    internal orientation, 382–383

425

Printed in the United States
By Bookmasters